Methodology of Educational Research

MES-54

For

Master of Education [M.Ed.]

By

Anjula Singh

B.Com, MA (Eco),
B.Ed, M.Ed (IGNOU)

Useful For

IGNOU, KSOU (Karnataka), Bihar University (Muzaffarpur), Nalanda University, Jamia Millia Islamia, Vardhman Mahaveer Open University (Kota), Uttarakhand Open University, Kurukshetra University, Seva Sadan's College of Education (Maharashtra), Lalit Narayan Mithila University, Andhra University, Pt. Sunderlal Sharma (Open) University (Bilaspur), Annamalai University, Bangalore University, Bharathiar University, Bharathidasan University, HP University, Centre for distance and open learning, Kakatiya University (Andhra Pradesh), KOU (Rajasthan), MPBOU (MP), MDU (Haryana), Punjab University, Tamilnadu Open University, Sri Padmavati Mahila Visvavidyalayam (Andhra Pradesh), Sri Venkateswara University (Andhra Pradesh), UCSDE (Kerala), University of Jammu, YCMOU, Rajasthan University, UPRTOU, Kalyani University, Banaras Hindu University (BHU) and all other Indian Universities.

Closer to Nature  We use Recycled Paper

GULLYBABA PUBLISHING HOUSE PVT. LTD.

ISO 9001 & ISO 14001 CERTIFIED CO.

Published by:

GullyBaba Publishing House Pvt. Ltd.

Regd. Office:
2525/193, 1st Floor, Onkar Nagar-A,
Tri Nagar, Delhi-110035
(From Kanhaiya Nagar Metro Station Towards Old Bus Stand)
Call: 9991112299, 9312235086
WhatsApp: 9350849407

Branch Office:
1A/2A, 20, Hari Sadan,
Ansari Road, Daryaganj,
New Delhi-110002
Ph.011-45794768
Call & WhatsApp:
8130521616,8130511234

E-mail: hello@gullybaba.com, **Website**:GullyBaba.com

New Edition

ISBN: 978-93-82688-38-9

Disclaimer: Although the author and publisher have made every effort to ensure that the information in this book is correct, the author and publisher do not assume and hereby disclaim any liability to any party for any loss, damage, or disruption caused by errors or omissions, whether such errors or omissions result from negligence, accident, or any other cause.

If you find any kind of error, please let us know and get reward and or the new book free of cost.

The book is based on IGNOU syllabus. This is only a sample. The book/author/publisher does not impose any guarantee or claim for full marks or to be passed in exam. You are advised only to understand the contents with the help of this book and answer in your words.

All disputes with respect to this publication shall be subject to the jurisdiction of the Courts, Tribunals and Forums of New Delhi, India only.

Note: Selling this book on any online platform like Amazon, Flipkart, Shopclues, Rediff, etc. without prior written permission of the publisher is prohibited and hence any sales by the SELLER will be termed as ILLEGAL SALE of GPH Books which will attract strict legal action against the offender.

Preface

Progress in any filed is directly linked with research and innovation. Our problems and difficulties in the field of education necessitate a purposeful and sustained research effort. Research in every sphere and more so in the field of education is the demand of the day. The educational programmes of modern India cannot be run on age-old lines. Educational reform and progress need a dedicated and competent team of research scholars.

This GPH book "Methodology of Educational Research (MES-054)" covers various aspects of educational research. It may serve as a useful reference for students, classroom teachers or administrations who are interested in conducting research in education. All important aspects of educational research have been included for the producer of research interested in the interpretation and application of research findings.

The book is written specially in question & answer format to provide students the instant gratification of a correct answer. In this book, I have tried to solve all possible questions from the exams' point of view. Solutions of previous years question papers have also been included to help students to understand the unique examination structure. I hope that this book would be a favourite study material for the students.

An attempt has been carefully made to present this book more useful and meet the requirement and challenges of the course prescribed by IGNOU University.

I wish you a successful and rewarding career ahead. Feedback in this regard is solicited.

– Anjula Singh

Acknowledgement

My compliments go to the **GullyBaba Publishing House (P) Ltd.,** and its meticulous team who have been enthusiastically working towards the perfection of the book.

Their teamwork, initiative and research have been very encouraging. Had it not been for their unflagging support, this work wouldn't have been possible. The creative freedom provided by them along with their aim of presenting the best to the reader has been a major source of inspiration in this work. Hope that this book would be successful.

– Anjula Singh

Publisher's Note

The present book of the MES series is targeted for examination purpose as well as enrichment. With the advent of technology and the Internet, there has been no dearth of information available to all; however, finding the relevant and qualitative information, which is focused, is an uphill task.

We at **GullyBaba Publishing House (P) Ltd.,** have taken this step to provide quality material which can accentuate in-depth knowledge about the subject. GPH books are a pioneer in the effort of providing unique and quality material to its readers. With our books, you are sure to attain success by making use of this powerful study material. Provided book is just a reference book based on the syllabus of particular University/Board. For a profound information, see the textbooks recommended by the University/Board.

Our site **gullybaba.com** is a vital resource for your examination. The publisher wishes to acknowledge the significant contribution of the Team Members and our experts in bringing out this publication and highly thankful to Almighty God, without His blessings, this endeavor wouldn't have been successful.

– Publisher

Topics Covered

Contents

Question Papers

1 EDUCATIONAL RESEARCH

An Overview

Research purifies human life. It improves its quality. It is search for knowledge. It shows how to solve any problem scientifically. It is a careful inquiry through search for any kind of Knowledge. It is a journey from known to unknown. It is a systematic effort to gain new knowledge in any kind of discipline.

When research seeks a solution of any educational problem, it leads to educational research. Curiosity, curiosities are natural gifts secured by a man. They inspire him to quest, increase his thirst for knowledge/truth. After trial and error, he worked systematically in the direction of the desired goal. His adjustment and coping with situations makes him successful in his task. Thereby, he learns and becomes wise, and prepares his own scientific procedure while performing the same task for second time.

The researching mind helps to understand, observe, control and predict the nature of phenomena including educational phenomena. Educational research, which essentially deals with social phenomena, uses both positivist and non-positivist approaches to generate new knowledge. There are a few steps in educational research, which a researcher is supposed to follow while conducting research. The scope of educational research is vast. Survey of research in education provides the broad areas of educational research. There are various types of studies conducted in educational research. These are both quantitative and qualitative in nature.

Q1. What were the methods of acquiring knowledge in historical perspective?

Or

Trace the historical development of different methods of acquiring knowledge.

Or

Describe some non-scientific methods of acquiring knowledge in historical perspective.

Ans. The methods by which man, from the earlier times, gaining knowledge can be classified under the following categories:

- **Tenacity:** It is the willingness to accept an idea/belief as valid knowledge because that idea/belief has been accepted for a long period of time. Tenacity requires no evidence for a belief except that the belief is already accepted. For example, to enter a religious place with the head covered and after removing the shoes, because it has always been like that. Such customs may have been enforced in order to safeguard the interests of the erstwhile elites, and have since then continued. Also, the meaning of belief goes on changing with time, place and conditions of existence, without changing or becoming flexible, one cannot choose between one of the available alternatives.
- **Intuition:** Intuition supposedly operates directly, without any intellectual effort or without any involvement of sensory processes. For example, designers, painters, poets, etc. pursue their creative activities by intuition. There is something in them, which tells them to apply their mind in a particular way. It appears to them that it is the only solution and there is no other alternative. This process cannot be discerned.
- **Authority:** Authority as a method of acquiring knowledge is the acceptance of an idea as a valid knowledge because some respected source, for example, to know the population one turns to census report, or a student looks at the dictionary for correct spelling. Obtaining knowledge by turning to customs or authorities is often economical of time and effort, but it sometimes leads to error. For instance, a scholar refused to look through a telescope when invited Galileo to view the newly discovered moons of Jupiter. He was convinced that the moons could not possibly be seen because Aristotle had not mentioned them in his discussions on astronomy. Therefore, when seeking advice from authorities, a researcher critically evaluates their

reliability and reserves the right to investigate and test their pronouncements to see whether he reaches the same conclusions. In choosing authorities and evaluating their claims to knowledge, the research should check not only the evidential of the authorities but also the arguments and evidence upon which they base their judgements.

- **Traditions and Customs:** Like authority, man derives knowledge from various social traditions and customs, which are handed down from one generation to another. For example, the way one should dress, the kind of food one need to eat, the god and goddesses one is supposed to worship are learnt from the members of the society through traditions and customs. These traditions and customs cannot be considered to be true knowledge unless they are examined and verified for their validity.
- **Personal Experience:** It is the most primitive and most familiar fundamental source of knowledge. When confronted with a problem, one often tries to recall or seek a personal experience that will help him reach a solution. Early man's observations and experience led him to appreciate that the part of the sky in which the sun rose and set varied. Modern man also acquires knowledge via personal experience – for example, we learn from personal experience to grow particular varieties of food grains or natural protection of plants from insects.

  Appealing to personal experience is a useful and common method of seeking knowledge. When it is not used critically, however, it can lead to incorrect conclusions. A person may make errors when observing or when reporting what he has seen or done. For example, observations and records of what was experienced may be poorly made; generalisations may be drawn on insufficient evidence or too few examples; incorrect conclusions may follow through prejudice; and evidence may be left out because it was not consonant with earlier experiences. Finally, there is always the danger of failing to recognise which were the salient features of the situation and which were irrelevant.

  The different methods of acquiring knowledge presented so far make few demands on their information and processes. In essence they assert that "we know this is true because (i) it has always been so, (ii) we feel and think it is so, (iii) the authority says it is so, or (iv) because our experience tells us it to be so".

The common thing in all these methods is that they all share an uncritical acceptance of their information and conclusion and limited skepticism about their method.

Q2. Explain the scientific approach for gaining knowledge.

[Dec-2011, Q.No.-3(a)]

Ans. With the advancement in science and technology, people started thinking in terms of scientific ways of looking at the world. As a result, the commonsense belief about happenings and phenomena of the world were replaced by the knowledge that is demonstrable or is based on evidence on which it can be tested by anyone who is oriented to the methods of science. Two strands of thought – rationalism and empiricism – hold grounds on the basis of which knowledge of the external world can be obtained. More exactly a combination of rationalism and empiricism is the scientific approach to gaining of knowledge.

(1) Rationalism

It is a way of thinking in which knowledge is developed through reasoning process alone. Information is carefully stated and logical rules are followed to arrive at acceptable conclusions. Rationalism involves deductive reasoning, inductive reasoning and a combination of both.

(i) Deductive reasoning (Syllogistic reasoning)

A significant contribution towards the development of a systematic method for obtaining reliable knowledge was made by the ancient Greek philosophers like Aristotle and his followers. Aristotle developed the syllogism, which can be described as a thinking process in which one proceeds from general to specific statements by deductive reasoning. It provides a means of testing the validity of any given conclusion or idea by proceeding from the known to the unknown. The syllogistic reasoning consists of (1) a major premise based on a self-evident truth or previously established fact or relationship; (2) a minor premise concerning a particular case to which the truth, fact, or relationship invariably applies; and (3) a conclusion. If the major and minor premise can be shown to be true, the conclusion arrived at is necessarily true. To use a sample example, consider the following proposition:

(a) All animals are mortal (major premise)
(b) Dog is an animal (minor premise)
(c) Therefore, dog will die (conclusion)

The method of syllogism or deduction, however useful has the following limitation:

- The conclusion of a syllogism is always derived from the content of premise. Therefore, if the premises are unrelated or if one of the premises is erroneous, the conclusion arrived at will not be valid.
- Another serious limitation of the deductive reasoning is its dependence upon verbal symbolism.
- Deductive reasoning can systematise what is already known and can identify new relationships as one proceeds from known to unknown, but it cannot be relied upon as sufficient method for securing reliable knowledge.

(ii) Inductive reasoning (Beconian System)

By sixteenth century, the Aristotelian method of syllogistic reasoning was being increasingly attacked. Of particular note in this connection was Francis Bacon (1561 – 1626), who argued against the practice, prevalent for centuries, of drawing conclusions from authoritative premises. As an alternative he maintained that researcher should, by careful observation, collect his own data and use there as the basis for making generalisations. The following is an example of inductive reasoning:

Every rabbit that has ever been observed has lungs;
Therefore, every rabbit has lungs.

In order to be absolutely certain of an inductive conclusion all instances must be observed. This is known as *perfect Induction* under Beconian system; it requires that the investigator examines every instance of phenomenon past, present and future. In practice therefore one generally relay upon Imperfect Induction. It arrives at a generalisation by observing only some instances that make up the class. To check the purity of water in a swimming pool, a health officer may take a single sample of water from the entire swimming pool. The size and representativeness of the instances observed largely determine whether one arrives at a sound conclusion. Through imperfect induction, an investigator merely arrives at conclusions of varying degrees of probability, for the possibility always exists that some unexamined instances of the class do not agree with his conclusion.

(iii) Inductive - deductive method or the scientific method

Both inductive and deductive methods have merits and demerits. A combination of both Aristotelian deductions with Beconian induction would help in getting valid knowledge. This new method is called inductive– deductive method or the scientific method.

According to **Mouly (1978**), "A back-and-forth movement in which the investigator first operates inductively from observations to hypotheses, and then deductively from these hypotheses to their implications, in order to check their validity from the stand point of compatibility with accepted knowledge. After revision, where necessary, these hypotheses are submitted to further test their validity at the empirical level. This dual approach is the essence of the modern scientific method and marks the last stage of man's progress towards sempirical science, a path that took him through folklore and mysticism, dogma and tradition, casual observation, and finally to systematic observation."

Therefore, scientific method uses both inductive and deductive reasoning to knowledge generation. It first makes use of inductive reasoning to formulate hypothesis to arrive at logical implications by using deductive reasoning.

Steps in the scientific method

Scientific method not only helps a person to arrive at the valid knowledge, but also helps all those who want to repeat them, to check them out with the same conditions and verify the results. The main steps in the scientific method are the following:

- **Sensing the problem:** Man comes across with certain hurdles, or difficulties while performing any kind of tasks. This leads him to sense or feel that there is a problem in the tasks, which needs to be solved.

- **Identification and definition of nature of the problem:** After sensing the problem, he identifies the problem and defines the nature of the problem in a precise manner so that the nature of the problem can be observed in the phenomenon and experimentation can be carried out.
- **Tentative solution to the problem or formulating hypothesis:** In order to reach solutions, man makes intelligent guesses about the possible solutions to the problem. These guesses are generally made on the basis of the observation of the facts by him.
- **Finding out implication of hypothesis through deductive reasoning:** The next step is to deduce the implications of hypotheses and know what is required to be observed if hypothesis is true.
- **Collection of evidence/data:** In order to find out validity of the implications, relevant evidences pertaining to the problem are collected through observation and experimentation or testing.
- **Verification of hypotheses:** Evidences or data collected are analysed to know whether they are in line with the hypothesis. The hypothesis is accepted to be true if it is supported by evidence and is rejected if it is not supported.

(2) Empiricism (Copernicus, Galileo and Darwin)

It is a way of gaining knowledge through observation of real events; that is known by experiencing through our senses. For the empiricist, it is not enough to know through reason alone. It is necessary to experience events through the senses, to see, hear, touch, taste and smell. Copernicus, Galileo and Darwin all based their important conclusions about nature largely on their observations of events. To illustrate further with an example, when we are ready to leave our home in the morning and see that the sky is dark and filled with clouds, and we hear approaching thunder, we are good empiricist if we take an umbrella our senses are telling us something.

Q3. What is the nature of science? Also, explain the general purposes of science.

Ans. From the earlier times, man has been curious about anything he could not understand. Slowly and gradually, he developed the scientific method of thinking and of investigating his problems, which today is producing astonishing results. It is an orderly system of searching for truth, which by basing conclusions upon factual evidence, and by using reasoning as a means of showing relationship between ideas, has given him better and more accurate answers to his many problems, not only in physical and biological sciences, but also in behavioural and social sciences. By attempting to apply this method of inquiry to behavioural and social sciences, the fields of psychology, economics, political science, sociology, anthropology, and education have become recognised as sciences. The term science, therefore, is now thought of as a method or attitude rather than a field of subject matter. It is described as a method of inquiry that permits man to examine the phenomenon of interest to him.

Science is based on certain beliefs and assumptions, which are briefly described as under:

- All events in nature are, at least to a degree, lawful or ordered, predictable and regular. This order, predictability and regularity of nature can be discovered through the activities of the scientific method.
- Truth can ultimately be derived only from observation. Scientist does not depend upon authority as a source of truth, but relies upon empirical observation. Thus, the phenomena that can actually be observed to exist are within the domain of scientific method.
- The scientist maintains a doubtful attitude towards data. He regards findings as tentative unless they are verified. Verification of the findings requires that other scientists must be able to repeat the observations and get the same results.
- The scientist is objective, impartial and logical in collecting and interpreting data or making observations. His personal bias does not in any way influence the truth and facts even when they are not in conformity with his own opinions.
- Scientist does not bother about the moral implications of his findings. He always deals with facts and does not consider what finding is good or what is bad for us.
- The ultimate goal of science is to integrate and systematic findings into a meaningful pattern or theory. The theory, however, is regarded as tentative and not the ultimate truth. It is subject to revision or modification as new evidence is found.

General purposes of science

The general purposes of science are explanation, prediction and control. These are described below:

Explanation of the phenomena: The essential purpose of science is to go beyond mere description of phenomena and provide explanation for them. For example, an iron piece sinks when thrown into the water whereas, a ship floats. The scientist wants to know the reasons for their occurrence. Having found possible causes for a particular happening or state of affairs, he has to build a generalisation that will explain how the factors influence the happening in order that he can relate the factors to a wider body of knowledge. Making a generalisation or building a framework provides an explanation for the phenomenon.

Control: The scientist often wishes to control conditions, which may have an adverse effect on human beings. Thus, he wishes to control the spread of malaria, or the conditions, which lead a child to be backward are reading. Although the purpose of scientists is to control natural events, but this objective is difficult to achieve. Scientists can predict, but cannot control any events.

Prediction: Scientists are not satisfied merely with formulating generalisations that explain phenomena; they also want to make predictions concerning the way generalisation will operate in new situations. Natural sciences have often been highly successful in elaborating such generalisation so that prediction is well – nigh certain. For example, the planet Pluto was predicted as existing years before it was actually identified. It is important to remember, however, that prediction in science does not necessarily mean foretelling the future.

Q4. Describe briefly positivism in educational research. Also, discuss its assumptions and limitations. [June-2011, Q.No.-2]

Or

What does positivism mean? What are the limitations of positivism and scientific method?

Ans. Science in the medieval period was primarily used in the service of religion. This can be observed from the fact that empirical science was not allowed to contradict theological dogma. For instance, if a dispute arose between knowledge gained through the senses and knowledge arrived at by religion or from church authority, the resolution was simple: truth lay with theology and any idea, which was in contradiction with theology, was summarily rejected.

In the *modern period,* science freed itself from the clutch of religion and began to dominate in the process of knowledge generation. Consequently, human being turned more observation and experimentation for establishing truth.

The term "positivism" was first coined by French philosopher Auguste Comte in the early nineteenth century. Comte, who is widely considered the first or modern sociologist, theorised that society goes through three stages:

- **Theological Stage:** The most primitive attempts are made to explain behaviour in term of spiritual or supernatural entities.
- **Metaphysical Stage:** Modified version of theological stage and sets out to explain behaviour in terms of spiritual abstractions, essences, or forces, which Comte regarded as depersonalised beings of the earlier, theological stage.
- **Final Positive Stage:** It dispenses with theological and metaphysical concepts and turns to observation and reason as means of understanding behaviour more simply; explanation now proceeds by way of scientific description.

Not only Comte but many other scholars also such as Bacon, Mill, Hume as well as the scholars of 'Vienna Circle' contributed to the development of the concept of positivism. The term has also been applied to the doctrine of a school of philosophy known as 'logical positivism', originated by the scholars of Vienna circle. *Logical Positivists* hold any statement in meaningless if it is not directly or indirectly verifiable.

Assumptions behind positivistic approach

Positivism derives its meaning from an acceptance of natural sciences as the paradigm of human knowledge. This has led the development of the scientific method as a means of knowledge generation. It is understood within the total framework of the principles and assumptions of science.

Determinism: The first assumption is determinism, according to which events have causes and are determined by other circumstances; these casual links can eventually be uncovered and understood. It is the ultimate aim of the scientists to formulate laws to account for the happenings in the world around them, obtaining thereby a firm basis for prediction and control.

Empiricism: The second assumption empiricism, which holds that certain kinds of reliable knowledge can only originate in experience, which scientifically means that acceptance of a theory or hypothesis depends on the nature of empirical evidence for its support. 'Empirical' here means that which is verifiable by observation or experienced. Thus, in empirical science, the scientist first gathers data on the basis of experience, then he classifies or if possible, qualifies data, tries to discover relationship in the classified and quantified data, and ultimately by gradual approximation he reaches the truth.

Parsimony principle: The third assumption underlying the work of the scientist is the principal of parsimony, the basic idea behind which is that phenomena should always be explained in the most economical way possible.

Generality: The fourth assumption is that of generality which forms the essential aspect of both the deductive and inductive methods of reasoning. Indeed, historically speaking, it was the problematic relationship between the 'concrete particular' and 'abstract general' that resulted in two competing theories of knowledge – the rational and the empirical.

The limitations of positivism and scientific method

In spite of the scientific enterprises proven success, especially in the field of natural sciences, its ontological (theory of being or existence) and epistemological (theory of knowledge) bases have been the focus of sustained and sometimes vehement criticism. Beginning in the second half of the nineteenth century, the limitations of the positivism were pointed out by the best intellectuals in Europe.

- The fundamental limitation of the positivistic paradigm is that it reflects a mechanistic and reductionist view of nature by which definition excludes notions of choice, freedom, individuality, and moral responsibility.
- The quantification of human behaviour and experience, which results in the depersonalisation of self. No matter how exact measurement may be, it can never give us an experience of life, for life cannot be weighed and measured on a physical scale.
- The bias and restricted image of humans comes about because the social scientists (wedded to positivism) concentrate on the repetitive, predictable and invariant aspects of person, on 'visible externalities' to the exclusion of the subjective world.
- Positivistic paradigm fails to take account of our unique ability, as human beings, to interpret out experiences and represent them to ourselves.
- Positivism is said to ignore the world in which the meanings are developed by active subjects through their life experiences.
- The findings of positivistic social science often said to be of little consequences to those for whom they are intended namely teachers, social workers, counselors, personnel, managers, etc.

- The more efforts, it seems, the researchers put into their scientific experimentation in the laboratory by restricting simplifying and controlling variables, the more likely they are to end up with a 'pruned, synthetic and constructed version of the whole social reality'.

Q5. What are the alternate or anti or non-positivist approaches?

Or

Explain the terms phenomenology, ethnomethodology and symbolic interaction.

Or

What do you mean by ethnomethodology? [Dec-2012, Q.No.-3(d)]

Ans. The anti-positivism movement in different disciplines of the social sciences is represented by three schools of thought — phenomenology, enthnomethodology and symbolic interactionism. A common thread of running through the three schools is concern with phenomena, that is, the things we directly apprehend through our senses as we go about our daily lives, together with consequent emphasis on qualitative as opposed to quantitative methodology.

(1) Phenomenology

The term phenomenology derives from the Greek phainomenon, whose root words are phainein: appear; and logia: science or study. Developed as a philosophy, by Edmund Husserl (1859-1938), phenomenology is a "reasoned inquiry into the world of appearances, that is, anything of which one is conscious" (Stewart and Mickunas, 1990, p. 3).

The goal is to study experience as it occurs in consciousness, in an attempt to glimpse the phenomenon in its immediacy as it is experienced, before the phenomenon has been overlaid with explanations as to causes or origins. To study the experience of phenomena as they appear in consciousness and in so doing apprehend their authentic reality, phenomenologists turn their attention to the life-world of the individual, the world of everyday lived experience (Munhall, 1994). In the attempt to grasp the essence or core structure of experience, that is, naked experience free of extraneous details, Husserl proposed the researcher engage in a process of "phenomenological reduction" in which all beliefs, assumptions and pre-conceived notions regarding the phenomena to be studied are identified, made explicit, and then set aside or "bracketed" (Beck, 1994). The researcher takes nothing for granted, is aware of preconceptions and sets them aside, and seeks to adopt an attitude of "wonder in the face of the world" (Fink, quoted by Merleau-Ponty, 1996, p. xiii). Subjects' descriptions of the experience are the raw data upon which the researcher reflects in order to discover the nature of the phenomena, intuit their essence or underlying structure, and describe them (Parse, Coyne and Smith, 1985; Spiegelberg, 1982).

Although phenomenologists differ among themselves on particular issues, there is fairly general agreement on the following points which can be taken as distinguishing features or their philosophical viewpoint:

- A belief in the importance and the primacy of subjective consciousness;
- An understanding of consciousness as active as meaning bestowing;
- A claim that there are certain essential structures to consciousness of which we can gain direct knowledge by a certain kind of reflection.

Various strands of development may be traced to the phenomenologist movement; transcendental phenomenology of Husserl is one of them. It comprises two concepts:

(i) Intentionality: It refers to consciousness, to the internal experience of being conscious of something; thus the act of consciousness and the object of consciousness are intentionally related, knowledge of intentionality requires that we be present to ourselves and to thing in the world, that we recognise that self and world are inseparable components of meaning. Intentional acts are objectifying while feeling act are non-objectifying.

Example: I saw night sky with the feeling of wonder. In this example, night sky is the intentional object and feeling of wonder is the act of consciousness.

The perception of night sky remains as concrete, independent, intentional experience, while, the feeling act of wonder may or may not continue to exist.

Intentionality comprises of two aspects:

(a) ***Noem:*** It refers not the real object but the phenomenon. For example, not the tree but the appearance of tree. Noema is the 'perceived as such' and 'textual'.

(b) ***Noesis:*** It is the act of perceiving. It is the perfect 'self-evidence' and 'structural'.

The working of Noema-Noesis relationship, the textural (noematic) and structural (noetic) dimension of phenomena, and the derivation of meanings is an essential function of intentionality.

(ii) **Intuition:** It is a 'primary inborn talent' directed towards producing solid and true judgement concerning everything that presents itself. It is regarded as a distract capacity of a pure and attentive mind born from the light of reason alone.

The self if an intuitive thinking being, a being who doubts, understand, affirms, denies, whishes for or against, senses, imagines. All things become clear and evident through an intuitive-reflective process through a transformation of what is seen; first intuitively in the manner in which it is presented and then in the fullness and clarity of an intuitive- reflective process.

(2) Ethnomethodology

Ethnomethodology is concerned with how people make sense of their everyday world. More especially, it is devised at the mechanisms by which participants achieve and sustain interaction is a social encounter the assumption they make the convention they utilise and the practices they adopt. Ethnomethodology, then seeks with understanding social accomplishments in their own terms; it is concerned with understanding them from within.

Harold Garfinkel (1979), *"to treat practical activities, practical circumstances, and practical sociological reasoning as topics of empirical study and by paying the most commonplace activities of daily life the attention usually accorded to extraordinary events, seeks to learn them as phenomena in their own right".*

In identifying the 'taken for granted' assumptions characterising any social situation and the ways in which the people involved make their activities rationally accountable, ethnomethodologists use notion like:

(i) **Indexicality** is the ways in which action and statements are related to the social contexts producing them,

(ii) **Reflexivity** is the ways in which all accounts of social settings–description, analysis, criticism, etc. and the social settings occasioning them are mutually interdependent.

(3) Symbolic Interactionism

Symbolic interactionism is a social theory based on the work of George Herbert Mead (1863-1931) and his student Herbert Blumer (1900 – 1987). It conceives of the self as a social rather than psychological entity. Human behaviour is understood as social behaviour made up of 'social acts'. Symbolic interactionism can be described as:

An approach in sociology, which focuses on the interaction of human beings and the roles they have. The model of the person in symbolic interactionism is active and creative rather than passive (Holloway 1997:150).

Woods, (1979), identified three basic postulates (assumptions) regarding this school of thought.

(i) ***Human beings act towards things on the basic of the meaning they have for them.*** Human beings inhabit two different worlds:

- *'Natural' world* wherein they are organisms of derives and instincts and where the external world exists independently of them, and
- *'Social' world* is the world of symbols, like languages, enables them to give meanings to objects.

This attribution of meanings, this interpreting, is what makes them distinctively human and social. Interactionists therefore focus on the world of subjective meanings and the symbols by which they are produced and represented. This means not making any prior assumptions about what is going in an institution, and taking seriously, indeed giving priority to inmates' own accounts. Thus, if pupils appear preoccupied for too much of the time – 'being bored', 'having a laugh', etc. the interactionist is keen to explore the properties and dimension of these processes.

(ii) ***Attribution of meaning to objects through symbol is a continuous process.*** Action is not simply a consequence of psychological attributes such as drives, attitudes or personalities, or determined by external social facts such as social structure or roles, but results from a continues process of meaning attribution which is always emerging a state of flux and subject to change. The individual constructs, modifies piece together, weighs up the pros and cons and bargains.

(iii) ***This process takes place in a social context, individuals align their actions to those of others***. They do this by 'taking the role of other', by making indications to 'themselves' about others likely responses. They construct how other wish or might act in certain circumstances, and how they themselves might act. They might try to 'manage' the impressions other have of them, put on a 'performance', try to influence others, etc.

In focussing on the interaction itself as a unit of study, the symbolic interactionist creates a move active image of the human being and rejects the image of the passive, determined organism. People are constantly undergoing change in interaction and society is changing through interaction.

Q6. Explain meaning and characteristics of research.

Ans. Research is considered as the application of scientific method in solving the problems. It is a systematic, formal and intensive process of carrying on the scientific method of analysis. It emphasises objective verification of generalisation. It involves logical analysis of problems and devising of appropriate methodologies for gathering relevant data, their analysis and interpretation. According to W.S. Monroes, "Research may be defined as a method of studying problems whose solution are to be derived partly or wholly from facts."

Main Characteristic of research

Best and Kahn summarised the following characteristics of research to clarify its spirit and meaning.

- Research is directed towards the solution of a problem. The ultimate goal is to discover cause and effect relationship between variables.
- Research emphasises the development of generalisations principles of theories that will be helpful in predicting future occurrences. Research is more than information retrieval, the simple gathering of information.
- Research is based upon observable experienced of empirical evidence. Research rejects revelation and dogma as methods of establishing knowledge and accepts only what can be verified by observation.
- Research demands accurate observation and description. Researchers may choose to use quantities measuring devices or qualitative descriptions of their observations. Only reliable and valid data gathering procedures should be utilised.
- Research involves gathering of new data from primary or first-hand sources or using existing data for a new purpose. It should add to what is known.
- Research activity is more often characterised by carefully designed procedures that apply rigorous analysis. It is rarely a blind, shotgun investigation or an experiment just to see what happens.
- Research requires expertise. The researcher knows what is already known about the problem, has searched related

literature carefully and is also thoroughly grounded in the terminology, concepts and technical skills necessary to understand and analyse the data gathered.

- Research strives to be objective and logical, applying every possible test to validate the procedures employed, the data collected and the conclusions reached. The researcher tries to suppress bias and emotions in analysis.
- Research involves the quest for answers to unsolved problems. However, previous important studies are deliberately replicated to confirm or to raise questions about their conclusions.
- Research is characterised by patient and unhurried activity. It is rarely spectacular.
- Research is carefully recorded and reported. Each important term is defined limiting factors are recognised, procedures are described in detail, references are carefully documented, results are objectively recorded, and conclusions are presented with scholarly caution and restraint.
- Research sometimes requires courage. Many scientific discoveries were made in spite of the opposition of political and religious authorities. Modern researchers in such fields as genetics, sexual behaviour and even business practices have aroused violent criticism from those who personal convictions, experiences or observations were in conflict with some of the research conclusions.

Q7. Discuss the nature of research in education.

Or

Define educational research. Explain its characteristics and limitation.

Or

Discuss the limitations of an educational research.

[June-2011, Q.No.-3(e)]

Ans. Research in education is a disciplined attempt to address questions or solve problems through the collection and analysis of primary data for the purpose of description, explanation, generalisation and prediction. The following are the important definitions of Educational Research:

- "The systematic and scholarly application of the scientific method, interpreted in its broader sense, to the solution of educational problems; conversely any systematic study designed to promote the development of education as a science can be considered educational research". *(Georg G. Monly)*

- "Educational Research is that activity which is directed towards the development of a science of behaviour in educational situations. The ultimate aim of such a science is to provide knowledge that will permit the educator to achieve his goals by the most effective method". *(Travers, M.W.)*

  Thus, Educational Research is to solve educational problem in systematic and scientific manner.

Characteristics of educational research

Educational Research characterises as follows:

- It is highly purposeful.
- It deals with educational problems regarding students and teachers as well.
- It is precise, objective, scientific and systematic process of investigation.
- It attempts to organise data quantitatively and qualitatively to arrive at statistical inferences.
- It discovers new facts in new perspective, i.e. it generates new knowledge.
- It is based on some philosophic theory.
- It depends on the researchers ability, ingenuity and experience for its interpretation and conclusions.
- It needs interdisciplinary approach for solving educational problem.
- It demands subjective interpretation and deductive reasoning in some cases.
- It uses classrooms, schools, colleges department of education as the laboratory for conducting researches.

Limitation

"In spite of the application of scientific method and refinement of research techniques, tools and designs, education as other social and behavioural sciences has not attained the perfection and scientific status of physical sciences," (Koul, 984). Our deficiencies stem primarily from (1) a lack of appreciation of research as the vehicle for scientific growth, and (2) a parallel lack of a theoretical framework on which to structure empirical findings to orient the efforts of the perfection.

Educational Research has not been able to establish generalisations equivalent to the physical sciences. Again, there is lack of unanimity among researchers in the field of facts and explanations. It is because of these limitations that Ary *et al.* (1972) pointed out that educational like other social sciences would never realise the objectives of science as completely as the physical sciences. Some of the limitations of the educational research are as following:

(1) Complexity of subject-matter: Educational research deals with the complex nature of human subjects. It has unlimited number of variables acting independently and in interaction. Educational research has to deal with all the individual differences of its subjects and the impact of group on the individual with all its diversities.

(2) Difficulties in Observation: Observation of human behaviour is more subjective and thus more difficult than the observation of physical or biological phenomena. Thus, it has a direct impact on the interpretation and conclusion of the study.

(3) Difficulties in Replication: It is difficult to make educational research as objective as it is in the physical science. Similarly, it lacks precision and replication of physical science. Educational phenomena are singular events thus replication and objectivity becomes difficult in educational researches.

(4) Interaction of Observer and Subjects: Here both the observers and subjects are living organism so the natural behaviours of the subjects are difficult in the presence of the observer. The observer's presence may change the situation, i.e. the natural behaviour of human subject.

(5) Difficulties of control: The rigid control of experimental conditions as it is found in the physical science is not possible in education research. Here the researcher has to deal with human subjects with all their moods, phantasies, individual variations and many variables simultaneously.

(6) Measurement problems: The tools used for measurement in educational researches are not so valid and reliable as those used in physical sciences.

- The relative lack of orientation of educators towards research is reflected in the correspondingly inadequate status of research. There is dire shortage of qualified researchers.
- Before any significant improvement can be expected in the educational enterprise, there is need for a new discipline of education totally committed to research as the basis for educational and social progress.
- The recruitment of educational research trainees must be highly selective and their training particularly rigorous. A greater research sophistication on the part of all teachers is also essential.
- There is need for the effective dissemination of research findings. There is a parallel need for an insightful synthesis of empirical structure.

Q8. What is the scope of educational research?

Ans. Education as a field of knowledge has two major dimensions. First, education as an academic discipline and second, education as an area of practice. As a discipline, it has its own concepts and propositions. But these concepts and propositions can be understood and explained with the help of knowledge drawn from cognate disciplines like psychology, sociology, philosophy, economics, etc. Hence, one finds content areas in education such as psychology of education, sociology of education, philosophy of education, economics of education, etc. As an area of practice, education operates at both vertical and horizontal level as well as at macro and micro-level. At macro-level, educational operations take place at societal or national level. At micro-level, education operates at the institutional and classroom level. Thus, scope of education can be classified into several ways.

Classification by major emphasis of cognate disciplines in education: Study of educational phenomena needs an understanding of the knowledge in cognate disciplines like psychology, sociology, philosophy, economics, management, etc.; hence, educational research can be conducted in these interdisciplinary areas such as psychology of education, philosophy of education, sociology of education, management of education, etc.

Classification by levels of education: Formal education takes place at different levels such as pre-primary, primary, secondary, senior secondary, and tertiary or higher levels. Therefore, educational research can be conducted at these levels of education.

Classification by modes of providing education: There are two major modes of providing education. These are face-to-face and distance education modes. Therefore, educational research can be conducted on the problems related to face-to-face and distance education modes.

Classification by curriculum areas–researches in subject matter, innovative techniques and ideas, and teaching methodologies: Research studies can be conducted in various curriculum areas at school and higher education levels. In all these curriculum areas, educational research pertaining to various aspects of curriculum such as planning, design, development, and evaluation can be undertaken.

Classification by educational operation at macro and micro-levels: At macro-level, research studies can be undertaken on the problems pertaining to educational planning, national policy formulation, implementation of policies, manpower planning, etc. At micro-level, various processes involved in the functioning of educational institutions as well as classroom operations can be studies. For example, teaching-learning process, student assessment, examination, school budget, school processes, etc. can be studied.

Classification by the research methods used: Since the nature of educational phenomena varies from one phenomenon to another, it would not be worthwhile to use the same research methods. Hence, we make use of different research methods, which may be used to study different educational phenomena. These are experimental method, descriptive method, historical method, philosophical method, case study method, etc.

Q9. What should be the priority areas of researches in education?

Ans. The problem of determining priorities in educational research is complex and becomes essentially a subjective issue. Each researcher may have his priorities common or uncommon to others. These priorities may be assigned in terms of individual needs and capacities, social targets, finances, value patterns, consideration of time and funds, and utility of a research problem. In this context, the Education Commission (1966, pp. 322-323) has noted that:

The priorities in educational research at the national level, from the point of view of the educational planners or administrators, may be very different from similar priorities at lower levels, or from the point of view of teachers.

The Commission, therefore, did not favour any rigid framework of priorities. It has suggested that the decisions about the priorities should be taken by the Education Research Council in the Ministry of Education at the national level, by the State Department of Education at the state level and by the universities, teacher training colleges or institutes and teachers interested in the research work.

The Third, Fourth, Fifth and Sixth Surveys of Research in Education (Buch, 1987 and 1991; NCERT, 1997 and 2006) and Educational Research and Innovations Committee (ERIC) of the National Council of Educational Research and Training have suggested some priority areas in educational research keeping in view the National Policy of Education-1986: Programme of Action (1986, 1992) and the role of education in total programme of national development.

- Research and policy making in education affect each other. This relationship suggests that research in the development of policy concerns; policy studies in science and technology education; effectiveness of policy issues and dissemination of findings related to such issues; use of qualitative and participatory approaches involving triangulation of methodologies in resolving policy issues and concerns should be given priority.

- Priority may be given to research studies designed to identify educational needs and problems of the scheduled caste and scheduled tribe children, rural girls, and children from economically deprived sections of the society. In this connection, studies on learning with interdisciplinary research, including bio-chemical and neuro-physiological factors, may be undertaken. Such studies will have immediate implications for the education of the children from the disadvantaged and deprived sections of the society.
- Another priority area in the field of education is the fulfilment of the Constitutional Directive of Article 45 relating to the provision of free and compulsory elementary education for all children up to the age 14. Studies, which will help to extend the educational programmes, formal and non-formal, to all children, especially belonging to scheduled castes and scheduled tribes including nomadic, semi-nomadic and denotified communities; hill areas and slums; and economically weaker sections of the society may be conducted.
- The dropout rate in school education is very high for various reasons and it is not likely to decrease very much in the near future. While every attempt should be made to increase the holding power of the school, we should also think of non-formal education as a possible alternative. Studies should be conducted to evolve organisation and methods of self-learning so that children in school learn better and those who drop out from school are not left out of the country's educational effort.
- The children from the scheduled castes, scheduled tribes, and the economically deprived sections of the society need educational opportunities as much as children from the other sections of society. How can opportunities be made equal? How can the effects of deprivation in the early life of infants be counteracted by social and educational intervention? These are some of the important problems, which need immediate attention of the researches.
- The programme of vocationalisation of secondary education was started in 1976. Since then it has been implemented in 10 States and 5 Union Territories. A number of other states are also in the process of introducing vocationalisation. However, in

spite of the best efforts of central and state-governments, the scheme of vocationalisation of education has not yet picked up the desired momentum. There have been many factors responsible for the slow progress. Research relating to the study of such factors, namely causes for failure of vocational education programme in the states and remedial measures, models of linkage between vocational education and industries in organised/unorganised sectors, absence of a well coordinated management system, unemployability of vocational pass-outs, mismatch between demand and supply, reluctance in accepting the concept of vocationalisation by the society, absence of proper provisions for professional growth and career advancement for the vocational pass-outs, etc. should be undertaken on priority basis.

- In view of the rate of population growth, we may not be able to provide the necessary educational facilities to the increasing number of students. The requirement of number of schools and teachers will be so large that the necessary resources are not likely to be available. Research is needed to explore the new techniques and alternative strategies of education. Studies on the formulation of decentralised/area specific interventions for education of children with special needs, girls, children belonging to linguistic and religious minorities should be undertaken for achieving the goals of access and equity.
- Schooling is a real problem for the children living in sparsely populated areas. In many parts of the country, there is concentration of population along river belts for obvious reasons. But many states have hill areas and dry areas, where population is scattered. How to provide schooling facilities to the children in such areas? The traditional models of schooling facilities do not seem to work. In this context, Mitra (1989) suggests that with the rapid expansion of facilities for T.V., radio, video and films, it is necessary to consider seriously their use for education. He is of the opinion that education of children in far flung hill, dry and tribal areas through distance mode needs serious consideration by researchers.
- The system of education in the country should make significant contribution towards developing suitable educational opportunities for the physically, mentally and socially challenged

children with reference to inclusive education. This needs special research efforts for designing suitable training and orientation programmes for teachers and developing suitable instructional aids and materials for teaching such type of children.

- The identification and nurture of talent is another priority area of research in view of the rate of innovation and change in both technological and social spheres.
- The scientific and technological development have not been matched by corresponding advance in human character and values. Research is needed in value education for fostering universal human values, and eliminating obscurantism, religious fanaticism, violence, superstition and fatalism.
- Research is needed to explore how the existing educational structure and content can be altered, enhanced and modified to bring about faster economic growth and social change. In this connection, research programme on problems like lifelong/recurrent education, work and productivity oriented education, education and self-reliance education and social mobility, strategies of human resources development, studies in education finance, administration and planning including management of systems and cost effectiveness, need immediate attention of research workers.
- The problems of the classroom, the teacher and the students, child development and processes of learning, and changing needs should also find place among the priority areas of educational research.
- Research and innovations are the two vital ingredients for the qualitative improvement of education. In this context, Leonardo de la Cruz, Head, ACEID, UNESCO, Bangkok, in his introductory address at UNESCO sponsored National Workshop on Educational Research (1989) remarked that one crucial area of target for such research and innovation if of course the educationally disadvantaged groups.
- At the higher education level, there is need for conducting evaluative studies to assess the impact of autonomous colleges and autonomous teaching departments, rural institutes/universities and academic staff colleges in providing quality education to college and university students.

- Open and distance education is also an important priority area of research. The impact of open schools and universities at the national and state levels in achieving the goal of Education for All need to be explored with the help of comprehensive surveys, longitudinal, experimental and evaluative studies.
- Teacher education also falls in the list of priorities. In this area, there is need for the reformulation of foundation or theory components of pre-service teacher education programme at elementary and secondary levels.
- The World Bank considers support for education to be an important part of its work for economic development. It believes this to be justified by research evidence. The 1980 policy paper on education issued by the Bank has drawn upon research and discusses educational research and research needs. It urges that research should be pursued into education as a social force interacting with society and the economy as part of the development process and as an individual learning process concerned with the determinants of leaning, application of skills, retention (Husen and Kogan, 1984).

Q10. What are the steps in educational research?

Or

Describe various steps in education research.

Ans. As the educational research is the application of scientific method to the study of educational problems, the steps in educational research, therefore, are more or less identical to those of scientific method. Following is a listing and brief description of the steps in the research process.

The research problem: Educational research starts with the selection of a problem that the researcher identifies from the area or field of his interest. It must be a question that can be answered through scientific inquiry. The problem should be such that can be clearly and precisely stated. The statement of the problem must be complete. It must be presented in a form that makes absolutely clear what data or evidence must be obtained in order to solve the problem.

Formulation of hypotheses: Educational research should make use of carefully formulated hypotheses. These may be formally stated or implied. In formulating hypotheses, the researcher should keep in mind that the hypotheses are tentative generalisations about the nature of the difficulty under consideration, calling attention to fundamental relationships or possible solution. The manner of formulating hypotheses is an important aspect of educational research and the researcher should give much thought to it.

The method to be used: The selection of research method to be used is of utmost importance in the research process. It refers to the general strategy followed in collecting and analysing the data necessary for solving the problem. The researches are generally classified in three categories: (i) Historical; (ii) Descriptive; and (iii) Experimental. The method or approach used in the study is dictated by the nature of the problem and the type of data required for answering the questions relating to the problem.

Data collection: Whereas the research method describes the overall approach to the problem, this step is concerned with the procedures and techniques to be adopted for data collection. It refers to the nature of the sample to be chosen for study, and selection and development of data gathering devices such as tests, questionnaires, rating scales, interviews, observations, checklists, and the like.

Analysis and interpretation of data: Good research is characterised by the care taken in the analysis and interpretation of data. It includes the selection of appropriate quantitative and qualitative techniques to be used for processing the data collected for the study.

Reporting the result: This is the last and important step of the research process. It is characterised by carefully formulated inferences, conclusions, or generalisations. The researcher must report his procedures, findings, and conclusions with utmost objectivity to others who may be interested in his study and its results.

Q11. What are the types of studies/researches in Educational Research?

Ans. Based on the two major paradigms, positivist and non-positivist, studies in educational research can be broadly categorised in two heads:

Quantitative Studies/Research: Quantitative studies are based on positive paradigm. It includes the following:

- **Experimental Studies** aims at investigating cause-effect relationships between variable in a given educational phenomena. The variable associated with the cause is independent variable and the variable associated with the effect is dependent variable.
- **Quasi–Experimental Studies** Quasi means 'seemingly, but not really'. Experimental studies follow true experimental design in which it is possible for the researcher to assign subjects randomly to groups or exercise full control over the scheduling

of experimental conditions. On the contrary, such conditions are not present in quasi-experimental design. The same kinds of problems studied in experimental research can be investigated using quasi- experimental research, but it is not possible for the research to assign subjects randomly to groups or exercise full control over the scheduling of experimental conditions.

- **Correlational Research** is a form of descriptive research concerned with determining the extent of relationship existing between variables. ***Example:*** relationship between the performance on intelligence test and performance on science achievement test.

Qualitative Studies/Research: Qualitative studies are based on non-positivist paradigm. It includes the following studies:

- **Descriptive Studies** are concerned with studying 'what exists'. It interprets and explains the educational phenomena. There are various forms of descriptive studies. For example, case studies investigate a particular case, i.e. an educational institution, a student, a teacher, a single system of education, etc. surveys of different forms also come under descriptive studies. Developmental studies attempt to investigate the change in the characteristics of children with their growth and development. Content analysis is concerned with the classification quantification and comparison of a given content, which may be from a document, or transcription of a speech or the communication between two or more people.
- **Historical Research** attempts to examine past events in order to draw their relevance for the present and for future like. There are various type of historical research namely, (i) bibliographic research, (ii) legal research, (iii) studying the history of scientific and philosophical ideas, (iv) Studying the history of educational institutions and organisation.
- **Philosophical Research:** The major emphasis of philosophical research is on analysing meaning and nature of educational concepts, and proposition and their relevance to educational practice. These studies also make an analysis of epistemology, metaphysics, and axiology of a particular educational process or educational thought.

Q12. What do you understand by the paradigm?

Ans. The idea of social construction of rationality can be pursued by considering Kuhn's idea of scientific paradigm. Thomas Kuhn, himself a historian of science, contributed to a fruitful development in the philosophy of science with his book *The Structure of Scientific Revolutions* published in 1962. It brought into focus two streams of thinking about what could be regarded as scientific, the Aristotelian tradition with its teleological approach and the Galilean with its causal and mechanistic approach. It introduced the concept of paradigm into the philosophical debate.

Definition and Meaning of Paradigm of Research

Paradigm derives from the Greek verb for "exhibiting side by side". In lexica, it is given with the translations "examples" or "table" of changes in form and differences in form. Thus, Paradigms are the ways of organising information so that fundamental and abstract relationships can be clearly understood.

The idea of paradigm directs attention to science as having recognised patterns of commitments, questions, methods, and procedures that underlie and give direction to scientific work. Kuhn focuses upon the paradigmatic elements of research when he suggests that science has emotional and political as well as cognitive elements. We can distinguish the underlying assumptions of a paradigm by viewing its discourse as having different layers of abstractions. The layers exist simultaneously and are superimposed upon one another. The concept of paradigm provides a way to consider the divergence in vision, custom, and tradition. It enables us to consider science as having different sets of assumptions, commitments, procedures and theories of social affairs. A paradigm determines the criteria according to which one selects and defines problems for inquiry and how one approaches them theoretically and methodologically. A paradigm could be regarded as a cultural manmade object, reflecting the dominant notions about scientific behaviour in a particular scientific community, be it national or international, and at a particular pointing time. Paradigms determine scientific approaches and procedures, which stand out as exemplary to the new generation of scientists – as long as they do not oppose them. A revolution in the world of scientific paradigms occurs when one or several researchers at a given time encounter anomalies or differences, for instance, make observations, which in a striking way to not fit the prevailing paradigm. Such anomalies can give rise to a crisis after which the universe under study is perceived in an entirely new light. Previous theories and facts become subject to thorough rethinking and revaluation.

There are three normal aspects of scientific research:

- Determination of the class of significant facts that the paradigm has shown to be particularly revealing of the nature of things in the field, and an attempt to increase the accuracy and reliability of facts.

- Matching of facts with theories, and
- Empirical work to articulate the paradigm theory, including a comparative study of various theories or generalisation with a view to deciding which one is better.

The normal scientific research is a puzzle solving activity, which includes not only solutions of problems that have not been solved before but also of problems that have not been solved so well. The new paradigm determines the problems that need to be solved; others are set aside. Sharing a paradigm does not necessarily mean having "shared values". However, lack of shared interpretation does not hinder the progress of research in the paradigm.

In a field of research, during the pre-paradigm stage there are frequent debates on legitimate methods, problems, and their standard solutions. When a paradigm is established, there is a general consensus in the research community on these issues. However, in the course of regular research, new and unsuspected issues crop up for which there are no readymade solutions. The attempt to solve them enriches and refines the paradigm; it leads to new theories, not all such theories are paradigm theories. During the pre-paradigm stage and during the crisis that develops in the existing paradigm, many speculative unarticulated theories come up which can point the way to a new paradigm.

Q13. How are paradigm, research and knowledge generation interrelated?

Ans. Research and knowledge generation

Research is an activity, which is carried out in a systematic way to find answers to questions. The questions which research seeks to answer may pertain to relationships between variables. The systematic exploration of the relationships leads to finding relational statements, which can be termed as laws. The laws help in understanding events or phenomena in the environment. The laws may be integrated to constitute a theory. In this sense, theorisation can be considered a goal of research. Also, since theorisation involves exploring several relational statements and integrating them, it is a complex process which requires a programmatic endeavour. And it is through the process of theorisation that research contributes to fund of knowledge, which can be seen to have a structure of its own; and this structure is concertised in terms of hypotheses, laws and theories. Thus, it can easily be seen that research is an organised search to find answers to questions, which ultimately makes contribution to knowledge generation process.

Research knowledge generate and Paradigm

Knowledge generation is directly an outcome of research activity, and, since a paradigm determines the research process in terms of influencing its assumptions, methods procedures, it has a determining influence on the knowledge generation process. From what has been elaborated on the nature and function of paradigm it can be seen that a paradigm goes to systematise the knowledge generation process, which proceeds as the development of a science as area or a set of phenomena is brought under study or close scrutiny. Then the relevant factors and variables are identified. Research or study correlates the variables and parameters, which may be found to be related to one another. Information about the phenomena under study is systematically integrated as theories begin to develop. If needed, the researcher may move from correlation to causality through systematic and controlled manipulation of variables (experimentation). This leads to establishment of a body of knowledge (theory) as the outcome of the study. Depending on the nature of the phenomenon under study, laws may be formulated and systematised. Ultimately, the established body of knowledge is used, according to necessity, in the resolution of problems or a source of further inquiry. Thus, a paradigm contributes to knowledge generation process, as it is an indispensable part of research.

Research and Paradigm

Research in social sciences is influenced by different intellectual traditions having different assumptions about the social world. On the basis of these varying assumptions, each tradition has its own particular set of questions, methods and procedures. With particular set of commitment, questions, methods and procedures, each tradition presents a paradigm. That is why a paradigm determines the criteria according to which a researcher selects and defines problems of inquiry. The paradigmatic elements form the rules of the game or disposition that govern and guide the day-to-day practices. They give definition and structure to the practices of research. A researcher trained in a particular tradition learns to see, feel, think and act as 'directed' by the paradigmatic elements in that tradition. These dispositions, the particular ways of seeing, feeling thinking and acting towards the world are implicit in the way in which the researcher defines the scope and the boundary of his inquiry. The concept of paradigm helps us understand the divergence in vision, custom and tradition. Paradigms explain social sciences as having different sets of assumptions, commitments, procedures and theories of social phenomena. It is in these disagreements that we have basic issues about values and visions of social order.

Paradigm in social science/educational research:

- In well-defined disciplines, which have developed over centuries, such as natural sciences, it is relatively easy to point out the paradigm that guides the research activities in that area. When social sciences emerged in the nineteenth century, they tended to regard the natural sciences as sciences as scientific models, but without awareness that the social scientist is part of a process of social self-understanding.

  The positivistic paradigm of social science research and knowledge generation is based on the philosophical ideas of the French philosopher, Auguste Comte, who accepted the natural science paradigm and turned to observation and reason as means of understanding human behaviour, More simply, explanation proceeded by way of scientific description. Comte consciously introduced the new science of society. The thought that it would be possible to establish it on a positive basis, just like the other sciences, which served as necessary preliminaries to it. Social phenomena were to be viewed in the light of laws and theories of natural sciences and investigated empirically; just like physical phenomena.

  Comte's position was to lead to a general doctrine of 'positivism' which held that all genuine knowledge is based on sense experience and can only be advanced by means of observation and experimentation. Following in the empirical tradition, it limited inquiry and belief to what can be firmly established and in thus abandoning metaphysical and speculative attempt to gain knowledge by reason alone. Positivist paradigm thus contributed to the development of social science research and generation of knowledge.

- Educational research faces the problem of having any prevailing paradigm because the very content of education and consequently that of educational research is multifaceted in nature. Education is a socially contrived process, intended to provide desired influences on individuals. The influencing factors included the learning material, teacher's role, conditions in school, or any other situation, where teaching-learning take place, interpersonal relationships arising out of interactions of various kinds, and also other factors in the community life that obtain in the form of social-cultural and economic aspects in the society. These factors and conditions, when created and utilised in educational environment, bear relationships that are educationally relevant. Devising relevant educative influences requires knowing the varied relationships that exist between and among the various attributes of learners and those of environment with the help of which their behaviours are sought to be modified. This brings to focus one major pursuit of educational research: to undertake an endeavour, to identify and discover a matrix of relationships, which constitutes the basic know-how for designing educational programmes and systems. This has to be continuous process since some news knowledge, regarding relationships between the availability of different educational inputs and the changing conditions to make in socio-economic political life, is required for relevant adjustments and modifications in ongoing educational programmes. This makes educational research multifaceted in content. And so, one single prevailing paradigm for educational research seems to be unsuitable.

Q14. Explain the meaning and characteristics of quantitative research paradigm in education. Why is this paradigm criticised in educational research?

Or

Discuss the main characteristics feature of paradigm of quantitative research paradigm.

Ans. The quantitative paradigm in educational research can be covered under the umbrella of social research, and is akin to natural science paradigm or positivistic paradigm. It is also known as empirical-analytical paradigm. In this paradigm, reality is treated as 'a given' or 'out' there in the world as objective. Knowledge is considered as something that can be acquired, and the communicated in tangible form. It is granted that human beings reason in deterministic fashion to the situations they encounter that every phenomenon that occurs has a cause. With these assumptions, the researcher, under the influence of this paradigm, seeks objective, external, quantifiable explanatory, verifiable and replicable data. According to this paradigm, human behaviour is rule-governed and the objective of the researcher is to identify the law-like regularities in the social-educational affairs and to manipulate them as we do with the objects in the physical world. This paradigm demands an analytical approach. Social/educational world is a world determined a number of factors, which simultaneously impact and interact with each other. If interrelated variables are identified, the specific causal relations can be established. It is granted that true knowledge is formalised knowledge. So, the variables of inquiry should be made clear and precise prior to starting to conduct research. Concepts need to be operationalised. Operationalisation of variables and reliability of measures receive considerable importance under this paradigm. Generalisations so reached will be testable or verifiable and hence meaningful. Thus, the paradigm falls in tune with the positivistic paradigm according to which any statement or proposition is meaningful if and only if it is verifiable, directly or indirectly.

Formal knowledge relies on mathematics for theory construction. Quantification eliminates or reduces ambiguity in the collected data. This paradigm favours logical inductive method to be adopted for hypothesis testing. Thus, empiricism, determinism, parsimony, generality, verifiability and replicability are some of the most important elements of this paradigm. Much of the research in social sciences and in education, as on date, is committed to this paradigm.

Characteristics/Different aspects of the paradigm of quantitative educational research

The paradigm of quantitative educational research has been presented here along with certain characteristics feature of it:

Basic assumptions: Regarding the nature of reality, the paradigm holds that a single tangible reality exists. This can be fragmented into variables. In this paradigm, the perceptions of the objects, events or processes are studied. In respect of inquirer-respondent relationships, the inquirer maintains distance from the object of inquiry so that reactivity is prevented. Regarding the truth statements (generalisability) the quantitative paradigm leads to nomothetic body of knowledge; truth statements are considered to be of enduring value and 'context-free'. Regarding causality it holds that for each effect there is a cause; controlled experiment can detect cause, concerning the relation to values, the inquiry is considered 'value-free', methodology being 'objective'.

Approach: The quantitative paradigm in educational research gives more importance to generation of universal arguments after natural sciences paradigm. They are more for the general view of the phenomenon under study.

Goals: The quantitative paradigm aims at establishing facts and testing of theories. A prior theory often guides inquiry. Statistical descriptions of facts present relations and intend to predict.

Research design: In the quantitative paradigm the research design in well specified; it is predetermined and gives the details in such a way that replication studies are possible. Hypotheses are formulated at the beginning of the study and the way they would be treated statistically, are given at the outset. The sample used is mostly selected randomly and the effort to control extraneous variables is made. Thus, the research designs are well knit and deterministic.

Methods: Methods in this paradigm are quantitative for precision and objectivity as well as mathematically manipulable. Methods generally used are experimental, survey, cross-sectional longitudinal, etc. These methods use structured observation tools for collecting data.

Tools: Quantitative paradigm in educational research prefers non-human data collection devices which allow the researchers to be objective. The tools generally in use are inventories, scales, questionnaires, tests, structured observation and interview.

Setting: Laboratory conditions are preferred because as a whole this ensures control.

Method of analysis: Quantitative paradigm in educational research follows a deductive approach. Statistical analyses are essentially used. Computer nowadays is an indispensable tool for data analysis.

Rigour, trustworthiness, and authenticity: The desirable characteristics of quantitative educational research are, as a whole, represented by internal validity, external validity, reliability and objectivity possessed by a piece of research.

Nature of findings: Research studies using quantitative paradigm have techniques to minimise bias and so the observations ultimately lead to objective findings, which are the goals of any significant piece of research education.

Limitations of quantitative paradigm in educational research

In recent years, strong counter pressures against quantification have emerged. They question the very assumptions on which the supposed superiority of the quantitative paradigm in educational research has been based. The following are some to the major limitations of the quantitative research paradigm.

Context stripping: Educational research situation, by its very nature, comprise numerous variables. Precise quantitative approach that focuses on selected subsets of variables, necessarily 'strip' from consideration, through approximate controls and randomisation, other variables that exist in the context of a particular piece of research in education. These 'stripped' variables might, if allowed to exert their effects, greatly alter findings.

Such exclusionary research designs, while increasing the theoretical rigour of a study, may detract from its relevance, that is, its applicability or generalizability because their outcomes can be properly applied only in other similarly truncated or contextually stripped situations (another laboratory, for example).

Exclusion of meaning and purpose: The main content of educational research is human behaviour which unlike that of physical objects, cannot be understood without reference to the meaning and purpose attached by human actors to their activities. Quantitative data, it is assumed cannot provide such rich insight into human behaviour. This sets serious limitation to the applicability of quantitative research paradigm.

Insider-outsider view: The 'outsider' view brought to bear upon an inquiry by an investigator (or the hypothesis proposed to be tested) may have little or no meaning within the 'insider' view of the studied individuals, groups, societies or cultures. Quantitative data, it is affirmed, are not useful for uncovering the 'insider' view. The theories concerning the study, to be valid, demand that all aspects or contexts of the educational research situation should be taken into consideration, which, by its very nature, is not possible under the quantitative paradigm.

Theory-ladenness of facts: Quantitative approach to research involving the verification or falsification of hypotheses assumes the independence of theoretical and observational characteristics of variables. If an inquiry is to be objective, hypotheses must be stated in ways that are independent of the ways in which the facts needed to test them are collected. But, it now seems established beyond doubt that theories and facts are quite 'independent' – that is, facts are facts only within some theoretical framework. Thus, a fundamental assumption of the quantitative research paradigm is exposed as dubious. If hypotheses and observations are not independent, 'facts' can be viewed only through a theoretical 'window' and objectivity is undermined.

Under-determination of theory: This limitation of the quantitative research paradigm is also known as the problem of induction. Not only are the facts determined by a theory window through which a researcher looks for them, but different theory windows might be equally well supported by the same set of facts. Although it may be possible, given a coherent theory, to derive by deduction what facts ought to exist, it is never possible, given a coherent set of facts, to arrive by induction at a single, independent theory. For example, while a million white swans can never establish, with complete confidence, the proposition that all swans are white, one black swan can completely falsify it. The proposition of the quantitative research paradigm that it can, by its methods, ultimately converge on the 'real' truth is thus brought sharply into question.

Value-ladenness of facts: Just as theories and facts are not independent, neither are values and facts, indeed, it can be argued that theories are themselves value statements. Thus, putative 'facts' are viewed not only through a theory window, but through a value window as well. The value-free posture of the quantitative research paradigm is thus compromised.

Q15. Explain the need for quantification in educational research.

Ans. While the first step in the development of science is the accumulation and clarification of observed events or phenomena, it soon becomes necessary to quantify these observations, for only quantification can provide the precision necessary for classification in a more mature science. In fact, the more advanced is the science, the greater is the need for it to go beyond enumeration, towards ever greater precision in measurement in order to permit the more adequate analysis of phenomena through mathematical manipulation.

Educational research data can be classified into two broad categories: qualitative data or attributes–for example, colour, intelligence and honesty and quantitative data for example, IQ, grade point average, height, etc. Generally, quantitative data are most easily processed when they are converted into numerical values. Quantification not only facilities their manipulation, but also increased the precision with which they can be analysed.

It is common knowledge that mathematics and statistics are prominently used in educational research, specifically in measurement and data analysis. For data collection, different variables (or attributes) characterising educational research situations are to be precisely measured in terms of numerical values; thus, the variables are quantified. These quantified variables are subjected to appropriate statistical techniques for data analysis in keeping with the objectives of the study. But, it has been quite often seen, even in the case of doctoral research study in education, that the researchers neither make a mention of the limitations of the quantitative procedure they employ, nor do they shown any evidence of their awareness of the limitations of the quantitative procedure they adopt for analysis of data. Every statistical technique of data analysis can be applied for specific objectives and purposes.

Criticism against quantification may be answered by taking the stance that the use of quantification works! Even if assumptions underlying the use of numbers and their manipulation may not be strictly adhered to by the researcher, quantification works quite well. While the educational researcher does not, of his own sweet will, disregard important assumptions in the assignment of numbers of the measures of variable or attribute being measured, he knows that he often cannot satisfy all such assumptions. Also he knows from experience as well as from his study of previous researches that taking sufficient care and employing adequate skill he can use his measures to get reasonable approximations of the variables under study along with the relation between them. He then can properly test and check his results to find their agreement with 'reality'. When he is able to achieve this, much he is in a position to employ mathematical/statistical methods to help him make reasonable inferences about what is 'out there' in the educational research situation.

Educational researchers are not unaware of the fact that statistical tests of significance have certain assumptions behind them. A sincere educational researcher need not be frightened about the violation of the assumptions when he has to use a statistical test. A researcher should rest on positive thinking that use of quantification in educational research has been highly successful. When increasing sophistication in measurement is possible with the help of computer, the use of quantification in educational research will be more desirable than posing challenge, problem and restriction.

Q16. Write short notes on the following:

(a) Types of paradigm in educational research

Ans. The two types of paradigm in educational research are:

'Positivist paradigm' or 'Quantitative research Paradigm': Modelled on the natural science paradigm it emphasises on empirical quantifiable observations, which lend themselves to analysis by means of mathematical tools. The task is to establish causal relationships leading to explanation.

'Non-Positivist' or 'Qualitative research' Paradigm: 'Non-Positivist' or 'Qualitative research' Paradigm is derived from the humanities with an emphasis on holistic and qualitative information.

(b) Use of quantitative research paradigm in education

Ans. The paradigm of quantitative research in education can be made use of to help the researcher when s/he has to design the investigation keeping in view a clear scheme of operation. S/he can visualise a framework, which will depict all aspects involved in the study such as the nature of data, their sources, the condition under which they can be obtained, devising instruments for collecting them, and ways as to how the data would be analysed. In other words, the emphasis of a given study varies in accordance with the perspective the researcher holds or the set of premises the researcher has for viewing the phenomenon under study. If the researcher has to design a strictly controlled experiment, he bases the entire study on the premise that the phenomenon can be rendered into a mathematical model or a quantifiable structure of variables. Similarly, when the concern of the study is the precision in discernment of characteristics of a concept and its relationships with other concepts, the approach is essentially quantitative. This is how the quantitative research paradigm in education works.

Q17. Explain the meaning of research paradigm.

Ans. Philosophers and sociologists of science have attempted to understand and describe the complexity of thought that guides definitions of 'Science'. They have used the concept of 'Paradigm of capture the idea that definitions of science (whether natural or social) are the products of shared understanding of reality – that is, worldviews (complete complex ways of seeing and sets of assumption about the world and actions within it). Used in this way, the concept has a grand scope, describing whole world of thought.

Analysing the different ways Kuhn has used the concept paradigm, Masterman (1970), has observed that Kuhn's twenty-one senses of paradigm fall into three main groups, viz. *metaphysical paradigms or metaparadigms, sociological paradigms* and Artefact Paradigms or construct paradigms. When Kuhn equates paradigm with a set of beliefs, with a myth, with a new way of seeing it, with an organising principle governing perception itself, and with something, which determines a large area of reality, it is clearly a metaphysical notion or entity, rather than a scientific one. When he defines paradigm as a universally recognised scientific achievement, as a concrete scientific achievement, etc., it is clearly a sort of sociological paradigm. Finally, Kuhn uses paradigm in a more concrete way, as an actual textbook or classic work, as supplying tools, more linguistically, as a grammatical paradigm, illustratively, as an analogy; and more psychologically, as a Gestalt – figure and as a an anomalous pack of card, it is nothing but a sort of artifact paradigms or construct paradigms.

Commenting on these different usages of paradigm, Masterman (1970), offers the following meanings— *sociologically*, "The Paradigm is something which can function when the theory is not there"; and *philosophically*, "A paradigm is an artifact which can be used as a puzzle solving device; not a metaphysical world – view; and finally, A paradigm has got to be a concrete 'Picture' used analogically; because it has got to be a 'way of seeing."

Q18. What is the scope for alternative paradigm in education?

Or

Differentiate between objective and subjective assumptions about reality (ontology).

Ans. Education is a process, a design for causing anticipated learning in individuals. This learning represents changes in individuals, which are basically intrinsic but get manifested in action forms in different situations in an individual's life. There would also be a qualitative improvement in the life of collectivities. In other words, Education has direct focus of the quality of life of individual in society under given conditions.

Educational practice pertains to deriving substance from the overall body of disciplinary knowledge for formulating them into translate curricular forms, making choices of curricular components and also deciding the modes of transacting them. Such actions for selectivity make education and action oriented, practice based programme or activity.

If one looks for concepts in education, one does find them in plenty, such as, curriculum, syllabus, work experience, drop out instruction, etc. However, there are many concepts, which are used in education such as learning, motivation, habits, intelligence, instructional system, cultural heritage, etc. It is often said that these are concepts from other disciplines, 'borrowed' into education. Thus, the broad canvas of education encompasses a multiple of concepts from different disciplines. Since each concept emerges from a particular disciplinarian perspective, their connotation changes when used in other disciplines. Therefore, while trying to understand education, one has to have an interdisciplinary attitude.

The idea about the nature of education presented clearly indicates the scope for viewing educational phenomena differently from different perspectives. These perspectives are as follows:

Conceptions of viewing reality

Ever since the methods of social science have been applied to the study of education and its problems, a controversy and debate has resulted. Educational research has at the same time absorbed two competing views of social science:

Traditional View: This view holds that social sciences are essentially the same as the natural sciences and are therefore concerned with discovering natural and universal laws regulating and determining individual and social behaviour.

Radical View: This emphasis how people differ from inanimate natural phenomena and, indeed, from each other. **(Cohen and Manian, 1994)**

Thus, both represent strikingly different ways of looking at social reality.

The objective and subjective views of reality

Paradigms may be considered as models for understanding reality and are described using the following categories: ontology, epistemology, human nature and methodology (Burrell and Morgan, 1979) (Figure 1.1).

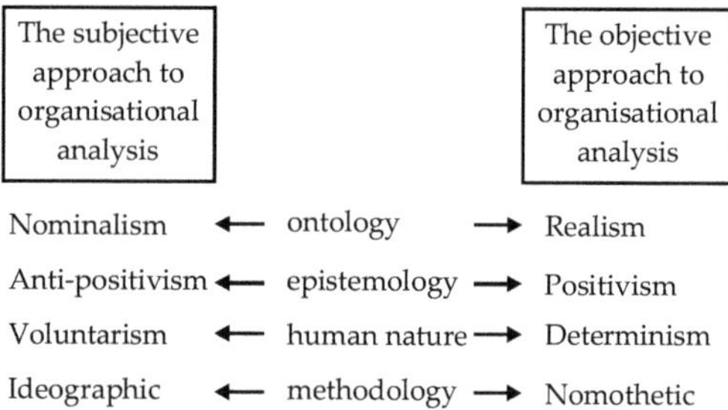

Fig 1.1: The subjective-objective dichotomy for analysing assumptions about the nature of social science

Source: *Burrell and Morgan (1979)*

(1) The nature of Reality (ontology)

(i) **Nominalism (subjectivist)** objective of thought are merely words and that there is no independently accessible thing constituting the meaning of a word.

(ii) **Realism (objectivist)** objects have an independent existence and are not dependent for it on the knower.

For example, in a seminar on social crises, scholars were discussing the issue of corruption.

- One group of scholar asserted –'it is an established fact that corruption as a social issue exists in all societies.' *Realism (Objectivist).*
- The other group of scholars dissented, countering that corruption is a social construct and its existence in the society is dependent upon the perception of people in any given society. They argued that corruption does not exist 'out there', waiting for the others to discover it. *Nominalism (Subjectivist).*

(2) The nature of knowledge and knowing (Epistemological)

(i) **Anti-Positivism (Subjectivist)** they hold that the very notion of 'truth' is problematic. Except for certain principles about the physical world, there are few truths that constitute universal knowledge. A poem or drawing is as legitimate a portrait of life experiences as a research report. It is soft, unscientific and idiosyncratic knowledge.

(ii) **Positivism (Objectivist)** truth exists 'out there'. In doing research, you will search for truth- or truths (multiple perspectives). Knowledge is hard, objective and tangible. It will demand of researchers as an observer's role.

For a concrete understanding of research paradigms vis-à-vis selection of research methods, please see Table 1.1.

Table 1.1: Selection of research paradigms and research methods

Research paradigms	Research approach	Research methods	Examples
Positivism	Quantitative	Surveys	• Attitude of distance learners towards online based education
		longitudinal,	• Relationship between students' motivation and their academic achievement.
		cross-sectional, correlational, experimental and quasi-experimental and ex-post facto research	• E? ect of intelligence on the academic performances of primary school learners
Anti-positivism	Qualitative	Biographical,	• A study of autobiography of a great statesman.
		Phenomenological,	• A study of dropout among the female students
		Ethnographical,	• A study of attitude of school new hired teachers
		case study	• A case study of a open distance learning Institution in a country.
Critical theory	Critical and action-oriented	Ideology critique,	• A study of development of education during the British rule in India
		action research	• Absenteeism among standard ? ve students of a primary school

Although, each of the paradigms has corresponding approaches and research methods, still a researcher may adopt research methods cutting across research paradigms as per the research questions she proposes to answer.

(3) The nature of Human Agency (Human Nature)

(i) **Determinism (Objectivist)** assume that human actions are predictable and hence, controllable.

(ii) **Voluntarism (Subjectivist)** unpredictability is the hallmark of human action; the goal is to describe and interpret how people make sense of and act in their words.

(4) Methodology

(i) **Nomothetic (objectivist)** views world of natural phenomena as being hard, real and external to the individual. Investigators will choose from a range of traditional potions- surveys, experiments, etc. Scientific investigation characterised by procedures and methods designed to discover general laws.

(ii) **Ideographist (Subjectivist)** views the social world as being of a much softer, personal and humanly created kind. Investigators will choose from a comparable range of recent and emerging techniques-accounts, participant observation, personal constructs, etc. The principle concern is with an understanding of the way in which the individual creates, modifies and interprets the words in which s/he finds himself/herself, taking qualitative as well as quantitative aspect. It has emphasis on the particular and individual and understanding of individual behaviour.

Q19. What is qualitative research? Mention the characteristics of Qualitative Research. Give a brief account of its background and nature.

Ans. Qualitative research is designed to reveal a target audience's range of behaviour and the perceptions that drive it with reference to specific topics or issues. It uses in-depth studies of small groups of people to guide and support the construction of hypotheses. The results of qualitative research are descriptive rather than predictive.

Definition of qualitative research

Qualitative research is defined as multi-method in focus, involving an interpretive, naturalistic approach to its subject matter (Denzin and Lincoln 1994).

Qualitative research can be characterised as the attempt to obtain an in-depth understanding of the meaning and definitions of the set presented by informants, rather than the production of a quantitative measurement of the characteristic or behaviour.

Characteristics of qualitative research

Best and Kahn (2002, pp. 184-185) has quoted ten themes proposed by Patton (1990, pp. 40-41) which highlight the following main characteristics of qualitative research:

- Qualitative research makes use of naturalistic inquiry. It aims at studying real world situations as they unfold naturally without any manipulation and pre-determined constraints on outcomes.
- It employs inductive or 'bottom-up' approach. The researcher generates new hypotheses and grounded theory form data collected during fieldwork. It aims to discover important categories, dimensions, and interrelationships. In the process of induction, the researcher begins by exploring genuinely open questions rather than testing theoretically derived (deductive) hypotheses. The data used to develop concepts and theories that help the researcher to understand the phenomenon.
- Most of the common research objectives in qualitative research aim at description, exploration, and discovery using 'wide-angle' and 'deep-angle' lens approach so as to examine the breadth and depth of phenomenon and to learn more about it. The whole phenomenon under study is "understood as a complex system that is more than the sum of its parts; focus on complex interdependencies not meaningfully reduced to a few discrete variables and linear, cause-effect relationships".
- The behaviour of the subjects under study is assumed to be fluid, dynamic, situational, social, contextual and personal. The behaviour is studied in the natural environments not under the controlled conditions.
- Qualitative research makes use of qualitative data, which are gathered from natural settings. These include "detailed, thick description; inquiry in depth direct quotations capturing people's personal perspectives and experiences". The researcher attempts to observe and describe the settings as they are, maintaining what Patton calls "emphatic neutrality". The total emphasis is on understanding of the situation in all its complexity by not proving something, not advocating, not advancing personal opinions and views, but researcher

includes his personal experiences and emphatic insight as part of the relevant data while taking a "neutral non-judgemental stance towards whatever content may emerge".

- Purposive sampling is the dominant strategy in qualitative research. The researcher uses small samples. He has direct contact with and gets close to the people, situation, and phenomenon under study. He collects qualitative data using in-depth interviews, participant observation, field observation, field notes and open-ended questions. The researcher is the primary data collection instrument, "researcher's personal experiences and insights are an important part of inquiry and critical to understanding the phenomenon". The data are in the form of words, images, and categories.
- Qualitative research emphasises "unique case orientation". It assumes each case is special and unique. Cross-case analysis follows from and depends on the quality of individual case studies.
- The analysis of qualitative data requires organising raw material into logical, meaningful categories, and examining them in holistic fashion for interpretation to others. The reports are narrative with contextual description and direct quotations from research participants.

The characteristics described above indicate that qualitative research is not one single method or strategy for research but a wide range of discrete strategies and methods. These strategies normally have one thing in common that they analyse complex and unique data through exploration. Qualitative research is concerned with the opinions, experiences and feelings of individuals producing subjective data. It is a "kind of research that produces findings not arrived at by means of statistical procedures or other means of quantification" (Strauss and Corbin, 1990, p. 17). Whereas quantitative research seeks causal determination, prediction, and generalisation of findings, qualitative research seeks understandings, exploitation and explanation to similar situations.

Background and Nature of Qualitative research

Qualitative research has a long and distinguished history. It has originated in the disciplines of sociology and anthropology and gradually being applied in other social science disciplines; education include. Qualitative research is a field of inquiry in its own right. A complex, interconnected family of terms, concepts, and assumptions surround the term qualitative research. These include the traditions associated with foundationalism, positivism, post-positivism, post-foundationalism, post structuralism, and the many qualitative research perspectives, and for methods, connected to cultural and interpretative studies (Denzin and Lincoln, 2003, p3). There are separate and detailed literatures on the many methods and approaches that fall under the category of qualitative research. Each method is based on a specific understanding of its object. However, qualitative methods cannot be regarded independently of the research process and issue under study. They are specifically embedded in the research process and are best understood and described using a procedural perspective.

Q20. What is the scope of qualitative research?

Ans. The following quote succinctly delineates the meaning and scope of qualitative research:

Denzin and Lincoln, 2003, *"Qualitative research is an interdisciplinary, trans-disciplinary, and crosscuts the humanities and the social and physical sciences Qualitative research is many things at the same time. It is multi-paradigmatic in focus. Its practitioners are sensitive to the value of the multi-method approach. They are committed to the naturalistic perspective and to the interpretive understanding of human experience. At the same time, the field is inherently political and shaped by multiple ethical and political positions.*

Qualitative research embraces two tensions at the same time. On the one hand, it is drawn to a broad, interpretive, post experimental, post- modern, feminist, and critical sensibility. On the other hand, it is drawn to more narrowly defined positivist, post- positivist, humanistic, and naturalistic conceptions of human experience and its analysis. Further, these tensions can be combined in the same project, bringing both postmodern and naturalistic or both critical and humanistic perspectives to bear."

In the academic social sciences, the most frequently used qualitative research approaches include the following:

- Ethnographic Research, used for investigating cultures by collecting and describing data that is intended to help in the development of a theory. This method is also called "ethnomethodology" or "methodology of the people". An example of applied ethnographic research is the study of a particular culture and their understanding of the role of a particular disease in their cultural framework.
- Critical Social Research, used by a researcher to understand how people communicate and develop symbolic meanings.

- Ethical inquiry, an intellectual analysis of ethical problems. It includes the study of ethics as related to obligation, rights, duty, right and wrong, choice, etc.
- Foundational Research, examines the foundations for a science, analyses the beliefs, and develops ways to specify how a knowledge base should change in light of new information.
- Historical Research allows one to discuss past and present events in the context of the present condition, and allows one to reflect and provide possible answers to current issues and problems. Historical research helps us in answering questions such as: Where have we come from, where are we, who are we now and where are we going?
- Grounded Theory is an inductive type of research, based or "grounded" in the observations or data from which it was developed; it uses a variety of data sources, including quantitative data, review of records, interviews, observation and surveys.
- Phenomenology describes the "subjective reality" of an event, as perceived by the study population; it is the study of a phenomenon.
- Philosophical Research is conducted by field experts within the boundaries of a specific field of study or profession, the best qualified individual in any field of study to use an intellectual analysis, in order to clarify definitions, identify ethics, or make a value judgement concerning an issue in their field of study their lives.

Q21. Discuss the history and criticism of qualitative research.

Ans. The history of qualitative research is vast and sometimes complex. Different scholars have tried to make several divisions starting from early 19th century to till the end of 20th century.

Denzin and Lincon have divided the 20th century history of qualitative research into five moments, which are as follows:

Traditional Period (Early 1900 s to World War II): In this period, qualitative researcher wrote "Objective" colonialising accounts of field experiences that were reflective of the positivist scientist paradigm written.

Modernist or Golden phase (1950 to 1970 s): In this phase rigorous qualitative studies of important social processes, including deviance and social control in the classroom and society took place. This was a moment of creative fermant.

Blurred genres (1970 - 1986): In this phase, the qualitative researchers had a full complement of paradigms, method and strategies to employ in their research. A plethora of theories were available to choose from, viz. symbolic interactionism, ethnomethodology, phenomenology, semiotics or feminism, critical theory, structuralism are some of the alternative paradigm. A plethora of theories were available to choose from viz. Symbolic interactionism, ethnomethodology, phenomenology, Semiotics or feminism, critical theory, structuralism, etc.

Crises of representation (mid 1980s): After the works by scholars like Marcus, 1988, Geertz, 1988 issues such as validity, reliability and objectivity, previously believed to be settled, once more become problematic. Writer continued to challenge older models of truth and meaning. Questions like whether other standard should be applied for assessing qualitative research were raised.

Fifth moment (recent situation): The search for grand narratives is being replaced by more local, small-scale theories filled to specific problems and particular situations.

From the history of qualitative research the following points can be summarised:

- Each of the earlier moments is still operating in the present.
- An embarrassment of choices now characterises the field of qualitative research.
- We are in a moment of discovery and rediscovery.
- Qualitative research act can no longer be renewed from within a neutral or objective positivist perspective.

Criticism of Qualitative Research

Qualitative research has some limitations also which are mentioned as under:

- Subjective bias is a constant threat to objective data gathering tools and analysis techniques. For example, an individual may intentionally attempt to exhibit an artificial behaviour when he knows that he is being observed during observation. Similarly, during an interview, the interviewees may not respond freely, frankly and accurately. There is a constant danger of subjectivity on the part of an observer/interviewer during observation/interview.
- The findings of qualitative research lack generalisations because of the nature and size of samples used for data collection. The samples are small in size and mostly purposive. Pure

subjectivity in the selection of such samples undermines their credibility.

- Qualitative research utilises a variety of methodologies in studying a phenomenon in holistic perspective. In certain cases, it is difficult to focus on complex interdependencies of its parts and understand the meaning of the phenomenon as a whole.

Q22. Give a tentative outline of doing Qualitative research in Education.

Ans. A qualitative research proposal consists of two essential elements:

- What the research wants to learn more about (the study's conceptual framework);
- How this will be implemented (its design and methodology);

Proposals for qualitative research typically have the following sections:

(1) Introduction
 (i) Theoretical/conceptual framework
(2) Research questions
 (i) Broad questions
 (ii) Focussed research questions
(3) Design choices (plan)
 (i) Overall approach and rationale
 (ii) Selection of the research site and population
 (iii) Data gathering procedure
 (iv) Tentative coding: domain identification
 (v) Data analysis procedures
(4) Data interpretation
(5) Credibility, Validity and Reliability
 (i) Establishing trustworthiness
 (ii) Personal biography of the researcher
 (iii) Ethical considerations
(6) Reporting
(7) Bibliography
(8) Appendices

(1) Introduction

(i) **Conceptual framework and theoretical position:** A model that includes the key concepts that are used to understand reality and the relationships among the concepts. It describes the topic and how it is framed, the research problem to be investigated, the general and specific research questions and the potential significance of the study. While presenting the conceptual framework, the researcher should clearly indicate the theoretical stand because different approaches have their theoretical assumptions. Generally speaking these approaches orient towards three basic positions:

(a) **Symbolic interactionism** concerned with studying subjective meaning and individual ascriptions of sense

(b) **Ethnomethodology** interested in routines of everyday life and their production;

(c) **Phenomenology** seeks to understand the lives experience of a small member of people.

(2) Research Questions

The formulation of research questions in concrete terms is guided by the aim of the study. Clear ideas about the nature of research questions that are pursued are also necessary for checking the appropriateness of methodological decisions. Frame the Study as responding to one or two general questions followed by a few sub questions. Frame the questions in a non-directional manner. They should not imply the cause and effect or suggest measurement. Also, expect that the question will evolve as the research unfolds as qualitative research refines and redefines as it emerges, you should expect change.

(3) Design Choices

(i) The design and methodology section serves two major purposes:

  (a) It represents a plan- the road map- for the conduct of the study.

  (b) It preserves the design flexibility that is a hallmark of QR

(ii) Design choice includes the following:

  (a) **Overall strategy and rationale:** Why you are fall a particular genre (Phenomenology, Ethnomethodology, Symbolic interactionism) in your study.

  (b) **Site or population:** It should clearly indicate whether the intensity and amount of data you can generate would help you fully respond to the research questions.

  (c) **Sampling Strategies:** It should indicate the following:

  - A priori determination of sample structure
  - Theoretical determination of sample structure
  - Gradual selection of sample

(d) **Data gathering procedure:** It should indicate the different types of techniques to be used for data collection. Techniques like participant observation, in- depth interviews, Artefacts, Focussed Group Discussion, Small group discussion, life histories, document research, archival research, etc.

(e) **Data management and Analysis procedure:** It should indicate about the data analysis technique. There are three ways:

- Ongoing analysis versus analysis at the end
- Structured or open ended analysis
- Analysis related to qualitative genre.

Then coding scheme, classification, categorisation, identification and content analysis takes place.

(4) Interpretation of Data

(i) Going back to theoretical framework with analysis.

(ii) How do one's findings compare with other findings in other contexts?

(iii) Where are the convergences and the departures?

(iv) How can one explain these with theory?

(v) Grounded theory - generation theory from 'below'.

(5) Credibility, Reliability and Validity

No single, universal, therefore totalising interpretation of truth. Verisimilitude is a criterion for 'veracity'.

(i) Specify what techniques and methods were used to ensure integrity of research

(ii) Specify researchers own position and assumptions

(iii) Ensure regulation at levels of: (a) Methodology; (b) Data; (c) Investigator; (d) Theory.

(6) Reporting

Reporting is the reflection of your analysis and interpretations several models of reporting exist.

(i) A chronology of events or descriptive life history

(ii) Thematic (in relation to)

(iii) Critical episodes

For excellent score, read GPH book.

2 RESEARCH PROBLEM

An Overview

One of the most difficult phases of the graduate research project is the choice of a suitable problem. Beginners are likely to select a problem that is much too broad in scope. This may be due to their lack of understanding of the nature of research and systematic problem solving activity. A careful survey and review of related enables a researcher to define and delimit the problem in terms of the nature of variables and scope. The review makes a researcher up-to-date on the work, which others have done and thus enables him to state the objective specifically. It helps to avoid unintentional duplication of well established findings.

The selection of a suitable problem is not an easy task. It is a major reasonability to commit oneself to a problem that will inevitably require much time and energy, which is so academically significant. The main sources of problem selection include: professional literature, inference from theories, professional experience and social, economic, political and technological changes.

Once the selection, definition and evaluation of the research problem have been accomplished the formulation of hypothesis is the most important step in the research process. The derivation of a suitable hypothesis goes hand in hand with the selection of a research problem. It gives definite point and direction to the study, prevents blind search and indiscriminate gathering of data and helps to delimit the field of inquiry.

After the identification of research problem, a researcher is required to write a research proposal. It is a plan for the research highlighting the theme of the research in the form of a title of the research problem; its specific objectives an hypothesis(es); the method and design of the study including details about the selection of sample(s) and tools analysis of data using quantitative and qualitative techniques, bibliography; time framework and financial budget.

Q1. Explain the meaning and importance of review of related literature.

Ans. A research problem arises from a theoretical and empirical framework. Thus, both conceptual and research literature are to be reviewed for this purpose. The review helps in identifying the latest research trends pertinent to a problem. It clarifies what is already known and also what is unknown and unexplored. An analysis of the related literature eliminates the possibility of duplication of what has already been done.

Importance

Review of the related literature, besides allowing the researchers to acquaint themselves with the current knowledge in the field or area in which they are going to conduct their research, serves the following specific purposes:

- The review of related literature enables the researchers to define the limits of their field. It helps the researchers to delimit and define their problem. To use an analogy given by Ary *et al.* (1972: 56), a researcher might say: 'The work of A, B and C has discovered this much about my question; the investigations of D have added this much to our knowledge. I propose to go beyond D's work in the following manner'. The knowledge of related literature brings the researcher up to data on the work, which others have done and thus to state the objectives clearly and concisely.
- By reviewing the related literature, the researchers can avoid unfruitful and useless problems. They can select those areas in which positive findings are very likely to add to the knowledge in a meaningful way.
- Through the review of related literature, the researchers can avoid unintentional duplication of well-established findings. It is of no use to replicate a study when the stability and validity of its results have been clearly established.
- The review of related literature gives the researcher an understanding of the research methodology, which refers to the way the study is to be conducted. It helps the researcher to know about the tools and instruments, which proved to be useful and promising in the previous studies. The advantage of the related literature is also to provide insight into the statistical methods through which validity of results is to be established.

- The final and important specific reason reviewing the related literature is to know about the recommendations of the previous researchers listed in their studies for further research.

Q2. Describe the procedure, which the researcher should adopt in identifying related literature and in locating, selecting and utilising the primary and secondary sources of information in the library.

Ans. The researchers must follow a specific procedure of logical searching. They should get a clear-cut picture of their own problem; otherwise, reading will be a random one. If they have grasped the general nature of their problem, then they should proceed on research for library material.

A library provides source of primary and secondary information. A researcher should be familiar with the library, its facilities and services.

Members of the library are usually issued a 'library card', which gives them access to the stacks. They can go through the stacks for an independent searching of books and other reference materials.

Members may also take the help of library staff in their search for such materials. After using the books or any other reference materials, it is desirable for the readers to leave them on the study tables so that library staff will return them to their proper place on the shelve. Sometimes a reference is not available in the library. In such a situation, the reader must consult the 'union catalogues' which lists reference found in other libraries. Such reference can be obtained by: (i) inter-library loan system; (ii) requesting an abstract or translation of the portion of a desired reference and (iii) requesting materials in different formats (micro-film/microfiche; CD-ROM and online soft copy).

Card Catalogue in the Library

The card catalogue is the index to the entire library collection. It lists the details of publications found in the library, with the exception of serially published periodicals.

Generally, the card catalogue contains author, title and subject cards arranged alphabetically. A great deal of information about a book can be found on the cards. Besides the title of the book and the name of the author, the reader will find the date of birth of the author, the edition, the publication data, the number of pages, and the name and location of the publisher. Other items listed on the cards are bibliographies, maps, portraits, illustrations, tables, series (if any) in which a book appears and a brief description of the book–whether the book is a translation and who did the translation.

Library Classification Systems

Library classification systems provide ingenious ways of systematising the placement and location of books. Every system is based upon a methodology that is logical and orderly to the smallest detail. The two principal systems of library classification in the USA are the Dewey Decimal system and the Library of Congress system.

The Dewey Decimal system is a decimal plan with the numbers running from 001 to 999.99. The Library of Congress system is particularly used in large libraries. It provides 20 main classes instead of 10 of the Dewey Decimal system. The system uses letters of alphabet for the principal headings and numerals for further sub-grouping.

In a library, all books have a call number of letter that appears in the upper left-hand corner of the author, subject or title card, and on the back of the book. These call numbers or letters are used to arrange the books serially on the library shelves and within each classification, the books are arranged alphabetically by author's last name, and deal with history, theory, research, philosophy, as well as the structure and fabric of education.

Library searching guidelines

As a researcher, the following 'library searching guidelines' suggested by Van Dalen (1973, p.88), may be of great use to you in identifying the best available resources pertaining to your problem.

- Before using a library, familiarise yourself with its layout, facilities, services, and regulations.
- Learn how to use the micro-form readers, photocopiers, and mechanical aids.
- In the stacks and in the periodical, reference, reserved book, and rare book rooms, note where materials that you will use frequently are placed.
- Schedule your work session in a library when you will encounter the least competition for resources and services
- Make out call slips for all or most of the books needed in one work session.
- Copy all information that the librarian needs to obtain each reference for you, and before closing the periodical index or card catalog, recheck and rectify any errors or omission.
- Arrange to spend a block of time in the library that is sufficient to accomplish a specific task.

- When little time is available; clear up questions that can be answered quickly through the help of reference books that are readily available.
- Before initiating search for materials in a library, write down questions that cover precisely the information you wish to locate and group the questions in accordance with the areas in the library where the answers may be found.
- Compile a list of the present and any previous names of periodicals, organisations, government agencies, collectors of statistics, libraries and museums with special collections, and outstanding authorities in your field.
- Keep a list of the best reference books, indexes, handbooks, historical studies and legal references in your area of specialisation.
- Obtain copies of the best bibliographies and reprints of significant research studies for your files.
- Note which periodicals regularly or occasionally print bibliographies, reviews of literature, or such other reference material and the issues in which they appear.

Q3. What are different sources of information for review of literature?

Ans. The various source of information are as follows:

Encyclopaedia of Education: These are very huge and multivolume publications. The spirit of the material of a good encyclopaedia is always scholarly. It gives far complete and balanced selection of topics accurately representing education at all stages and in its various aspects. They are the works of experts in the various areas of education. Organisation of their contents is usually alphabetical.

- **Encyclopaedia of Education Research:** It was prepared by Walter Scott Monroe under the auspices of the American Educational Research Association in 1941 and it was revised in 1950. It aims to present a critical evaluation, synthesis and interpretation of research studies in education. Its new edition has a much wider coverage including reports of educational research not only in the USA, but also in other countries.
- **Encyclopaedia of Modern Education:** It was prepared by Henry D. Rivilin and H. Schueller, which was published in New York in 1943 by the Philosophical Library. It is the work of over 200 eminent contributors and covers the entire fields of education.

- **Encyclopaedia of Education Research**: It was prepared under the auspices of Education Research Association, was edited by Chester Harries and published by Macmillan, New York. It is not merely a revision of earlier editions, but a completely rewritten volume that has attempted to put into a new prospective the findings of research.
- **Encyclopaedia of Childcare and Guidance:** It was published in 1968 by Garden City, New York, Doubleday and Co. It is a comprehensive work on the problem of childhood. It also suggests ways to deal with such problems.
- **Encyclopaedia of Philosophy:** It was published in 1967 by Macmillan-Free Press, New York. It is an authoritative and comprehensive reference work covering both Western and Eastern thought ancient, medieval and modern.

Research Periodicals: Information about new ideas and developments often appear in periodicals long before it appears in books. There are many periodicals in education and in other closely related areas that are the best sources for reports on recent research studies. Such periodicals give much more up-to-date treatment to current questions in education than books possibly can. They also publish articles of temporary, local or limited interest that never appear in book form. The periodicals of proper dates are the best sources for determining contemporary opinion and status, presents or past.

It has been estimated that there are about 2100 journals that are specifically related to the field of education. In all such journals one may also find articles of interest devoted to psychology, philosophy, sociology and other subjects.

All those engaged in educational research should become acquainted with certain educational periodicals and they should also learn to use the indexes to them. Knowledge about the editor of a periodical, the names of its contributors, and the associations or institutions publishing it may serve as clues in judging the merit of the periodical.

Ulrich's Periodicals Directory: A Classified Guide to a Selected List of Current Periodicals, Foreign and Domestic, 12th ed. (New York: Bowker, 1967) provides a comprehensive list of periodicals relating of education. In this directory, periodicals are grouped in a subject classification and are alphabetically arranged. Each entry includes title, subtitle, date of origin, frequency of publication, annual index, cumulative indexes and item characteristics of each periodical.

In India, many periodicals are published by some associations or institutions. They provide a medium for dissemination of educational research and exchange of experience among research workers, teachers, scholars and others interested in educational research and related fields and professions.

Abstracts: Abstracts include brief summaries of the contents of the research study or article. They serve as one of the most useful reference guides to the researchers and keep them abreast of the work being done in their own field and also in the related fields.

In India, the Ministry of Education and Social Welfare, Government of India (now Ministry of Human Resource Development), New Delhi, since 1995 has been issuing India Education Abstracts every three months. It abstracts the contents of books and periodicals on education published in India in English and Hindi. Most of the Indian journals are indexed in various issues. The abstracts appear under the following subject heading; Philosophy of Education; Educational Psychology; Measurement and Testing; Examinations; Students and Students Organisations; Educational and Vocational Guidance; Teacher Education and Training; Curriculum; Basic Education; Health and Physical Education; Primary, Secondary, Higher, Vocational and Technical Education; and Social Education.

Many professional periodicals and yearbooks, in India and abroad, include some reviews of research and technical discussions of educational problems in one or all the issues of their series.

Newspapers and Pamphlets: Many articles of particular interest to a researcher may be located through pamphlets and newspapers. Current newspapers provide up-to-date information on speeches, seminars, conferences, new trends and a number of other topics. Old newspapers, which preserve a record of past events, movements and ideas, are particularly useful in historical inquiries. Some libraries catalogue pamphlets and newspapers in their reference sections.

Government Documents: Government documents are a rich source of information. They include statistical data, research studies, official reports, laws and other materials that are not always available elsewhere. These are available in national, regional, states as well as local-level government offices.

Monographs: Monographs are also major sources of information on ongoing research. In the USA, universities and teachers' colleges publish many research studies in education in the form of monographs. A few examples of these are supplementary educational monographs, educational research monographs and lincoln school monographs. In England also, various institutes of education publish monographs from time to time. In India, only some universities and research organisations publish a limited number of monographs.

Theses and Dissertations: Theses and dissertations are usually preserved by the universities that award the authors their doctoral and masters degrees. Sometimes these studies are published in whole or in part in various educational periodicals or journals. Because the reports of many research studies are never published, a check of the annual list of theses and dissertations issued by various agencies is necessary for a thorough coverage of the research literature.

Computer-generated Reference Materials: School Research Information Service (SRIS), Direct Access to Reference Information (DATRIX) and Psychological Abstract Search and Retrieval Service (PASAR) in the USA provide a number of computer-generated reference sources that may save a great deal of time and effort of the researchers. SRIS operated by Phi Delta Kappa (Bloominton, IN) provides a computer printout of abstracts for a moderate fee. DATRIX, a development of the University Micro-films (Ann Arbor, MI) provides computerised retrieval for Dissertation Abstracts, from 1928 to date. The researchers can procure information on microfiche or Xerographic copy of the complete dissertation, which they need, form University Micro-films, on payment. The PASAR furnishes printouts of abstracts of psychological journal articles, monographs, reports and parts of books for a moderate fee.

Research sometimes requires courage. The history of science reveals that many important discoveries were made in spite of the opposition of political and religious authorities. The Polish scientist Copernicus (1473-1543) was condemned by church authorities when he announced his conclusion concerning the nature of the solar system. His theory that the sun, not the earth, was the centre of the solar system in direct conflict with the older Ptolemaic theory, angered supporters of prevailing religious dogma, who viewed his theory as a denial of the story of creation as described in the book of Genesis. Modern researchers in such fields as genetics, sexual behaviour, and even business practices have aroused violent criticism from those whose personal convictions, experiences or observations were in conflict with some of the research conclusions.

Q4. Describe the procedure which researcher should adopt in organising the related literature in a systematic manner.

Ans. After making the comprehensive survey of the related literature, the next step for the researcher is to organise the pertinent information in a systematic manner. It should be done in such a way as to justify carrying out the study by showing what is known and what remains to be investigated in the topic of concern.

The organisation of the related literature involves recording the essential reference material and arranging it according to the proposed outline of the study.

Recording Reference Information: Once pertinent information has been identified, the researcher should record certain essential information for locating the material on 3×5 inch index card to serve as a bibliography card. To make writing of the final report simpler, it is desirable that the information recorded in the bibliography card should appear, in content and style, exactly as it will appear in the final report.

The basic information in the bibliography card should include name of the author with last name first; title of the book or article; name of the publication (for articles); name of the publisher; date of publication; volume number, page numbers; and library call number (for books). If some of this information is not available, the specified space should be left blank so that the missing information can be included immediately upon locating references.

Recording Contest of References: After recording the essential information on the bibliography cards, it is necessary to arrange the cards according to the location of the material in the library. For example, the researcher may list together all cards pertaining to the material located in the periodical section. Similarly, all the material located in the reserve section may constitute another list, and so on. Then the researcher should make a systematic review of the material located in a specific section of the library and after reviewing each reference on the list, he should proceed to another list.

All the information likely to be used in the final report should be recorded on 4×6 inch card to serve as content card. The information to be recorded on the content cards will depend on the source from which it is taken. If it is from a primary source, it may include brief bibliographic information comprising author's last name, brief title of the report, specific page numbers on which information is located; sentence statement of the problem; brief description of the study; statements of findings or conclusion, or both; a card code as to the aspect of the research to which the material most closely relates.

The information to be recorded from the secondary source is somewhat different from the primary source. Turney and Robb (1971, p.55) have given the following suggestions for recording information from a secondary source:

- Provide brief bibliographic information (as with a primary source).
- Record on a single card only those statements that are related to the same topic (if all the information cannot be placed on one card, continue statements on another card and staple on the first card).
- Paraphrase, in complete statements, the most relevant ideas. Record direct quotations only if they are stated concisely and effectively, and if paraphrasing might change meaning.
- Place a page number and a paragraph number after each separate statement indicating its location in the reference in case you need to review it again.
- Code the cards (probably in the upper-right hand corner) according to topic(s) to which it most closely relates.

Preparation of the Related Literature Report: For the preparation of the report of the related literature, the researcher should arrange the bibliographic and content cards according to the proposed outline of the problem. This can be done with the help of card code.

The report of the related literature should begin with an introductory paragraph describing the organisation of the report. After the introduction, the researcher should present the studies most relevant to each aspect of the proposed problem outline. Studies with similar and contradictory results should be reported side by side without using excessive space.

Q5. Give a brief account of some important referencing styles.

Ans. The few important referencing styles are as under:

Address

Abdul Kalam, A.P.J. (2005). *How to add value to distance education.* Address of the President of India at the 16th Convocation of IGNOU (March 5). New Delhi. (http://www.presidentofindia.nic.in/sripts/eventslatest1.jsp?id=836)

Book Chapter

Kulandai Swamy, V.C. (2002). *Open and Distance learning, and concerns of access and equity.* In H.P. Dikshit et al (Eds.), Access and Equity: Challenges for open and distance learning. New Delhi: Kogan Page India.

Journal article

Chaudhary, S.V.S., and Bansal, K. (2000). Interactive radio counselling in IGNOU: A study Journal of Distance Education, 15(2), 37-51.

Conference Paper

Joshi, M.M. (1998). *'Higher education in India: Vision and action.'* Country paper presented at UNESCO World conference on Higher Education at the 21st century, Paris, October 5-9.

Research Report

Panda, S., Raza, R., Khan, A.R., Garg, S., and Gaba, A. (2004). Study on programme completion and learner persistence and dropout in distance education. Unpublished research report. IGNOU, New Delhi and International Research Foundation for Open Learning, Cambridge.

Books

Singh, Anjula (2014). *Philosophical and Sociological Perspectives.* New Delhi: Gullybaba Publishing House (P) Ltd.

Q6. Describe the important sources for selecting a research problem.

Ans. After selecting the broad area, the researcher must narrow it down to a highly specific research problem. He must state the specific question whose answer he seeks through the application of scientific method.

It is not possible to all the educational problems that need to be researched. Each researcher selects a problem because of his own unique needs and purposes. There are, however, some important sources which helpful to a researcher for selecting a problem.

Professional Experience

One of the most fruitful sources of problems for the beginner in research is his own experience as a professional educator. In the classroom, there is a dynamic interaction between teacher and pupil, between pupil and pupil, and between pupils and materials.

This interaction provides a rich source of problems to be solved through educational research. Classrooms lectures and discussions suggest many stimulating problems to be solved. The teacher may be confronted with a number of behavioural problems in the classroom. He has to make decisions about the probable effects of classroom instruction on pupil behaviour so as to establish a relationship between instructions objectives, learning experiences and pupil change. The pupil behaviour may be analysed in terms of his achievement, interests, intelligence, aptitudes, motivation and personality. The teacher has to make decisions about teaching methods and techniques. He may study the effectiveness of a particular method of teaching so as to base classroom instructions upon empirical evidence rather than upon his biased impressions. For instance, a teacher in a secondary school may wish to investigate whether the problem-discussion method is more effective in the teaching of civics to tenth grade students in comparison to lecture method.

The classroom is not the only source of problems for the teacher. The experience of the pupils, their attitudes, home environment, peer influences, socio-economic status, and motivation level are rich sources of problems.

The educational administrators may find subjects of research in the areas concerning decision-making, scheduling, teacher placement, instructional supervision, and several other-matters with which they are concerned. Different professional personnel in the field of education view the educational scene from different angles and they may encounter many problems of research in their own perspective.

Contacts and discussion with research oriented people, attending conferences, seminars and listening to the learned speakers are helpful in identifying research problems. Active membership in organisations, which are concerned with the improvement of educational system usually, brings one into close contact with crucial problems and issues concerning education.

Inference from Theory

A second important source of research problem lies in the inferences that can be drawn from various educational and psychological theories known to the researcher. The application of general principles involved in various theories to specific classroom situation makes an excellent starting point for research. It will help to determine whether a particular theory can be translated into actual practice. Learning theories, personality theories, theories of intelligence, theories of motivation, sociological theories and many others provide rich sources of topics for research in classroom situations. It is only through the application of scientific method, that we can profitably test the validity scope and practicability of various theories in educational situations.

Professional Literature

Among the sources of problems, one has to be thoroughly acquainted with the literature in the field of one's interest. The study of professional literature will not only expose a research to pressing research problems but also suggest the way in which research is conducted. Research reports, bibliographies of books and articles, periodicals, research abstracts, yearbooks, dictionaries and research guides suggest areas that need research. Some specialised sources as the *Encylopaedia of Educational Research, Dissertation Abstracts International,* the *Hand-book of Research on Teaching, Psychological Abstracts* and similar publications provide rich sources of problems. The publications like *Research Needs in the Study of Education* (1968) and the *Third Indian Year Book of Education: Educational*

Research (1968), *Surveys of Research in Education* (1973, 1979, 1987, 1991, 1997, 2006) are exclusively devoted to identifying and bringing into sharp focus the varied research needs in the different areas and aspects of Indian education. All published research reports generally conclude by making suggestions about further research. Such suggestions help a researcher to consider how the procedures employed could be adapted to solving other problems, or how a similar study could be undertaken in a different field or subject area or with a different sample or subjects.

Replication or extension of completed research studies is also a profitable and worthwhile activity for a beginner in research. There is a common feeling that once a study has been conducted, it should not be repeated. Repeating a study at different times on different groups, in different contexts and places increases the extent to which the research findings can be generalised and provides additional evidence of the validity of the findings.

Sometimes research studies are criticised for weakness in design, tools, treatment and analysis of data, contradictions and inconsistencies in the results, and so on. A valuable and worthwhile contribution can be made by repeating such studies after making necessary modifications in the design and procedures so as to correct or modify the findings for their inconsistencies.

Technological and Social Changes

Technological and social changes demand development of new courses and curriculum for students in educational institutions. All these developments constantly bring froth new problems for research. The use of hardware and software in classroom instructions, the training of teachers in the methodology of teaching through team teaching, micro-teaching, simulation, computers, etc. are being advocated by the educations all over the country. All such innovations in education need to be carefully evaluated through research process.

Q7. Define a research problem. Discuss how to evaluate the selected research problem on the basis of certain criteria.

Ans. After the problem has been selected, the next task is to define it in a form amenable to research. According to Whiteny (1964, pp.80-81):

To define a problem means to put a fence around it, to separate it by careful distinctions from like questions found in related situations of need.

The researcher must be certain that he knows exactly what his problem is before he begins work on it. Specifying a problem explicitly and narrowing it down to workable size are extremely important at the very star. According to Monroe and Engelhart (1928):

To define a problem means to specify it in detail and with precision. Each question and its subordinate questions to be answered are to be specified. The limits of the investigation must be determined. Frequently, it is necessary to review previous studies in order to determine just what is required to be done. Sometimes it is necessary to formulate the point of view or educational theory on which the investigation is to be based. If certain assumptions are made, they must be explicitly noticed.

In the formal definition of the problem, the researcher is required to describe the background of the study, its theoretical basis and underlying assumptions, and state the problem in concrete, specific, and workable questions.

All questions raised must be related to the problem. Each major issues or element should be separated into its subsidiary or secondary elements, and these should be arranged in logical order under the major division.

A good statement of a problem must clarify exactly what is to be determined or solved. It must restrict the scope of the study to specific and workable research questions. The most important step in this direction is to specify the variables involved in the questions and define them in operational terms.

Evaluation of the Problem

When considering problem, which a researcher may undertake for investigation, he is required to ask himself a series of questions about it. These questions are helpful in the evaluation of the problem on the basis of personal suitability of the researcher and that on social value of the problem. All these questions must be answered affirmatively before the study is undertaken.

Is the Problem Researchable?

There are certain problems that may not effectively solved, through the process of research. The question such as, "Is it good to provide sex education in the secondary schools?" is a value question and can be answered only on the basis of value judgement. The educationists, parents, students, and teachers may provide answer to such type of questions, but in practice, questions involving philosophical issues are hardly answered by scientific investigation. Science cannot provide answer to philosophical and ethical questions. A reasonable problem is always concerned with the relationship existing between two or more variables that can be defined and measured.

Therefore, research cannot be used in developing solutions to philosophical and ethical issues. The point that is being emphasised here is that the problem must be stated in workable research questions that can be answered empirically. For instance, the above question might be rested as,

"What is the effect of sex education in the secondary schools on the attitudes of adolescent girls towards premarital indulgence in sex?" the researcher can be design a study to obtain information on this type of question that can be used in developing a solution to the ethical question, "Is it good to provide sex education in the secondary school?"

Is the Problem New?

There is no purpose in studying a problem, which had already been adequately investigated by other researchers. In ignorance, a researcher undertakes a study, which is neither new nor original. He, therefore, spends time needlessly on a problem already investigated by some other researcher. To avoid such duplication, it is essential to examine very carefully the record of previous studies completed in one's field. The researcher should not select a problem until he is convinced that it is really a new problem and has not been investigated so far. However, this does not mean that a problem, which has been investigated in the past, is no longer worthy of study. A researcher may repeat a study when he wants to verify its conclusions or to extend the validity of its findings in a situation entirely different from the previous one.

Is the Problem Significant?

The questions of the significance of the problem usually relates to what a researcher hopes to accomplish in a particular study. What is his purpose in undertaking to solve the particular problem he has chosen? When new knowledge does he hope to add to the sum total of what is known? And what values is this new knowledge likely to have? All these questions are directed to the researcher. Unless these questions can be answered clearly by him, the problem should not be selected for research.

The research should show that the study is likely to fill the gaps in the existing knowledge, to help resolve some of the inconsistencies in previous research, or to help in the reinterpretation of the known facts. The findings should become a basis for theory, generalisations or principles and should lead to new problems for further research. However, if the findings lack apparent implications, then they must, at least, have some practical application.

Is the Problem Feasible for the Researcher?

A problem may be a good one from the point of view of three criteria mentioned above, yet it may not be feasible in view of some of the personal aspects of a researcher discussed below:

Researcher competencies: The problem should be in an area in which the researcher is qualified and competent. He must be familiar with the existing theories, concepts and laws in order to identify a worthwhile problem.

Interest and enthusiasm: The problem should be one in which the researcher is genuinely interested and about which he is truly enthusiastic. It should be meaningful and arouse real curiosity of the researcher.

Financial consideration: The problem should be one, which is financially feasible. The researcher should ascertain whether he has the necessary financial resources to carry on the investigation of the selected problem. He must have an estimate of the expenditure involved in data gathering equipment, printing, test material, travel and clerical assistance. If the research project is an expensive one, the researcher may determine the possibility of getting financial assistance from the state and private agencies and central organisation like the University Grants Commission, the National Council of Educational Research and Training, the Indian Council of Social Sciences Research, National Council for Teacher Education, and Distance Educational Council (IGNOU).

Time requirements: The problem should one that can be studied and completed in the allotted time. It is worthwhile to plan for the time that will be needed for the development and administration of tools, processing and analysis of data, and writing of the research report.

Administrative considerations: In addition to personal, financial and time requirements, the researcher should consider the kinds of data, equipment, specialised personnel, and administrative facilities that are needed to complete the study successfully. The researcher must ascertain whether the pertinent data are available and accessible to him.

Q8. Explain the meaning and importance of hypothesis.

Ans. The term hypothesis consists of two words: hypo and thesis '*Hypo*' means tentative or subject to verification. '*Thesis*' means statement about the solution of a problem. Thus, the meaning of the term 'hypothesis' is a tentative statement about the solution of a problem.

In accordance with John W. Best (1963), 'it is a shrewd guess or inference that is formulated and provisionally adopted to explain observed facts or conditions and to guide in further investigation'. According to J. Mouly George (1970) 'hypothesis is an assumption or proposition, whose tenability is to be tested on the basis of the compatibility of its implications with empirical evidence and with previous knowledge'.

The hypothesis, in a very general way, is defined as the tentative solution to the problem. It is a proposition or a statement, which implies that this may, perhaps be the answer to the problem and needs to be tested for being established as a fact. According to Van Dalen (1956), 'a hypothesis serves as powerful beacon that lights the way for the research worker'. It simply means that the hypothesis tells the researchers what to do, how to do and why to do all that in the context of problem-solution. For example, 'a very bright student fails in the examination'. A researcher gets concerned with the problem and wants to know why, in spite of being bright, the student has failed. After reviewing various factors and circumstances that might have been responsible for this failure, the researchers make a conjecture that the student might have been seriously ill at the time of examination. This conjecture is the form of a hypothesis and determines what the researchers should do to verify whether it is a fact or not. They visit the house of the student to meet parents and enquire about the student's health at the time of examination. The entire thing is determined by the hypothesis that they had developed.

Hypothesis refers to a conjectural statement about the solution of the problem, which the researchers verify on the basis of relevant information collected by them. it is said to be an informed or shrewd guess, inferences, supposition or hunch about what may be the solution of the problem or answer to a question. It is a statement which is tested and which implies linkages and non-linkages between variables in terms of their relationships, association, differences and prediction, after which the testing are either accepted or rejected. It is a possible explanation for the puzzling condition or event that concerns the researcher.

Importance of Hypotheses

The importance of a hypothesis is generally realised in the studies, which aim to make predictions about some outcome. Since experimental studies aim at making predictions about the outcome of the experiment, the role of a hypothesis is considered to be utmost importance. A hypothesis is recommended for all major studies to explain observed facts, conditions or behaviour and, hence it serves as a guide in the research process. The hypothesis saves time and energy of a researcher in gathering extensive empirical date and in detecting relevant relationships between variables. Without a hypothesis, the researcher would find it difficult, laborious and time-consuming to identify pertinent facts needed to explain the problem under investigation. A hypothesis provides definite point to inquiry, aids in establishing direction in which to proceed and helps in delimiting the field of investigation by identifying the specific facts on which to concentrate and specifying the facts which are to be weeded out.

- A hypothesis provides tentative explanations of facts and phenomena. Such explanations, if held valid, lead to generalisations, which help significantly in understanding a problem and thereby extend the existing knowledge in the area to which they pertain.

- A hypothesis provides direction to research. It represents specific objectives and thus helps in identifying the type of data needed to test the proposition. It helps in the selection of relevant facts and variables that the researcher needs in this study. A hypothesis provides basis for selecting the samples and the research procedures to be used in the study. Data analysis techniques (qualitative and quantitative) needed are also implied by the hypothesis. It also helps the researcher to delimit their study in scope so that it does not become broad or unwieldy.
- A hypothesis provides basis for reporting the conclusions of the study. It is convenient for a researcher to test each hypothesis separately and draw conclusions relevant to each hypothesis.

Q9. Discuss the various types of hypothesis.

Ans. Generally, hypotheses are classified into two types:

Directional Hypothesis

It is the one, which stipulates the direction of the expected difference or relationships. For example, 'engineers will have more mechanical interests than the doctors'.

Non-directional Hypothesis

It is one, which does not specify the direction of the expected difference or relationship. For example, 'There is a difference in the mechanical interests of engineers and doctors'.

A research hypothesis can be in any one of the following forms:

- Declarative form
- Null form
- Question form

In *declarative form,* the researcher makes a positive statement. For example, 'The mechanical interests of engineers are significantly more than that of doctors'.

In *null form*, the researcher makes a statement that no relationship exists, e.g., 'There is no significant difference in the mechanical interests of engineers and doctors', and the difference that the researcher has found by measurement is only by chance. Because of this sort of no difference assertion of the null hypothesis, this is called by some as a hypothesis of null difference.

The null hypothesis is used for denying many other forms of researcher hypothesis also. For example,

- If a researcher's hypothesis says that there is a correlation between two variables, the null hypothesis declares that there is no correlation if the entire population is taken; and whatever correlation comes is due to sampling chance.
- If the researcher's hypothesis says that distribution of a trait in a population is not normal, the null hypothesis would say that it is normal and non-normality in the sample taken is merely due to sampling chance.

They are also called the testing hypothesis when declarative hypothesis is tested statistically by converting them into a null form. The statisticians use the null hypothesis because it is testable statistically.

In the question form hypothesis, a question is asked as to what will be the outcome instead of stating what outcome is expected, e.g., 'Is there any difference in the mechanical interests of engineers and doctors?' After knowing in detail about the word hypothesis, its sources, qualities and types, we are in a position to formulated hypotheses. For any research problem, it is generally possible to derive more than one hypotheses.

Researchers formulate hypotheses by using both induction and deduction approaches. One of the goals of the research is to produce or formulate a principle or a theory, which will provide answers to practical problems.

Now in order to be plausible and have a chance of coming out true, the hypothesis must emanate from the study of previously discovered facts and theories, which the researchers might have field.

Q10. Discuss the criteria of a good hypothesis.

Or

What are the characteristics of a good Hypothesis?

Ans. A good hypothesis should meet the following criteria:

- **It should be stated as far as possible in simple terms:** Stating the hypothesis in simple terms not only makes their meaning clear to others, but also helps in their testability. Moreover, the simplicity of statement provides a basis for a clear and easily comprehensible report at the completion of the study.

  A hypothesis should not make use of the vague terms or constructs. It is quite useless to formulate a hypothesis that makes use of terms or constructs which do not convey the intended meaning to the reader. The researcher should make use of such terms that are generally accepted for naming a phenomenon.

- **It should be consistent with most known facts:** A hypothesis should not be inconsistent with a substantial body of established facts. They should be grounded in the well-established theories and laws. Consider the hypothesis, 'There is no relationship between the self-concept of adolescent male students and their rate or physical growth.' This hypothesis is not worth testing because the preponderance of evidence supports the relationship between self-concept and rate of physical growth.

  A hypothesis, however, cannot be consistent with all known facts because is so many areas the facts themselves contradict one another. In such cases, it is worthwhile to formulate hypotheses that resolve the contradiction.
- **It should be limited in scope:** Hypotheses of global significance are not usable as they are not specific and simple for testing drawing conclusions. The beginning researchers, however, are overly ambitious in their initial efforts and formulate hypotheses of global significance. It is partly because to their earnestness and partly because it takes maturity of viewpoint to realise how little can be accomplished in a specific period. It is desirable to formulate hypotheses that are simple to test, yet are highly significant. Sometimes it is of course possible to state a rather broad research hypothesis and derive a number of operational hypotheses from it.
- **It should be amenable to testing within a reasonable time:** The researchers should not select a problem, which involves hypotheses that are not amenable to testing within reasonable specified time. They must know that there are problems that cannot be solved for a long time. These are problems of immense difficulty that cannot be profitably studied because of the lack of essential techniques or measures.
- **It should state the expected relationship between variables:** A satisfactory hypothesis should state explicitly an expected relationship between the variables.
- **It should be testable:** A hypotheses should be formulated in such a way that they can be tested or verified. Such hypotheses enable the researcher to determine; by observation, whether those consequences that are derived deductively, actually occur or not. If the hypotheses are not testable, it would be impossible

either to confirm or contradict them and therefore they do not help the researcher to draw conclusions. For example, the hypothesis: 'The NCC programme promotes the all-round adjustments for the high-school students would be hard to test because of the difficulty of defining and measuring all round adjustment. Moreover, it would be difficult for the researcher to isolate other factors that might contribute to the adjustment of high-school students.

- **It should be clearly and precisely stated:** When hypotheses are clearly stated that usually avoid the use of general terms such as personality, intelligence and social class in their statements. On the other hand, the researcher may use 'personality as measured by the Sixteen Personality Factor Questionnaire, 'intelligence as measured by Raven's Progressive Matrices' or 'social class as defined by socio-economic status scale by Jalota et al'. The clear statement of hypotheses generally involves concise technical language and definition of terms that are better defined that those in common language.
- **It should be amenable to testing within a reasonable time:** The researchers should not select a problem, which involves hypotheses that are not amenable to testing within reasonable specified time. They must know that there are problems that cannot be solved for a long time. These are problems of immense difficulty that cannot be profitably studied because of the lack of essential techniques or measures.
- **It should state the expected relationship between variables:** A satisfactory hypothesis should state explicitly an expected relationship between the variables.

Q11. State how the hypotheses are tested.

Ans. Hypotheses are possible explanations, which account for the factors, events, or conditions that the researcher attempts to understand. After they are formulated according to the criteria, they are subjected to the empirical as well as logical testing:

(1) Some hypotheses are simple and can be tested directly. In most situations, however, they are complex and cannot be so tested. They have to be tested in terms of their deducted consequences. In scientific thinking process, the hypotheses involve deduction of consequences. Suppose a researcher wants to test the hypothesis: "Affluence leads to immorality"; he cannot test this

hypothesis directly and he has to proceed indirectly. He might deduce the consequences emanating out of the situation of affluence, e.g., great consumption of liquor, thereby leading to loss of reason, giving rise to greater crime rates, adultery, fast driving, etc. It would then be considerably convenient to test the hypothesis in terms of its deduced consequences. Indirect method of handling research problems involves intricate and complex procedures. Intellectual and disciplined effort is needed for the deduction of consequences. In this way, the researcher does not test the hypothesis, but tests the deduced consequence of the hypothesis. Once all the deduced consequences, after testing, come out to be true, the hypothesis is confirmed. If some of the consequence are true and some others not, the hypothesis needs to be examined afresh.

In order to test the hypothesis in terms of deducted consequences, it is necessary to collect evidence by selecting or developing data collecting instruments, to analyse the data, and then to interpret results in the light of the hypothesis and its deduced consequences. Any hypothesis then will be confirmed it the evidence agrees with the deduced consequences.

The necessary conditions for confirmation are:

(i) All factual evidences collected through tests or other means should correspond with the deduced consequences.

(ii) The test situations or data collecting tools should take into account all factors and conditions that are suggested by the consequences.

(iii) The consequences are logically deduced from the hypotheses.

(2) The absence of conflict with the other satisfactorily proved generalisations lends support to the correctness of a hypothesis.

(3) A hypothesis is also confirmed to correct if the predictions made on its basis prove to be successful.

Q12. Explain the meaning of Research Proposal and describe its various types.

Ans. A Research Proposal is "a written statement of the research design that includes a statement explaining the purpose of a study and a detailed systematic outline of a particular research methodology."

The research proposal drawn up by the investigator is the result of a planned, organised and careful effort and basically contains the following:

(1) Broad goals of the study
(2) The specific problem to be investigated
(3) Details of the procedures to be followed
(4) The research design offering details on:
    (i) The sampling Design
    (ii) Data collection methods
    (iii) Data analysis
(5) Time frame of the study
(6) The budget, detailing the costs with reference to specific items of expenditure.

    The initial draft of the proposal is a tentative plan or a blue-print, which is submitted to the experts for scrutiny, comments, suggestions and modification.

Types of Research Proposal

There are three types of research proposals. The categorisation is generally made keeping in view the type and purpose of the study.

- The most common research proposal is of the type that is prepared by those who undertake research for their degree of diploma in education. In most of the institutions/universities, submission of a well planned research proposal is a general requirement for researchers while persuing a degree or diploma course. These proposals are prepared by the researchers either under the guidance of their approved supervisors or a committee of experts.
- The second category of research proposal is one that is submitted by a researcher to NGO or governmental organisation for financial support, which is provided by the concerned agency after the scrutiny and evaluation of the proposal by a committee of experts.
- The third category of research proposal is submitted by school, college or university academics to research organisations, such as university, the Indian Council of Social Science Research, the National Council of Educational Research and Training, National Institute of Open Schooling, Distance Education Council (DEC-IGNOU), or any other autonomous research organsiation.

Q13. Explain the procedure used in the preparation of a research proposal or synopsis.

Ans. A worthwhile research study is likely to result only from a carefully planned and well-designed proposal. The following categories of information should appear in the research proposal.

Introduction

The introductory part of the proposal should include the following information:

(1) **The Title:** The title of the research proposal should do no more than name the topic. It should be so worded that it suggests the theme of the study. In selecting a title, the researcher should consider two things:

(i) The title should not be burdened by pompous words and should not include terms of unscientific, rhetorical, argumentative, emotional, or biased nature. The language in the title should be professional in nature but not pedantic.

(ii) The title should not be too lengthy or too involved. It should be specific to the area of study.

(2) **Statement of the Problem:** Statement of the problem is not exactly the same as the title of the thesis. It has a definite place in the introduction and is an attempt to focus on a clear goal. Statement of the problem should primarily be an expansion of the title. It should be either in question form or as a declarative statement. The major question or statement may be followed by several minor questions or statements and explanations.

(3) **Review of Related Literature:** It is always desirable for research workers to devote some time in reviewing the related literature to know the studies already conducted in the field and to ensure that what they are going to do is not just a repetition of the previous work. Under this section, the research worker should report some significant and landmark studies in the area of the research in hand. As far as possible, the latest studies should be mentioned giving evidence that the research worker is well versed with the latest position of research in the area of work.

(4) **The Hypotheses:** Questions that the research is designed to answer are usually framed as hypotheses to be tested on the basis of evidence. This step establishes the problem and the logic underlying the research study. It gives direction to the

data gathering procedure. It is in the light of the hypotheses that the relevance of data to be collected is judged.

(5) **Significance of the Study:** A research proposal should show the worth and urgency of the study. It should indicate clearly how the results of the research could influence educational theory or practice.

(6) **Definition of Terms and Concepts:** It is necessary to define all unusual terms and concepts that could be misinterpreted. The technical terms or words and phrases having special meaning need to be defined operationally. We seldom come across unanimous definition or modes of measurement for certain concepts and terms, such as intelligence, motivation, achievement, etc., and in such situations, it becomes obligatory on the researcher to provide an operational definition of such terms or concepts by stating how the variables will be measured and interpreted.

(7) **Delimitations of the Study:** Boundaries of the study should be made clear with reference to (a) the scope of the study by specifying the areas to which the conclusions will be confined, and (b) the procedural treatment including the sampling procedures, the techniques of data collection and analysis, the development of measuring tools and their use in the study.

(8) **Basic Assumptions:** Assumptions are statements of ideas that are accepted as true. They serve as the foundation upon which the research study is based.

The researchers in writing their proposal should select their basic assumptions with care and be particularly aware of certain common errors.

Method, tools and techniques

Under this section, the method employed for the research should be explained. Occasionally, a research study may employ more than one method. In that case, all such methods should be mentioned. It is not sufficient to give theory behind the method, but it is more important to explain how this method will be used in a particular study. The investigator should also describe the main tools and techniques, which may be employed for data collection. The tools may be described in two categories: (a) standardised tools and (b) tools developed by the investigator. In case of standardised tools, information about their validity and reliability should be furnished. In case of the tools developed by the investigator, the procedure to be followed for the development of tools should be described in brief.

Data analysis

A paragraph indicating the procedure to be followed for analysing the data should be indicated. If any statistical technique is to be used, it should be referred. It is not sufficient to mention only the name of statistical technique, but it must be clarified for what purpose a particular technique will be used. A technique will be justified only in terms of objectives of the study.

Bibliography

In each research, proposal, the researcher should give a list of books, journals, and other documents that he has used in selecting the problem, which he may use during the tenure of study.

Time Schedule

The researcher should also prepare a realistic time schedule for completing the study within the time available. Dividing a study into phases and assigning dates for the completion of each phase helps the researcher to use his time systematically.

Budget

The research proposals, which are submitted to government, private or autonomous agencies for financial assistance should also include a budget proposal estimating the funds required for travel expenses, typing, printing and cyclostyling, purchase of equipment, tools, books and other materials.

3 DATA COLLECTION AND ANALYSIS

An Overview

A method of data collection is the procedure that a researcher physically uses to obtain research data from research participants. Since the research problem is always associated with a larger population, it may not be possible to arrive at generalisation that would be applicable with a larger population, it may not be possible to collect empirical evidence from such a larger population. Hence, there is need of having a small population from which the relevant evidence can be gathered. This small population is the representation of the larger population and is called the sample. The process of selecting a small population from the large population is called sampling. A sampling plan should specify how the elements are drawn from the large prevent population and also how many elements are drawn. Blalock(1960) states that all sampling plans can be brought under two categories such as non-probability sampling and probability samplings.

In order to arrive at empirical solution to the research problem, you need to collect data or evidences from the representative population or sample. The instruments that are employed to collect new facts or to explore new fields are called tools. It is of vital importance to select suitable instruments and tools. Different tools are used to collect different types of data. The use of a particular research tool depends upon the type of research proposal. The researcher may use one or more of the tools in combination for this purpose. Such tools or methods of data collection include tests, interviews, questionnaire, observation, etc.

Q1. Differentiate and draw relationship between Sample and Population.

Or

Discuss the concept of sample.

Ans. A population is composed of the entire group of people that could possibly be included in your study. A sample is a subgroup of individuals selected from that population. Unless the population is small, when you conduct your research you could not possibly study every individual within the potential study population, so you study a subgroup or sample. As researchers choose a sample for study, they need to make sure that the sample is representative of the larger population. When there is a representative sample, the researcher will be able to generalise to the population.

For instance, a researcher intends to study the learning styles of B.Ed. teacher trainees enrolled in IGNOU. Since each year about 10,000 students enroll in IGNOU's B.Ed. programme, it is not possible to collect data from all students. Hence, the researcher may decide to select a sample of 500 or 1000 students for the purpose of collection of data. This selection is called sample and 10000 enroll students will be come in population for this research.

Sampling can save time and money! After research is conducted and researchers determine characteristics of the sample, then generalisations can be made about the entire population. (Johnson and Christensen, p.222) It is unrealistic to expect an entire population to participate in a study (unless the population is extremely small) therefore, sampling is an accepted alternative. Even when researchers intend to study an entire population, this may not be possible because of people who refuse to participate or because of others who cannot be contacted. Again, a sample is what is needed for the study.

Q2. What do you understand by the sample size? Do you think that the larger the sample size is the better generalizability of the research findings? Justify your answer.

Ans. An important consideration in judging the credibility of research is the size of the sample. In most studies, there are restrictions that limit the number of subjects, although it is difficult to know when the sample is an important consideration in judging the credibility of research is the size of the sample. In most studies, there are restrictions that limit the number of subjects, although it is difficult to know when the sample is too small.

Most researchers use general rules of thumb in their studies, such as having at least 30 subjects for correlational research, and at least 15 subjects in each group in an experiment. In surveys that sample a population, often a very small percentage of the population must be sampled, for example less than 5 or even 1 per cent. Of course if the survey sample is too small, it is likely that the results obtained cannot characterise the population. Formal statistical techniques can be applied to determine the number of subjects needed, but in most educational studies, these techniques are not used.

In educational research, a major consideration with sample size is concluding that a study with a relatively small sample that found no difference or no relationship is true. For example, suppose that you are studying the relationship between creativity and intelligence and, with a sample a of 20 students, found that there was no relationship. Is it reasonable to conclude that in reality there is no relationship? Probably not, since a probable reason for not finding a relationship is because such a small sample was used. In addition to the small number of subjects, it is likely that there may not be many differences in either creativity or intelligence, and without such differences, it is impossible to find that the two variables are related. That is, with a larger sample that has different creativity and intelligence scores, a relationship may exist. This problem, interpreting results that show no difference or relationship with small samples, is subtle but very important in educational research since so many studies have small samples.

If a greater precision of results in an investigation is needed, the sample should be larger. Greater precision is sometimes needed when one is dealing in areas where difference are likely to be small.

Krejcie and Morgan (1970) have developed a table (see Table 3.1) which may be referred to by the researcher for determining the size of a sample.

Table 3.1: Determining the size of a random sample

N	S	N	S	N	S
10	10	220	140	1,200	291
15	14	230	144	1,300	297
20	19	240	148	1,400	302
25	24	250	152	1,500	306
30	28	260	155	1,600	210
35	32	270	159	1,700	313
40	36	280	162	1,800	317
45	40	290	165	1,900	320
50	44	300	169	2,000	322

55	48	320	175	2,200	327
60	52	340	181	2,400	331
65	56	360	186	2,600	335
70	59	380	191	2,800	338
75	63	400	196	3,000	341
80	66	420	201	3,500	346
85	70	440	205	4,000	351
90	73	460	210	4,500	354
95	76	480	214	5,000	357
100	80	500	217	6,000	361
110	86	550	226	7,000	364
120	92	600	234	8,000	368
130	97	650	242	9,000	368
140	103	700	248	10,000	370
150	108	750	254	15,000	375
160	113	800	260	20,000	377
170	118	850	265	30,000	379
180	123	900	269	40,000	380
190	127	950	274	50,000	381
200	132	1000	278	75,000	382
210	136	1100	285	10,00,000	384

Notes: N=population size; S = sample size

Source: *Krejcie and Morgan, 1970*

From Table 3.1, it is evident that the size of the sample decreases at an increasing rate as the population size increases. But this may not be the case always as you can find from the table that the sample size is 382 for a population of 75,000, whereas it is 384 for a population of 10,00,000. But according to Borg and Gall (1979), sample size should be large where:

- there are many variables;
- only small differences or small relationships are expected or predicted;
- the sample will be broken down into small groups;
- reliable measures of the dependent, variable are unavailable.

However, Garrett (1962) has cautioned that if size of the sample is less than 25, there is often little reason for believing such a small group of units to be adequately descriptive of any population. Therefore, for getting better evidence from the sample, the size of the sample should be larger.

Q3. Discuss the various sampling methods.

Or

Explain the different types of probability sampling with suitable examples. [Dec-2012, Q.No.-2]

Ans. Sampling is a method of selecting units of analysis such as households, people, consumers, companies etc from a population (universe) of interest to a manager. By analysing the data collected from the sample, you draw inferences about the population parameters. In other words, sampling is employed to throw light on the population parameter.

It can be of two types: probability sampling and non-probability sampling.

Probability Sampling (Random Sampling)

A probability sampling is a method of sampling that ensures that every unit in the population has a known non-zero chance of being selected. Please note that every potential sample need not have the same chance of selection. Practitioners have been using various forms of random selection, the most popular being a random number table. Today, computers have replaced the random number table and the software generates the random numbers in a scientific manner very fast.

There are quite a few variant of random sampling:

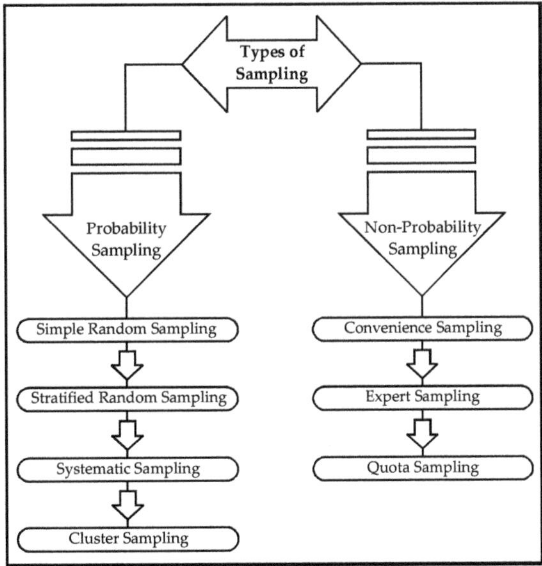

Fig. 3.1: Types of Sampling

Probability Sampling

Probability sampling involves the selection of a sample from a population, based on the principle of randomisation or chance. Probability sampling is more complex, more time-consuming. However, because units from the population are randomly selected and each unit's probability of inclusion can be calculated, reliable estimates can be produced along with estimates of the sampling error, and inferences can be made about the population.

The following are the most common probability sampling methods:

Simple Random Sampling: Simple Random Sampling is the foundation of Probability Sampling. It is a special case of probability sampling in which every unit in the population has the same chance of being selected. If you have to select n units out of N units, every possible selection of n units must have the same probability.

For example, a bank wants to do a study on the customers' perception of its service quality in the last 12 months with regard to the savings bank account holders. First, you have to prepare the sampling frame for this study. You can go through that bank's records and get a complete list of saving bank account holders. This is your sampling frame. Suppose your sampling frame contains 500 account holders and you have to select 50 out of this 500 and interview them. How to actually draw a sample of 50 account holders out of the 500 account holders?

One method is to prepare 500 small paper slips, each giving the account holder's name and account number. Put these slips in a container, shuffle the container thoroughly and then select 50 slips one after the other from the container.

Stratified Sampling: This method is useful when the population consists of a number of heterogeneous subpopulations and the elements within a given subpopulation are relatively homogeneous compared to the population as a whole. Thus, population is divided into mutually exclusive groups called strata that are relevant, appropriate and meaningful in the context of the study. A simple random sample, called a subsample, is then drawn from each strata or group, in proportion or a non-proportion to its size. As the name implies, a proportional sampling procedure requires that the number of elements in each stratum be in the same proportion as in the population. In non-proportional procedure, the number of elements in each stratum are disproportionate to the respective number in the population. The basis for forming the strata such as location, age, industry type, gross sales, or number of employees, is at the discretion of the investigator. Individual stratum samples are combined into one to obtain an overall sample for analysis.

Imagine that you are working as a Marketing Manager in a Consumer Product company and you are studying the customer attitudes towards your product in order to improve your sales. Suppose there are three typical cities that will influence your sales. Suppose the customers within each city are similar and between cities are vastly different. Selection of the customer for the study has to be a random sample of customer chosen from each city so that meaningful and reliable inferences can be drawn, which in turn will enable the marketing manager to develop suitable strategies. This is an example of stratified random sampling.

Systematic Sampling: This procedure is useful when elements of the population are already physically arranged in some order, such as an alphabetised list of people with driving licences, list of bank customer by account numbers. In these cases one element is chosen at random from first *k* element and then every kth element (member) is included in the sample. The value *k* is called the *sampling interval.* For example, suppose a sample size of 50 is desired form a population consisting of 100 accounts receivable. The sampling interval is Thus, a sample of 50 accounts is identified by moving systematically through the population and identifying every 20th account after the first randomly selected account number.

Systematic random sampling is very easy and less time consuming. The precision of systematic random sampling is higher than simple random sampling.

The chance of selecting a non-representative sample is very high in this method of sampling especially when there is a correlation between the place of the unit in the population list and the characteristics of the unit that should be observed. Here it is possible that using the "k" you jump over some specific units and select in case different units of the population.

Multistage Sampling: This method of sampling is useful when the population is very widely spread and random sampling is not possible. The researcher might stratify the population in different region of the country, then stratify by urban and rural and then choose a random sample of communities within these strata. These communities are then divided into city areas as clusters and randomly consider some of these for study. Each element in the selected cluster may be contacted for desired information.

For example, for the purpose of a national pre-election opinion poll, the first stage would be to choose as a sample a specific state (region). The size of the sample, that is the number of interviews, from each region would be determined by the relative populations in each region. In the second stage, a limited number of towns/cities in each of the regions would be selected, and then in the third stage, within the selected towns/cities, a sample of respondents could be drawn from the electoral roll of the town/city selected at the second stage.

Multi-phase sampling is designed to make use of the information collected in one phase to develop a sampling design in a subsequent phase. A study with two phases is often called double sampling. The first phase of the study might reveal a relationship between the family consumption of non-aerated beverages and the family income and this information would then be used in the second phase to stratify the population with family income as the criterion.

The essence of this type of sampling is that a subsample is taken from successive groups or strata. The selection of the sampling units at each stage may be achieved with or without stratification. For example, at the second stage when the sample of town/cities is being drawn, it is customary to classify all the urban areas in the region in such a way that the elements (town/cities) of the population in those areas are given equal chances of inclusion.

This method needs careful design. The inference about sample and final analysis is a bit complicated and should be based and adapted on the procedure of the sampling and different methods were used.

Cluster sampling (Area Random Sampling: One of the problems encountered with probability sampling methods is that you have to apply sampling procedure to a population that is scattered across a number of wide geographic regions. In these cases, you will have to cover a lot of distance in order to have access to the units you propose to sample.

Suppose you want to do a simple random sample survey of all the residents in India who belong to the highest income category. Your interviewers will have to do a tremendous amount of travelling. It is for this reason cluster-sampling method is followed. The steps involved in cluster sampling are:

- Divide the population into a number of clusters bases on geographic boundaries
- Select a random sample of clusters from this population of clusters
- Either measure all units within the randomly chosen clusters or do further random sampling each cluster.

Strictly speaking, when you measure all the units in the selected clusters, the procedure is called cluster sampling. Suppose you do further sampling within each cluster by adopting a simple random sampling or stratified random sampling, the procedure becomes a *multistage sampling.*

Non-probability Sampling

The fundamental difference between non-probability sampling and probability sampling is that in non-probability sampling procedure, the selection of the sample units does not ensure a known chance to the units being selected. In other words, the units are selected without using the principle of probability.

Even though the non-probability sampling has advantages such as reduced cost, speed, and convenience in implementation, it lacks accuracy in view of the selection bias. Another negative point of the non-probability sampling is its inability to generalise results from the sample to the population. It is mandatory in inferential statistics to use only probability sampling for valid conclusions. Non-probability sampling is suitable of pilot studies and exploratory research.

Convenience Sampling: Using college and university students in studies involving attitudes towards co-education is basically a matter of convenience. In consumer panel studies, you may use clients who are available to you as your respondents for giving their opinion on products and services. In many research projects, you simply look for volunteers to participate. This is how the convenience sampling is done. For heaven's sake, don't generalise results based on convenience sampling.

Expert Opinion Sampling: Expert Opinion Sampling involves gathering a set of people who have the knowledge and expertise in certain key areas that are crucial to decision-making. In qualitative methods of demand projection for a new product, you use the expert opinion method to arrive at a reasonable forecast. The advantage of this sampling is that it acts as a support mechanism for some of your decisions in situations where virtually no data are available. The major disadvantage is that even the experts can have prejudices, likes, and dislikes that might distort the results.

Quota Sampling: In simple terms, quota sampling is stratified random sampling without probability principle being applied to the selection of the sample units. Suppose in an opinion study, you want both men and women to participate. You know that in the population category of interest, 65 per cent are men and 35 per cent are women. If your sample size is fixed at 200, you will have a quota of 130 men and 70 women. It doesn't matter how you get them as long as you have met the quota. There are some socio-economic studies where quota sampling is the only way out because of practical considerations. You can do the descriptive statistics, graphs, charts, and summary table and stop there. That is it. Drawing any possible conclusions from a quota sampling will be highly tentative. None of the statistical inference techniques should be applied when you have followed quota sampling or for that matter any non-probability sampling procedure.

Q4. Discuss the concept of sampling error.

Or

What do you mean by sampling error? Explain with examples.

[June-2012, Q.No.-3(a)]

Ans. Sampling error arises from estimating a population characteristic by looking at only one portion of the population rather than the entire population. It refers to the difference between the estimate derived from a sample survey and the 'true' value. The measures estimated from the samples are called statistics, and will tend to differ more or less from sample to sample drawn from the same population due to fluctuations of sampling. Measures descriptive of a population, on the other hand, are called parameters and are to be thought of as fixed reference value. The difference the sample estimate (statistics) and the population value (parameter) is called error.

Sample studies are subject to sampling and non-sampling errors, which are of a random and/or of a constant nature. Mouly (1963, pp. 169-170) has classified these errors in a four-way classification table which is shown in figure 3.2.

	Random	Systematic
Sampling	A	B
Measurement	C	D

Fig. 3.2. Errors of Sampling

The cells A and B refer to sampling errors while C and D refer to non-sampling ones.

The errors which are due to sampling and of which the average magnitude can be determined are called sampling errors. Cell A refers to the unavoidable errors that occur whenever sampling is done and some shift in the sample statistics is caused by selecting at random any individual who may be high, low or average in the trait in question. For example, if the researcher has decided to select a sample of 50 students in a study of achievement motivation and has already chosen the first 49, the 50th student, selected at random, high in achievement motivation, will, therefore, cause some shift in the sample statistics in the upward direction.

Cell B refers to constant errors of sampling. These are also called errors of bias in sampling, that is, errors which do not cancel out but which lean systematically in one or the other direction of the population value. For example, the researcher would probably introduce a bias in his data by drawing a sample some favoured locations. When the magnitude of systematic errors is large, the data are of limited use for drawing out of the generalisations about the population.

Whatever the procedure of sampling, there are also due to faulty tools of measurement, incomplete coverage of sample or non-response, defects in data collection, etc. These biases produce errors, which are known as non-sampling errors. These are also called measurement errors and are represented in figure 3.2 by the cells C and D. The errors in the cell C refer to random errors of measurement and are due to the unreliability of the testing. On any measuring instrument, most individuals are likely to be mismeasured to some degree due to errors in the procedures of observation, interviewing, coding, non-response, etc. These errors are called as variable response errors and they tend to cancel each other in the long-run.

Cell D refers to systematic errors of measurement. It concerns biases, which include all the discrepancies between our observations and the quantities we aim to measure of the systematic non-cancelling types. For example, if in the testing of a sample of students for general mental ability, the researcher unintentionally allows an extra time of 2 minutes for the test, there will probably be a systematic tendency for the sample statistics to be higher than it should be, and therefore, there will be a bias in the measurement of mental ability. The size of such biases is unknown in practice. The square of the total error is the sum of squares of sampling and non-sampling error. That is:

$$(\text{Total error})^2 = (\text{Sampling errors})^2 + (\text{non-sampling errors})^2.$$

This relationship may be illustrated by means of the three sides of a right-angled triangle shown in figure 3.3.

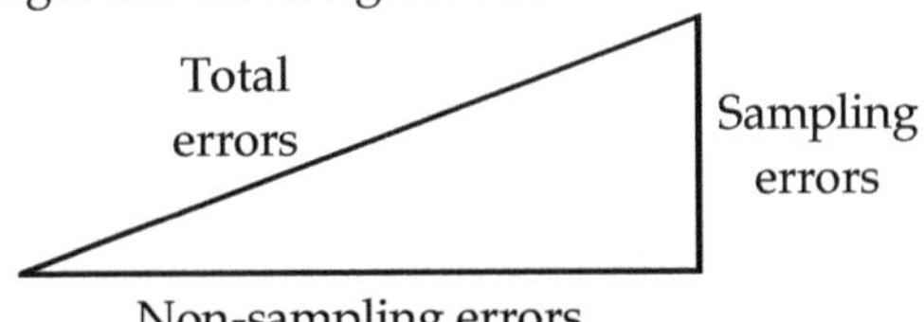

Fig. 3.3. Relationship between Total, Sampling and Non-sampling Errors

The total error can be represented by the hypotenuse and its length depends on the length of two other sides representing sampling and non-sampling errors. Thus, the total error cannot be shorter than either of the errors. The magnitude of sampling errors can be minimised to any value sometimes by a change in sample design, and always by selecting more sampling units, either in the form of more clusters or more individuals. By taking large sample, random sampling errors cancel each other to the point that the sample statistics will tend to stabilise close to the population parameter. Of the non-sampling errors, the random or variable, response errors may be reduced either by taking more observations per individual (s), interviewers or by improving the precision of the methods of observation. The magnitude of non-sampling errors may be mostly due to bias or systematic error of measurement, which can be minimised only through better survey methods, i.e. through improving the questionnaire or, the fieldwork, or the coding and processing of data, etc.

Q5. Classify the tools of research on the basis of purpose they serve in research process.

Or

Differentiate between norm-referenced and criterion-referenced tests. [June-2013, Q.No.-3(d)]

Ans. A researcher will require many data gathering tools and techniques, which may vary in their complexity, design, administration and interpretation. Each tool or technique is appropriate for the collection of certain type of evidence or information. The researcher has to select from the available tools, which will provide data, he requires for the testing of the hypotheses.

Tests consist of a series of tasks, which the subject is required to perform. They are designed to measure general mental ability or intelligence; special abilities or aptitudes; creativity; achievement; personality traits and adjustment, interests and values.

Cronbach (1964, p.21) defines a test as a systematic procedure for comparing the behaviour of two or more persons at a particular time; or one or more persons at different times.

Classification of tests

The classification of the test may be made in term of their purpose, that is, the type of psychological traits that they describe and claim to measure, for example, tests of general intelligence, tests of aptitudes, tests of achievement, etc. The tests may be non- standardised, teacher made or standardised. Another classification is made on the basis of types of responses which an item requires, e.g., paper-pencil tests and performance tests.

Standardised test versus teacher made test

Standardised test are those test, which are validated over a large sample. This sample acts as a norm group for various kinds of variables you include in your study. The validity and reliability of these tests are established with the help of various statistical measures. Such test also standardised content, procedure of test administration, procedure of scoring and interpretation for the users. Standardised tests are widely accepted and used by the researchers. On the other hand, you may like to develop tests on your own to collect evidences on various aspects pertaining to functioning of a school or educational system. For example, a teacher may like to develop a test to assess students' performance in Mathematics. S/he may not go for establishing validity and reliability of the test, as the purpose is limited.

Power tests versus speed tests

Power tests do not have time limits. The test taker is give ample time to complete all the test items. It is he, who decides when to hand over the answer sheet to the examiner. On the other hand, speed tests specify time limits. The test taker has to complete tasks within the prescribed time limit. Tests used in various kinds of entrance examinations are generally speed tests. For example, the B. Ed entrance test by IGNOU every year expects candidates to complete the test paper in two hours. This is an example of speed test.

Group tests versus individual tests

The distinction between group tests and individual tests is made on the basis of the way they are administered on the students. When a test can be administered to a large number of subjects, it is called a group test. Group tests are economical, easy to administer and score. Generally, researchers prefer group tests. But there are specific situations where the researcher needs individual tests. These tests are required when the purpose of the researcher is to obtain detailed information about particular respondents. Administration of individual test requires expertise and experience on the part of the researcher.

Paper-pencil tests versus performance tests

Paper-pencil tests require respondents to write the answers to the questions by putting a tick mark, encircling or underlining one of alternative answers given to a test item. Sometimes, the respondents are also asked to provide the answers by writing a word, a phrase of a sentence. The common achievement tests developed and used by teachers in schools and colleges are examples of the paper-pencil tests. Performance tests expect respondents to respond to the questions by manipulating some cards, block, etc. Such tests are generally administered to young children in pre-primary classes in order to assess their mental and mathematical abilities.

Verbal tests versus non-verbal tests

When the emphasis of a test is on reading, writing or speaking, it is called a verbal test. In education, we find many verbal tests. The common example is achievement test used by a teacher. Non-verbal tests comprise numerals or drawings. Respondents need to provide their answers by analysing the drawings. Non-verbal tests are used in many entrance tests as part of the non-verbal reasoning. Many intelligence tests like Raven's Progressive Matrices, use non-verbal methods to test the intelligence of the respondents.

Objective tests versus subjective tests

In the objective tests, there is agreement among two or more evaluators on the correctness of the answer. But when there is no agreement between two evaluators on whether an item is correct or incorrect, the test is a subjective one. Essay tests are subjective tests but multiple-choice tests; true-false, etc. are objective tests.

Norm-referenced tests and criterion-referenced tests

Tests can be classified into norm-referenced tests and criterion-referenced tests based on the method of interfering test results. In norm-referenced tests, the results of the students are described in forms of certain norms decided for a known group. Thus, the performance of a student is described in terms of the relative position s/he holds in a participator group. For example, student 'X' has secured first position in the class or student 'Y' has stood first in the Central Board of Secondary Education (CBSE) Examination. In the first case, the performance of the student is described in terms of his position in class, whereas in the second case it is described in terms of the national norm, i.e. CBSE norm.

Criterion referenced tests describe the performance of students in terms of certain criteria or standard what a student can perform is specified by a criterion test. For example, student 'A' can type 50 words per minute without error. Students 'B' can spell and words out of 10 words correctly in English spelling test. Thus, 50 words per minute and 8 words out of 10 words are criteria or standards fixed by the test developers. The objective of such test is to achieve the criterion by the students.

Projective versus Non-projective test of personality

Students' personality characteristics and adjustment problems can be measured with the help of projective and non-projective tests. Projective tests are used to assess students' personal-social adjustment. Through these tests, students are provided a series of ambiguous forms or pictures and asked to describe what they see in the forms of pictures. Forms their description, we analyse what they have projected onto the forms or the pictures. Roschach Inkblot Test and Thematic Apperception Test are example of projective tests.

Non-projective tests include problem checklists and personality inventories. Problem checklists consist of a list of problems, which students face in these lines and they are asked to choose the problems, which concern them the most. The problems may be related to their study, family, health, friends, school, etc. For example, 'I do not pronounce certain words correctly', 'I cannot get along well with my classmates'. Personality inventions are similar to problem checklists but they contain a series of questions to which students are expected to answer by circling 'yes' or 'no' or '?' for uncertain. The questions are asked in the areas of health, socio-emotional adjustment, self-confidence, socio-ability, etc.

Q6. What criteria will you use for assessing the worth of a test?

Or

Discuss the characteristics of a test one should look for while selecting different kinds of tests for gathering data.

Or

Describe the procedures to find out the reliability of a test.

[June-2012, Q.No.-3(d)]

Or

Briefly explain the considerations for selecting a good test.

[Dec-2011, Q.No.-3(e)]

Or

Explain criterion validity with the help of suitable examples.

[June-2011, Q.No.-3(b)]

Ans. In selecting tests for collecting data in research situation, researcher must evaluate their validity, reliability and usability. These evaluative criteria are considered desirable for a good test.

Validity

The test, as a data collection tool, must produce information that is not only relevant but free form systematic errors; that is, it must produce valid information. In general, a test is valid if it measures what it claims to measure. A test, however, does not possess universal and eternal validity. It may be for use in one situation but invalid if used in another.

There are different types of validity including:

Content validity: Content validity is essentially applied only to tests of proficiency and of educational achievement. It is estimated by evaluating the relevance of the test items, in relation to instructional objectives and actual subject matter studied, individually and as a whole. This form of validity is based upon judgement of several subject experts and test specialists, careful analyses of instructional objective, and the actual subject matter studied. This analysis is rational as well as judgement, and therefore, the content validity is sometimes also named as rational or logical validity.

Criterion-related validity: In some situations of decision-making especially in selection or classification, the decision is based on an individual's expected future performance as predicted from the test score. A test, which predicts the kind of behaviour it was intended to predict (e.g. success in a job) is said to possess predictive validity. This validity, therefore, refers to the association between present results as indicated by a test and future behaviour; and in order to determine the predictive validity of a test, the results from it must be compared with the actual performance in future. If a test is designed to select students for some engineering course, for example, scores on the test must indicate a significant positive correlation with ultimate success in this field. While establishing the predictive validity of a test, a follow up study is required. The researcher administers a test, makes his prediction, tries the treatment suggested by these predictions, and obtains a record of the outcome. The outcome may be the employee's production on a job, the school marks, the doctor's satisfaction with his job after joining the medical profession and the like. A researcher studies predictive validity when his primary interest is in some outcome, which he wants to improve by some professional decisions.

In many situations for which tests are developed, some cumbersome technique or method of collecting information is already in use. If the existing technique is considered useful for decision-making, the first question in validation is whether the new test agrees with the present source of information. If they disagree, the new test, in spite of its good qualities, can certainly not be a substitute for the original technique. The agreement between the test and the existing cumbersome technique, for which the test is developed, is estimated by an empirical comparison. Both the test and the original technique are applied to the same subjects and the results are compared. For example, tests developed for some clinical diagnosis are compared with the opinions framed by a psychiatrist. This type of empirical check on agreement is called concurrent validation, because the two sources of information lead to nearly the same results. The validity of the newly developed test thus established is called concurrent validity.

In case of predictive validity, the record of the outcome may be termed as criterion. While investigating concurrent validity, the test is proposed as a substitute for some other existing cumbersome technique. The information obtained through this technique acts as criterion. In both the cases, the information obtained through the newly developed test is related to criterion, and therefore, the two types of validities are also termed as criterion-related validity. It is worth nothing that whilst predictive validity refers to the association between the present results and future behaviour, the concurrent validity is concerned with the test's ability to provide an estimate of present behaviour.

Construct validity: Construct validity is concerned with the meaning and interpretation of the test scores obtained in terms of psychological or theoretical constructs. A construct is a trait, ability, temperament, or attitude which is hypothesised to explain certain aspects of behaviour such as 'Achievement Motivation', Intelligence', 'Creative Thinking' or 'Test Anxiety'. Construct validity is thus concerned not only with the test itself, but also with the theory which seeks to explain, or to account for the results which are obtained when test is used.

Construct validity is established through a long-continued experimentation based on imagination, reasoning and observation. First imagination suggests that a construct X accounts for the test performance. The researcher then reasons, "If that is so, then individuals with a high score should have characteristics or attribute Y". An experiment is performed and observations are made, and if the expectation is confirmed, the interpretation is supported. But as various deductions are tested, some of them prove to be inaccurate. The proposed interpretation is then altered either by invoking a different concept, by introducing an additional concept, or by altering the theory of the concept itself. The process of construct validation is the same as that by which scientific theories are developed.

Reliability

A test must be reliable, that is, it must have the ability to consistently yield the same results when repeated measurements are taken of the same individuals under the same conditions. If an individual receives a score of 60 on an achievement test, for example, and is assigned a rank, he should receive approximately the same rank when the test is administered on the second occasion.

Repeated measures of an attribute, characteristics or a trait by a test may produce different results. These may be due to either a real change in behaviour or to the unreliability of the test itself. If the variation in the results is due to a real change in behaviour, the reliability of the test is not doubtful. However, if the variation is due to the test itself, then the test is either internally inconsistent or can have little predictive value.

There are four procedures in common use for assessing the reliability of a test. They include:

The test-retest method: In this method, the same test is re-administered shortly after the first administration, and the two sets of scores are correlated to obtain the reliability of the test. The chief disadvantage of this method is that if the time interval between the two administrations of the test is short, the immediate memory effects, practice and the confidence induced by familiarity with the test material may over-estimate the reliability of the test. On the other hand if the time interval is long, the real changes in behaviour in terms of growth may under-estimate the reliability of the test. Owing to the difficulties in controlling conditions, which influence test scores on the second administration of the test, the test-retest method is generally less useful than the other methods.

The equivalent or parallel forms method: This method requires that two equivalent or parallel forms of a test are prepared, administered to the same group of subjects and the results in terms of two sets of test scores are correlated to obtain the reliability of the test.

In drawing up parallel forms, care has to be taken to match test materials for content, difficulty and form; and precautions must be taken not be have the items in the two forms too similar. When the parallel forms are virtually identical, reliability is too high. On the other hand, when parallel forms are not sufficiently alike, reliability will be too low. It is also worth noting that practice effects are not eliminated by this method. In spite of all these limitation, the parallel forms method of determining reliability is widely used.

The split half method: In this method, the test is first divided into two equivalent 'halves' and the scores on the half of the items are correlated with the scores on the other half. From the reliability of the half-test, the self-correlation of the whole test is then estimated by Spearman Bown Prophecy formula. The items of the test can be divided into two sets in a variety of ways. This method of reliability measures the internal reliability of the test, and if the two halves do not correlate highly, it suggests that they are not measuring the same thing. Moreover, the method has the advantage of controlling the fatigue and practice effects. The main criticism of the method is that a test can be divided into two halves in a number of ways, and therefore, the correlation between the scores on the two halves may not have unique values.

The rational equivalence method: This method of reliability is evolved to get an estimate of the reliability of a test, free from the objections raised against the methods discussed. Two forms of a test are defined as equivalent when corresponding items are interchangeable; and when the inter-item correlations are the same for both the forms. Two internal consistency formulae developed by Kuder-Richardson are often used to obtain coefficients of equivalence for tests where one point is given for every correct answer and zero for a wrong answer.

Usability

The usability of a test includes objectivity, economy of time and cost, simplicity and ease of administration, scoring and interpretation in using test for collecting data in a research study. A test should yield objective results, that is, the results should be independent of personal judgement of the researcher using the test. The tests that can be administered in a short period of time are likely to gain co-operation of the subjects and to save the time of all those involved in the test administration. The cost involved in the construction or administration of a test should be limited. The simplicity and ease of administration, scoring and interpretation are important factors in selecting a test, particularly when the expert advice is not easily available. The tests should be interesting and fascinating to the subjects so as to gain their tests co-operation.

Q7. Describe the procedure of developing a test.

Ans. Test development is an independent, advanced and technical area of research and is based on well developed theory of psychometrics.

When a researcher sets out to construct a test, there are several factors that determine his operation and line of action. These factors include the area, the age group and the grade for which the test is to be developed. The approach of the researcher will depend on whether the test is designed for general purposes or some specific purpose. But in spite of all such factors, there are some general principles and procedures which one has to follow while constructing a test.

Planning: The construction of a test must starts by a consideration of the limitations under which the test has to be developed. It includes a detailed set of specifications as to the purpose of the test and the time, cost and resources at the disposal of the researcher or test-maker. The nature of the population for which the test is constructed has to be defined. The length of the test, type and nature of the test-items and method of scoring the test are also some basic considerations, which are to be planned in advance.

Preliminary draft: While preparing the preliminary draft of the test, the researcher or test maker must consult the existing test in the concerned area. Such tests are helpful in constructing the items for the test. The test maker may also create some original items of his own to cover the attribute or trait adequately. The preliminary draft must have more than double the items required for the test. For ability and attainment test, it is necessary to compile a large number of items of suitable difficulty. A rough idea of the difficulty of the items can be obtained by trying out a few items on a small group of subjects from the population. The items are then edited and carefully worded instruction, which indicate briefly the nature and purpose of the test, the nature of the task, with a few examples, must be supplied with the test. The final manuscript of the preliminary draft is then submitted to experts for their opinion and criticism. It is also worthwhile to administer the final manuscript of the preliminary draft to a small group of subjects from the population and check the answers. It is called 'small-group try out' of the test. This procedure may suggest further modification. After the necessary modifications in the light of experts' suggestions and 'small-group try out', the preliminary draft is printed. For recording the responses of the subjects, a separate answer sheet must also be printed which may be enclosed with the booklet of the preliminary draft.

The tryout: At this stage, the preliminary draft is administered to a large random sample of the population for which the test is constructed. The size of the sample for tryout is usually taken as 370, because it helps the test maker to get the indices of difficulty and discrimination quickly for selecting good items for the final test with the help of the Table developed by J.C. Flanagan.

At the tryout stage, the time limit should be generous. The test may be so timed that nearly 90 per cent individuals in the sample complete the last item. In case of speed test, the time limit that produces a good scatter of scores without fatigue should be fixed.

The test booklets along with their answer sheets are collected and scored with the help of a scoring key.

Item analysis: The major objective of item analysis is the improvement of total score reliability or of total score validity, or both, and the achievement of better item sequences and types of score distribution. Item analysis procedures provide for each item of the test of ability, two indices-one of its difficulty and another of its power to discriminate between the good and the bad performers on the test. Many kinds of such indices have been proposed. One begins by arranging the answer sheets from the highest to the lowest obtained score. From the arranged answer sheets, the top 27 per cent and the bottom 27 per cent of the answer sheets are separately taken. Next, the proportions of the two groups passing a given item are found. Entering Flanagan's Table with the proportion of successes in the two groups, read the Biserial r from the intersecting column and row in the body of the table. The Biserial r will be the discriminative power or the validity index of an item. The mean of the two proportions is the difficulty index of an item. Garrett (1962, p. 368) suggests that items with validity indices of 0.20 or more and difficulty indices of 0.40 to 0.60 are regarded as satisfactory. Items having zero or negative validity are useless and must be discarded or they must be carefully examined for ambiguities, inaccuracies and other errors. It is worth noting that the items for non-cognitive tests are selected only on the basis of validity index. In such type of tests, there is no question of the difficulty value of an item as the subject is required to respond to a series of statements or questions in 'yes' or 'no', 'agree' or 'disagree', or in a similar way, to indicate his feelings or opinions.

Final draft: The selected items are put in the final draft of the test which is administered to as large a sample as is practicable for estimating the parameters of validity, reliability and norms.

Q8. Define a questionnaire. Discuss its various types.

Ans. A questionnaire is a device consisting of a series of questions dealing with some psychological, social, educational, etc; topic(s) sent or given to an individual or a group of individuals, with the object of obtaining data with regard to some problems under investigation. Goode and Hatt (1952, p. 33) state that in general the word 'questionnaire' refers to a device for securing answers to a series of questions by using a form which the respondent fills in himself. Bar et. al. (1953, p. 65) define questionnaire as a systematic compilation of questions that are administered to a sample of population from which information is desired.

Questionnaire is a popular means of collecting all kinds of data in research. It is widely used in educational research to obtain information about certain conditions and practices, and to inquire into opinions and attitudes of an individual or a group. A questionnaire is either administered personally to a group of individuals as to a group of individuals or it is mailed to them to save time and money in travel. In the former situation, the person administering the tools has an opportunity to establish rapport with the respondents, to explain the purpose of the study to the respondents, and to explain the meaning of questions to the respondents that may not be clear to them. In the latter situation, the mailed questionnaire is probably both the most used and most used and most abused data gathering research tool. It is mostly used when the individuals from whom we desire information cannot always be contacted personally without the expenditure of great deal of time and money in travel.

Classification of Questionnaires

The questionnaires can be classified in terms of the nature of the questions, which are used. Questions may be asked in a closed or an open form. The researcher may use one type exclusively or both in combination. Questionnaires that call for short or check responses are known as closed form or restricted type. They include a set of questions to which respondents can reply in a limited number of ways. The respondent is invariably permitted to reply only with 'yes' or 'no', or 'no-opinion', or is requested to select answer from a short list of possible responses. He is asked to place a tick (√) mark in a space provided on the answer sheet or he may be requested to underline a response. Sometimes he is asked to insert brief answers of his own. For certain type of information, the closed type of questionnaire is useful, because it is easy to respond, takes little time and effort to fill out is relatively objective and is fairly easy to tabulate and analyse. While using closed-type of question items, it is advisable to provide for unanticipated responses by allowing an 'open' category or response with a request, 'please specify' or 'kindly mention' which enables the researcher to properly tabulate and classify such responses. The following example illustrates such type of question items:

Please tick (√) the reasons given below for not introducing the 'grade system marking' by your school.

- Non-availability of administrative guidance and support ( )
- Non-availability of academic guidance and support ( )
- It is time-consuming ( )
- It is not effective in overcoming the defects of numerical making ( )
- It cannot be changed and adopted according to the local institutional needs ( )
- Any other, please mention ( )

....

....

The open-form or unrestricted type of questionnaire calls for a free response in the respondent's own words. The form of the questions is unstructured and no clues are provided to the respondent. The open form of questions provides for greater depth of response and the greatest advantage of this type of questions is freedom that is given to the respondent to reveal his opinion and to clarify his response. However, the responses to such type of questions are sometimes difficult to tabulate, organise and interpret. The following example illustrates this type of question:

State the reasons for not introducing the 'Grade-System of Marking' in your school.

....

....

Q9. What are the various factors that need to be considered while constructing a questionnaire?

Ans. A questionnaire needs to be constructed very carefully. It requires both competences and ability on our part. The following points need to be taken into consideration while constructing a questionnaire.

Reflection of the purposes of research: A good questionnaire must reflect the objectives of the research problem through specific questions contained in it. Each question must communicate to the respondents its objective so that analysis and interpretation of responses are made properly. Moreover, the covering letter of the questionnaire should indicate the purposes of the research.

Make the question more precise: The following principles given by Best (1977, pp. 160-162) may be considered to make questions precise.

- Properly define terms that otherwise could easily be misinterpreted. For example, "What work did you do in the year 2012?" This question is subject to various interpretations.
- Hence needs precision in its statement.
- Be careful in using adjectives and adverbs that have no agreed upon meaning. Words like 'rarely', 'occasionally', 'scarcely', 'hardly' may be interpreted differently; hence should be carefully used.
- Beware of double negative. The Distance Education Council should not fund the institutions that do not meet its requirements. This statement may be stated as: The Distance Education Council should fund only those institutions, which fulfil its requirements/conditions.
- Avoid the double-barreled questions. Break it into two questions. For example, the question 'Do you agree that distance education is cost-effective and promote democratisation of education?' Can be split into two separate questions.
- Be careful of inadequate alternatives. For example, in the questions 'Are you employed? Yes/No'. It does not specify the nature of employment to the respondents.
- Underline a word if you wish to indicate special emphasis.
- When asking for rating or comparisons a point of reference is necessary. For example, 'The temperature of place 'A' is (hot, warm or cool)' needs to have a point of reference like 'in comparison to place B.
- Phrase questions so that they are appropriate for all respondents. For example "How many counselling sessions for a course do you attend in a month?" may not be appropriate for all distance learners as there is provision of intensive counselling sessions in many cases.

- Design questions that will give a complete response. The question "Do you watch television?" does not reveal the TV viewing habit of respondents.
- Provide for the systematic qualifying of responses. For example, five alternatives to a question may be ranked and given some numerical weightage in a systematic manner. For example, in the case of a 3 point scale A may be 3 pt, B may be 2 pt, and C may be 1 pt. based on the type of questions asked.

Information level of respondents: The assumptions about the expertness of the respondents in a particular field of the amount of information he possesses should not be unrealistic. The information elicited by the questionnaire must lie within the respondent's present level of information.

Social Acceptance of Responses: the questions must provide the respondent a range of responses, which meets his criteria of social acceptability. A question constitutes a threat to the respondent's ego if he is required to give an answer, which he feels is socially unacceptable response to a question. The annoying of embarrassing questions must be avoided.

Leading questions: The questions should be objective with no leading suggestions as to the most appropriate response. For example, in a question "Would you say that you are in favour of co-education in secondary schools?", it is easier for the respondents to answer 'yes' than 'no'. In answering 'yes' he is merely agreeing with the language of the question. It is more difficult to respond, "no", since this response seems to contradict, or at least goes counter to the ideas of the person who worded the question.

Sequence of question: first, the question should be limited to a single idea or to a single reference. Secondly, the questionnaire maker needs to give thought to the arrangement of the questions in a questionnaire. Questions should be presented in a good psychological order by adopting the 'funnel approach'. This is a procedure of asking the most general or the most unrestricted questions first and following it with successively more specific and restricted questions.

The form or type of questions: Another importance consideration that weighs in the matter of constructing a questionnaire may contain closed or open type of questions. Each type of question has its merits and limitation and the questionnaire framer must decide which type is more likely to supply the information required.

Length of the questionnaire: A questionnaire should contain either closed type of questions, or open type of questions or both.

Expert Opinion: It is advisable to get all the help from experts for planning and constructing the questionnaire. Questions should be submitted to the experts for criticism and modified accordingly.

Q10. Define a checklist and explain the procedure used in its construction.

Ans. A checklist is a simple device consisting of a prepared list of items, which are thought by the researcher to be relevant to the problem being studied. After each item a space is provided for the observer to indicate the presence or absence of the item by checking 'yes' or 'no', or a type of number of items may be indicated by inserting the appropriate word or number. A checklist draws the attention of the observer to relevant factors and enables him to record the data quickly and systematically. Thus, the responses to the checklists items are a matter of 'fact', not of 'judgement'.

The checklist is an important tool in gathering facts for educational surveys that is for checking of library, laboratory, games facilities, school buildings, textbooks, instructional procedures, etc. Checklists are sometimes used in the form of a questionnaire, which are completed by the respondent rather than by the observer.

Construction of a Checklist

The researcher should examine carefully the checklists, which have already been prepared and used by other researchers in various fields of educational research. He should then determine the items on which he requires information for his investigation. The items thus determined may be arranged in logical and psychological order. There are various ways of writing and arranging the items in a checklist.

Kempfer (1960) has suggested four ways and the researcher may make use of all or some of them to serve his purpose best.

- The form in which the observer or respondent is asked to check all items found in a situation. For example, put a tick (√) in the blank provided before each game played in your school.

  ____________ Football
  ____________ Hockey
  ____________ Cricket
  ____________ Volleyball
  ____________ Basketball

- The form in which questions with a 'yes' or 'no' are asked to be encircled, underlined or checked in response to the items given. For example, Does your University have a Teacher' Union?

- The form in which items are positive statements and the respondent or observer is asked to put a tick (√) in the space provided on the right of the item. For example,
  Our School has a Student's Union. ( )
- The form where items can best be put in sentences and the observer or respondent is asked to check, underline or encircle the appropriate word/words.
  For example, the school organises debates weekly, fortnightly, monthly, annually, irregularly. The items of the checklist should be phrased in such a way that they are discriminative in quantity. It will increase the validity of the checklist. A preliminary tryout of the checklist may also helpful in making the tool more objective.

Q11. Define a rating scale and describe its various types.

Ans. An observer may be asked to judge the behaviour he observes and classify it into categories. This is essentially the task he performs when completing a schedule, but he can also be asked to give a numerical value or rating to his judgement. By 'rating' is meant the judgement of one person by another. In the words of Barr, Davis and Johnson(1953): Rating is a term applied to expression of opinion of judgement regarding some situation, object or character. Opinions are usually expressed on a scale of values.

Rating scale refers to a scale with a set of points, which describe varying degrees of the dimension of an attribute being observed.

The rating scale procedures exceed all psychological measurement methods that depend upon human judgement, for popularity, use and ease of administration. They are used in the evaluation of individuals, their reactions and in the psychological evaluation of stimuli. Rating scales are also used to record quantified observations of a social situation. They may be used to describe the behaviour of individuals, the activities of an entire group, the changes in the situation surrounding them, or many other types of data.

Forms of Rating Scales

A number of rating techniques have been developed which enable the observers to ascribe numerical values or rating to their judgements of behaviour. According to Guilford (1954, p. 263), these techniques have given rise to five broad categories of rating scales:

Numerical scales: In the typical numerical scale, a sequence of defined numbers is supplied to the rater or to the observer. The rater or the observer assigns to each stimulus, to be rated, an appropriate number in line with these definitions or descriptions.

In such type of scales, sometimes zero is placed at the 'indifferent' category and negative numbers below it. But Guilford (1954, p. 264) does not favour the use of negative rating numbers as this type of scale may be unnatural to those observers or raters who are not well versed in algebra. The use of zero may also trend to suggest a break in the scale and thus destroy 'continuity' of the scale.

It has been seen that observers or raters usually avoid terminal categories. If such categories (0 and 10) are not included, observers or raters would tend to avoid categories 1 and 9 and thus the range of ratings gets shortened. To avoid this shortcoming, it is suggested to expand the scale beyond the categories, which a researcher wants to include in his scale. For example, if a researcher wants an effective scale of seven points, he may make use of additional two categories so that desired dispersion of seven point rating is achieved.

In some numerical scales, the observer or rater is not provided with numbers, which he has to use in making judgements. He has to report in terms of descriptive 'cues' and then the researcher assigns numbers to them. For example, while rating performance in a drama, the cues may be the following: very good; average; poor; very poor. To those cues, the number 1 through 5 may be assigned by the researcher.

Graphic scales: The graphic scale is the most popular and the most widely used type of rating scale. In this scale, a straight line is shown, vertically or horizontally, with various cues to help the rater. The line is either segmented in units or it is continuous. If the line is segmented, the number of parts can be varied. Examples of such a scale are illustrated as under:

How effective was presentation of material aids in the class by the teacher?

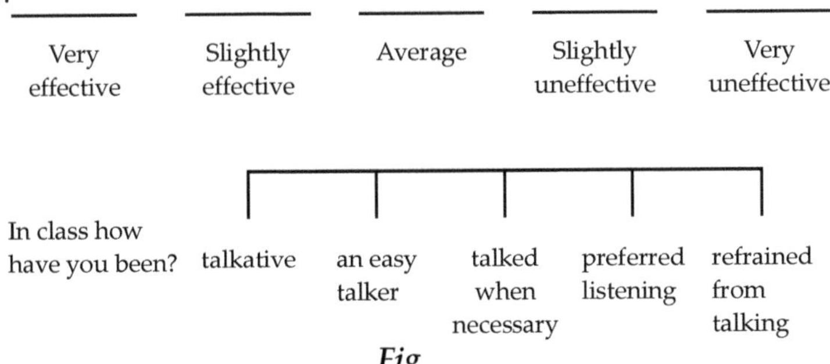

Fig

Standard scales: In standard scales, a set of standards is presented to the rater. The standards are usually objects of some kind to be rated with pre-established scale values. In its best form, this type is like that of the scales for judging the quality of handwriting. The scales of handwriting provide several standard specimens that have previously been spread over on a common scale by the methods of equal-appearing interval or pair comparisons. With help of these standard specimens, a new sample of handwriting can be equated to one of the standards or judged as being between two standards.

Rating by cumulated points: The unique and common feature of rating by cumulated points is in the method of scoring. The rating score for an object or individual is the sum or average of the weighted or unweighted points. The 'Checklist method' and the 'Guess-who technique' belong to this category of rating.

Guilford (1954, p. 271) suggests that the checklist item may be in multiple choice form rather than in true-false. For example, while rating the performance of personnel in their work assignment, the items like the following may be used:

Cooperative with other	***His relations with public are:***
-enthusiastically	-outstanding
-willingly	-creditable
-indifferently	-acceptable
-grudgingly	-poor
-defiantly	-detrimental

Forced choice ratings: In 'Forced-choice Rating' methods, the rater is asked, not to say whether the rate has a certain trait or to say how much of a trait the rates has but to say essentially whether he has more of one trait than another of a pair.

Q12. What are the various factors need to be considered while constructing a rating scale?

Ans. The following considerations may be taken in view while constructing a rating scale:

- The trait to be rated must be clearly defined and described in objective and unequivocal terms.
- The number of steps in the scale should neither be too many nor too less. Generally, 5 on 7 point scales are preferred.
- The directions to the rater must be clear and comprehensive.
- The items in the rating scale may be arranged in ascending or descending order.
- The number of characteristic to be rated need to be limited.
- The rater needs to be well informed of the characteristics to be rated.
- The rater should be instructed to skip the rating of characteristics of which s/he no knowledge.

- Some space may be provided for the rater to write additional material in the form of comments.

Q13. Explain the various advantages and disadvantages of rating scale.

Ans. Advantages of Rating Methods

There are some advantages of rating methods when compared with the method of pair comparisons and method of rank order.

- Rating methods consume much less time than methods of pair comparisons and rank order.
- They are far more interesting to the raters, especially if graphic methods are used.
- Rating methods can be used with raters who have minimum of training.
- They can be used with large numbers of stimuli.
- They have much wider range of application and can be used for teacher-ratings personality ratings, school appraisal, sociological surveys, etc.
- Best ratings can be presenting one stimulus to rater at a time.

Limitation of rating scale

Since ratings are based on human judgement, they are subject to personal biases or subjectivity. Major limitations are as follows:

- **Generosity error:** Raters generally rate high if they find that the rate is known to them. As a result, high ratings are given in almost all cases. This is also called the *'error of leniency'*.
- **The error of central tendency:** Quite often, raters ten to rate the individuals on the middle of the scale and avoid rating on the extremes of the scale.
- **The halo-effect:** Sometimes the rater forms a general opinion about the individual's merit. As a result, his ratings on specific traits are influenced by this general impression. It is difficult to get rid of this influence, which causes him to carry qualitative judgement from one trait to another.
- **The logical error**: Very often, the raters find logical connections between certain traits and accordingly give similar ratings for these traits. This apparent logical coherence of the traits increases inter-correlation among them.
- **The constant error:** When a rater has the tendency to rate others in the opposite direction from himself in a trait, the constant error occurs. For example, if a person is very sincere in his activities, he would rate others as not sincere constantly.

- **The proximity error:** Accident traits are rated similarly by the raters. This gives rise to high inter-correlation among them than the remoter-ones, because of their closeness or proximity.

Q14. Define an attitude scale and describe the procedure followed in the construction of an attitude scale.

Ans. An attitude scale or an opionnaire is designed to measure the attitude or belief of an individual towards an object, event, or a phenomenon. Thurstone (1929) defines an attitude as the degree of positive or negative effect associated with some psychological objects. By a psychological object, he means any institution, ideas, symbol, phrase, job, etc. Attitude of an individual is basically, his reaction to an object, situation or proposition in favourable or unfavourable ways. Attitude scale is always in the form of a continuum, which ranges from favourablesness through neutral to unfavourableness. An attitude scale consists of a set of statements about the particular psychological object. While writing statements for an attitude scale, the following criteria as listed by Edwards (1957) need to be taken into consideration.

- Avoid statements that refer to the past rather than to present.
- Avoid statements that are factual or capable of being interpreted as factual.
- Avoid statements that may be interpreted in more than one way.
- Avoid statements that are irrelevant to the psychological object.
- Avoid statements that are likely to be endorsed by almost every one or almost no one.
- Keep the language of the statements simple, clear and direct.
- Statement should be short and should contain only one complete thought.
- Statement with universals such as all, always, name should be avoided.
- Statement should be in the form of simple sentences.
- Avoid the use of double negatives.

Construction of scale

- A large number of statements with favourable and unfavourable opinions towards the psychological objects are written. For example, in preparing an attitude scale to measure students' attitude towards the use of computers in the teaching-learning process, items such as the following may be written.
  (i) Computers help in the teaching-learning process.
  (ii) Use of computers in the teaching-learning process consumes a lot of instructional time.

- The number of favourable and unfavourable statements in the scale needs to be equal. All the statements are edited. In the beginning of the scale, clear directions are given regarding how to mark their answers, namely, by putting a mark or by putting a circle around the answer.
- Scoring weights of 5, 4, 3, 2, and 1 are used for SA, A, U, D, and SD for the statements with favourable opinion and the scoring weights of 1, 2, 3, 4, and 5 are used for SD, D, U, A and SA for the statements with unfavourable opinion. An individual score on a particular attitude scale is the sum total of this ratings on all items.
- Once the draft scale is ready, it is administered to a sample of at least 200 subjects selected from the population of the study. Scoring of the items is done as per the scoring weights decided for different items.
- The final detecting of the items to the scale are made on the basis of t-value. For this, item wise analysis of the responses is carried out. On the basis of the total scores obtained by the respondents, the upper 25 per cent obtaining the highest scores and the lower 25 per cent obtaining the lowest score are taken. A rate of 't' is found out based on the responses of upper and lower group to the individual statement. Finally, 20 to 25 statements with the largest t-values ($t>1.75$) are selected for the final draft of the attitude scale.
- The reliability of Likert type attitude scale is computed by the split-half method. The validity of the scale is decided by comparing it with other similar standarised scales.

Q15. Describe the different types of attitude scale and their limitations.

Ans. There are two types of attitude scale. These are as follows:

Method of Equal-Appearing Intervals

The method of equal-appearing intervals was originally devised by Thurstone and Chave (1929) and has been modified subsequently in the light of research findings. This technique involves the following steps:

- **Collecting and editing of statements:** A large number of statements, which express varying degrees of intensity of feeling or opinion towards a psychological object are collected. They are collected by making an extensive study of the literature, by consulting experts and research workers. Collected statements are edited from the viewpoint of the criteria for developing statements for the attitude scale.

- **The sorting procedure:** The statements are then given to the experts or judges for classification. Each judge is informed of the purpose of the scale and is asked to classify each statement on an eleven point scale. This is done by printing each statement on a separate card and judges are then asked to sort each card in one of eleven piles, presumably forming a continuum, according to degree of favourableness or unfavourableness of each statement with respect to the psychological object under study.
- **Selection of statements for the final scale:** As a result, of the sorting or rating procedure, the number of judges for each statement under different categories is found out. Then $Q(=Q_3 - Q_1)$ and the median or scale value for each statement are computed. The items for the final scale are selected on the basis of Q and median or scale values, i.e. the items should be fairly and evenly spread on the scale continuum, and Q-values of the selected statements should as low as possible. Vernon (1963, p. 154) recommends that:

  On a 9-point scale, Q-values should seldom exceed 2.00 and an average of less than 1.50 should be aimed at.

  The median or scale values indicate the spread of statements on the scale continuum, and Q or inter-quartile range is a measure of the spread of the middle 50 per cent of the judgements. When there is good agreement among the judges in judging the degree of favourableness or unfavourableness of statement, Q will be small compared with the value obtained when there is relatively less agreement among the judges.

  The final form of the scale is then constructed by selecting 30 to 35 statements which are most relevant, least ambiguous and which cover or represent the different intensities of the attitude. They are then arranged in a random order.
- **Reliability and validity:** The reliability of the attitude scale developed by following the method of equal-appearing intervals is obtained by spilt-half method.

Limitations: Equal-appearing intervals scale has been criticised on account of several limitations.

- The large number of persons, whose co-operation is required to develop such a scale, may not be available.

- The scale can be developed only after considerable effort, thereby making it somewhat cumbersome.
- It needs a good deal of time to construct, which sometimes may not be available.
- Respondents may not like to attempt the scale as it requires considerable reading on their part.

Method of Summated Ratings

The method of summated ratings was introduced by Likert (1932). The method appears to yield similar results to that devised by the method of equal-appearing intervals. The coefficient of correlation between the two types of scales was reported as high as+0.92 in a study by Edwards and Kenny (1946). It has been claimed by Likert (1932), Hall (1934), and Edwards and Kenney (1946) that the method of summated rating is simpler, easier and less laborious than that developed by Thurstone. Moreover, it has been found that the time required to construct an equal-appearing interval scale is approximately twice that required by the method of summated ratings. In terms of these advantages, the method of summated ratings tends to be used more frequently by the researchers in opinion research.

Limitations: There are major two limitations of this method:

- It requires a great deal of decision-making
- It fails to measure true attitudes if respondents are concerned with looking good or meeting expectations of the instructor

Q16. What is meant by observation technique? What are the various types of Observation techniques?

Ans. Observation is the process in which one or more persons observe what is occurring in some real-life situation, and classify and record pertinent happenings according to some planned scheme. It is used to evaluate the overt behaviour events, and the contexts surrounding the events and behaviours in controlled and uncontrolled situations. Observation is useful technique of collecting authentic evidence in descriptive educational research.

Type of observations

Observation technique can be classified in two ways. These are:

Participant or non-participant observation: Observation may be either participant or non-participant. In the participant observation, the observer becomes more or less one of the group under observation. In such situations, the observer will be in sight of the person being observed and may actually take part in some activity with the observed individual or group. The observer may play any one of several jobs in observation, with varying degrees of participation, as a visiting stranger, an attentive listener, an eager learner, or a more complete role as participant observer.

In the non-participant observation, observer takes a position where his presence is not disturbing to the group. He may follow in detail the behaviour of one individual or may describe one or two behaviour characteristics of dozen or more individuals. In this type of observation, a one-way vision screen that permits the observer to see the subject but prevents the subject from seeing the observer, is useful.

Structured and unstructured observation: Observation may also be classified as unstructured and structured. Unstructured observation is mainly associated with participant observation and it is often an exploratory technique. The structured observations are much too formal and they are designed to provide systematic description to test casual hypotheses. Structured observations are executed in controlled situations like classroom or laboratory settings. Interaction analysis of the classroom verbal behaviour of a teacher is an example of structured observation. Structured observations start with relatively specific formulations. There is much less choice with respect to the content of observation. The observer sets up in advance categories of behaviour in terms of which he wishes to analyse the problem, and keeps in mind the time limit under which has to make the observation. In the unstructured observations, it may not be possible to categorise behaviour in advance of observation. Instead of using predetermined categories, the observer considers aspects of behaviour in terms of their context or the situations of which they are part.

Q17. What are the stages of Observation? Give its limitations.

Ans. As a good research technique, observation needs proper planning, expert execution, and adequate recording and interpretation.

Planning for Observation

Observation as a research technique must always be directed for a specific purpose. It is neither haphazard nor unplanned. The planning for observation includes definition of specific activities or units or behaviour to be observed, the nature of the groups of the subjects to be observed, the scope of observation-individual or group, determination of the length of each observation period, deciding about the tools to be used in making the observation and recording, etc.

According to Good (1966, pp. 244-245) planning for observation includes the following factors:

- An appropriate group of subjects to observe.
- Selection and arrangement of any special condition for the group.

- Length of each observation period, interval between periods, and number of periods.
- Physical position of the observer and possible effect on the subject(s).
- Definition of specific activities or unit of behaviour to be observed.
- Entry of frequencies or tallies in the record, as a total for the entire observation period or by sub-division of time within the observation period.
- Scope of observation, whether for an individual child or for a group.
- Form of recording, including consideration or mechanical techniques and such quantitative factors as number, time, distance, and spatial relationships.
- Training of the observer in terms of expertness.
- Interpretation of data collected through observation.

Execution of Observation

An expert execution of observation includes:

- Proper arrangement of specific conditions for the subject or subjects to be observed.
- Assuming the proper role or physical positions for observing.
- Focussing attention on the specific activities, or units of behaviour under observation.
- Handling well the recording instruments to be used.
- Utilising the training and experience fairly well in terms of making the observation and recording the facts.

Recording and Interpreting the Observation

The recording of the observation data may either be simultaneous or soon after the observation. In the former case, the observer on recording his observation data simultaneously with the occurrence of the phenomena observed. In the latter case, the observer undertakes to record his observations not simultaneously with his actual observation process, but immediately after, he observed for a unit of time while the details are still fresh in his mind.

In viewing, classifying and recording behaviour, the observer must take utmost care to minimise the influence of his biases, attitudes and values on the observation report. The observer should know what he is looking for in a given situation and should carefully and objectively record relevant data. The subjectivity on the part of an observer is partly due to his emotional involvement, his selective perception and his different powers of recall. In order to overcome the biases introduced by the human observer, various mechanical instruments are used to obtain a more accurate record of events. The use of cameras, tape-recorders, stop-watch, binoculars audiometer, stethoscope, light meter, thermometers, one-way vision screen of mirror, etc. allows behaviour to be measured to a degree of accuracy which could not be achieved by the human observer. It is advisable to develop an observation form or schedule while making observations. The specific behaviours to be observed and recorded should be listed on this form. The observation form should be simple and the behaviours listed on it may be clearly specified and examples given where necessary.

Limitations of observation

Observation as a technique of research suffers from certain limitations. They are:

- Subjectivity of the researcher influences the process of observation and recording of data.
- The phenomenon may be distorted through the very act of observation.
- The observer may like to record the information, which he is interested in.
- The samples of behaviour being observed may not provide the sufficient basis for drawing conclusions.
- The validity and reliability of observation depends upon the competency of the observer.
- Sometimes, the people being observed become conscious and do not behave naturally.
- It is slow and laborious process.
- Obtained data may be unmanageable for the researcher to classify and interpret scientifically.

Q18. Explain the concept of an interview and the stages to be followed in an interview. [June-2012, Q.No.-3(b)]

Ans. The interview is a process of communication or interaction in which the subject or interviewee gives the needed information verbally in a face-to-face situation. Although the interview is generally associated with counselling or psychotherapy, it can be used effectively to collect useful information about individuals in many research situations.

Type of interview

Interview can be classified into different categories on the basis of their purposes, design or structure which are as follows:

Research and clinical interview: In experiments, historical, and surveys research, interview is used as a technique to collect evidences to prove hypotheses or to find out solutions to research questions. Such type of interview is called 'research interview'. On the other hand, in a clinical situation, psychiatrist or social worker uses interview to obtain information about the interviewee's personal problems, for the purpose of diagnosis and treatment. Such interview is called 'clinical interview'.

Individual and group interviews: When we interview one individual at a time, it is called 'individual interview'. On the other hand, the interview, which is carried out for a group of individuals is called 'group interview'. The size of the group should not be too large or too small. The optimum size is approximately 10 to 12 persons (Good, 1966).

Structured, semi-structured and unstructured interviews: Interviews are classified as structured, semi-structured and standardised depending on the procedure of the research design which are discussed as follows:

- **Structured interview:** In structured interview, the procedure of interview is pre-determined or standardised. Each interviewee is asked a set of questions. The interview or interviewer cannot rephrase the questions or words in the interview schedule. It is formal in nature and is less flexibility in the process. But the advantage is that it is easy to interpret the data obtained from the interview as there is uniformity maintained in the process throughout with each interviewee.
- **Semi-structured interviews:** In semi-structured interview, there is more flexibility in the process of interview in comparison to structured interview. The interviewer can deviated from the predetermined questions or words and change wording of the questions or their order of presentation. It provides the scope to probe deeper into the interviewee's psyche. It provides a mixed framework for analysis as the interviewer may use his own feelings and judgements while analysing and interpreting the data.
- **Unstructured interviews:** Unstructured interviews do not mean that the questions to be asked and the procedure to be followed are not pre-decided. Of course, they are, but the interviewer has the absolute freedom to restructure the questions or the process of interview. Sometimes, the researcher stands with a certain topic (s) and proceeds on with the same as the main focus. Unstructured interviews generate large amount of data as the interviewer goes on probing into in order to elicit the required information. Hence, it poses problems to the researcher in analysing and interpreting data.

Stages

There are three stages, which needed to be followed in interview. These are:

Preparation for the interview: It is necessary to plan for the interview carefully if it is effective in obtaining the required information. The interviewer must decide exactly what kind of data the interview should yield, whether the structured or unstructured procedure will be more useful, and how the results of the interview should be recorded. It is advisable to try out the interview on another person before using it for actual investigation. This may reveal the deficiencies that should be corrected before the actual execution of the interview. The interviewer must have a clear idea of the sort of information he needs, and accordingly he may prepare an interview schedule with a list of questions, which will extract that information.

Conducting the interview: In the execution of an interview, a harmonious relationship between the interviewer and interviewee is most essential. A good rapport helps the interviewee to feel at ease and express himself willingly. In order to establish a good rapport, the interviewer should greet the interviewee in a friendly manner so as to get him settled in the new situation in a relaxed manner.

An interviewer generally should start with a pleasant conversation and ask factual non-threatening questions in the beginning.

The interviewer should try to redirect the interview to more fruitful topics when he feels that the required information and data are not emerging. He should wind up the interview before the respondent (interviewer) becomes tired. A well prepared interview schedule ensures good use of limited interview time; it makes interviewing multiple subjects (interviewees) more systematic and comprehensive; and it keeps interactions between the interviewer and interviewee focussed.

Recording of the interview: Recording the interview is an important as preparation for the interview or conducting of the interview. The interview may make use of a schedule, a structured format, rating scale or a tape recorder to record the responses of the interview. The use of a tape recorder during the conduct of interview not only eliminates the omission, distortions, elaborations and other modifications of data usually found in written interviews, but it also provides an objective basis for evaluating the adequacy of the interview data in relation to the performance of the interviewer. The use of tape recorder also permits the interviewer to devote full attention to the interviewee and saves much time of the interviewer, which he may have to utilise in recording the responses during or after the interview. The conscious and unconscious selection of the interview data by the interviewer is also avoided in a tape recorded interview. If a tape-recorder is not available, the interviewer may take notes of responses. The notes should include unusual and significant behaviour as well as the responses to questions of the interviewees.

Q19. Define sociometry. Discuss various sociometric techniques.

Or

As a teacher, how could you use sociometric techniques for understanding dynamics in your class? [June-2011, Q.No.-4]

Ans. The term Sociometry is defined as the measurement of the social relationships that exists among the members of a group. Sociometric techniques attempt to describe attractions or repulsions between group members by asking them to indicate whom they would select or reject in various situations. Such techniques are used in various educational situations to study social adjustment, group, dynamics, learning, motivation, discipline, and other problem areas that involve social relations.

Numerous sociometric techniques are used to measure social interaction within groups, but *sociogram, sociometric matrix, and guess-who technique* are most frequently used in educational research.

Sociogram

The sociogram is often used by the classroom teacher, counselor, or psychologist to study the interpersonal relationships of groups. In the research situations, it is used to study the problems of learning, motivation, discipline, and group dynamics.

To construct a sociogram, the researcher generally begins with the question such as "With whom would you most like to work on a small group project? Give your first, second and third choice." Each member of the group is provided with a form on which he can write the names of the members he has chosen. The group members are assured that the information given by them will be held in strict confidence. If there are boys and girls in the group, then the boys may be represented by triangles and girls by circles. A choice may be represented by a single pointed arrow (→), a mutual choice by an arrow pointing in opposite directions (↔). Rejections may be represented by dotted lines (…). The members who are chosen most often are referred to as 'stars', those not chosen by other as 'isolates'. Small groups made of members who choose one another are 'cliques'.

The next step in the construction of a sociogram is the tabulation of the choices made by the group members.

The next step is to construct a sociogram. A sociogram provides a diagrammatic picture of the group's relationships. The following procedure is used in constructing the sociogram.

- Place the names of the stars in the centre of the sociogram, using triangles to denote boys, and circles to denote the girls.
- Place the names of those receiving the next highest scores (in circles and triangles) near the names in the centre but far enough to permit the drawing of lines connecting triangles and circles.
- Place the isolates (who receive no scores) and the seldom chosen individuals around the outer area of sociogram.
- Use lines to choices and arrow heads to show direction of choice. A solid line might be used for a first choice, a broken line for second choice, and a dot-dash line for third choice. Sometimes different colours are also used for first, second and third choices.

Sociometric Matrix

A sociometric matrix is a rectangular arrangement of numbers indicating the choices made by the members of a group. An example of a 4 × 4 matrix (four rows and four columns) is shown in the following Table 3.2.

Table 3.2. A Sociometric Matrix of Four Member Group for a Two Choice Question

Student	Rakesh	Kamal	Moti	Prakash
Rakesh	0	1	1	0
Kamal	1	1	0	0
Moti	1	0	1	0
Prakash	0	1	0	0
Total	2	3	2	0

In this example, the question asked was, "With whom would you like to work on a group project? Choose two mates". In the matrix shown in Table 3.2, the numeral 1 is used to indicate a choice, while 0 is used to indicate no choice. It is seen from the matrix that Rakesh has chosen Kamal and Moti. These choices can be shown by Rakesh → Kamal and Rakesh ↔ Moti. It is also seen that Moti has chosen Rakesh and so the choice is reciprocal. It can be shown as Rakesh ↔ Moti. By adding the choices in each column, it is easy to find the extent to which any group member is chosen by others in the group. In this example, Kamal has been chosen three times and so he is most popular (star). Prakash has not been chosen at all and is termed an 'isolate'.

Various soicometric indices are computed from the scoiometric data. The choice status is the measure of the extent to which a member is chosen by his group. The index is calculated by the following formula:

$$CS_j = \frac{\sum c_j}{N-1}$$

In which

CS_j = the choice of status of the individual j

$\sum c_j$ = the sum of the choices in the subject column A, B, C, D, etc.

N = the number of the individual in the group.

In the above example, the choice of status of Kamal is 3/3 = 1, Moti is 2/3 = 0.66, and Prakash is 0/3 = 0.

'Social Expansiveness' is another measure. It indicates the extent to which the group members tend to choose others. The formula for computing this index is:

$$E = \frac{\sum c_{ij}}{N}$$

In which

E= index of expansiveness

$\sum c_{ij}$ =the sum of all choices made by all group members

N = the number of individuals in the group.

Guess-Who Techniques

The Guess-Who technique was developed by Hartshorne and May (1929), for use particularly with child raters. In this technique, a student is asked to read each descriptive statement presented to him and then to write down the name of the student who best fits that description. The student may be use more than one name for each statement, and he is also allowed to use his own name. Examples of statements that might be used in this kind of technique are:

- There is a person who is always doing little things to make others happy.
- There is a person who is disliked by others and has lots of enemies.

The scores for each student is the sum of the number of times he is chosen for each descriptive statement. It the positive statement indicates socially desirable qualities and the negative statement indicates undesirable ones, the total score will be the algebraic sum. For example, if a student is mentioned positively 9 times and negatively 3 times, his total score will be + 9 + (–3) = + 6. If there are several positive and negative statements for a number of behavioural attributes, it is possible to get a score for each attribute for each student of the group. These scores are useful in the study of individual roles and serve as measure of his reputation.

Q20. Write short notes on the following:

(a) Limitation of attitude scale

Ans. Main limitations of the attitude scales are as follows:

- An individual may not express his real attitude; instead express socially acceptable opinions only.
- An individual may not know about his real attitude
- An individual may not have faced a real situation for which he is expected to express the attitude. Hence, it is difficult for him/her to express the attitude towards a phenomenon clearly.
- Equal obtained by respondents do not necessarily mean equal favourableness to a phenomenon.
- Individual tend to respond according to what they should feel rather than what they actually feel.

(b) Areas applicable to observation research

Ans. There are many areas where observation can be used as a technique of research. Wragg (1999) has provided following examples of areas applicable to observational research.

Personal traits: The traits of either the teacher or the pupils for example, whether the teacher is warm or aloof, whether certain pupils appear to prefer collaboration or description.

Verbal interaction: What teachers and pupils talk to each other, who does the talking and about what, question and answer, choice of vocabulary and language register.

Non-verbal: Movement, gesture, facial expressions, like smiles and frowns.

Activity: The nature of pupils' tasks, what the teacher does.

Management: How the teacher manages pupil behaviours, the use of resources, the organisation of group or individual work.

Professional skills: Questioning, explaining, arousing interest and curiosity.

Affective: Teachers' and pupils' feeling and emotions, interpersonal relationships.

Cognitive: The nature and level of thinking in classroom: for example, the level of reasoning necessary to answer a question, or the degree of understanding pupils to have a topic or concept.

Sociological: The roles people play, norms, codes, the effects of social background status, power.

(c) Schedule

Ans. Schedule is a device consisting of a set of questions, which are asked and filled in by an interviewer in a face to face situation with another person. It differs from the questionnaire in that the former is administered personally to a respondent or a group of respondents while the latter is usually mailed. The schedule has many advantages over the questionnaire. It is administered personally and therefore it provides opportunity to the researcher to establish rapport with the respondents. This helps the researcher to explain the nature and purpose of the investigation and to make the meaning of the questions clear to the respondents if they misinterpret a question or give incomplete or indefinite responses. The schedule also economises time and expense of the investigation. It ensures almost all complete and usable returns. A schedule has some limitations also. It may not be possible to contact personally all the respondents either individually or in a group.

4 ANALYSIS AND INTERPRETATION OF DATA

An Overview

A research report stands on the quality of the facts and data on which it is based. It is important to indicate that an excellent research design and a very representative sample are not sufficient to ensure good results if the analysis rests on incorrect data. The importance of constructing an appropriate and accurate instrument for measuring and collecting data is absolutely necessary. The different scales of measurement depend on the type of research and the type of data being collected. Generally, all data collected for any research study are either quantitative or qualitative. Quantitative data are either parametric or non-parametric. Parametric data are measured data on interval or ratio scales of measurement. Ratio scales measurement are almost non-existent in psychological and educational research setting except in the area of psycho-physical judgement. Non-parametric data are obtained by applying nominal or ordinal scales of measurement. These data are either counted or ranked.

Data in raw form may have little meaning to the researcher until they have been classified, organised and analysed with the help of various appropriate quantitative and qualitative techniques. Statistical techniques have contributed greatly in gathering organising, analysing and interpretation numerical data. The process of numerical data through statistics calls for competence in the use of statistical methods and for understanding to know the strengths and the weaknesses of the statistical methods which he uses so that he may not mislead or be mislead by such methods. Besides these methods, descriptive statistical measures are used to describe the characteristics of a sample or population in totality. But descriptive measures limit generalisation to the particular group of observed individuals. To overcome this problem sampling statistics are useful to generalise the inference about population from the observations of the characteristics of a sample. The next problem is to determine how well a researcher can infer or estimate the parametrefrom particular statistics. For making such inference about the parameters, we generally make use of parametric and non-parametric tests.

The methods used in analysis of qualitative data include questionnaire based data in the form of responses to open-ended questions; field notes, and records of observation; responses to inquiries in depth, capturing people's perspectives and experiences during unstructured interview, etc.

Q1. Discuss the nature of data.

Or

What do you mean by data? Identify its various types.

Or

What are the characteristics of qualitative and quantitative data?

Or

What are the characteristics of a quantitative data?

[June-2011, Q.No.-3(a)]

Ans. The data collected from various sources through the use of different tools and techniques generally comprise of numerical figures, ratings, narratives, responses to open-ended questions, quotations, field notes, etc. The nature of data depends mostly upon the type of tool or technique used by researcher in their collection. Some data are collected in the form of numerical figures (quantitative) and some are in the form of symbols or narratives (qualitative). In research, usually two types of data:

Quantitative Data

Quantitative data are obtained by applying various scales of measurement. The experiences of people are collected in a way to fit into standard responses to which numerical values are attached. These data are close-ended and hardly provide any depth or details. Quantitative data are either parametric or non-parametric. Parametric data undergo interval or ratio scale measurement. For example, in measuring reaction time, we make use of ratio scale measurement. The score on a psychological test or inventory is an illustration of interval scale measurement. Non-parametric data are obtained by applying nominal or ordinal scales of measurement. These data are either counted or ranked.

Characteristics of quantitative data may include:

- generally have geographic locations (coordinates);
- are often large in volume (databases, reports, etc.);
- come from a variety of often heterogeneous sources;
- have variability of resolution (details) and scales that sometimes hamper their compilation and integration;
- have a high degree of complexity;
- are needed at varying temporal frequency (e.g., hourly, daily, monthly, yearly), depending on the phenomena or subject under consideration;
- are available in varying forms and formats; and
- more and more available in digital or electronic versions.

Qualitative Data

Qualitative data are verbal or symbolic. The detailed descriptions of observed behaviours, people, situations and events, are some examples of qualitative data. For example, the responses to open-ended questions of a questionnaire or a schedule, first hand information from people about their experiences, ideas, beliefs, and selected content or excerpts from documents, case histories, personal diaries and letters are other examples of qualitative data.

Characteristics of Qualitative Data:

- Emergent and natural
- Interpretative
- Non-random and hypothetical
- Inductive and insightful
- Researchers represent the fundamental instruments essential to the success of a qualitative research study
- Context sensitive
- Contributes to the construction of concepts, theories and previously unknown abstractions as opposed to theories that already exists

Q2. Explain the nature and organisation of Quantitative data.

Ans. Quantitative data consists of tools and tests based on scales of measurement: nominal, ordinal, interval or ratio. *Ratio scale measurements* are almost non-existent in the educational studies except psycho- physical judgements. In this measurement, the experiences of people are fit into standard responses to which numerical values are attached.

Nominal scales: Nominal scales of measurement are used when a set of objects among two or more categories are to be differentiated on the basis of qualitative difference. Usually, a number of symbols or numerals are chosen to represent all objects in a given category, thus taking the advantage of the property of identity. We may assign individuals to such categories as sex (male and females), nationally (Indian and Americans), educational level (school students and college students), professional rank (lecturers, readers and professors), etc.

Each individual can be a member of only one category and all the members of the category have the same defined characteristics. Nominal scales are non-orderable and the only arithmetical operation applicable to such scales is counting, the mere enumeration of individuals in each category, class or set. The nominal scale is primitive form of measurement and the statistical techniques based on counting are permissible in this type of measurement.

Ordinal scales: The ordinal scales of measurement correspond to quantitative classification of a set of objects. The sets or classes of objects are ordered on some continuum in a series ranging from lowest to highest according to the characteristics we wish to measure. The ranking of students in class for height, weight or scholastic achievement are the examples of ordinal scale of measurement. It may be noted that the successive intervals between consecutive points on the ordinal scale may not be equal throughout the entire scale. Suppose we place three students Ram, Sham and Ali, in order of height, Ram tallest, and assign the number 3, 2 and 1 respectively. All we have is information about serial arrangement. We cannot say that Ram, is as much taller than Sham as Sham is taller than Ali, even through the three numbers assigned to them are equally spaced on the scale of measurement. The common arithmetical operations – addition, subtraction, multiplication, and division – cannot be legitimately used with ordinal scales, but statistical procedures based on ranks are appropriate.

Interval scales: If we actually measure the height of the three students Ram, Sham and Ali by using a metre scale and find their heights to be 185 cm, 172 cm and 159 cm, respectively, then we have measurements on a scale of equal units. This scale of measurement is called an interval scale. By this type of measurement we can make some exact and meaningful decisions. We can say that Ram is 13 cm taller than Sham and 26 cm taller than Ali. We can also infer that the difference in heights between Ram and Ali is twice than that between Ram and Sham.

Rating scales: The fourth and highest level of measurement is the ratio scale. All the four operations of addition, subtraction, multiplication and division can be used with ratio scales. All statistical techniques are permissible with such scales. These scales have all the characteristics of interval scales, with the additional advantage of a true zero point. It is possible to indicate the complete absence of an attribute. For example, the zero point on a centimetrescale indicates the complete absence of length or height.

The quantitative data are either parametric or non-parametric.

(1) **Parametric data:** These data are measured on interval or ratio scale measurement. In educational research, we would be mostly dealing with interval scale measurement. For example, the marks obtained by M.Ed. distance learners enrolled with IGNOU provide data on interval scale. In interval scale, the difference between consecutive points on scale are equal over the entire scale but have is no zero point (point of reference) on it in absolute senses. It is chosen conventionally or arbitrarily. An intelligence test, an aptitude test or an attitude scale are based on interval scale.

(2) **Non-Parametric data:** These data are provided by nominal and ordinal scales of measurement. These data are either counted or ranked. Usually a number of symbols or numerals are chosen to represent all objects in a given category, thus taking the advantage of the property of identity in the number system.

There are certain properties of numbers that must have parallels in the observed phenomena.

(i) ***Property of identity:*** a number has identity system. Every number is unique and no other number is exactly the same.

(ii) ***The property of order:*** in this number system, numbers have their order or rank, i.e. one number being greater than other number.

(iii) ***The property of additivity:*** In the system of numbers, summing of a certain number with certain other number can be added, they can also be subtracted, multiplied and divided.

The quantitative data, parametric or non-parametric, collected through the administration of various tools on selected samples or samples are raw.

Organisation

Organisation of data includes editing, classifying and tabulating quantitative information.

- Editing implies checking of the gathered raw data for accuracy, usefulness and completeness.
- Classification refers to dividing the data into different categories, classes, groups or heads. For this, the researcher is guided by the nature of the problem, the hypotheses to be verified, or by the responses or characteristics of the samples, he has selected. If the problem or hypotheses, for example

involved the difference between attitudes of male and female teachers towards co-education at the secondary school stage, the categories of male and female serving in government and private aided schools would be clearly indicated. In some situations when the group is sufficiently homogeneous, no breakdown into categories or subgroups is necessary and it is desirable to describe the group as a whole. However, in the situations where the group is sufficiently heterogeneous it is desirable to divide the group into homogeneous sub-groups or categories that have in common some distinctive attributes for the purpose of analysis.

- Tabulation is the process of transferring classified data from data gathering tools to the tabular form in which they may be systematically examined. This process may be performed in a number of ways. In simple and less sophisticated types of research, hand sorting and tabulating procedures are usually employed. More extensive and sophisticated investigations make use of card-tabulating process.

Q3. Discuss the nature and organsiation of qualitative data.

Ans. Qualitative data are verbal and other symbolic materials. These include detailed descriptions of observed natural behaviours in a real life setting, free from the constraints of more conventional procedure. It is an in-depth verbal description of a phenomenon. The goal is to capture the richness and complexity of observed behaviour that occurs in natural settings. The observation data are in the form of words rather than numbers. These data comprise the description of the setting or physical environment, social interactions, physical activities, non-verbal communications, planned or unplanned activities and interactions.

The detailed description of people, situations and events in the form of responses of open-ended questionnaires or interviews schedules are other examples of qualitative data. These data are also the description of individual's experiences, knowledge, opinions, beliefs and feelings of a social phenomenon. The selected content or excerpts from documents, case histories, personal diaries, and letters also provide data, which are qualitative in nature.

Qualitative data provide first hand information to the researcher about some phenomenon in depth. The extent of depth and detail will vary depending upon the nature and purpose of particular research study. Data of qualitative nature are neither systematic nor standardised. But they permit a researcher to understand situations and events as seen and felt by him, and also by others. For example, the responses to open-ended questions are longer and detailed which help a researcher to understand in depth the points of view of other people, their level of emotion, their characteristics, their attitudes and values, and their experiences. Similarly data gathered through participant observation or an open-ended unstructured interview which are mostly descriptive in nature specify some basic information pertaining to the place, the persons present, nature of settings, type and nature of various types of interactions and activities during the interview or observation.

Organisation

The qualitative data gathered through open-ended questionnaires, participant observations and in depth interviews are voluminous. They are not systematically and logically arranged. There is a need to organise and classify them into specific patterns, categories and descriptive units for analysis and interpretations. For this it is necessary to make some copies of the data.

Patton (1982) suggests to make four copies and store one complete copy in a safety deposit box as these data are unique and priceless.

The second copy should be used for further treatment of the data through out.

The third copy may be used to fill the missing gaps, if any, identified during their scrutiny by the researcher. Additional notes can also be recorded in this copy.

The organsiation of qualitative data involves a lot of cutting and pasting for which fourth copy may be utilised.

After making the copies, you can start with the actual classification and organisation of the data for which there are no formal or universal rules. The classification and organisation of qualitative data in various units, patterns or categories requires a creative approach and a lot of perseverance on the part of a researcher.

As a first step, you may go through the contents of the data carefully and note down the comments in the margins or attach small pieces of paper with your written notes using staples/tags.

The next step is to arrange the data in topics for which you may use abbreviations. The abbreviated topics are written either in the margins of the relevant data or on a slip of paper which may be attached with the relevant page.

The process of classifying or labeling the various kinds of data and preparing a 'data index' is an essential step in the organisation of qualitative data. In case of large data, it is not possible to develop a simple classification system. In such cases, we may make use of computers, which are helpful in developing systematic and comprehensive classification schemes.

Q4. Illustrate the procedure for classifying and tabulating quantitative data into frequency distribution.

Ans. We will illustrate the procedure in two cases as follows:

When the range of data is small

We have available the following data as scores of 50 distance learners in a course of their B.Ed. Programme.

22	25	28	26	30	29	23	22	21	26
27	25	24	25	20	22	25	26	27	24
23	24	26	28	25	27	24	23	25	23
24	29	25	27	26	23	21	24	25	26
20	24	25	29	30	27	22	23	23	21

These scores are raw and may have little meaning until they are classified in some systematic order. The method of classification is called frequency distribution.

We will illustrate the method by using the above data of scores. Inspection of the data shows that some scores occur more than once. For example, there are two 20s, three 29s, four 27s, six 26s and so on. This suggests that we may arrange the data in columns, as shown in the Table 4.1

Table 4.1 Frequency distribution of scores of B.Ed. distance learners

Scores (X)	Tallies	Frequency (f)
30	II	2
29	III	3
28	II	2
27	~~IIII~~	5
26	~~IIII~~ I	6
25	~~IIII~~ IIII	9
24	~~IIII~~ II	7
23	~~IIII~~ II	7
22	IIII	4
21	III	3
20	II	2
		N = 50

In one column, we may arrange the scores in descending or ascending order and in the other, we record by tallies the number distance learners who achieved these scores. Where we have to record five tallies we mark four as IIII and fifth is made across the four. The tallies are then totaled in the next column. This column provides us the list of number of time each scores occurs.

It is known as frequency of that score and is generally designated as 'f'. Such an arrangement of the data is known as frequency distribution. The value of the scores is generally represented by the symbol X.

In this example, maximum score is 30 and minimum score is 20. In this way, we have only eleven classes. Bu the when the range (i.e. interval between the highest score and the lowest score) is large we classify in as many classes as there are scores value, we shall have large number of classes. In such situations, we reduce the number of classes by arranging the data in arbitrarily defined classes of variables.

When the range of data is large

For large range of data, we will consider the following scores of 100 distance learners in course of M.Ed. Programme.

53	68	66	48	85
68	76	70	86	84
36	68	82	76	78
72	91	92	60	40
64	80	63	62	81
93	65	77	64	73
68	63	60	74	88
76	80	75	89	83
93	76	69	71	73
77	74	83	79	66
63	76	72	66	84
85	66	80	63	65
72	65	73	53	46
79	55	71	95	63
63	76	75	64	85
82	82	62	88	100
75	93	71	68	88
70	74	86	68	61
71	75	71	73	82
80	76	75	86	62

The distribution of above scores shows that the highest score is 100 and lowest score is 36. The range is 100 – 36 = 64. Therefore, the distribution of scores can be conveniently arranges by dividing the range of 64 into ten or more class intervals if the classes are taken to be of 5 points each and we take the starting point 35, then the scores within the range 35 to 39, that is, all score with the values 35, 36, 37, 38 and 39 will be grouped together to form the lowest class.

All the scores from 40 to 44, i.e. 40, 41, 42, 43 and 44 will form the next class. Similarly, we shall group all scores within the ranges 45 to 49, 50 to 54 and so on. The highest class interval will 100-104. The frequency distribution of the data will be represented as under in the table 4.2.

Table 4.2 Frequency distribution of scores of 100 M.Ed. distance learners

Class Intervals	Tallies	Frequency (f)
100-104	I	1
95-99	I	1
90-94	~~IIII~~	5
85-89	~~IIII~~ ~~IIII~~	10
80-84	~~IIII~~ ~~IIII~~ II	12
75-79	~~IIII~~ ~~IIII~~ ~~IIII~~ II	17
70-74	~~IIII~~ ~~IIII~~ ~~IIII~~ III	18
65-69	~~IIII~~ ~~IIII~~ IIII	14
60-64	~~IIII~~ ~~IIII~~ ~~IIII~~	15
55-59	I	1
50-54	II	2
45-49	II	2
40-44	I	1
35-39	I	1
		N = 100

Q5. Explain the various methods of graphical representation of data.

Ans. Graphical representation often facilitates the understanding of a set of data. If the graph is well drawn, it is usually easier to read and interpret data. Four methods of graphical representation of data are in general use:

Histogram

The graph usually drawn to represent a frequency distribution is called a Histogram. A histogram is a set of rectangles (vertical bars) each proportionate in width to the magnitude of a class interval and proportionate in area to the number of frequencies concerning the classes' intervals. In a histogram, the variables (class-intervals) are always shown on X-axis and the frequencies are taken on the Y-axis. In constructing, a histogram there should not be any gap between two successive rectangles, and the data must be in exclusive form of classes. However, we cannot construct histogram for distribution with open-end classes and it can be quite misleading if the distribution has unequal class intervals.

Procedure: To prepare a histogram we may proceed as follows:

Step 1: Draw a horizontal line at the bottom of graph paper along which mark off units to represent the class intervals. It is usual to start with the class intervals of lowest values.

Step 2: Draw a vertical line through the extreme end of the horizontal axis along which mark off units to represent the frequencies of the class intervals. Choose a scale, which will make the largest frequency (the height) of the polygon approximately 75 per cent of the width of the figure.

Step 3: Draw rectangles with class unit as base, such that the areas of rectangles are proportional to the frequencies of the correspondingly classes.

The histogram (fig 4.1) plotted from the data given in Table 4.3 as follows:

Table 4.3 Test scores of 100 College Students

Class Interval	Mid Points	Frequency	Cumulative frequency	Cumulative percentage frequency
44.5 – 49.5	47	1	1	1.00
49.5 –54.5	52	1	2	2.00
54.5 – 59.5	57	2	4	4.00
59.5 – 64.5	62	2	6	6.00
64.5 – 69.5	67	1	7	7.00
69.5 – 74.5	72	15	22	22.00
74.5 – 79.5	77	14	36	36.00
79.5 – 84.5	82	18	54	54.00
84.5 – 89.5	87	17	71	71.00
89.5 – 94.5	92	12	83	83.00
94.5 – 99.5	97	10	93	93.00
99.5 – 104.5	102	5	98	98.00
104.5 – 109.5	107	1	99	99.00
109.5 – 114.5	112	1	100	100.00
		N = 100		

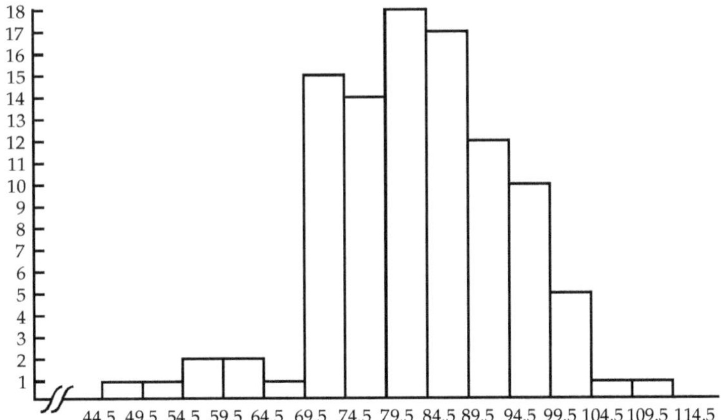

Fig. 4.1: Histogram plotted from the data of table 4.3

Frequency polygon

A frequency polygon is the figure with many angles obtained by connecting the mid-points of the class intervals just outside the histogram with the mid-points of the tops of rectangles by straight lines. The area under frequency polygon is the same as that under the corresponding histogram. This is because the area of the triangular strips out of the frequency polygon would be equal to the area outside the histogram included in the frequency polygon.

Procedure for frequency polygon: The first two steps are identical with those used in the construction of the histogram. The third step to be followed is given as under:

Step 3: Directly above the point on the horizontal axis representing the mid-point of each class interval, plot the points at a height proportional to the frequencies. Join these points by straight lines. The frequency polygon for distribution of Table 4.3 is shown in Figure 4.2.

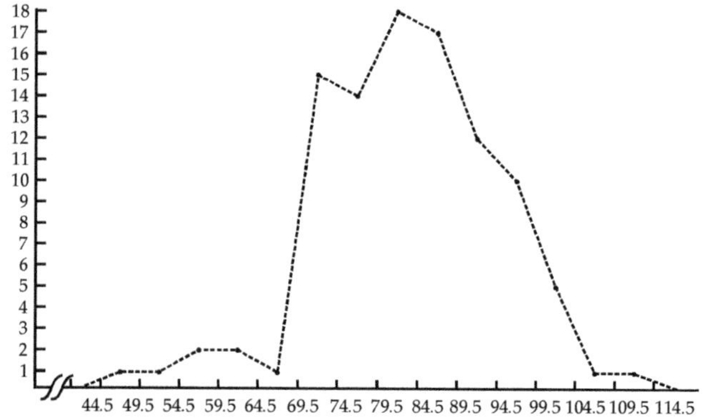

Fig. 4.2: Frequency Polygon plotted from the data of table 4.3

Cumulative Percentage Curve or Ogive

The cumulative percentage curve or ogive differs from the cumulative frequency curve in that frequencies are expressed as cumulative percents of N on the vertical axis instead of as cumulative frequencies. In column (5) of Table 4.3, the cumulative frequencies are expressed as percentage of N. After finding cumulative percentage frequencies, we may then plot these frequencies corresponding to upper exact limits of class intervals. A curve joining the points thus obtained is called *cumulative percentage curve or ogive.*

The cumulative percentage curve or ogive of the distribution represented in Table 4.3 is illustrated in Figure 4.3:

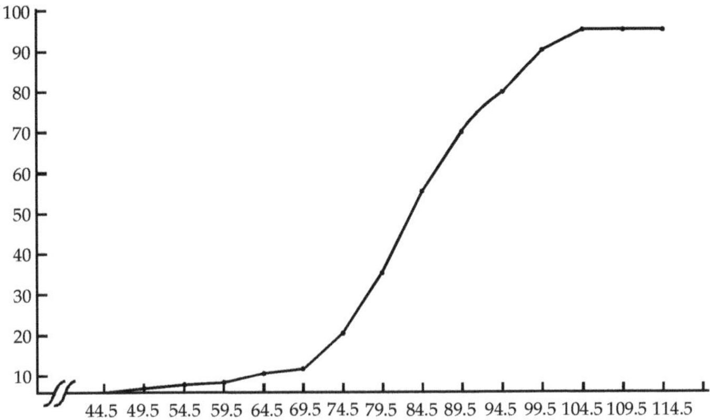

Fig. 4.3: Cumulative Percentage Curve or Ogive plotted from the data of table 4.3

Uses of Ogive

- Percentiles and percentile ranks are determined quickly, fairly and accurately from the ogive when the curve is carefully drawn and the scale divisions are precisely marked.
- A useful overall comparison of two or more groups is provided when ogives representing their sources are plotted upon the same horizontal and vertical axes.
- Percentile norms are determined directly from ogive.

Q6. Define and compute different measures of central tendency.

Ans. Measures of central tendency are measures of the location of the middle or the center of a distribution. The definition of "middle" or "center" is purposely left somewhat vague so that the term "central tendency" can refer to a wide variety of measures. Measures of central tendency are the best way to reduce a set of data and still retain part of the information. Main measures of central tendency are:

Mean of ungrouped data

$$\text{Mean}(\overline{X}) = \frac{\sum X}{N}$$

Where $\sum X$ indicates the sum of the values of all the observations, and N is the total number of observations. Compute the arithmetic mean for ungrouped data. For example, now consider the monthly salary (₹) of 10 employees of a firm:

2500, 2700, 2400, 2300, 2550, 2650, 2750, 2450, 2600, 2400

If we compute the arithmetic mean, then:

$$\overline{X} = \frac{2500 + 2700 + 2400 + 2300 + 2550 + 2650 + 2750 + 2450 + 2600 + 2400}{10}$$

$$= \frac{25300}{10} = ₹2530.$$

Therefore, the average monthly salary is ₹ 2530.

Mean of grouped data: When the observations are classified into a frequency distribution, the midpoint of the class interval would be treated as the representative average value of that class. Therefore, for grouped data the arithmetic mean is defined as:

$$\overline{X} = \frac{\Sigma fx}{N}$$

Where,

x is midpoint of various classes,

f is the frequency for corresponding class, and

N is the total frequency, i.e. $N = \Sigma f$,

To simplify calculations, the following formula for arithmetic mean may be more convenient to use.

$$\overline{X} = A + \frac{\sum fd}{N} \times i$$

Where A is an arbitrary point,

$$d = \frac{X - A}{i},$$

i = size of the equal class interval.

Remark: A justification of this formula is as follows. When $d = \frac{X - A}{i}$, then $X = A + id$.

Multiplying throughout by f, taking summation on both sides and dividing by N, we get:

$$\overline{X} = A + \frac{\sum fd}{N} \times i$$

This formula makes the computations very simple and takes less time.

Median

Median may be defined as the *middle value* in the data set when its elements are arranged in a sequential order, that is, in either ascending or descending order of magnitude. It is called a middle value in an ordered sequence of data in the sense that half of the observations are smaller and half are larger than this value. The median is thus a measure of the *location or centrality* of the observations. The median can be calculated for both ungrouped and grouped data sets.

Ungrouped Data: In this case, the data is arranged in either ascending or descending order of magnitude.

- If the number of observations (N) is an odd number, then the median (Med) is represented by the numerical value corresponding to the positioning point of $\frac{(N+1)}{2}$ ordered observation. That is,

  Med = Size or value of $\left(\frac{N+1}{2}\right)^{th}$ observation in the data array.

- If the number of observations (N) is an even number, then the median is defined as the arithmetic mean of the numerical values of:

  $\left(\frac{N}{2}\right)^{th}$ and $\left(\frac{N+1}{2}\right)^{th}$ observations in the data array. That is,

$$\text{Med} = \frac{\left(\frac{N}{2}\right)^{th}\text{observation} + \left(\frac{N}{2}+1\right)^{th}\text{observation}}{2}$$

Grouped Data: To find the median value for grouped data, first identify the class interval which contains the median value or $\left(\frac{N}{2}\right)^{th}$ observation of the data set. To identify such class interval, find the cumulative frequency of each class until the class for which the cumulative frequency is equal to or greater than the value of $\left(\frac{N}{2}\right)^{th}$ observation. The value of the median within that class is found by using interpolation. That is, it is assumed that the observation values are evenly spaced over the entire class interval. The following formula is used to determine the median of grouped data:

$$\text{Med} = L + \frac{\left(\frac{N}{2}\right) - cf}{f} \times i$$

Where,

L=lower class limit (or boundary) of the median class interval,

cf = cumulative frequency of the class prior to the median class interval, that is, the sum of all the class frequencies upto, but not including, the median class interval.

f = frequency of the median class

i = width of the median class interval

N = total number of observations in the distribution

Mode

Mode is also a measure of central tendency. This measure is different from the arithmetic mean, to some extent like the median because it is not really calculated by the normal process of arithmetic. The mode, of the data, is the value that appears the maximum number of times.

In an ungrouped data, for example, the foot size (in inches) of ten persons are as follows:

5, 8, 6, 9, 11, 10, 9, 8, 10, 9

Here, the number 9 appears thrice. Therefore, mode size of foot is 9 inches.

In grouped data, the method of calculating mode is different between discrete distribution and continuous distribution. In discrete data, For example, find the mode of the following data set:

48 44 48 45 42 49 48

The mode is 48 since it occurs most often.

For continuous data, usually we refer to modal class or group as the class with the maximum frequency (as per observation approach). Therefore, the mode from continuous distribution may be computed using the expression:

$$\text{Mode} = L + \frac{f_1 - f_0}{2f_1 - f_0 - f_2} \times i$$

Where,

L = lower limit of class,

f_1 = frequency of model class

f_0 = frequency of preceding class

f_2 = frequency of succeeding class

i = class interval

Q7. The following table gives the daily profits (in₹) of 195 shops of a town. Calculate mean and median.

Profits	No. of Shops
50 – 60	15
60 – 70	20
70 – 80	32
80 – 90	35
90 – 100	33
100 – 110	22
110 – 120	20
120 – 130	10
130 – 140	8

Ans. The calculations of mean and median are shown below:

Class Intervals	f	Mid-value (X)	$u=\frac{X-95}{10}$	fu	Less than c. f.
50-60	15	55	–4	–60	15
60-70	20	65	–3	–60	35
70-80	32	75	–2	–64	67
80-90	35	85	–1	–35	102
90-100	33	95	0	0	135
100-110	22	105	1	22	157
110-120	20	115	2	40	177
120-130	10	125	3	20	187
130-140	8	135	4	32	195
Total	195			–95	

$$\overline{X} = A + \frac{\sum fu}{N} \times h = 95 - \frac{95}{195} \times 10 = ₹90.13$$

Since $\frac{N}{2} = \frac{195}{2} = 97.5$, the median class is 80 – 90 and, therefore, L= 80, $h = 10,\ f = 35,\ c.f. = 67.$

$$\text{Thus, Med.} = L + \frac{\frac{N}{2} - c.f}{f} \times h$$

$$\therefore \text{Med.} = 80 + \frac{97.5-67}{35} \times 10 = ₹88.71$$

Q8. The following table gives the distribution of marks by 500 students in an examination. Obtain median of the given data.

Marks	0-9	10-19	20-29	30-39	40-49	50-59	60-69	70-79
No. of Students	30	40	50	48	24	162	132	14

Ans. Since the class intervals are inclusive, therefore, it is necessary to convert them into class boundaries.

Class Intervals	Class Boundaries	Frequency	'Less than' type c.f.
0 – 9	-0.5 – 9.5	30	30
10 – 19	9.5 – 19.5	40	70
20 – 29	19.5 – 29.5	50	120
30 – 39	29.5 – 39.5	48	168
40 – 49	39.5 – 49.5	24	192
50 – 59	49.5 – 59.5	162	354
60 – 69	59.5 – 69.5	132	486
70 – 79	69.5 – 79.5	14	500

Since $\frac{N}{2}=250$, the median class is 49.5 – 59.5 and, therefore, L= 49.5, $h=10,\ f=162,\ c.f.=192$

$$\text{Thus, Med.} = L+\frac{\frac{N}{2}-c.f}{f}\times h$$

$$=49.5+\frac{250-192}{162}\times 10 = 53.08 \text{ Marks}$$

Q9. Calculate Mode from the following given data-set.

Mid-value	15	25	35	45	55	65	75	85
Frequency	5	8	12	16	28	15	3	2

Ans. A series with 'Mid-values' is first to be expanded as a series with class intervals, as under:

Expansion of Mid-values as class-intervals for the estimation of Mode

Mid Values	Class Intervals	Frequency
15	10 – 20	5
25	20 – 30	8
35	30 – 40	12
45	40 – 50	16
55	50 – 60	28
65	60 – 70	15
75	70 – 80	3
85	80 – 90	2

Class interval 50 – 60 is the one with highest frequency. This is the modal class interval, as the frequencies are increasing or decreasing in a systematic pattern. The actual value of Mode is,

$$\text{Mode} = L+\frac{f_1-f_0}{2f_1-f_0-f_2}\times i = 50+\frac{28-16}{2(28)-16-15}\times 10 = 50+4.8 = 54.8$$

Q10. What do you understand by measures of variation? Explain its types.

Ans. A numerical measure that can be used to throw some light on the scatter or the homogeneity of data is called a measure of variation. The various measure of variability are as follows:

- **Range:** The range is defined as the difference between the highest (numerically largest) value and the lowest (numerically smallest) value in a set of data. Among the various measures of dispersion, the range is the simplest one. This measure can be applied where a researcher require a quick result. Range is easy to calculate and simple to understand and this is its merit. It can be safely used when variations are not much, but it may give a misleading result if there are one or two abnormal items. Also, the demerits of the range are that it has no further algebraic properties and cannot be applied for open end distribution.

In symbols, this may be indicated as:

$R = H - L,$

Where,

R = Range; H = Highest Value; L = Lowest Value

For grouped data, the range may be approximated as the difference between the upper limit of the largest class and the lower limit of the smallest class.

- **Mean deviation:** The mean deviation is the arithmetic mean of absolute difference between the items in a distribution and the average of that distribution. Theoretically, mean deviation can be computed from the mean. However, in actual practice the mean is frequently used in computing the mean deviation. Under this method, algebraic signs (+,-) are ignored while taking the deviations from average. For un-grouped data, the formula is:

$$\text{M.D. from mean} = \frac{\sum |X - \overline{X}|}{N}$$

Where, the two bars indicated that the sign of the difference within the two bars is taken as positive.

The co-efficient of Mean deviation for un-grouped and grouped data, the formula is:

$$\text{Coefficient of M.D.} = \frac{\text{M.D}}{\overline{X}}$$

- **Standard Deviation:** The standard deviation is the most familiar, important and widely used measure of variation. It is a significant measure for making comparison of variability between two or more sets of data in terms of their distance from the mean. Standard deviation may be defined as the square root of the arithmetic mean of the squares of deviations from arithmetic mean of given distribution. This measure is also known as root mean square deviation. If the values in a given data are dispersed more widely from the mean, then the standard deviation becomes greater. It is usually denoted by σ. The square of the standard deviation(σ^2) is called variance.

Standard deviation is calculated by using the following formula:

$$\sigma = \sqrt{\frac{\sum (X - \overline{X})^2}{N}}$$

Where,

σ = standard deviation, X = observations, $\overline{X}$ = arithmetic mean,

$\sum (X - \overline{X})^2$ is the sum of the squares of deviations,

N is the number of observations.

For grouped data:

$$\sigma = \sqrt{\frac{\sum f (X - \overline{X})^2}{N}}$$

Where,

N is the sum of frequencies.

If the collected data are very large, then considering the assumed mean is more convenient to compute standard deviation. In such case, the formula is slightly modified as:

$$\sigma = \sqrt{\frac{\sum fdx^2}{N} - \left(\frac{\sum fdx}{N}\right)^2} \times c$$

Where, c = common factor, $dx = \frac{m - A}{c}$.

Q11. Prove that mean deviation from median is less than that measured from any other value.

Or

Calculate the mean deviation from mean and median from the following data:

Marks:	**0-10**	**10-20**	**20-30**	**30-40**	**40-50**
No. of students:	**6**	**28**	**51**	**11**	**4**

Ans.

Marks	f	M.V(X)	cf	fX	$X - \overline{X}$	$f\lvert X - \overline{X}\rvert$	f|X–Med.|
0-10	6	5	6	30	–17.9	107.4	108.84
10-20	28	15	34	420	–7.9	221.2	227.92
20-30	51	25	85	1275	2.1	107.1	94.84
30-40	11	35	96	385	12.1	133.1	130.46
40-50	4	45	100	180	22.1	88.4	87.44
				2290		657.2	649.5

Mean deviation from Median

$$\frac{N}{2}=\frac{100}{2}=50^{th}\text{item}$$

$$\text{Med.}=L+\frac{N/2-cf}{f}\times i$$

$$=20+\frac{50-34}{51}\times 10$$

$$M.D_{Med.}=\frac{\Sigma f|X-Med.|}{\Sigma f}=\frac{649.5}{100}=6.49$$

Mean deviation from Mean

$$\overline{X}=\frac{\Sigma fX}{\Sigma f}=\frac{2290}{100}=22.9$$

$$M.D_{\overline{X}}=\frac{\Sigma f|X-\overline{X}|}{\Sigma f}=\frac{657.2}{100}=6.57$$

Since, $M.D_{Med.}<M.D_{\overline{X}}, 6.49<6.57$

Hence, it is proved that mean deviation from median is less than that measured from any other value.

Q12. Calculate the standard deviation from the mean for the following series:

Sales	No of days
40-50	10
50-60	15
60-70	25
70-80	30
80-90	12
90-100	8

Ans.

Sales (X)	No. of days(f)	Mid-value	dx = (m – 65)/10	dx^2	fdx	fdx^2
40 – 50	10	45	-2	4	-20	40
50 – 60	15	55	-1	1	-15	15
60 – 70	25	65	0	0	0	0
70 – 80	30	75	1	1	30	30
80 – 90	12	85	2	4	24	48
90 – 100	8	95	3	9	24	72
	N = 100				$\Sigma fdx = 43$	$\Sigma fdx^2 = 205$

$$\sigma = \sqrt{\frac{\sum fdx^2}{N} - \left(\frac{\sum fdx}{N}\right)^2} \times i = \sqrt{\frac{205}{100} - \left(\frac{43}{100}\right)^2} \times 10$$

$$\sqrt{2.05 - 0.1849} \times 10 = 1.36510 = 13.65$$

Q13. Find mean and standard deviation of the following distribution:

Age (in years)	No. of Persons
Less than 20	0
Less than 25	170
Less than 30	280
Less than 35	360
Less than 40	405
Less than 45	445
Less than 50	480

Ans. Less than type frequencies are given in the question. These are first converted into frequencies of various mutually exclusive classes.

Calculation of mean and S.D.

Let $u = \frac{X - 32.5}{5}$

Class Intervals	No. of Person (f)	Mid-value (X)	u	fu	fu^2
20-25	170	22.5	–2	–340	680
25-30	110	27.5	–1	–110	110
30-35	80	32.5	0	0	0
35-40	45	37.5	1	45	45
40-45	40	42.5	2	80	160
45-50	35	47.5	3	105	315
Total	480			–220	1310

$$\overline{X} = 32.5 - 5 \times \frac{220}{480} = 30.21 \text{years}$$

$$\sigma = \sqrt{\frac{\sum fu^2}{\sum f} - \left(\frac{\sum fu}{\sum f}\right)^2} \times i$$

$$\sigma = \sqrt{\frac{1310}{480} - \left(\frac{-220}{480}\right)^2} \times 5 = 7.94 \text{years}$$

Q14. Define normal distribution. What are its basic assumptions? What are the characteristics of normal probability distribution curve?

Or

Discuss the assumptions of Normal Probability Curve (NPC).

[Dec-2011, Q.No.-3(c)]

Ans. The normal distribution, also called the normal probability distribution happens to be most useful theoretical distribution for continuous variables. It is approximation to binomial distribution. Whether or not p is equal to q, the binomial distribution tends to the form of the continuous curve when n becomes large at least for the material part of the range. In fact, that corresponding between binomial and the normal curve is surprisingly close even for low values of n provided p and q are fairly near equality. The limiting frequency curve, obtained as n, becomes large and is called the normal frequency curve or simply the normal curve.

It is defined and given by the following probability function:

$$P(X) = \frac{1}{\sigma\sqrt{2\pi}} e^{\frac{-(x-\mu)}{2\sigma^2}}$$

X = Values of the continuous random variable

μ = Mean of the normal random variable

e = Mathematical constant approximated by 2.7183

π = Mathematical constant approximated by 3.1416

Assumptions

The normal distribution is based on the following set of assumptions:

- **Independent Causes:** the forces affecting the event must be independent of one another, i.e. they are independent of each other.
- **Conditions of Symmetry:** The operation of causal forces must be such that the deviations from mean on either side is equal in number and size.
- **Multiple Causation**: The causal forces must be numerous and of approximately equal weight or importance.

Characteristics/Properties of Normal Distribution/Normal Curve

Normal distribution curve has the following properties/characteristics:

Perfectly Symmetrical and bell shaped: The normal curve is perfectly symmetrical and bell shaped about mean. This means that if we fold the curve along its vertical axis at the centre, the two halves would coincide.

Unimodal Distribution: It has only one mode, i.e. it is unimodal distribution.

Equality of Mean, Median and Mode: In a normal distribution, mean, median and mode are equal, i.e.

$\overline{X}$ = Med. = Mode

Asymptotic to the Base Line: Normal curve is asymptotic to the base line on either sides, i.e. it has a tendency to touch the base line but it never touches it. This is clear as follows:

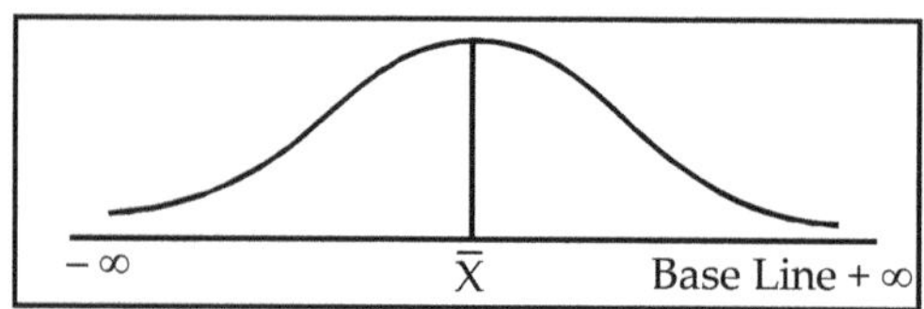

Fig. 4.4: Normal Curve is Asymptotic to the Base Line

Range: The normal curve extends to infinity on either side, i.e. it extends $-\infty$ to $+\infty$.

Total Area: The total area under the normal curve is 1.

Ordinate: The ordinate of the normal curve at the mean is maximum.

Mean Ordinate: The mean ordinate divides the whole area under the curve into two equal parts, i.e. 50 per cent on the right side and 50 per cent on left side.

Equidistance of Quartiles: In a normal distribution, the quartiles Q_1 and Q_3 are equidistant from the median, i.e.

$$Q_3 - \text{Med.} = \text{Med.} - Q_1$$

Quartile Deviation: In a normal distribution, the quartile deviation is 2/3 times the standard deviation, i.e.

$$\text{Q.D.} = \frac{2}{3}\text{S.D.}$$

Mean Deviation: In a normal distribution, the mean deviation is 4/5 times the standard deviation, i.e.

$$\text{M.D.} = \frac{4}{5}\text{S.D.}$$

Points of Inflexion: The normal curve has two points of inflexion (i.e. the points where the curve changes its curvature) at $\overline{X} - 1\sigma$ and $\overline{X} + 1\sigma$. In other words, the points of inflexion occurs at $\overline{X} \pm 1\sigma$, i.e. at $\overline{X} - 1\sigma$ and $\overline{X} + 1\sigma$. This is clear from the figure 4.5 given below:

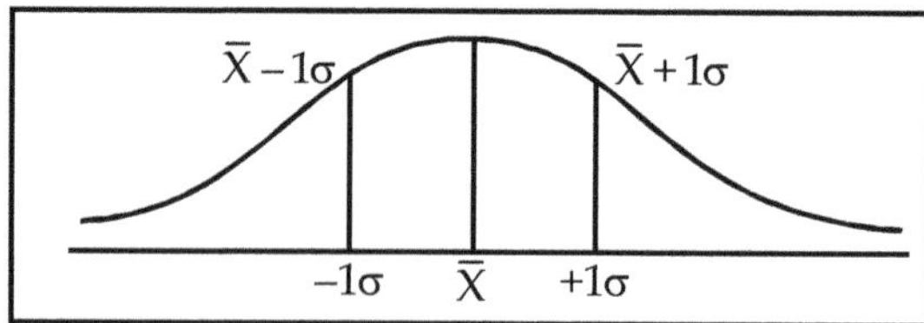

Fig. 4.5: Points of Inflexion in Normal Curve

Continuous Probability Distribution: Normal distribution is a distribution of continuous variables. Therefore, it is called continuous Probability Distribution.

Constants: The constants of normal distribution are denoted by the following symbols:

Mean $= \overline{X}$ or μ or m , Moment coeff. of Skewness $= \sqrt{\beta_1 = 0}$

S.D. $= \sigma$, Moment coeff. of Kurtosis $= \beta_2 = 3$

Variance $= \sigma^2$

Main Parameters: The normal distribution has two parameters namely mean $(\overline{X})$ and standard deviation (σ). The entire distribution can be known from these two parameters.

Areas Property: One of the most important properties of normal curve is the area relationship property. The total area under the normal curve is 1. It has been found that:

- Area under the normal curve between $\overline{X} - 1\sigma$ and $\overline{X} + 1\sigma$ is 0.6826, i.e. $\overline{X} + 1\sigma$ covers 68.26 per cent area under the normal curve.
- Area under the normal curve between $\overline{X} - 2\sigma$ and $\overline{X} + 2\sigma$ is 0.9545, i.e. $\overline{X} \pm 2\sigma$ covers 95.45 per cent are under the normal curve.
- Area under the normal curve between $\overline{X} - 3\sigma$ and $\overline{X} + 3\sigma$ is 0.9973, i.e. $\overline{X} \pm 3\sigma$ covers 99.73 per cent are under the normal curve.

The following figure illustrates the area property:

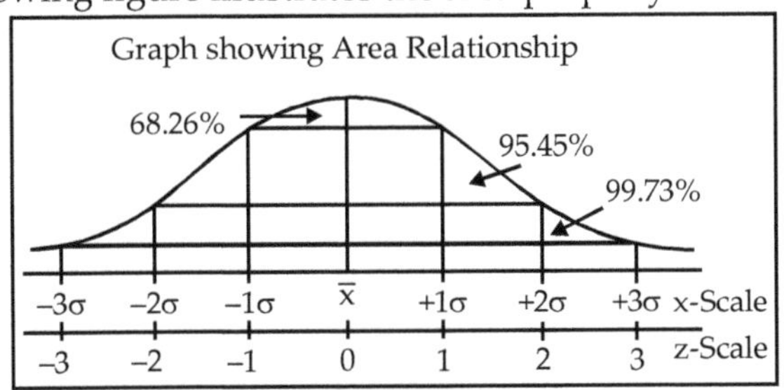

Fig. 4.6: Area Property of Normal Curve

Q15. Discuss the uses of normal probability distribution with suitable examples.

Ans. The various uses relating to normal distribution are studied under the following heads:

Finding areas when $\overline{X}$ and σ of normal variate are given

In order to find the area under the normal curve, firstly we transform the given value of normal variate in to Z-variate. For example, if $\overline{X} = 30$, σ=5 and X=35, will be transformed in to the standard normal variate as follows:

$$Z = \frac{35-30}{5} = 1 \qquad \text{where} \quad Z = \frac{X-\overline{X}}{\sigma}$$

Thus, for X=35, the standard normal variate (SNV) is 1.

After Z-transformation, Table of Area under the normal curve is consulted.

Finding $\overline{X}$ and σ when the area under normal curve is given

When the area under the normal curve is given, then we can find the mean $(\overline{X})$ and standard deviations (σ) of the normal distribution.

For examples:

In a normal distribution, 31 per cent of the items are under 45 and 8 per cent are over 64. Find $\bar{x}$ and σ of the distribution.

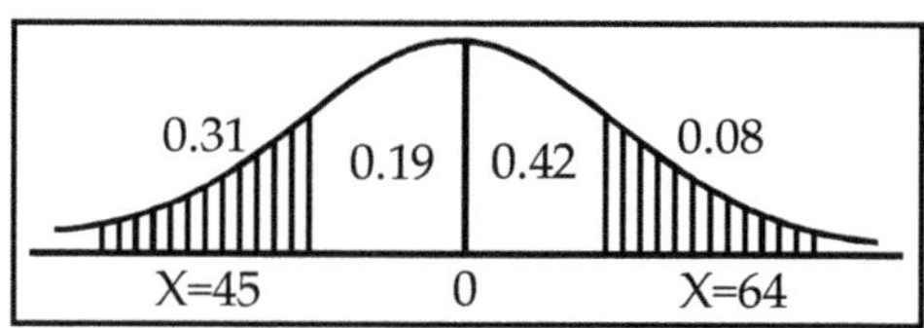

$$Z = \frac{X-\overline{X}}{\sigma}$$

Value of Z corresponding to 0.50–0.31=0.19 area=–0.5 (From the table)

$$\therefore -0.5 = \frac{45-\overline{X}}{\sigma} \text{ or } -0.5\sigma = 45-\overline{X} \text{ or } \overline{X}-0.5\sigma = 45 \qquad \text{...(i)}$$

Value of Z corresponding to 0.5–0.08=0.42 area=+1.41 (From the table)

$$\therefore 1.41 = \frac{64-\overline{X}}{\sigma}$$

or $1.41\sigma = 64-\overline{X}$

or $\overline{X}+1.41\sigma = 64$ ...(ii)

Solving the two equations

$\overline{X}-5\sigma = 45$

$\overline{X}+1.41\sigma = 64$

$-\quad -\qquad -$

$-1.91\sigma = -19$

$\Rightarrow \sigma = 10$ approx.

Substituting the value of σ in equation (i)

$\overline{X}-5(10) = 45$

$\overline{X}-5(10) = 45$

$\overline{X}-5 = 45$ or $\overline{X} = 50$

$\therefore \overline{X} = 50, \sigma = 10$

Finding Minimum and Maximum Score amongst the Highest and Lowest Group

When the $\overline{X}, \sigma$ and proportion of highest and lowest groups are given, then we can find the minimum and maximum score amongst the highest and lowest group. The following examples illustrate the procedure:

The wages of 5,000 workers were found to be normally distributed with mean ₹2,000 and standard deviation ₹120. What was the lowest wages amongst the richest 500 workers?

Given N=5,000, $\overline{X} = 2000$, σ=120

Proportion of richest workers $= \frac{500}{5000} = \frac{1}{10} = 0.10$

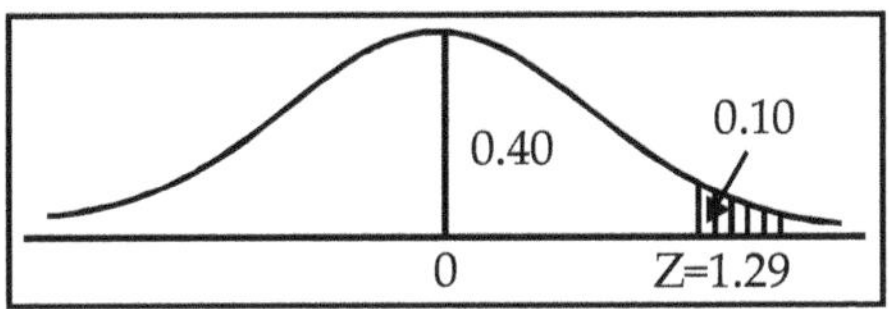

The value of Z corresponding to 0.40 area=1.29

We know that: $Z = \frac{X - \overline{X}}{\sigma}$

$$1.29 = \frac{X - 2000}{120} \Rightarrow X - 2000 = 154.8 \Rightarrow X = ₹2154.8$$

Thus, the lowest wages among the richest 500 workers in ₹2154.8

Fitting of Normal Curve

The following example, illustrate the procedure of fitting the normal curve.

Fit a normal curve to the following data by the method of ordinates:

Variable:	**0-10**	**10-20**	**20-30**	**30-40**	**40-50**
Frequency:	**3**	**5**	**8**	**3**	**1**

For fitting the normal curve, we compute $\overline{X}$ and σ

Computation of $\overline{x}$ and σ

Variable	f	M.V. (x)	d	d' = d/i	fd'	fd'^2
0-10	3	5	–20	–2	–6	12
10-20	5	15	–10	–1	–5	5
20-30	8	25	0	0	0	0
30-40	3	35	+10	+1	+3	3
40-50	1	45	+20	+2	+2	4
	N = 20				$\Sigma fd' = -6$	$\Sigma fd'^2 = 24$

$$\overline{X} = A + \frac{\sum fd'}{N} \times i = 25 + \frac{-6}{20} \times 10 = 22$$

$$\sigma = \sqrt{\frac{\sum fd'^2}{N} - \left(\frac{\sum fd'}{N}\right)^2} \times i = \sqrt{\frac{24}{20} - \left(\frac{-6}{20}\right)^2} \times 10 = 10.53$$

After finding the $\overline{X}$ and σ, we adopt the following procedure:

Variable (1)	M.V. (X) (3)	$Z = \frac{X - \overline{X}}{\sigma}$ (4)	Value of Ordinate from Ordinate Table (5)	$fe = \frac{Ordinate \times N \times i}{\sigma}$ (6)
0-10	5	–1.61	.1092	2.07 = 2
10-20	15	–.66	.3209	6.09 =6
20-30	25	.28	.3836	7.28 = 7
30-40	35	1.23	.1872	3.55 = 4
40-50	45	2.18	.0371	0.7049 = 1
				N = 20

Q16. Discuss any two methods of computing correlation.

Ans. There are many situations in which we may not have scores and have to deal with data in which differences in a given attribute or trait can be expressed only by ranks or classifying an individual into one of several descriptive categories. There are two method of computing correlation in such kind of data, namely product moment correlation and rank order correlations.

Product Moment Correlation

In some situations, the data for two variables X and Y are expressed in interval or ratio level of measurement and the distribution of these variables have a linear relationship. Moreover, the distributions of the variables are uni-modal and their variances are approximately equal. In such situations, we may make use of product moment method of correlation. It is also called Pearson's r.

Calculation of Pearson's r from ungrouped data: When the 'N' (size of the sample or group) is small or the raw scores are small numbers, there is no need of grouping the data and we may make use of the following formula.

$$r_{xy} = \frac{N\Sigma xy - \Sigma x.\Sigma y}{\sqrt{\left[N\Sigma x^2 - (\Sigma x^2)\right]\left[N\Sigma y^2 - (\Sigma y^2)\right]}}$$

In which

x = Deviation of the X measures from the assumed mean

y = Deviation of the Y measures from the assumed mean

The value of Pearson's r can also be obtained from the original measures with the help of the following formula:

$$r_{xy} = \frac{N\,\Sigma XY - \Sigma X.\Sigma Y}{\sqrt{\left[N\Sigma X^2 - (\Sigma X^2)\right]\left[N\Sigma Y^2 - (\Sigma Y^2)\right]}}$$

Calculation of Pearson's r from grouped data: When N is large or even moderate in size, the best procedure is to group data in both variables X and Y and to from a scattergram.

The values from the scattergram may be used in the following formula:

$$r_{xy} = \frac{N\,\Sigma fxy - \Sigma fx.\Sigma fy}{\sqrt{\left[N\Sigma fx^2 - (\Sigma fx^2)\right]\left[N\Sigma fy^2 - (\Sigma fy^2)\right]}}$$

Rank order correlation

Rank order correlation is the simplest method of correlation. It is also known as the Spearman rank order coefficient of correlation and is denoted by ρ (rho). This method is used when the data are available only in ordinal form of measurement (ranked) rather than in interval form, or if the number of paired variables is fewer than 30.

Computation of the Spearman rank coefficient of correlation

Where Ranks are Given: Where actual ranks are given to us the steps required for computing rank correlation are:

- Take the differences of the two ranks, i.e. $(R_1 - R_2)$ and denote these differences by D.
- Square these differences and obtain the total ΣD^2.
- Apply the formula, $\rho = 1 - \frac{6\Sigma D^2}{N(N^2-1)}$.

Where Ranks are not given: When we are given the actual data and not the ranks, it will be necessary to assign the ranks. Ranks can be assigned by taking either highest value as 1 or the lowest values as 1. But whether we start with the lowest value or the highest value we must follow the same method in case of both the variables.

Equal Ranks: In some cases, it may be found necessary to rank two or more individuals or entries as equal. In such a case it is customary to give each individual an average rank. Thus, if two individuals are ranked equal at fifth place, they are each given the rank $\frac{5+6}{2}$, that is 5.5 while, if three are ranked equal at fifth place, they are given the rank $\frac{5+6+7}{3} = 6$. In other words where two or more items are to be ranked equal, the rank assigned for purposes of calculating coefficient of correlation is the average of the ranks which these individuals would have got had they differed slightly from each other.

Where equal ranks are assigned to some entries an adjustment in the above formula for calculating the rank coefficient of correlation is made.

The adjustment consists of adding $\frac{1}{12}(m^3 - m)$ to the value of ΣD^2 where 'm' stands for the number of items whose ranks are common. If there are more than one such group of items with common rank, this value is added as many times the number of such groups. The formula can thus be written $R = 1 - \frac{6\left\{\Sigma D^2 + \frac{1}{12}(m^3 - m) + \frac{1}{12}(m^3 - m) + ...\right\}}{N^3 - N}$.

Q17. Compute the product moment r from the following data in two variable X and Y for 11 students.

X:	25 28 32 27 29 30 26 31
Y:	50 52 60 55 53 56 51 51

Ans. For computing the values of $\sum x$, $\sum y$, $\sum x^2$, $\sum y^2$ and $\sum xy$, we proceed as under:

X	Y	x	y	x^2	y^2	xy
25	50	–2	–5	4	25	10
28	52	+1	–3	1	9	–3
32	60	+5	+5	25	25	25
27 AM	55 AM	0	0	0	0	0
29	53	+2	–2	4	4	–4
30	56	+3	+1	9	1	3
26	51	–1	–4	1	16	4
31	51	+4	–4	16	16	–16
		$\Sigma x = +12$	$\Sigma y = -12$	$\Sigma x^2 = 60$	$\Sigma y^2 = 96$	$\Sigma xy = 19$

$$r_{XY} = \frac{N\sum xy - (\sum x)(\sum y)}{\sqrt{\left[N\sum x^2 - (\sum x)^2\right]\left[N\sum y^2 - (\sum y)^2\right]}}$$

$$= \frac{(8)(19) - (12)(-12)}{\sqrt{\left[(80)(60) - (12)^2\right]\left[(8)(96) - (-12)^2\right]}}$$

$$= \frac{296}{\sqrt{(336)(624)}}$$

$$= \frac{296}{457.891} = 0.646$$

Q18. Calculate the Pearson's r between marks obtained by 25 students in science and arithmetic given in the following table.

Marks in science (Y)	Marks in Arithmetic (X)				Total
	30 – 39	40 – 49	50 – 59	60 – 69	
30 – 39	3	1	1	–	5
40 – 49	2	6	1	2	11
50 – 59	1	2	2	1	6
60 – 69	–	1	1	1	3
Total	6	10	5	4	25

Ans.

Marks in Science		x / dx / dy	Marks in Arithmetic (x)							
			30-39	40-49	50-59	60-69				
		x	34.5	44.5	54.5	64.5				
(y)	y	dx / dy	–1	0	1	2	f	fdy	fdy^2	fdxdy
30-39	34.5	–2	3 [6]	1 [0]	1 [–2]	0 [0]	5	–10	20	4
40-49	44.5	–1	2 [2]	6 [0]	1 [–2]	2 [–4]	11	–11	11	–3
50-59	54.5	0	1 [0]	2 [0]	2 [0]	1 [2]	6	0	0	0
60-69	64.5	1	0 [0]	1 [0]	1 [3]	1 [2]	3	3	3	3
		f	6	10	5	4	25	–18	34	4
		fdx	–6	0	5	8				
		fdx^2	6	0	5	16				
		fdxdy	8	0	–2	–2				

Here, $\sum fdx = 7$, $\sum fdx^2 = 27$, $\sum fdxdy = 4$

$\sum fdy = -18$, $\sum fdy^2 = 34$, $N = 25$

Substituting these value in the formula for computing r

$$r = \frac{N\sum dxdy - (\sum fdx)(\sum fdy)}{\sqrt{\left[N\sum fdx^2 - (\sum fdx)^2\right]\left[N\sum fdy^2 - (\sum fdy)^2\right]}}$$

$$= \frac{(25)(4) - (7)(-18)}{\sqrt{\left[(25)(27) - (7)^2\right]\left[(25)(34) - (-18)^2\right]}}$$

$$= \frac{226}{\sqrt{(626)(526)}}$$

$$= \frac{226}{573.83} = 0.39$$

Q19. Calculate the ranks correlation coefficient for the following data of marks of 2 tests given to candidates for a clerical job:

Preliminary Test:	92	89	87	86	83	77	71	63	53	50
Final Test:	86	83	91	77	68	85	52	82	37	57

Ans. Calculation of Rank Correlation Coefficient:

Preliminary test X	R_1	Final test Y	R_2	(R_1-R_2) D^2
92	10	86	9	1
89	9	83	7	4
87	8	91	10	4
86	7	77	5	4
83	6	68	4	4
77	5	85	8	9
71	4	52	2	4
63	3	82	6	9
53	2	37	1	1
50	1	57	3	4
N = 10				$\Sigma D^2 = 44$

$$R = 1 - \frac{6\sum D^2}{N^3 - N}$$

$$= 1 - \frac{6 \times 44}{990}$$

$$= 1 - 2.67$$

$$= 0.733$$

Thus, there is a high degree of positive correlation between preliminary and final test.

Q20. Calculate coefficient of correlation by means of ranking method from the following data:

X:	40	50	60	60	80	50	70	60
Y:	80	120	160	170	130	200	210	130

Ans. Calculation of Rank Coefficient of Correlation

X	R_1	Y	R_2	$D = R_1 - R_2$	D^2
40	8	80	8	0	0
50	6.5	120	7	–0.5	0.25
60	4	160	4	0	0
60	4	170	3	1	1
80	1	130	5.5	–4.5	20.25
50	6.5	200	2	4.5	20.25
70	2	210	1	1	1
60	4	130	5.5	–1.5	2.25
N = 8				$\Sigma D = 0$	$\Sigma D^2 = 45.00$

In this question in X series, the values 60 and 50 are repeated thrice and twice. The average rank for the value 60 is 4 (3+4+5)/3 while for the value 50 it is 6.5 (6+7)/2. In both the cases, the correlation factor will be $\frac{1}{12}(3^3 - 3)$ and $\frac{1}{12}(2^3 - 2)$. In series Y, the 130 is repeated twice. The average rank for the value 130 is 5.5 (5+6)/2. In this case, correction factor will be $\frac{1}{12}(2^3 - 2)$.

Appling the formula,

$$R = 1 - \frac{6\left[\Sigma D^2 + \frac{1}{12}(m_1^3 - m_1) + \frac{1}{12}(m_2^3 - m_2) + \frac{1}{12}(m_3^3 - m_3)\right]}{(N^3 - N)}$$

$\Sigma D^2 = 45, m_1 = 3, m_2 = 2, m_3 = 2, N = 8$

By substituting values in the above formula, we get

$$R = 1 - \frac{6\left[45 + \frac{1}{12}(3^3 - 3) + \frac{1}{12}(2^3 - 2) + \frac{1}{12}(2^3 - 2)\right]}{8(8^2 - 1)}$$

$$= 1 - \frac{6(45 + 2 + 0.5 + 0.5)}{8(63)} = 1 - \frac{6(48)}{504} = 1 - \frac{288}{504} = 1 - 0.571 = 0.429$$

Q21. Describe the nature of parametric tests and assumptions on which the use of parametric tests are based.

Or

Parametric tests are most powerful tests for testing the significance, explain.

Ans. Parametric tests are useful and are the most powerful tests for testing the significance or trustworthiness of the computed sample statistics. Parametric tests are the tests that have parameters or limits, i.e. where there are lower limits say '0' (zero) and upper limit say '100'. For example, in a scholastic achievement test, a student may have a least score as zero or a highest score as 100. Such type of tests are called size parametric tests.

A 'population' is a collection or aggregate of entities or individuals such as animals, machines and plants. A population can be finite or infinite in number and existent by hypothetical in character. To study the population characteristics or behaviour, instead of enumerating the entire population, we observed a few individuals from the population, which comprises a sample. This process is termed as sampling and here sample characteristics are utilised to approximately determine or estimate the population.

For example, on examining a particular product, we arrive at a decision of purchasing or rejecting the product. The error involved in such an approximation is known as 'sampling' error' and is inherent and unavoidable in any sampling scheme. There are various sampling schemes, but the most commonly used one is random sampling. This is the sampling scheme, in which each individual of the population gets an equal chance of being selected in the sample.

The population characteristics such as mean, median and standard deviation are known as 'parameters' of the population, whereas the corresponding characteristics of the sampling are called 'statistic'. To illustrate, suppose a researcher at a university is interested in knowing what proportion of students at the university smoke. To investigate this question, he asks 50 students of a class whether they smoke and found that 20 of them do. Thus, the percentage of students who smoke in the class is 40. On the basis of this information, he constructs the following chart to represent his problem:

Group	**Characteristic of Concern, i.e. Percentage of Smokers**
Population – all students of the the university	**Parametre–** Percentage of students at university who smoke
Sample – all students of a class	**Statistic** – 40 per cent of the class smoke

Assumptions

The use of parametric tests are based on certain assumptions, these are:

- When the variables described are expressed in interval or ratio scales and not in nominal or ordinal scales of measurement.

- When the population values are normally distributed.
- When the samples have equal or nearly equal variances. This condition is known as equality or homogeneity of variances and is particularly important to determine when the samples are small.
- When the selection of one case in the sample is not dependent upon the selection of any other.

Q22. What are the inferences regarding the means of large sample and small samples?

Or

How inferences will be drawn regarding means of large numbers?

Or

Explain the concept of standard error of mean.

[June-2013, Q.No.-3(c)]

Ans. The inferences regarding the means of large and small sample are as follows:

Large Samples

Suppose we wish to measure the general intelligence of scheduled caste high school students of a certain city using a non-verbal test of intelligence. It would be a difficult task to measure the general intelligence of all the high school scheduled caste students of the city, and hence, we must usually be satisfied with a sample drawn from this population. This sample should be as large and as randomly drawn as possible to represent adequately all the scheduled caste high school students of that city. If we select a large number of random samples of 100 scheduled caste high school students each from the population of all scheduled caste high school students in the city, the mean values of general intelligence for all samples would not be identical. A few would be relatively high, others relatively low, but most of them would tend to cluster around the population mean. This variation of sample means is due to what is known as sampling error. The sample mean will not only vary from sample but will also usually deviate from the population mean. Each of these sample means can be treated as a single observation and we can set up their frequency distribution. This distribution is known as 'sampling distribution of the means'.

According to the Central Limit Theorem, if large-sized samples, greater than 30 in size, are selected at random from a population:

- The distribution of sample means will be normal and it will possess all the characteristics of a normal distribution.

- The average value of the sample means will be same as the mean of the population.
- The distribution of the sample means around the population mean has its own standard deviation. This standard deviation is known as the standard error of the mean and is denoted as SE_M or σ_M.

The standard error of a mean gives us a clue as to how far such sample means may be expected to deviate from the population mean. It tells us how large the errors of estimation are in any particular sampling situation.

The formula for the standard error of the mean in a large sample is:

SE_M or $\sigma_M = \frac{\sigma}{\sqrt{N}}$ in which

σ = Standard deviation of the sample

N = The number of cases in the sample

The SE_M can be thought of as the standard deviation of a distribution of sample and around the fixed population mean of all high scheduled caste students. In case of large samples, the sampling distribution is assumed to be normal.

Confidence intervals and levels of confidence: Suppose we have drawn a large sample from a population to obtain measures of a variable (e.g. test score) and computed the mean (M) for the sample. Using the central limit theorem and normal curve concept, we can say that the sample M has 95 per cent chance of being within 1.96 standard error units M_{pop} (mean population). In other words, a mean for a random sample has a 95 per cent chance of being within $1.96\sigma_m$ units from M_{pop}. It may also be said that there is a 99 per cent chance that the sample mean lies within $2.58\sigma_M$ units of M_{pop}. More specifically, we can say that there is a 95 per cent probability that the limits $M \pm 1.96\sigma_M$ spans the population means M_{pop}. By the same reasoning we can say that there is a 99 per cent probability that the limits $M \pm 2.58\sigma_M$ encloses M_{pop}. Such limits are called as confidence intervals. These limits are also called as 'fiduciary limits' and the confidence placed in the interval defined by the limits as containing the M_{pop} is called the 'fiduciary probability'. These limits help us to adopt particular two levels of confidence. One is known as 5 per cent level or .05 level, and the other as the 1 per cent or .01 level. The .05 level of confidence indicates that the probability is .95 that it falls outside of these limits. By the same reasoning, .01 level of confidence indicates that the probability is .99 that M_{pop} lies within in the interval $M \pm 2.58\sigma_M$, and .01 that it falls outside of these limits.

Small Samples

When the number of cases in the sample is less than 30, we may estimate the value of σ_m by the formula:

$$SE_M = \frac{S}{\sqrt{N}}$$

Where,

S = Standard deviation of the small sample

$$S = \sqrt{\frac{\Sigma x^2}{N-1}}$$

Here,

Σx^2 = Sum of the squares of deviations of scores from the Mean in the sample

N = Total number of cases in the sample

For small samples, it may be noted that we should not assume that sampling distribution of means is distributed normally. It was in about 1815 when William Seely Gosset developed the concept of small sample size. He found that the distribution of small sample means were somewhat different from the normal curve. Such a distribution was named t-distribution. When the size of the sample is small, the t-distribution lies under the normal curve, but the tails or ends of the curved are higher than the corresponding parts of the normal curve.

For small samples, it is necessary to make use of selected points as given in the t-table provided in the annexure. As the sample increases, the t values approach the values of the normal probability table. In the use of t values, we make use of important concept of degrees of freedom.

Degrees of freedom

For finding the standard deviation of small sample, we make use of (N-1) in the large sample for calculating standard deviation (S) instead of N. The difference between N and (N-1) may seem very slight, especially when N is reasonably large, but there is a very important difference in the meaning. In the formula (N-1) is known as the number of degrees of freedom and is denoted by the symbol df. By freedom, we mean freedom to vary.

Q23. What is the significance of difference between independent means of large and small sample?

Ans. Test the significance of the difference between the means of two independent small samples involving one tailed and two tailed test. Means are said to be independent or uncorrelated when computed from samples drawn at random from totally different and uncorrelated groups.

Large Samples

The frequency distribution of large sample means drawn from the same population falls into a normal distribution around M_{pop} as their measures of central tendency, and it is reasonable to expect that frequency distribution of the difference between the means computed from samples drawn from two different populations will also tend to be normal, with a mean of zero and a standard deviation that is called the SE of the difference between means. Such a SE is denoted by d_M that can be estimated from the SEs of the two means, σ_{M_1} and σ_{M_2}. The formula is

$$SE_{\text{diff. between means}} = \sqrt{\sigma_{M_1}^{2} + \sigma_{M_2}^{2}}, \qquad \text{...(i)}$$

Where,

σ_{M_1} is the SE of the mean of the first sample,

σ_{M_2} is the SE of the mean of the second sample,

N_1 is the number of cases in the first sample and

N_2 is the number of cases in the second sample.

By way of illustration, let us apply the above formula to a typical problem. Two groups, one of 95 boys and the other of 64 girls of the tenth grade, were given the same word-building test. The result is summarised in Table 4.4:

Table 4.4 Means and Standard Deviations of Two Independent Large Samples

Statistics	Boys	Girls
N	90	60
Mean (M)	25	24
Standard deviation (σ)	5	4

Assuming that our samples are random, it is to be ascertained whether the difference between the means 25 and 24 is significant.

Using the formula(1), we compute the SE of the difference between the two means.

$$SE_{\text{diff. between means}} = \sqrt{\frac{(5)^2}{25} + \frac{(4)^2}{24}} = 1.29 \left(\sqrt{\frac{\sigma_1^{2}}{N_1} + \frac{\sigma_2^{2}}{N_2}} \right).$$

The obtained difference between the means of the boys and girls is 1 (i.e. 25-24), and the SE of this difference (σ_{d_M}) is 1.29.

To determine whether boys and girls actually differ in word-building ability, we shall set up a null hypothesis. This hypothesis asserts that the difference between the population means of boys and girls is zero and that, except for sampling errors, mean differences from sample to sample will

all be zero. In accordance with the null hypothesis, we assume a sampling distribution of difference to be normal with the mean equal to zero, $M_{pop}\,(boys) - M_{pop}\,(girls) = 0$. The deviation of each sample difference,

M boys – M girls, from this central reference point is equal (M boys – M girls) $-M_{pop}\,(boys) - M_{pop}\,(girls)$, or (M boys – M girls) – 0. The deviation of each sampled difference given in terms of standard measure would be the deviation by the SE, which gives us a Z-value in terms of the general formula.

$$Z = \left| \frac{M_1 - M_2}{Se_{diff.\,between\,means}} \right| \qquad \text{...(ii)}$$

Fig. 4.7 shows a sampling distribution of Z ratios.

Using formula (2),

$$Z = \frac{1}{1.29} = 0.78.$$

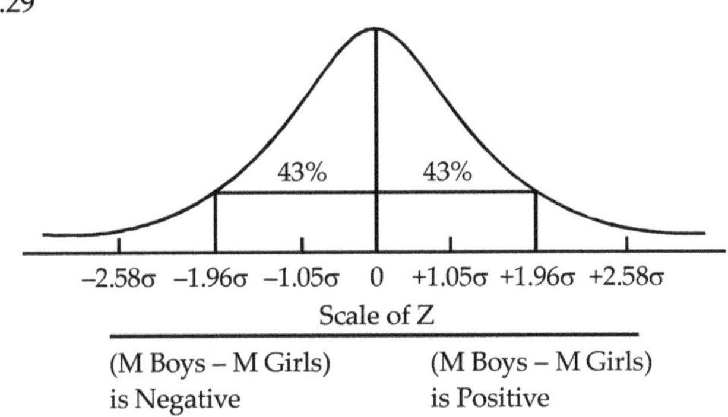

Fig. 4.7 Sampling distribution of Z with a mean of zero

From the normal table, we know that 28 per cent × 2 or 56 cent of the cases in a normal distribution fall between the mean and $\pm 0.78\sigma d_M$, and 46 per cent of the cases fall outside. This means that under the null hypothesis, we can expect Zs as large as ± 0.78 to occur 'by chance' 46 times in 100 comparisons of the means of samples of tenth grade boys and girls on the word-building test.

For the sake of convenience, the researchers have 0.05 for accepting or rejecting a null hypothesis. From normal table, we read that ± 1.96 mark off points along the baseline of a normal distribution of the left and right of which lie 5 per cent of the cases (2.5 per cent at each end of the curve). When a value is 1.96 or more, we reject a null hypothesis at 0.05 level of significance. The Z-value of 1.51 in our problem falls short of 1.96 that does not reach the 0.05 level. Accordingly, we retain the null hypothesis and conclude that tenth grade boys and girls actually do not differ in mean performance on the word-building test.

Furthermore, from the normal table, we know that $M \pm 2.58$ mark off points to the left and right of which lie 1 per cent (0.5 cent at each end of the curve) of the cases in a normal distribution. If the Z-value is 2.58 or more, we reject the null hypothesis at 0.01 level, and the probability (P) is that not more than once in 100 trails would a difference of this size arise if the true difference $(M_{pop1} - M_{pop2})$ were zero.

Small Samples

The formula provided by Fisher for testing a difference between means computed from uncorrelated samples is:

$$t = \frac{|M_1 - M_2|}{\sqrt{\left(\frac{\Sigma x_1^2 + \Sigma x_2^2}{N_1 + N_2 - 2}\right)\left(\frac{N_1 + N_2}{N_1 N_2}\right)}} \quad \text{...(iii)}$$

where M_1 and M_2 are means of the two samples Σx_1^2 and $\Sigma x_2^2 =$ sums of squares of the deviations from their respective means in the two samples, and N_1 and N_2 are the number of cases in the two samples.

The appropriate t critical value for acceptance or rejection of the null hypothesis would be found for $N_1 + N_2 - z\,df$, using the t-table. When we are hypothesising a direction of difference, rather than the mere existence of such difference, 5 per cent area or 1 per cent area of rejection is either at the upper tail or the lower tail of the curve. For example, the 0.05 level is read from 0.10 (P/2 = 0.05) and 0.01 level from 0.02 column (P/2 = 0.01).

To illustrate the use of formula (3), let us test the significance of the difference between mean scores of five boys and eight girls, all 13-year-old on an interest test using data of Table 4.5.

$N_1 + N_2 - 2 = 5 + 8 - 2$

Using formula (3),

$$t = \frac{29 - 27}{\sqrt{\left(\frac{104 + 226}{5 + 8 + 2}\right)\left(\frac{5 + 8}{5 \times 8}\right)}}$$

Table 4.5 Scores of Five Boys and Eight Girls on an Interest Test

Boys			Girls		
X_1 ($N_1 = 5$)	$X_1 = X_1 - M_1$	X_1^2	X_2 ($N_2 = 8$)	$X_2 = X_2 - M_2$	X_2^2
23	–6	36	36	9	81
25	–4	16	27	0	0
33	4	16	18	–9	81
35	6	36	32	+5	25
29	0	0	24	–3	9
			29	2	4
			22	–5	25
			28	1	1
		104	216		226
			$M_2 = 27$		

$$= \frac{2}{\sqrt{\left(\frac{330}{11}\right)\left(\frac{13}{40}\right)}} = \frac{2}{\sqrt{9.75}} = 0.64.$$

The critical values of t for rejection of null hypothesis in the t-table for (5 + 8 – 2) or 11 df are 2.20 at 0.05 and 3.11 levels. Since the obtained t-value is 0.64, it does not equal or exceed the t critical value necessary for rejection of the null hypothesis at the 0.05 level for 11 df. The null hypothesis is accepted and we conclude that there are no significant differences in the mean interest scores of 13-year-old boys and girls.

Q24. Compute standard error of difference to a problem in which two groups, one of 81 male and the other 49 female distance learners of M.Ed. were given a test in course I. The data are summarised as under:

	Male	Female
N	81	49
Mean (M)	34.5	38.4
Standard Deviation	6.12	5.11

Ans. Using the formula,

$$SE_{\text{diff. between means}} = \sqrt{\sigma_{M_1}^{2} + \sigma_{M_2}^{2}}$$

$$= \sqrt{\frac{(6.12)^2}{81} + \frac{(5.11)^2}{49}} = 0.997$$

Q25. Test the significance of the difference between the means of the following test scores of achievement in English of 5 boys and 8 girls of class V.

Score of Boys: 10, 12, 20, 22, 16

Scores of Girls: 24, 15, 6, 20, 12, 17, 10, 16

Ans.

Boys X_1	$x_1 = (X_1 - M_1)$	x_1^2	Girls X_2	$x_2 = (X_2 - M_2)$	x_2^2
10	–6	36	24	9	81
12	–4	16	15	0	0
20	4	16	6	–9	81
22	6	36	20	5	25
16	0	0	12	–3	9
$\Sigma x_1 = 80$		$\sum x_1^2 = 104$	17	2	4
			10	–5	25
			16	1	1
			$\Sigma x_1 = 120$		$\sum x_2^2 = 226$

Mean of boy's of scores

$$M_1 = \frac{\sum x_1}{N_1} = \frac{80}{5} = 16$$

Mean of girl's scores

$$M_2 = \frac{\sum x_2}{N_2} = \frac{120}{8} = 15$$

Formula for testing the significance:

$$t = \frac{|M_1 - M_2|}{\sqrt{\left(\frac{\Sigma x_1^2 + \Sigma x_2^2}{N_1 + N_2 - 2}\right)\left(\frac{N_1 + N_2}{N_1 N_2}\right)}} = \frac{|16-15|}{\sqrt{\left(\frac{104+226}{5+8-2}\right)\left(\frac{5+8}{5\times 8}\right)}}$$

$$= \frac{1}{\sqrt{9.75}} = 0.32$$

The t critical values for the rejection of null hypothesis for (5 + 8 – 2) or 11 df are 2.20 and 3.11 at .01 levels. Since the obtained t value is 0.32, it does not equal or exceed the t critical value for 11 df, the null hypothesis is accepted and we conclude that there is no significant difference in the means of the two groups.

Q26. Test the significance of difference between the means of two dependent samples.

Ans. Means are said to be dependent or correlated when obtained from the scores of the same test administered to the same sample on two occasions. This experimental design is called single group method, when the same test is administered to equivalent samples, which the individuals who make up the groups have been matched person for person, by one or more characteristics. The formula used for testing the significance of the difference between means obtained in testing the significance of the difference between means obtained in the initial and final testing is:

$$t = \frac{|M_1 - M_2|}{\sqrt{\sigma_{m_1}{}^2 + \sigma_{m_2}{}^2 - 2r_{12}\sigma_{m_1}\sigma_{m_2}}} \quad ...(i)$$

where σ_{m_1} is the SE of the initial test mean, σ_{m_2} is the SE of the final test mean and r_{12} is the correlation between the scores in the initial and final tests.

The following example will illustrate the use of the above formula.

In a test of achievement, the following data were obtained in the initial and final tests. Is there any significant improvement in the final test?

Initial test $N = 12$

$M = 42.66$

$\sigma = 12.63$

$\sigma_{m_1} = 3.65$

Final test $N = 12$

$M = 50.66$

$\sigma = 15.74$

$\sigma_{m_2} = 4.54$

r between the two tests = 0.94

In the above example,

$$t = \frac{|M_1 - M_2|}{\sqrt{\sigma_{m_1}{}^2 + \sigma_{m_2}{}^2 - 2r_{12}\sigma_{m_1}\sigma_{m_2}}} = \frac{|42.66 - 50.66|}{\sqrt{(3.65)^2 + (4.54)^2 - 2 \times 0.94 \times 3.65 \times 4.54}}$$

$= 4.92$

Since there are 12 students, we have 12 pairs of scores and 12 difference, the df becomes 12 – 1 or 11. To test the hypothesis that there is significant improvement in the final test, we would make us of the tailed test. In the one-tailed test, we see that the table value of t for 11 df at the 0.05 level of significance is 1.80 and at the 0.01 level of significance is 2.73. Since our t-value (i.e. 4.92) is much larger than the 0.01 level, it may be concluded that improvement from the initial to the final test is significant. Thus, the hypothesis stating that the students have made a significant improvement in the final test is accepted.

Q27. Test the significance of the difference in means of Mastery Test, which was administered on two occasions to a group of 12 seventh class students, before and after providing remedial instruction to the students for improving performance in Hindi.

Mastery test before providing remedial instructions:

Mean (M_1) = 32.66

S.D. (σ_1) = 12.08

$\sigma_{M_1} = 3.45$

Mastery test after providing remedial instructions:

Mean (M_2) = 32.66

S.D. (σ_2) = 12.08

$\sigma_{M_2} = 3.45$

$r_{12} = 0.93$

Ans. By using the following formula:

$$t = \frac{|M_1 - M_2|}{\sqrt{\sigma_{m_1}{}^2 + \sigma_{m_2}{}^2 - 2r_{12}\sigma_{m_1}\sigma_{m_2}}} = \frac{|32.66 - 40.66|}{\sqrt{(3.45) + (4.34)^2 - 2(0.93)(3.45)(4.34)}}$$

$= 4.93$

Q28. What is meant by analysis of variance? Describe its assumptions.

Or

Explain some of the basic assumptions of analysis of variance.

[June-2012, Q.No.-3(c)]

Ans. We use Z and t-tests to determine whether there is any significant difference between the means of two random samples. Suppose we have six random sample and we want to determine whether there are any significant differences among their means.

For this, we would have to use $\frac{6(6-1)}{2} = 15t$ tests to determine the significance of the difference between the six means by taking two means at a time. This procedure is cumbersome and time consuming. The technique of analysis of variance would make it possible to determine if any of the two of the means differ significantly from each other by a single test, called F test, rather 15t tests. The F test enables us to determine whether the sample means differ from one another (between group variance) to a greater extent than the test scores differ from their own sample means (within groups variance) using the ratio:

$$F = \frac{\text{Variance between groups}}{\text{Variance within groups}}$$

The significance of F ratio is determined from Table D of the Appendix. This table indicates the F critical values necessary to reject the null hypothesis at selected levels of significance.

Analysis of variance has certain basic assumptions underlying it. Johnson (1961) presents certain assumptions, which should be fulfilled in the use of this technique:

- The population should be normal. This assumption, however, is not especially important. Eden Yates showed that even with a population departing considerably from normality, the effectiveness of the normal distribution still held. Besides the findings of Eden and Yates, the study of Norton cited by Guilford (1965, pp. 300-301) also points out that F is rather insensitive to variations in the shape of population distribution.
- All the groups of a certain criterion or of the combination of more than one criterion should be randomly chosen from the sub-population having the same criterion or having the same combination of more than one criterion. For instance, if we wish to select two groups in a school population, one of the third grade and the other of the fourth grade, we must choose randomly the respective subpopulations. This assumption is the keystone of the analysis of variance technique. Failure to fulfil this assumption gives biased results.
- The sub-groups under investigation should have the same variability. We should test this assumption before we run through the analysis of variance. Otherwise, a false interpretation of the results may follow. This assumption is tested either by applying Bartlett's test of homogeneity or by applying Hartley's test.

Q29. Discuss the computing process of analysis of variance.

Ans. In the analysis of variance (one-way), we examine the relationship between one independent and one dependent variable. The analysis consists of following steps:

- The variance of the measures (scores) for the randomised groups are combined into one composite group known as the total groups variance (V_t).
- The mean value of the variances of each of these groups computed separately, is known as the within-groups variances' (V_w).
- The difference between the total' groups variance and within-group variance is known as the between-groups variance ($V_t - V_w = V_b$).
- The F-ratio is computed as:

$$F = \frac{V_b}{V_w} = \frac{\text{Variance Between Groups}}{\text{Variance Within Groups}}$$

It may be noted that the within-groups variance represents the sampling error in the distributions. It is also referred to as the error variance or residual. The between-groups variance represents the influence of the variable under study or the experimental variable. If the 'between-groups variance' is not significantly greater than the 'within-groups variance', we may conclude that the difference between the means is probably due to sampling error. If the F-ratio is significantly greater, it means that the ratio of the 'between-groups variance' and 'within-groups variance' is probably too large of significance are read from the F-table. The Table indicates two different degrees of freedom, one for V_b (the numerator) and one for V_w (the denominator). The degrees of freedom for the within a group variance (V_w) is determined in the same way as it is computed for the t-test, i.e. the sum of the individuals, for all the sample groups minus the number of the groups. If there are K number of groups with n_1, n_2, n_3 ..... subjects in each group, then $(n_1 + n_2 + n_3 + ... - K)$ gives the degrees of freedom for 'within groups variance'.

Let us compute F-ratio for the following data, which have been obtained in an experimental study in which three groups, each group consisting of 5 randomly assigned students, were given a mastery (criterion) test after an audio-visual instructional programme in chemistry.

Group A		**Group B**		**Group C**	
X_1	X_1^2	X_2	X_2^2	X_3	X_3^2
19	361	21	441	17	289
16	256	21	441	24	576
22	484	17	289	25	625
25	625	26	676	29	841
23	529	21	441	19	361
$\Sigma X_1 = 105$	$\Sigma X_1^2 = 2255$	$\Sigma X_2 = 106$	$\Sigma X_2^2 = 2288$	$\Sigma X_3 = 114$	$\Sigma X_3^2 = 2692$

We will apply analysis of variance for testing the hypothesis that the mean performance of three groups do not differ significantly.

For the analysis of variance using the following steps:

Step 1: Correction $= \frac{(\Sigma x)^2}{N} = \frac{(\Sigma x_1 + \Sigma x_2 + \Sigma x_3)^2}{N}$

$$= \frac{(105 + 106 + 114)^2}{15} = \frac{(325)^2}{15} = 7041.67$$

Step 2: Total sum of squares (Total SS_t)

$SS_t = \sum x_1^2 + \sum x_2^2 + \sum x_3^2 - \text{correction}$

$= 2255 + 2288 + 2692 - 7041.67$

$= 7235 - 7041.67 = 193.33$

Step 3: Sum of squares between means of treatment (SS_b)

$$= \frac{(\sum x_1^2)}{n_1} + \frac{(\sum x_2^2)}{n_2} + \frac{(\sum x_3^2)}{n_3} - \text{correction}$$

$$= \frac{(105)^2}{5} + \frac{(106)^2}{5} + \frac{(114)^2}{5} - 7041.67$$

$= (2205 + 2247.2 + 2599.2) - 7041.67$

$= 7051.40 - 7041.67 = 9.73$

Step 4: Sum of Squares Within Treatments (SS_w)

$SS_w = SS_t - SS_b$

$= 193.33 - 9.73 = 183.60$

Step 5: Calculation of variances for each SS and analysis of the total variance into components

Each SS denotes a variance when divided by the degrees of freedom (df) allotted to it. There are 15 measurements in all and hence there are (N – 1) or (15 – 1) or 14 df in all which are allotted in the following manner:

If N = number of measures in all and K = number of groups, we have df for total sum of squares $(SS_t) = 15 - 1 = 14;$ df for within treatments $(SS_w) = 15 - 3 = 12$ and df for between means of treatments $(SS_b) = K - 1 = 3 - 1 = 2.$

To compute the mean square between (MS_b) and mean square within (MS_w), we divide the sum of squares between (SS_b) and the sum of squares within (SS_w) their respective degrees of freedom (df).

$$F = \frac{\frac{MS_b}{MS_w} = \frac{SS_b}{df_b}}{\frac{SS_w}{df_w}} = \frac{\frac{9.73}{2}}{\frac{183.60}{12}} = 0.318$$

Q30. What is the significance of Pearson's coefficient of correlation? Test the significance of difference between Pearson's coefficient of correlation of two samples.

Ans. The mathematical basis for the standard error of a Person's coefficient of correlation is rather complicated because of the difficulty in its nature of sampling distribution. The sampling distribution of r is not normal except when the population r is near zero and size of the sample is large (N = 30 or greater). When r is high (0.80 or more) and N is small, the sampling distribution of r is skewed. This is true also when r is low (0.20 or less).

A mathematically more sound method for making the inference regarding Pearson's, especially when its magnitude is very high or very low, is to convert r into Fisher's Z coefficient and find the standard error (SE) of Z. The sampling distribution of Z coefficient is normal regardless of the size of sample and N and the size of the correlation r. Furthermore, the SE of Z depends only upon the size of sample N, and is independent of the size of r.

The formula for standard error of $Z(\sigma_z)$ is

$$SE_z = \sigma_z = \frac{1}{\sqrt{N-3}} \quad \text{...(i)}$$

By way of illustration, consider an r between the scores on an intelligence test and on an achievement test in mathematics, obtained from a random sample of 84 male students of eighth grade. Using formula (1), the standard error of Z is

$$\sigma_z = \frac{1}{\sqrt{84-3}} = \frac{1}{9} = 0.111$$

For an r of 0.78, Table G of the Appendix gives a corresponding Z of 1.05. Since the sampling distribution of Z is normal, the confidence internal at. 95 level for the population of true Z is $Z \pm \sigma_z \times 1.96 = 1.05 \pm 0.111 \times 1.96$ or 0.83 and 1.26. The corresponding r's, from table of the Appendix, are 0.68 and 0.85, which give a well estimated interval within which we expect the population r with 0.95 confidence, that is, the chances are 95 in 100 that population r lies between 0.68 and 0.85. If we want a higher degree of confidence we can take the 0.99 level of confidence, for which the limits $1.05 \pm .111 \times 2.58$ or 0.76 and 1.34. The corresponding r's from Table G, are 0.64 and 0.87, that is, the chances are 99 in 100 that populations r lies between .64 and .87.

The exact method of determining the standard error of the difference between two r's is first convert the r's into Fisher's Z coefficients and then to determine the significance of the difference between the two Z's.

Significance of the difference between Pearson's Coefficient of Correlation

When we have two correlations between the same two variables, X and Y, computed from two totally different and unmatched samples, the standard error of a difference between two corresponding independent Z's is compared by the formula:

$$SE_{D_Z} = \sigma_{Z_1-Z_2} = \sqrt{\frac{1}{N_1-3}+\frac{1}{N_2-3}} \qquad ...(ii)$$

in which

N_1 and N_2 = sizes of the two samples.

The significance of the difference between two Z's is tested with the help of the formula

$$\overline{Z} = \frac{Z_1 - Z_2}{SE_{D_Z}} \qquad ...(iii)$$

To illustrate the use of the formula (3), let us consider the correlations of 0.70 and 0.62 computed between intelligence and academic achievement on the basis of the data, obtained from two groups of seventh grade students $(N_1 = 103)$ and $(N_2 = 124)$ from two different schools. To test significance of the difference between the two r's we shall convert them into Z coefficients. The corresponding Z's, from Table G, are 0.87 and 0.73. Using formula (2), the SE_{DZ} is

$$S_{D_Z} = \sigma_{Z_1-Z_2} = \sqrt{\frac{1}{103-3}+\frac{1}{124-3}} = 0.135$$

$$\overline{Z} = \frac{0.87-0.73}{0.135} = 1.036$$

The obtained Z value is less than 1.96 and hence is not significant at .05 level. This indicates that the correlation between general intelligence and academic achievement does not really differ in the two groups drawn from two different schools.

Q31. Explain the meaning and uses of Non-parametric tests. Describe the assumptions of non-parametric test on which the use of non-parametric tests are based.

Ans. Non-parametric tests do not require any assumptions about the parameters or about the nature of population. By non-parametric tests we mean those statistical tests which do not depend either upon the shape of the distribution or upon the parameters of the population mean, standard deviation, variance, etc. The assumption as to the normality or symmetricity of the population of the population distribution from which the samples have been drawn is not required for these non-parametric tests. Non-parametric tests are sometimes referred to as distribution free tests. In addition to this, these non-parametric test do not require measurements so strong as that requires by parametric tests.

Some advantages (or uses) of non-parametric tests are mentioned below:

- Non-parametric tests are distribution free, i.e. they do not require any assumption to be made about population following normal or any other distribution.
- Generally, they are simple to understand and easy to apply when the sample sizes are small.
- Most non-parametric tests do not require lengthy and laborious arithmetical computations and hence are less time-consuming.
- Non-parametric tests make fewer and less restative assumptions than do the parametric tests.
- There is no alternative to using a non-parametric test if the data are available in ordinal or nominal scale.
- Non-parametric tests are useful to handle data made up of samples from several populations without making assumptions.

Assumptions

- The nature of the population, from which samples are drawn, is known to be normal.
- The variables are expressed in nominal form, that is, classified in categories and represented by frequency counts.
- The variables are expressed in ordinal form, that is, ranked in or expressed in numerical scores, which have the strength of ranks.

Q32. Discuss the various non-parametric tests, which are used in the case of independent sample.

Ans. The most frequently non-parametric tests, which are used in drawing statistical inference in the case of independent or unrelated samples are:

Chi-square test

In situations where the members of a random sample are classified into mutually exclusive categories, we wish to know whether the observed frequencies (i.e. number of subjects in different categories on the basis of our observation) in these categories are consistent with some hypothesis concerning the relative frequencies. This can further be explained with the following example:

Suppose we have taken a very limited opinion in a small sample of 90 students of class X regarding their plan for opting Arts, Science or Commerce at a later stage. The opinion of students and their frequencies are as follows:

Arts	Science	Commerce
35	28	27

As the three streams are equally popular among the students, we now assume that the difference in frequencies of these three exclusive categories is only due to chance. Presently, the chi-square test is the most suitable measure to test the agreement between these observed and expected results. Chi-square is denoted as χ^2 and is defined by the following equation.

$$\chi^2 = \Sigma\frac{(f_o - f_e)^2}{f_e},$$

Where f_o is the observed or experimentally determined frequency and f_e is the expected frequency of occurrence based on some hypothesis.

When the square of the difference between observed and expected frequencies is divided by the expected frequency, in each case, the sum of these quotients is chi-square.

The Median Test

The Median test is used for testing whether two independent samples differ in central tendencies. It gives information as to whether it is likely that two independent samples have been drawn from populations with the same median. It is particularly useful whenever the measurements for the two samples are expressed in an ordinal scale.

In using the median test, we first calculate the combined median for all scores in both samples. Then both sets of scores at the combined median are dichotomised and the data are cast in a 2 × 2 table shown in Table 4.6.

Table 4.6. 2 × 2 Table for Use of Median Test

	Group I	Group II	Total
No. of scores above combined median	A	B	A + B
No. of scores below combined median	C	D	C + D
Total	A + C	B + D	

Under the null hypotheses, we except about the half of each group's scores to be above the combined median and about half to be below, that is, we would expect frequencies A and C to be about equal, and frequencies B and D to be about equal. In order to test this null hypothesis, we calculate, χ^2 using the following formula.

$$\chi^2 = \frac{N(|AD - BC| - N/2)^2}{(A+B)(C+D)(A+C)(B+D)}$$

The Mann-Whitney U Test

The Mann-Whitney U test is more powerful than median test. It is a most useful alternative to the parametric t test when the parametric assumptions cannot be met and when the measurements are expressed in ordinal scale values.

Suppose n_1 is the number of individuals in one of the two independent groups and n_2 the number of the individuals in the other. To apply the U test, we first combine the observations or scores from both groups, and rank these in order of increasing size. In this ranking, we have to consider the algebraic sign, that is, the lowest ranks are assigned to the largest negative numbers, if any. Then the ranks of each sample group are summed individually and represented as ΣR_1 and ΣR_2.

Next we calculate two U's using the formulae:

$$U_1 = n_1 n_2 + \frac{n_1(n_1+1)}{2} - \Sigma R_1$$

And $$U_2 = n_1 n_2 + \frac{n_2(n_2+1)}{2} - \Sigma R_2$$

In which

n_1 = number of individuals in first group

n_2 = number of individuals in second group

ΣR_1 = sum of ranks in first group

ΣR_2 = sum of ranks in second group

The two U's are also related by the equation:

$$U_1 = N_1 N_2 - U_2$$

The only one U needs to be calculated, for the other can be easily determined by this equation.

The Z-value of U can be computed by the formula:

$$Z = \frac{U - \frac{N_1 N_2}{2}}{\sqrt{\frac{(N_1)(N_2)(N_1+N_2+1)}{12}}}$$

It does not matter which U (the larger or smaller) is used in the computation of Z. The sign of Z will depend on which U is used, but the numerical value will be identical.

Q33. The following table gives the number of screws declared fit and also unfit by three inspectors X, Y and Z. Test the hypothesis that proportion of screws declared unfit by the three inspectors are same.

	Number of Screws			
Inspector	**X**	**Y**	**Z**	**Total**
Fit Screws	**50**	**47**	**56**	**153**
Unfit Screws	**5**	**14**	**8**	**27**
Total	**55**	**61**	**64**	**180**

Ans. Table for three inspectors is given:

	Number of Screws			
Inspector	X	Y	Z	**Total**
Fit Screws	50	47	56	153
Unfit Screws	5	14	8	27
Total	55	61	64	180

Here the frequencies are arranged in 2 × 3 contingency table, d.f = (2 – 1)×(3 – 1) = 1 × 2 = 2

Table for expected frequencies can be completed as given below:

Inspectors		**No. of Screws**		**Total**
	X	Y	Z	
Fit Screens	$\frac{55\times153}{180}=46.75$	$\frac{61\times153}{180}=51.85$	$\frac{64\times153}{180}=54.4$	153
Unfit Screws	$\frac{55\times27}{180}=8.25$	$\frac{61\times27}{180}=9.15$	$\frac{69\times27}{180}=9.6$	27
Total	55	61	64	180

Calculation for chi sequence χ^2:

f_o	f_e	$(F_o–F_e)$	$(F_o–F_e)^2$	$(F_o–F_e)^2/f_e$
50	46.75	3.25	10.5625	0.2259
5	8.25	–3.25	10.5625	1.28030
47	57.85	–4.85	23.5252	0.45366
14	9.15	4.85	23.5252	2.571060
56	54.4	1.6	2.56	0.070599
8	9.6	1.6	2.56	0.26667
	180			$\sum\left[(F_o–F_e)^2/f_e\right]=4.868189$

$$\chi^2=\Sigma\frac{(f_o-f_e)^2}{f_e}=4.868189$$

$\therefore \chi^2$ (4.868189) is greater than 1.96 therefore hypothesis is rejected.

Q34. Test the median between eighteen male and fourteen female teachers of co-educational institution. They were asked to express

their attitude towards co-education at the secondary school stage. Both the groups of teachers were administered an attitude scale and common median attitude score was worked out. The number of cases from both groups falling above and below the median score is shown in the following table:

	Below Median	Above Median	Total
Female Teachers	10	4	14
Male Teachers	6	12	18
Total	16	16	32

Ans. Using the formula for χ^2:

$$\chi^2 = \frac{N(|AD - BC| - N/2)^2}{(A+B)(C+D)(A+C)(B+D)}$$

$$\chi^2 = \frac{32(|(10)(12) - (4)(6)| - 32/2)^2}{(14)(18)(16)(16)}$$

$= 3.17$

Since the obtained value 3.17 of χ^2 for 1 df does not exceed the χ^2 critical value of 3.84 for a two tailed test at .05 level, the null hypothesis is retained and we may conclude that there is no difference in the attitude of male and female teachers towards co-education at the secondary school stage.

Q35. A researcher wished to evaluate the effectiveness of micro-teaching and simulation in developing certain teaching skills among student-teachers of a teacher training institution. He divided all the 40 students teachers of the college into two groups A and B by randomly assigning 20 to each of the groups. Group A was trained in various skills of teaching through micro-teaching and the Group B was trained through simulation technique. After a period of two months training, the student teachers were rated in the teaching skills by supervisors. The rating scores of the student teachers are given below:

Group A	Group B
90	46
78	42
75	65
72	61
75	64
83	82
73	69
80	66

74	56
67	48
63	68
45	44
55	85
84	83
89	71
77	87
70	76
58	50
47	59
92	79

Ans.

Group A	Rank	Group A	Rank
90	39	46	4
78	29	42	1
75	25.5	65	15
72	22	61	12
75	25.5	64	14
83	33.5	82	32
73	23	69	19
80	31	66	16
74	24	56	9
67	17	48	6
63	13	68	18
45	3	44	2
55	8	85	36
84	35	83	33.5
89	38	71	21
77	28	87	37
70	20	76	27
58	10	50	7
47	5	59	11
92	40	79	30
$N_1 = 20$	$\Sigma R_1 = 496.50$	$N_2 = 20$	$\Sigma R_2 = 350.50$

All rating scores are ranked from lowest to highest and the Mann Whitney U test is used to test the null hypothesis at the .05 level of significance using the following formulae:

$$U_1 = n_1 n_2 + \frac{n_1(n_1+1)}{2} - \Sigma R_1$$

$$U_1 = (20)(20)\frac{(20)(21)}{2} - 469.50 = 140.50$$

$$U_2 = (20)(20)\frac{(20)(21)}{2} - 350.50 = 259.50$$

Using the equation $U_1 = N_1N_2 - U_2$, we check

$140.50 = 400 - 259.50$

$140.50 = 140.50$

$$Z = \frac{U - \frac{N_1N_2}{2}}{\sqrt{\frac{(N_1)(N_2)(N_1 + N_2 + 1)}{12}}}$$

$$Z = \frac{140.50 - \frac{400}{2}}{\sqrt{\frac{(20)(20)(41)}{12}}} - 1.61$$

Since the obtained Z value of –1.61 does not exceed the Z critical value of 1.96 for a two-tailed test at 0.05 level, the null hypothesis is retained and it may be concluded that micro-teaching approach and simulation technique are equally effective in developing certain teaching skills among the student teachers.

Q36. Discuss the various non-parametric tests, which are used in the case of dependent sample.

Ans. A number of non-parametric tests are used in drawing inference in respect of dependent or related samples. These are:

(1) Sign Test: The sign test is the simplest type of all the non-parametric tests. Its name comes from the fact that it is based on the direction or the plus or minus signs of observations in a sample and not on their numerical magnitudes. The sign test can be of two types:

(i) **One-sample sign test:** In one-sample sign test, we set up the null hypothesis that + and – signs are the values of a random variables having the binominal distribution with $p = \frac{1}{2}$, i.e. $H_0 : p = \frac{1}{2}$ or that $\mu = \mu_0$

(a) **Procedure:** This test involves the following steps:

- Find the + and – sign for the given distribution. Put a plus (+) sign for a value greater than the mean value (μ_0), a minus (–) sign for a value smaller than the mean value and a zero (0) for a value equal to the mean value.

- Denote the total number of signs (ignoring zeros) by n and the number of less frequent signs by 'S'.
- Obtain the critical value (K) of less frequent signs (S) preferably at 5 per cent level of significance by using the following formula:

$$K = \frac{n-1}{2} - 0.98\sqrt{n}$$

- Compare the value of 'S' with the critical value (K). If the value of S is greater than the value of K (i.e. $S > K$) then the null hypothesis is accepted. If $S \le K$, the null hypothesis is rejected.

(b) **Alter:** The problem relating to one sample test can also be solved by using Binomial Probability Distribution. When the sample size is fairly small $(\text{i.e.}, n \le 25)$, we find probability of the less frequent signs p(S) by the sum of the probability of S of fewer S using the binominal distribution formula, ${}^{n}C_{x}q^{n-x}p^{x}$ with $p = \frac{1}{2}$. Then, we compare the above calculated value of probability with the expected value at 5 per cent level of significance, i.e. at $\alpha = 0.05$ for one tailed/two tailed tests. If the calculated probability P(S) is ≤ 0.05, null hypothesis is rejected and if $P(S) > 0.05$, the null hypothesis is accepted.

(ii) **Paired Sample Sign Test:** The sign test has very important applications in problems involving paired data such as data relating to the collection of an account receivable before and after a new collection policy; responses of mother and daughter towards ideal family size, etc. In such problems, each pair of sample values is replaced with a plus sign if the first value is greater than the second, a minus sign if the first value is smaller than the second or a zero if the two values are equal. Then we proceed in the same manner as in one-sample test.

When the sample size is fairly large (i.e. $n > 25$), we use the normal approximation to the binomial distribution to carry out the sign test. The value of 'z' can be computed as:

$$Z = \frac{S - np}{\sqrt{np(1-p)}}$$

Then we get the critical value of Z at the desired level of significance.

If the calculated value of Z happens to be less than the critical value, then we accept the null hypothesis. If the case is reverse, then we reject the null hypothesis.

(2) Wilcoxon's Signed-Rank Test: This is another non-parametric test, which has been developed by Sir Wilcoxon. This test is based on the ranking of the sample of observations. Like sign test, Wilcoxon's signed-rank test can be of two types:

(i) **Wilcoxon's One-Sample Signed-Rank Test:** In a one sample signed-rank test, we test the null hypothesis that $\mu = \mu_0$ against an appropriate alternative hypothesis at a desired level of significance.

Procedure: This test involves the following steps:

- Calculate the difference $d = x - \mu$ with algebraic signs.
- Assign ranks (ignoring the signs) to the difference in the increasing order of magnitude (i.e. from low to high) ignoring zero differences. In case of ties (i.e. when two or more values are the same), assign ranks to such pairs by averaging their rank positions.
- Put all the ranks against the +ve differences rank column (R^+) and all the ranks against the –ve rank column (R^-)
- Get the total number of ranks, n
- If $n \leq 25$, then calculate the value of the test statistic given by $T = \sum R^+$ or $\sum R^-$ ranks whichever is less.
- Then find the critical value of T from the Wilcoxon's T-table given in the appendix.
- If the calculated value of T is less than or equal to its critical value, then reject the null hypothesis. In the reverse case, accept the null hypothesis.

(ii) **Two Sample Signed Rank Test (or Paired-Sample Signed Rank Test):** The Wilcoxon's signed rank test has important applications in problem involving paired data. Such a test is widely used by the research scholars in their study of two related samples or matches pairs of ordinary data, viz. outputs of two similar machines, responses gathered before and after a treatment, etc. where we can find both the direction and magnitude of difference between the matched values. In these problems, we find the difference between each pair of values with algebraic signs. Then we proceed in the same manner as in the case of one sample signed rank test.

When N is large than 25, the sum of the ranks is approximately normally distributed. The sum of the ranks of the smaller of the like signed ranks is designated as T.

The value of Z is determined by the formula:

$$Z = \frac{T - \frac{N(N+1)}{4}}{\sqrt{\frac{N(N+1)(2N+1)}{24}}}$$

in which

N = number of pairs ranked

T = sum of ranks of the smaller of like signed ranks

Q37. The production manager of a large undertaking randomly paid 10 visits to the worksite in a month. The number of workers who reported late for duty was found to be 2, 4, 5, 1, 6, 3, 2, 1, 7 and 8 respectively. Using the sign test verify the claim of the production supervisor that on an average, not more than 3 workers report late for duty. Use 5 per cent level of significance.

Ans. Let $H_0 : \mu \leq 3$ against $H_1 : \mu > 3$ at 5 per cent level of significance.

Determination of Signs w.r.t. μ=3

X	Signs (X-3)	
2	–	No. of Plus Signs =5
4	+	
5	+	No. of Minus Signs =4
1	–	
6	+	No. of Zero = 1
3	0	
2	–	Total No. of Signs = n = 9 (ignoring 0's)
1	–	
7	+	
8	+	

From the above table, we get

Total no. of signs (ignoring zeros)=n=9

Number of less frequent signs=S=4

The critical value (K) of less frequent signs (S) at 5 per cent level is given by:

$$K = \frac{n-1}{2} - 0.98\sqrt{n} = \frac{9-1}{2} - 0.98\sqrt{9} = 4 - 2.94 = 1.06$$

Since number of less frequent signs S(4) is more than the critical value of K(1.06), i.e. S>K, the null hypothesis is accepted. It means that the sample data support the claim of the production supervisor.

Q38. A physical instructor claims that a particular exercise if done continuously for 7 days, reduced weight by 3.5 kg. Five overweight girls did the exercise for 7 days and their weights were observed as under:

Girls:	1	2	3	4	5
Weight before exercise:	70	72	75	71	78
Weight after exercise:	66	70	72	66	72

Making use of the sign test, verify the claim at α=0.05 that the exercise reduces the weight by at least 3.5 kg.

Ans. Denoting the mean weight before and after exercise by μ_1 and μ_2 respectively, we have the following,

$$H_0 : \mu_1 - \mu_2 = 3.5 \text{ against } H_1 : \mu_1 - \mu_2 < 3.5, \alpha = 0.05$$

Determination of Signs w.r.t. 3.5

Girls	X	Y	D = (X – Y)	Signs (D – 3.5)
1	70	66	4	+
2	72	70	2	–
3	75	72	3	–
4	71	66	5	+
5	78	72	6	+

From the above table, we get

No. of Plus signs=3; No. of Minus signs=2

The total no. of signs or n=5

Number of less frequent signs=S=2 The critical value (K) of less frequent signs (S) is given by:

$$K = \frac{n-1}{2} - 0.98\sqrt{n} = \frac{5-1}{2} - 0.98\sqrt{5} = 2 - 2.19 = -0.19$$

Since S>K, H_0 is accepted. It means that the sample data support the claim that the exercise if continuously done for 7 days reduces the weight by at least 3.5 kg.

Q39. Use Wilcoxon's signed-rank test to see if there is a difference between the number of days until the collection of an account receivable before and after a new collection policy. Use the 0.05 level of significance.

Before (X):	30	28	34	35	40	42	33	38	34	45	28	27	25	41	36
After (Y):	32	29	33	32	37	43	40	41	37	44	27	33	30	38	36

Ans. Let us take hypothesis H_0: There is no difference between the number of days before and after a new collection policy in the accounts receivable.

And H_1: There is a difference between the two.

Determination of Signed Ranks

X	Y	$d = X - Y$	$\|d\|$	Ranks (R) $\|d\|$ (± ignored)	Signed Ranks	
					R^+	R^-
30	32	–2	2	6	-	6
28	29	–1	1	3	-	3
34	33	1	1	3	3	-
35	32	3	3	9	9	-
40	37	3	3	9	9	-
42	43	–1	1	3	-	3
33	40	–7	7	14	-	14
38	41	–3	3	9	-	9
34	37	–3	3	9	-	9
45	44	1	1	3	3	-
28	27	1	1	3	3	-
27	33	–6	6	13	-	13
25	30	–5	5	12	-	12
41	38	3	3	9	9	-
36	36	-	-	-	-	-
Total				n = 14	$\Sigma R^+ = 36$	$\Sigma R^- = 69$

From the above table, it must be seen that the total number of ranks=n=14 (n≤25).

Since n<25, the test statistic is given by

T=smaller of two sums of the signed ranked=36

Looking at Wilcoxon's T-table at 5 per cent level for a two tailed test at n=14, we get the critical value of T=21

Since the calculated value of T is greater than its critical value, null hypothesis is accepted. It means that there is no significance difference between the number of days before and after a new collection policy.

Q40. Suppose a group of 26 delinquent children were initially rated for their social adjustment by a psychiatrist and then sent to a juvenile jail. After they were rated by a psychiatrist for social adjustment and then their initial and final adjustment rating scores were compared. The rating data are given in the following table:

50	47
54	52
62	63
39	31
56	52
51	42
58	51
60	49
48	42
46	42
42	40
53	56
40	36
51	50
56	42
60	48
57	47
43	48
45	37
52	39
61	60
62	52
48	42
39	45
41	42
39	40

Using Wilicoxon sign ranked test to test the rating score of children.

Ans.

Final adjustment score	Initial adjustment score	d	Rank of d	Rank with less frequent sign
50	47	3	7.5	
54	52	2	5.5	
62	63	–1	–2.5	2.5
39	31	8	17.5	

contd..

contd..

Final adjustment score	Initial adjustment score	d	Rank of d	Rank with less frequent sign
56	52	4	10	
51	42	9	19	
58	51	7	16	
60	49	11	23	
48	42	6	14	
46	42	4	10	
42	40	2	5.5	
53	56	–3	–7.5	7.5
40	36	4	10	
51	50	1	2.5	
56	42	14	26	
60	48	12	24	
57	47	10	21	
43	48	–5	–12	12
45	37	8	17.5	
52	39	13	25	
61	60	1	2.5	
62	52	10	21	
48	42	6	14	
39	45	–6	–14	14
41	42	–1	–2.5	2.5
39	49	–10	–21	21

The null hypothesis that there was no difference between in initial and final adjustment rating scores of the group was tested at .05 level of significance. Since the direction of the difference is not predicted, a two tailed region of rejection is appropriated.

T, the smaller of the sum of the like signed ranks

$= 2.5 + 7.5 + 12 + 14 + 2.5 + 21 = 59$

By using the following formula:

$$Z = \frac{T - \frac{N(N+1)}{4}}{\sqrt{\frac{N(N+1)(2N+1)}{24}}}$$

$$Z = \frac{59.5 - \frac{(26)(26+1)}{4}}{\sqrt{\frac{26(26+1)(2(26)+1)}{24}}} = 2.95$$

Since the obtained Z-value of 2.95 exceeds the Z critical value of 1.96 for a two-tailed test at the 0.05 level, the null hypothesis is rejected. We may conclude that the environment in the juvenile jail has considerably improved the social adjustment of delinquent children.

Q41. Write a short note on the various methods of analysis of qualitative data.

Ans. The objective in the analysis of qualitative data, gathered by a wide variety of methods and techniques, is holistic perspective and studying real-world situations as they unfold naturally, non-manipulatively and unobtrusively with openness to whatever emerges without predetermined constraints on outcomes. Keeping this objective in view, the analysis of qualitative data means studying the organised material in order to discover inherent facts. These data are studied from as many angles as possible either to explore the new facts or to reinterpret already known existing facts. The content analysis, inductive analysis and logical analysis are mostly used methods in analysis of qualitative material.

Q42. What is meant by content analysis? Explain its various approaches.

Or

Define content analysis and describe its uses.

Ans. Content analysis is concerned with the classification, organisation and comparison of the content of document or communication. Cartwright (1970, p. 424) uses the terms "content analysis" and "coding" interchangeably as both the processes involve objective, systematic, and quantitative description of any symbolic behaviour. Since content analysis is concerned with the classification, evaluation and comparison of the content of communication of document, it is sometimes referred to as "documentary activity" or "information analysis". The communication may be in the form of responses to open-ended questionnaire, conversation as a result of interview, or description of an observed activity. It may also be in the form of official records (census, birth, accident, crime, school, institutional and personal records), judicial decisions, laws, budget and financial records, cumulative records, courses of study, content/of text book, reference works, newspapers, periodicals or journals, prospectus of various educational institutions or universities, etc., direct quotations, and notes of an interview. The content can be analysed on two levels: (i) manifest level and (ii) interpretative level. Manifest level is the basic level of analysis, which aims at the descriptive account of data that is what was actually said with nothing read into it and nothing assumed about it. Interpretative level is the latent level of analysis. It is concerned with what was meant by the responses, what was inferred or implied.

Berelson (1952) has specified three broad approaches that a researcher may adopt in content analysis. These include:

Characteristic of Content: In this approach, the researcher is interested primarily in the characteristics of the content itself. He may focus either on the substantive nature of the content or upon the form of content.

Berelson (1952), as quoted by Cartwright (1970), has listed six uses, which are concerned primarily with substantive characteristics of the content.

- In the first two of these, the researcher either tries to describe trends in communication content over periods of time by employing methods for sampling the total flow of communication at successive points in time and to use the same system of classification throughout or he attempts to trace the development of scholarship in the publication of reputed scientific journals. For example, a researcher may study and record trends in articles on *concept of adult education* in the Indian context appearing in Surveys of Research in Education (Buch, 1973, 1979, 1987 and 1991). A scrutiny of the topics of research in distance education over a period from 1980 to 2008 appearing in various scholarly journals in an example to illustrate trends in their publications.
- In the next two uses, the researcher attempts to compare the content materials coming from different sources. He may be interested either to disclose international differences in communication content or to compare media or "levels" of communication.
- In the fifth use, the researcher may be interested in studying the role of various mass media in molding public opinion. For example differences in partisanship among newspapers, journals, radio and T.V. in the role of a certain voluntary organisation in the *National Literacy Mission Programmes* may be studied by some researcher to identify, which media favour more the role of the organisation in comparison to other.
- In the sixth use of the analysis of characteristics of systematic material, the observed substance of communication content is evaluated against standards adopted by the researcher.

Cartwright (1970) has pinpointed three other uses of content analysis in which the focus of the researcher is upon the *form* of the content.

- The first of these is concerned with the content analysis of propaganda so as to reveal the ways in which the propagandist pursues his objectives of influencing the public. The ways may include the themes or appeals employed by the propagandists.
- In the second use, the main concern of the researcher is to measure the *readability* of communication material. This may be done by grading such material on the basis of their difficulty of comprehension. Educators undertake such type of studies to make textbooks fit the age and mental level of different groups of students using various schemes.
- The third use confines to the discovery of the stylistic features of characteristics of literary products. The study by Miles (1951) pertaining to ratio of verbs to substantives in poetry since sixteenth century is an example of such type of content analysis.

Producers or Causes of Content: In the second major approach, the researcher attempts to draw valid inferences about the nature of the producers of the content or the causes of the symbolic material from the characteristics of the material itself. In some situations where the researcher cannot study the producer of the content (communicator) directly, but has access to the communicated material (content), this approach is used to make valid inferences about the nature of the producer of the content. In other situations, where a researcher can persuade an individual to produce symbolic behaviour as a response to standard conditions, the characteristics of such behaviour are generally taken as a very acceptable indication of the individual's own characteristics.

Assessment of psychological state of persons or groups using contents of clinical interviews, protective tests, biographies, autobiographies, diaries, letters and other personal documents illustrates second important use of content analysis.

Audience and Effects of Content: In the third major approach to content analysis, the researcher interprets the content so as to reveal something about the nature of its audience or its effects. He takes the content material as a basis for drawing inference about the characteristics of the *audience* for whom the material (content) is designed, or about the effects of communication.

Q43. Enumerate the steps included in content analysis.

Or

Discuss the procedure of content analysis as used in educational research. **[June-2011, Q.No.-3(f)]**

Ans. The following points describe the steps involved in the process and some issues relating to this operation.

Defining the Unit of Analysis

The unit (material) may be confined to single words, to phrases, to complete sentences, to paragraphs, or to even larger amounts of materials such as articles or to complete books. Either of these can be considered as an entity whose specified characteristics can be determined and analysed. Hayman (1968, p. 80) suggests that the unit shout be comprehensive enough to provide meaning through some content at least, but small enough not to allow subjectivity in it use.

Specifying Variables and Categories

Once the unit is defined, the researcher conducts its analysis so as to create reproducible or objective data for scientific treatment and generalisation beyond the specific set of symbolic material analysed. For converting symbolic material into objective data, it is necessary to specify the "variables" explicitly in terms of which descriptions are to be made. The variables are sometimes referred to as "dimensions" or "types of attributes". A few examples of such variables are: number of words, percentage of personal pronouns, attitudes towards privatisation, attractive traits of teachers, degree of confidence in a friend, etc. After the selection of some variables, viz. degree of confidence in a friend, there are many ways in which this variable may be broken down into categories as: (1) unqualified confidence, (2) qualified confidence (3) confidence and mistrust equally balanced (4) qualified mistrust, (5) unqualified mistrust, (6) question not asked by interviewer, (7) question asked, but answer not classifiable in above categories. A second classification of categories of the same variable may be: (1) high, (2) low, (3) not classifiable in either. It may be pointed out that if two independent persons were to be code the same material, one using the first set of categories and other using the second, they would come out with different descriptions of the same material. Hence, explicit specification of the system of categories used with each variable is necessary for reproducible analysis.

There is need for framing explicit rules specifying what features of the content are to be taken as indication that it falls in the one category rather than another. A statement of these rules constitute the operational definition of the category. These specific rules are helpful in arriving at an agreed system of coding if the analysis is conducted by two or more independent analysis.

Frequency, Direction and Intensity

Once the unit is defined and the variables alongwith their categories to be employed specified, the analyst will classify units, in the material to be analysed, according to frequency, direction and intensity. For frequency, the analyst merely counts the number of units, which fall into each of his categories.

Direction refers to whether the reference was favourable, unfavourable, or neutral. It might be pleasant-unpleasant, interesting-uninteresting, and threatening-non-threatening. Intensity indicates the emotional impact of the units analysed. Is it large or small, and in what direction?

Judging direction and intensity is more subjective than merely counting for frequency.

Contingency Analysis

The contingency analysis aims at considering the content within which the unit is found. A researcher should consider the favourableness or unfavourableness of single unit in the light of the remainder of the communication so that its real meaning might not be lost.

Sampling

One of the major and practical problems in content analysis is sampling. The unit, which a researcher analyses must be representative of the total material with which he is concerned, so that results can be generalised. Invariably a researcher undertakes the analysis of a specific content in order to reveal something about the universe of data than just those symbolic material with which he deals.

Conclusion and writing of the report

In the light of the analysis of the content, the analyst has to use all care and caution in arriving at the conclusions. It demands critical and logical thinking in summarising the findings. The analyst should not draw conclusions, which are inconsistent among themselves.

The report writing after the analysis of content needs highest level of scholarship on the part of the researcher. This is matter of exceptional strategy, which calls for creativity in addition to the qualities of imagination and ingenuity. The report must be elegant and objective.

Q44. Write notes on the following:

(a) Inductive analysis

Ans. Inductive analysis means identifying the patterns, themes, and categories that emerge out of analysis of the qualitative data. In this analysis, researcher looks for natural variation in data. For evaluation, according to Patton (1982, p. 306), "the study of natural variation will involve particular attention to variations in programme processes and how participants respond to and are affected by programmes". He describes these approaches as: (i) indigenous typologies, and (ii) analyst-constructed typologies.

- *Indigenous typologies* approach is called as the *emic* approach to analysis in anthropology. In this approach, cultural behaviour is studied in terms of the inside view of human events rather than imposed from cross-cultural classification of behaviour. In order to understand the thoughts and views of a particular group of people, it is necessary that the whole analysis of experience must be based on their concepts.
- In the *analyst-constructed typologies* approach, the researcher looks for patterns, categories and themes for which the participants of a programme do not have labels or terms, and the researcher himself/herself constructs topologies to explain variations and contrasts in activities, participants and others associated with the programme. The main objective of these typologies is to make descriptions based on an analysis of the patterns that appear in the data so as to make interpretations about the future of the programme.

Analytic induction is a major logic of qualitative research. The rule is as to take one case and develop a working hypothesis to explain it. Then take another case and examine whether the hypothesis can explain the new case. If it fails, revise the hypothesis to explain both cases. Then, take the third and repeat the same process of examining and revising the hypothesis. When you do not need to revise the hypothesis further and except that the hypothesis will, fit any new cases you might take, the hypothesis have been refined enough. Hence, the choice of cases to be examined has an important bearing on the trust worthiness of procedures of qualitative research. Not all qualitative research follows this approach but the inductive approach to design, field work and analysis is one of the most influential characteristics of qualitative inquiry.

(b) Logical analysis

Ans. Inductive analysis is used for representing patterns as dimensions of categories, either using participant-generated constructions or evaluator-generated constructions. It is sometimes useful to cross-classify different dimensions to generate new insights about how the data can be organised and to look for patterns that may not have been recognised in the initial inductive analysis. Logical analysis aims at creating potential categories by crossing one typology with another, and then moving back and forth between the logical construction and the actual data for creating a "new typology" using cross-classification matrices.

According to Patton (1982, p. 314): Creating cross-classification matrices is an exercise in logic. This procedure involves creating potential categories by crossing one dimension or typology with another, and then working back and forth between the data and one's logical constructions, filling in the resulting matrix. This logical system will create a new typology all parts of which may or may not actually be represented by the data. Thus, the analyst moves back and forth between the logical construction and the actual data in the ongoing search for understanding through description.

The researcher must be extremely careful in using this kind of analysis. He should be sensitive to interpreting the possibility of a category of activity or behaviour that has either has been overlooked in the data or that is logically a possibility in the setting but has not been manifested.

(c) Criticism of historical data

Ans. Historical data gathered with the help of primary and secondary sources are the solid basis of historical inquiry. Primary sources have been called as the first witnesses to a fact by Good, Barr and Scates (1941). Original documents or remains come under the category of primary sources. Secondary sources are the accounts of an event provided by a person who did not directly observe the event, object, or condition. In some situations, it is not possible to obtain primary data and in such situations, the researcher may have to rely on secondary sources.

In historical research, after the identification of data with the help of primary or secondary sources, the researcher subjects these data to rigorous analysis and evaluation, which is known as criticism of data. It involves dual processes of establishing the authenticity of the sources and of establishing the validity of its contents. The process of establishing authenticity of the data is called as external criticism and that of establishing the validity of their content is termed as internal criticism.

External criticism helps in checking the genuineness of the source of content. It determines whether it is what it appears or claims to be and whether it reads true to be original. It is confined to the detection of fraud. External criticism is also called lower criticism. After establishing the authenticity of the historical data, the data are subjected to internal criticism. It is also called as higher criticism and is concerned with the validity or truthfulness of the textual content of the document. It also concerned with the competence, good faith, bias and general reputation of the author of the document.

The check list given following which is provided by Good, Barr and Scates (1941) may be used in the processes of external and internal criticism of data of historical nature:

(1) Who was the author, not merely what was his name but what were his personality, character, position, and so forth?

(2) What were his special qualifications as a reporter - alertness, character, bias?

(3) What were his special qualifications and disqualifications as a reporter of the matters here treated?

   (i) How was he interested in the events related?

   (ii) How was he situated for observation of the events?

   (iii) Had he the necessary general and technical knowledge for learning and reporting events?

(4) How soon after the events was the document written?

(5) How was the document written, from memory, after consultation with others after checking the facts, or by combining earlier trial drafts?

(6) How is the document related to other documents?

   (i) Is it an original source; wholly or in part?

   (ii If the latter, what parts are original; what barrowed; where? How credible are the borrowed materials?

   (iii) How and how accurately is the borrowing done?

   (iv) How is the borrowed material changed; how used?

In the analysis of historical data, it is necessary to get answers to all the above listed questions so as to draw inferences relating to historical events.

(d) Analysis of case studies data

Ans. The main objective in the analysis of case study is to understand an individual or a unit in depth. A case or unit has been defined as a person, a family, a social or an ethnic group, a social institution or a village. In a phenomenon, some cases are related and an in-depth study of these cases is undertaken for unfolding the interactions between various factors influencing the phenomenon. It is a way of organising social data for the purpose of viewing social reality.

A case study probes deeply and analyses interactions between factors that explain present status or that influence change or growth. It is a longitudinal approach, indicating development over a period of time (Best and Kahn, 2002, p. 193). The subject of the case study is selected very carefully in order to assure that the subject is typical or even a prototype of that category of individuals, whom the researcher wishes to generalise about. The emphasis is on a typical nature of the 'case' rather than its uniqueness. In view of this, the researcher uses a multi-method approach, such as observation (especially participant observation for studying physical characteristics, social qualities or behaviour), interview (both structured and unstructured with subject, relatives, friends, teachers, counsellors etc; questionnaires, recorded data, etc. for in-depth study of an individual case, group of individuals or institutions like drug addicts, migrants workers, industrial workers, slum dwellers, educational institutions, old age homes, and other welfare agencies, business groups, delinquents, slow learners, etc. These studies are also concerned for the purpose of understanding the learners, etc. These studies are also learned conducted for the purpose of understanding the culture and development of variable relationships.

The analysis of case study data, gathered through observation, interview, questionnaires, rating scales, documents, etc., attempts to understand an individual or unit in depth. It tries to understand the 'case' in totality of its environment. The aim of analysis is not to study the present status of the case or unit but also to probe thoroughly its past. The emphasis is to observe events in terms of their location in space and time, and interpret results in the light of the relationships and interdependence of events.

It may be noted that case study data are subjective, and hence, subjective bias may intervene in their analysis and interpretation. A researcher should be skillful in isolating the significant variables from irrelevant ones in the analysis of case study data. The facts and results after the analysis must be reported precisely with utmost objectivity and judgement. The interpretation of results should be supported with adequate evidence and every precaution must be taken to detect faulty conclusions. The use of analytic induction may be made to discover important dimensions, interrelationships and antecedents to explain the case or cases.

(e) Analysis of ethnographic data

Ans. Ethnography as a naturalistic inquiry has been described primarily as a method of field study, which was used to understand the cultural characteristics of primitive people like African, American, Indian tribes by studying and analysing their language, customs and traditions, life styles, religious beliefs and practices, social relations, rules of conduct, political institutions and systems. Observation of patterns of action, interactions (verbal and non-verbal) between members of the tribe as well as between the tribe members and the researcher or his informants, and scrutiny of records and artefacts were generally used in data collection. Later on, for valid ethnographic studies, it was realised that the researcher or his informant should spend more time with group members of the particular tribe so that he is able to observe their activities in the natural social settings. For this, the researcher/informant has to learn the language of the tribe, participate in its activities, and finally he has to identify some members of the tribe with whom he develops a good rapport, who in turn provide information about the tribe.

The analysis of data in such studies involves explaining the events, answering "why" questions, attaching significance to particular happenings and events, and putting pattern of events into an analytic framework. It uses the process of synthesising the information from various sources such as observation, interview and field notes. The emphasis is on using inductive logic in which hypotheses are suggested by observations without preconceptions. The hypotheses are periodically re-evaluated on the basis of new observations, modifying them when they are inconsistent with the evidence. The analysis would be less statistically oriented than the analysis in an experimental or quantitative survey study. However, the statistics, if used, is descriptive rather than inferential. The main objective of the analysis is to understand the group or its members in as free and natural atmosphere as possible, i.e. "how the members of the group view the situation, how they interpret their own thoughts, words, and activities as well as those of others in the group." (Best and Kahn, 2002, p. 197).

Q45. Explain the strategies used in the validation of qualitative data.

Ans. Patton (1982, pp. 327-334) has listed the following major strategies for validation of results:

(1) **Rival Explanations:** Once the researcher after qualitative analysis has described the patterns and their explanations, it is important to look for rival or competing themes and explanations both inductively and logically. Inductively it implies looking for other ways of organising the data that might lead to different results. Logically it involves searching for other logical possibilities can be supported by the data. However, it may be noted that when considering rival hypotheses and competing explanations, the strategy to be employed by the researcher is not one of attempting to disprove the alternatives, but to look for data that support alternative explanations. In this strategy, the researcher should give due weightage to

supporting evidence and look for the best "fit" between data and analysis.

(2) Negative Cases: The search for negative cases and instances that do not fit within the identified pattern and their understanding is also important in the verification and validation of results.

(3) Triangulation (reconciling qualitative and quantitative data): This type of triangulation aims at comparing data collected through some kind of qualitative methods. It is highly likely that qualitative methods and quantitative methods will eventually lead to different findings and not a single and well integrated picture of the situation. It is because qualitatively data are commonly used for "generating hypotheses" or "describing hypotheses" and quantitative data are used to "analyse outcomes", or "verify hypotheses". However, in endorsing the notion triangulation, Trend (1978), quoted by Patton (1980), p. 330), maintains that it is useful to bring a variety of data and methods to bear on the same problem in order to reduce system bias in interpreting results of study. The findings of some studies could be strengthened by supplementing of qualitative approach with quantitative analysis.

(4) Triangulation (comparing multiple qualitative data sources): This type of triangulation involves comparing and cross checking consistency of data derived by different times using qualitative methods. It means:

(i) comparing observational data with interview data;

(ii) comparing observational data with questionnaire data;

(iii) comparing what participants of a programme say in public with what they say in private;

(iv) checking for the consistency the opinion of the participants about a programme over a period of time; and

(v) comparing the opinion of the participants of a programme with others who were associated with programme in one capacity or the other.

The triangulation of data sources within qualitative methods will seldom lead to a single totally consistent picture. But such triangulation is helpful to study and understand when and why there are differences.

(5) **Triangulation (multiple perspectives from multiple observers):** The aim of this kind of triangulation is to involve several observers or using several interviews so as to reduce the potential bias or subjectivity as a result of observation by single observer. For example, while observing a group of students during an activity, we may involve three observers and ask them to record all the aspects of the activity independently, and then compare the observation data of the three observers in order to judge the extent of agreement or disagreement between the observers.

(6) **Design Checks (keeping methods and data in context):** The nature of research design and methodology also contribute to distortion in results. Sampling gives rise to three types of errors. The errors may be due to:

(i) distortion in the situations that were sampled for observation;

(ii) distortion introduced by the time periods during which observations took place;

(iii) distortion because of selectivity of people who were sampled either for observation or interviews.

Thus, the researcher must be careful to limit results of his study to those situations, time-period, people and contents for which the data are applicable.

(7) **Evaluator Effects:** The presence of researcher during the observation or interview can distort the result of study. The distortion may be due to:

(i) reactions of programme participants and other associated with it to the presence of researcher,

(ii) changes in the researcher during the process of observation or interview;

(iii) biases of researcher; and

(iv) incompetence of the researcher.

The presence of a researcher during observation or interview may create a halo effect and consequently the participants of the programme are motivated to "show off". Their deviation from the normal behaviour will lead to distorted findings. It is desirable to undertake long-term observations for minimising the halo effect. Researchers sometimes become personally involved with programme participants and therefore lose their sensitivity to the full range of events occurring during the process of observation or interview. A record of the changes in the researcher, field notes and conversation with the people as associated with the programme are helpful to overcome evaluator effects.

5 METHODS OF RESEARCH

An Overview

Different techniques and tools of data collection, their analysis and interpretation depend on the nature of research activity being undertaken. The research activity may be of different kinds: philosophical, historical, descriptive, ex-post facto, experimental or action research.

Major focus of philosophical and historical approaches on insightful interpretation of facts, concepts and principles related to education system. Applications of such approaches of research help us to get clarity of concepts, events and ideas. Moreover, they help us to understand the present and to get future direction for education.

Descriptive research is the most significant approach in exploring the status of any event. Starting from benchmark studies upto evaluation oriented studies educational researcher employs various methods of descriptive studies.

Experimental research has its base in physical and natural science. Different kinds of experimental design have been evolved with a view to strengthen internal and external validity of experiments. While studying the casual factors contributing to occurrence of educational events, a researcher generally makes use of true experimental design. However, due to the complex nature of educational phenomena, it is not always possible to use time experimental designs in dealing with human situations. Moreover, the problem occurs in conducting controlled inquiry in educational setting. Hence, we make use of ex-post facto research to explain cause and effect relations in educational situations.

At the end, action research plays a major role in making every teacher and administrator responsive to solutions of various kinds of problems and taking active part in effective and efficient functioning of school system.

Q1. What are the major concerns of philosophical research in education?

Ans. The major concerns of philosophy pertain to three of its content areas: metaphysical, normative and analytical.

Metaphysical

The main function of philosophy is to raise basic questions about the nature of reality, the nature of universe, the nature of human being, the nature of beauty, etc., and to answer these issues through speculation. Answers of such questions help us to conceptualise the nature of education, nature of child and nature of development, etc.

Normative

The second concern of philosophy is to establish norms, standards or guidelines for the conduct of human affairs with reference to nature reality. This involves identification of human dispositions which are worthy of cultivation, pointing out the arguments why these dispositions are to be considered 'worthwhile'; and discussing how these excellences are to be nurtured or cultivated. Such issues can be directly associated with the aims and objectives of education, identification of appropriate methods and procedures of acquiring knowledge, etc.

Analytical

The third concern is to clarify the concepts, which are used as prime elements of any area of study. Such clarifications are made on the basis of appropriate arguments and exposition of underlying assumptions behind such analysis. It helps us to define knowledge and its components. Moreover the meaning the nature of various concepts are articulated through analytical inquiry.

Q2. Discuss the meaning, nature and areas of philosophical research in education.

Ans. Philosophical studies in education aim at:

- assessment of status of knowledge through analysis of meanings and relationships of different concepts and exposition of underlying assumptions, and
- a fruitful synthesis of ideas from different fields concerning educational theories and practices.

In other words, a researcher in the area of educational philosophy focuses on analysis of meaning and nature of different educational concepts and the relevance of different kinds of educational practices. He identifies appropriate norms and standards of educational practices through a cross examination of ideas reflected by different thinkers in the field of education.

Philosophical research in education focuses on:

(i) development of deep understanding of and fresh insights into educational concepts, theories, principles, issues and problems, and

(ii) making normative inducements, on and evaluations of educational practices.

It helps us to clarify concept like democracy, liberations, equality, secularism, nationalism, freedom, autonomy, authority and social justice in the context of education. Moreover, philosophical inquiry leads towards arriving at normative criteria for governing aims and objectives of education and parameters for curricular processes.

Major functions of philosophical studies in education are analysis and appraisal of arguments, statements and theories; synthesis and integration of such understanding with different aspects of educational system, viz. policy formulation, curriculum, teaching-learning processes, evaluation, teachers and learners expected roles, etc.

Hence, the use of intellectual processes of conceptualisation, logical analysis, synthesis and evaluation of ideas and thoughts remain in the forefront of philosophical inquiry. Education system needs sound theoretical and ideological basis in this context, philosophical research contributes towards building a normative framework for educational priorities, curriculum, curricular practices and management of education system through cross-examination of ideas reflected by different philosophers in the field of education.

Areas of Philosophical research in education

Studies of educational philosophy/contributions of educationists/philosophers

Ideas about education are clarified and expressed philosophically before putting them into actual practice. There is a direct impact of philosophy on education from the viewpoint of identifying aims and objectives, relevant contents, disciplines, methods, and evaluation processes.

A philosopher or a group of philosophers may express their ideas about various aspects of education system in different forms: speeches, discourses and writings. A researcher in education may be interested in making an analytical and critical appraisal of the educational philosophy of a thinker or a group of thinkers and present their ideas on education in a consolidated, formal, and systematised form.

The researcher intends to analyse educational philosophy/contributions of individual thinkers, schools of philosophy, scriptures, historical/cultural periods. For instance, the studies like 'educational thoughts of Gandhiji and their relevance to contemporary education', 'educational philosophy of B.R. Ambedkar and its relevance for social change', 'educational philosophy of Sri Aurobindo and its relevance for modern society', educational Philosophy of J.Krishna Murti and its implications for modern system of Indian education, etc. come under the category of describing and classifying the philosophical thoughts of individual thinkers and drawings its implications for present days education.

In such kind of studies, it is expected that the researcher must present a consistent and coherent account of ideas, and the basic assumptions and underlying these ideas. In the absence of this exercise, it becomes an activity of mere collection of facts from different sources and presenting them in order.

Study of the educational philosophy propounded by a particular school of thought

Philosophy can be classified under different schools of thought like idealism, naturalism, realism, existentialism, pragmatism, socialism, communism (dialectical materialism). Every school of thought projects its educational philosophy based on its ideology regarding the basic goals of education. Abstractions and formal statements governing principles and ideas of a school of thought on educational systems can also be considered as one of the areas of philosophical inquiry.

Study of the philosophical bases of curriculum

There are several issues related to theoretical as well as practical aspects of education, which have philosophical bases and can be resolved through rational means. Several questions raised in the criteria for identifying the desirable state of mind, etc., are the concern of an educational philosopher. For example, a study conducted on the concept of child according to Sri Aurobindo's philosophy may be placed under this area of research.

Study of the philosophical bases of instructional processes

Several ways and means of teaching have been grouped under different methods of teaching, but many questions are being raised about the meaning of terminologies, concepts, and activities highlighted under different methods. For instance, how does the term 'imparting' differs from 'instruction'? What is punishment and is there any need for "punishment" in education? A number of such philosophical questions related to the instructional processes need to be answered through analytical exercises. Through such exercises, clear-cut ideas are generated about the activities carried out in educational settings and appropriate norms are suggested from time for educational practices. For instance, a study conducted on 'The concept of child in Tagore's Philosophy' or 'The justification and role of negative education in child's development' fit into this area.

Study of the philosophical analysis of the contributions made by psychological theories to education

We are aware of the influence of developments in the field of psychology like 'developmental psychology', 'need theories' and 'concept formation' on educational process. At a particular time, one or other theory has been given importance in the educational field because of its popularity at that time. Very little research has been done to justify the relevance of psychological theories to educational situations. There is scope for philosophical inquiries about the relevance and scope of such theories as far as educational practices are concerned.

Study of the philosophical analysis of theories, which influence education

There can be several issues of education related to imbibing certain social ideals into the system. The issues like 'freedom of the classroom set up', 'autonomy of higher education institution', 'democratic values in education', 'equality of educational opportunities', and 'policies and practices of democracy in education', require philosophical analysis from time to time in order to accommodate the changes in societies. This help us in examining appropriate social aims and norms existing in a given educational set up and suggesting the norms for further development.

Understanding and analysing concepts philosophically

Concepts have social and historical context. Analysis of concepts also have philosophical context related to some educational problem. Identifying and defining various concepts and ideas and drawing its implications for education has also remained as one of the focuses of philosophical research. Moreover, analysis of view points and issues on education is also linked with philosophical research. A number of studies have been conducted on these lines such as, 'Mechanistic and organismic view points in Biology and their trace in Education' and Philosophy of Language analysis and its educational implications with special reference to Wittgenstein.

Philosophical research centred on certain themes

Philosophical inquiries are made on analysis of certain themes, its ontological and epistemological aspects, taking into account the assumptions of the representative schools of philosophy, and to synthesise viewpoints to provide premises for education. You will come across thematic studies like 'Experience as a major premise in Education', 'Conception and Perception of Environmental Education', 'Phenomenology in relation to Education', 'Nature and Development of Personality in the Bhagvad Geeta, and its Educational Relevance, 'Dilectialism in Indian Education', etc. These studies help us to evaluate the significance of certain themes or ideas in the context of education.

Q3. What are the various steps involved philosophical research?

Ans. Philosophical inquiry uses a few well-defined steps, which may be followed to make the inquiry successful. They are stated as follows:

(1) Identification of problem: The process of philosophical study starts with identification of appropriate problem of study. The problem may be concerned with the areas and issues of philosophy of education. At this stage researcher must ensure that the theme of the study is capable of yielding a system of thought. Sound rationale must be provided in the identification of the problem. As a beginner researcher, he will have to review available literature in the field of philosophy of education. The gaps and priorities in the field of philosophical research as reviewed by the experts will also help in this process.

(2) Collection of data: Keeping in view the theme identified and the preliminary questions raised therein, the researcher must collect all the possible information relevant to the form the available literature. The sources may be mostly of literacy nature, such as write-ups or expressed opinions of the philosophers concerned, and commentaries on the relevant philosophical works appearing in the forms of books, journals, transcriptions, recordings, research reports, etc. Mostly collection of such information is possible through intensive library work.

This stage is very crucial since the researcher will have to decide the relevance of the information and the way to collect it. We must be clear about the authenticity of the sources of the information and the nature of the information included therein. In other words, first, we should ensure about the genuineness of the sources of the information and, secondly, we should examine whether the information collected through the authentic source is reliable and meaningful for our study or not.

(3) Classification of information and interpretation: We should logically classify the information under different heads focussing on the theme of investigation. Then, we must interpret the information under each classification keeping in view the main questions we raise in specific context. Interpretation may follow different processes like description, comparison, appraisal, cross examination, etc., of different ideas or concepts in the context of major questions under consideration.

Interpretation of the information in philosophical research is a scholarly job, which rests on the analytical insight and the synthesising ability of the researcher. "The task of interpretation is chiefly that of ascribing a significance, meaning, purpose and relatedness to a common' end, and to an apparently heterogeneous mass of data" (Varma, 1965).

We may follow a logical process of interpretation and give substantive references to our judgements/comments but there is every possibility of reflecting our subjectivity in the process. Essentially a researcher studies others' ideas from his own point of view. However, conscious efforts must be made to detach ourselves as much as possible and interpret the ideas of others without getting carried away by our own biases. In this respect, the researcher's role is very much significant in philosophical analysis of information.

(4) Reporting the study: The last stage of the work may be identified with reporting of the study. In the report, a logical sequence is maintained between the different heads of classification and appropriate conclusions are drawn towards the end of presentation. At this stage, care is to be taken for clarity and precision of presentation. Moreover, appropriate references with quotations as well as notes necessary points of presentation are to be cited carefully in the report.

Q4. What is meant by historical research in education? What are its main characteristics?

Ans. Historical research has been defined as the systematic and objective location, evaluation and synthesis of evidence in order to establish facts and draw conclusions about past events. It involves a critical inquiry of a previous age with the aim of reconstructing a faithful representation of the past. In historical research, the investigator studies documents and other sources that contain facts concerning the research theme with the objective of achieving better understanding of present policies, practices, problems and institutions. An attempt is made to examine past events or combinations of events and establish facts in order to arrive at conclusions concerning past events or predict future events.

Main characteristics of historical research

Historical approach of research or 'historiography' has some unique features and is generally counted as one of the methods of scientific inquiry.

- It is not a mere accumulation of facts and data or even a portrayal of past events.
- It is a flowing, vibrant report of past events, which involves an analysis and explanation of these occurrences with the objective

of recapturing the nuances, personalities and ideas that influenced these events.

- Conducting historical research involves the process of collecting and reading the research material collected and writing the manuscript from the data collected. The researcher often goes back-and-forth between collecting, reading, and writing. For example, the process of data collection and analysis are done simultaneously, but they are not two distinct phases of research.
- It deals with discovery of data that already exists and does not involve creation of data using structured tools.
- It is analytical in that it uses logical induction.
- It has a variety of foci such as issues, events, movements and concepts.
- It records and evaluates the accomplishments of individuals, agencies or institutions.

Q5. Describe the value and scope of historical research in education.

Ans. Historical research has great value in the field of educational research because it is necessary to know and understand educational achievements and trends of the past in order to gain perspective on present and future directions. Knight (1934), as quoted by Good, Barr and Scates (1941, p. 243) has given the following analysis of the value of historical research:

- A knowledge of the history of schools and other educational agencies is an important part of the professional training of the teacher or the school administrator.
- Much of the work of the school is traditional. The nature of the work of the teacher and the school administrator is restrictive and tends to foster prejudices in favour of familiar methods. The history of education is the "sovereign" of educational prejudices.
- The history of education enables the educational worker to detect fads and frills in whatever form they may appear, and it serves as a necessary preliminary to educational reform.
- Only in the light of their origins and growth can be viewed the numerous educational problems of the present sympathetically and without bias by the teacher, the school administrator, or the public.
- The history of education shows how the functions of social institutions shift and how the support and control of education

have changed from very simple and local arrangements to those that are now somewhat centralised and complex.

- The history of education is an ally in the scientific study of education rather than a competition. It serves to present the educational ideals and standards of other times, and it enables social workers to avoid mistakes of the past.
- It inspires respect for sound scholarship and reverence for great teachers.

Scope

The subject matter of historical research may be of following types:

(1) General educational history of specific periods such as (a) ancient India, (b) A during British rule, (c) Independent India, etc.

(2) History of specific levels of education (a) primary education, (b) secondary education, (c) tertiary education, etc. in India.

(3) History of specific types of education such as (a) adult education, (b) distance education, (c) disadvantaged education, (d) women's education in India.

(4) Historical study of specific educational institutions such as (i) University of Mumbai, (ii) Aligarh Muslim University and so on.

(5) History of the role of the teacher in ancient India.

(6) History of specific components of education such as (a) curriculum, (b) text-books, (c) teaching-learning methods, (d) aims and objectives of education, (e) teacher-student relationships, (f) evaluation process and so on.

(7) History of national education policies in India.

(8) History of admission processes in professional/technical courses (medicine, engineering, management) in India.

(9) History of teacher education.

(10) Historical biographies of major contributors to education such as Mahatma Gandhi, Maharshi Karve, Maharshi Phule, Shri Aurobindo, Gurudev Tagore and so on.

(11) History of educational administration.

(12) History of public financing of education.

(13) History of educational legislation in India.

(14) History of educational planning.

(15) History of contemporary problems in India.

(16) Historical study of the relationship between politics and education in India.

(17) Historical study of the impact of the British rule in India.

(18) Comparative history of education in India and some other country/countries.

(19) Historical study of the system of state-sponsored inspection in India.

(20) Historical study of education in specific Indian states such as Maharashtra, Tamil Nadu, Madhya Pradesh, Rajasthan, etc.

In other words, historical research in education may be concerned with an individual, a group, an idea a movement or an institution.

If a historical study focuses on an entire country/society/system, i.e. if it is broad in scope, it is said to be a macro-level historical research. On the other hand, if its focus is narrow and includes a selective set of people or events of interest, it is said to be a micro-level historical research.

Q6. What are various steps in educational historical research?

Ans. In general, historical research involves the following steps:

(1) Selection of the Problem: A researcher may select a problem pertaining to the history of individuals, institutions, organisations, law, curriculum, administration, text-books, teacher education, equipment, important concepts and thoughts that have influenced education during a specific period of time in a given culture or sub-culture determined by religion, caste, sex, age or work. He may delimit his study to an era of events in a local, regional, or national setting, or he may study the trend of events in different areas, different societies, or different cultures. The historian may discover new knowledge, the meaning of which, when interpreted will provide answers about past events. Sometimes he may doubt an old interpretation of existing data and then attempts to provide a more satisfactory explanation of past events.

The researcher should exercise due care in selecting and delimiting the historical problem for investigation. He should check that the problem selected should not only be of historical and current significance, but answerable by available methods of research and by the available sources of data. Sometimes many worthwhile topics of historical importance may have to be discarded when adequate data are not available.

(2) Formulation of Hypotheses: The hypotheses that the researcher constructs for historical research are useful in explaining events, conditions or phenomena of the historical period in question. Sometimes it is argued that in such type of studies a researcher is merely interested in concrete events in their singularity, he has merely to check the validity and authenticity of facts about past events and arrange them in a chronological sequence. Therefore, the researcher may not formulate any hypotheses in such investigations. But the findings based on unstated hypotheses are ambiguous and do not explain or describe the structural interrelations of the phenomena under study. The reports of such findings relate what happened in the past but do not explain how and why the events occurred in a particular sequence. However, it must be noted that the hypotheses for historical research may not be formal hypotheses to be tested. Rather, they are written as explicit statements that tentatively explain the occurrence of events and conditions.

Some examples of hypotheses in educational historical research, viz. (i) The innovations in examination system at the secondary school stage in 1950s and 1960s were based upon the recommendations of Secondary Education Commission (1952-53); (ii) The Gurkul system has a significant effect upon education in ancient period; and (iii) The educational programmes and innovations of DPEP were based upon practices that previously have been tried and accepted during 1970s and 1980s, are presented as illustrations.

(3) Collection of Data: After the problem has been selected and stated and appropriate hypotheses or researcher questions have been formulated, the researcher has to collect all the data available so that research questions and hypotheses may be thoroughly answered and verified. The collection of data in historical research is a tedious and time-consuming process. The researcher usually sifts through the vast materials of human activity that testify about past events, and from these he identifies and selects data that are relevant to his problem. These data are classified into primary and secondary sources.

(i) Primary sources

Primary sources are eyewitness accounts and are the only solid bases of historical inquiry. Good, Barr and Scates (1941, p. 253) have called them as the "first witnesses to a fact". The original documents or remains come under the category of primary sources. They are available in written, pictorial and mechanical forms as under:

- **Personal records:** Certificates, diaries, autobiographies, affidavits, declarations, letters, wills, deeds, contracts, and original drafts of speeches, articles, books, and pamphlets.
- **Official records:** Legislative, judicial, or executive documents prepared by central or state governments, municipalities, panchayats or other local bodies, such as constitutions, laws, charters, court proceedings and decisions; data preserved by missionaries and other religious organisations such as financial records of the minutes of the meeting of managing or governing bodies; the information compiled by central or state education departments, special commissions, professional organisations, school boards, administrative authorities, such as the minutes of meetings, reports of committees and commissions, administrative orders, school surveys, annual reports, budget, attendance records, cumulative records of dramas, games musical and athletic events, and examinations.
- **Oral testimony of traditions and events:** Myths, folk tales, family stories, ceremonies, spoken account of a witness of an event, interviews with administrators, teachers, students, parents or guardians, school patrons, and prominent educationists.
- **Pictorial records:** Photographs, movies, micro-films, drawings, paintings, coins, and sculpture.
- **Mechanical records:** Photograph records of events and tape recordings of interviews, meetings, and speeches.
- **Remains or relics:** Fossils, skeletons, tools weapons, clothing, buildings, furniture, utensils, art objects, teaching materials, samples of examination question papers, samples of student work, and murals.

(ii) Secondary sources

Secondary sources are the accounts of an event provided by a person who did not directly observe the event, object, or condition. The person may have directly contacted an actual observer and talked with him or read an account by an observer. Since the testimony of the person is not that of an actual participant or observer, secondary sources are subject to an inherent danger of inaccuracy and distortion. For this reason, the researcher should rely as much as possible on primary sources and use the secondary sources only to bridge the gaps between the various pieces of primary data.

At times, however, it is not always possible to obtain primary data and in such situations, the researcher may have to rely on secondary sources. These situations, according to Mouly (1963, p. 208), are frequent in education where only fragmentary reports concerning the processes of education are available. He is the opinion that people in the past considered education so trivial that they did not bother recording anything about its nature or its organisation: and consequently, it is relatively difficult to identify suitable primary data to permit the conduct of a good historical research in education. The personal documents as diaries and personal letters also leave wide gaps for the researcher to get the required continuity without resorting to secondary sources.

Secondary sources, if used carefully, serve many useful purposes. They may acquaint a researcher to major theoretical issues in his field and to the work that has been done in the area under study. They may suggest possible solutions of the problem and working hypotheses and may introduce the researcher to important primary sources.

In the location of source materials in historical research, the card catalog, periodical indexes, bibliographies, reviews, dissertations, and research journals provide helpful guides. It may be noted that historical studies involve more intensive bibliographical work and library usage than any other type of research, and hence, the researcher should be careful while assembling full bibliographical information in his note-taking system to facilitate proper documentation.

(4) Criticism of Data: After the data have been identified, the researcher must learn to read them correctly as a basis for developing sound ideas of the past, which in turn may help in interpreting present trends and possibly in predicting future events. For this, the researcher subjects his data to rigorous evaluation, which is known as criticism of the data. It involves the dual processes of establishing the authenticity of the source and of establishing the validity of its contents.

The process of establishing authenticity of the data is termed as external criticism and that of establishing the validity of their content is termed as internal criticism.

(5) Interpretation of Data: After the data have been collected and criticised, the researcher turns himself to the task of interpretation of these data in the light of his problem.

Because of the unique nature of the historical data, the task of interpretation becomes complicated and acquires special significance. It requires greatest ingenuity and imagination on the part of the researcher.

The researcher in the historical type of investigation must be very cautions while dealing with 'cause and effect' relationship. Here his position is entirely different from a researcher of physical sciences who deals with very simple isolated laboratory phenomena. Historical causes are invariable complex and the historical researcher must accept the fact that he is not dealing with clear-cut cases of cause and effect.

Since history is actually a record of the chain of related events, it becomes very difficult for a researcher to interpret that one event in the chain was caused by the previous event in the chain. Furthermore, many conditions and circumstances interact and become responsible for a particular event. Therefore, it makes the task of the researcher difficult to assess accurately the influence of a particular event and to identify clear-cut cause-effect relationships.

The historical researcher must also be very cautious in his use of analogy in the interpretation of data. While drawing comparisons between one historical event and number of others, he must carefully make use of similarities as well as of differences.

The ultimate goal in the historical type of research is not only to establish facts but also to determine trends, which the data may suggest and to draw inferences from the data. The researcher must show an understanding of the sequence of events and must draw a vertical relationship of preceding facts with succeeding one along the time line. His goal should be one of synthesis and interpretation rather than mere summation.

(6) Writing of the Research Report: After the data have been interpreted, the researcher has to write a well-organised report of his study. The writing of historical research report needs the highest level of scholarship on the part of the researcher. This is a matter of expositional strategy, which calls for creativity in addition to the qualities of imagination and ingenuity. The researcher must be elegant and objective in his style of writing the research report.

The historical research report must be presented in the logical, chronological and topical order. Good, Barr and Scates (1941, p. 265) also recommend that an appropriate combination of the chronological and topical organisation of historical data, involving consideration of such influences or forces as political institutions, law, economics, geography, social conditions, war, national culture, art, literature, religion, great leaders, natural sources, etc. seems best.

Reports of historical research should neither be dull and unattractive nor too flowery and ornamental. They must follow precision, continuity, clarity and dignity in their style to give a sense of design and completeness.

Q7. How can we enhance the value of historical research?

Or

What are the limitation of historical research in education?

Ans. We must take care of following limitations of historical research in view of enhancing the credibility of historical studies in education.

Researcher's bias and values

As you know, the historical research is interpretative in nature. The researcher's bias, values and interests play a major role in selection of problem as well as interpretation of data. As a researcher, you must be aware of your bias, values and interests as well as others values and biases. Your openness in exposing your values and biases will provide an opportunity to others to see you interpretation of historical data in the context.

In case you present your bias and values from a particular school of thought or an ideology of a historian, you must make your points of view more clearly in your reporting. For example, the 'radical historians' do not believe in treating history of education to analysis of facts related to formal schooling and the efforts made to promote formal education, as 'liberal reform' oriented historians do. The radical historians visualise many cultural order currents that affect learning and social development of citizens. They see educational process with a broad framework of livelihood of people, interaction and conflict of different groups, the discriminatory treatment of women and minority groups, the connections between schools and polities and between education and social stratification. Your interpretation will depend on your bias towards either, 'liberal reform' thoughts or 'radial' thoughts presentism.

Influence of presentism

Another point to be kept in mind is regarding the influence of presentism in historical data. Many concepts and perspectives that have recent origin are very often imposed on interpretation of historical events. Hence, distorted meaning of historical events gets its place in interpretation. To avoid such bias towards presentism, as a researcher you must intent to discover how the various concepts were used in past and in its specific setting rather than attaching present meaning to them.

Use of concepts

Since, historian takes help of indifferent concepts to organise the past events therefore, concepts used by the researcher in dealing with historical data must be defined in the context of time setting. For instance, the concept of teacher as visualised today may not exist in the context of past agrarian society. If the researcher restricts himself to the concept of teacher as defined in a dictionary and tries to confine the role and status of teacher in educational developments, he may tie down his hands to a limited scope of formal school teacher hood.

The researcher must define concepts with a historical perspective. Various terms and concepts emerging in different disciplines like sociology (e.g., role bureaucracy, institution, anthropology culture, ethnic groups and psychology (e.g., motive, attitude, personality, creativity, development, needs) are used in interpretation of historical data. As a historical researcher, you must be aware of how these concepts are defined in social science discipline from which they originate. It must be ensured that they are used appropriately in historical research.

Assumptions behind causal references

Certain historians assume that humans act similarly across cultures and across time. However, others assume that history does not repeat itself. Historical events are unique. Occurrences at one point in history cannot be used to help explain occurrences at another point of time. As a researcher, you must be careful about these assumptions. For instance, historical explanation of events taking place under colonialism may not be juxtaposed to find meaning of events taking place in medieval era. You must take a holistic look into different circumstances associated with major events under study. In other words, if you restrict yourself to analyse the events in the context of specific antecedents and ignore other factors your analysis will have limited meaning. As a historian, you may not use causal links with certainty or in absolute terms. Rather you must carefully state causal relations with high probabilistic terms and references giving scope for others' interpretations and studies.

Generalisability

The question of generalisability in historical research is raised very often by critics. This is raised mainly due to data concerning historical events have limitations for generalisations. The historical researcher studies only a small portion of the phenomena that interest him. The data concerning an event may not be available in complete form and chronological order. Limited information may restrict the historians to draw generalisations about the events under study. As a researcher, you must strengthen your findings by increasing the sample data on which they are based. Hence, you must search for as many primary and secondary sources relating to the theme as possible. Wherever the evidence is limited, you should limit the generalisability of your interpretations accordingly.

Q8. Explain the meaning and nature of descriptive research.

Ans. Descriptive research studies are designed to obtain pertinent and precise information concerning the current status of phenomena and, whenever possible, to draw valid general conclusions from the facts discovered. They are restricted not only to fact finding but may often result in the formulation of important principles of knowledge and solution of significant problems concerning local, state, national and international issues. Descriptive studies are more than just a collection of data; they involve measurement, classification, analysis comparison, and interpretation. They collect and provide three types of information: (1) of what exists with respect to variables of conditions in a situation; (2) of what we want by identifying standards of norms with which to compare the present conditions or what experts consider to be desirable, and (3) of how to achieve goals by exploring possible ways and means on the basis of the experience of others or the opinions of experts.

Descriptive studies investigate phenomena in their natural setting. Their purpose is both immediate and long range. They constitute a primitive type of research and do not aspire to develop an organised body of scientific laws. Such studies, however, provide information useful to the solution of local problems and at times provide data to form the basis of research of a more fundamental nature.

Descriptive research differs from other types of research in purpose and scope. A clear-cut distinction can be drawn between descriptive studies and historical studies on the basis of time. The latter deals with the past and the former with the present. The limitations of descriptive investigations, however, are very similar to those of the historical inquiry in that cause and effect relationships are difficult to establish, and the time at which study is conducted is a critical factor in the interpretation of the data. The method of descriptive research, in contrast to an experiment, is relatively less scientifically sophisticated. Here the researcher does not manipulate the variables or arrange for events to happen. In fact, the events that are observed and described by him would have happened even though there had been no observation. Descriptive studies involve events that have already taken place and are related to a present condition.

Descriptive studies vary greatly in complexity. At one extreme, they constitute nothing more than frequency count of events to the study of local problems without any significant research purpose. At the other extreme, they attempt to ascertain significant interrelationships among phenomena.

Q9. Classify the descriptive research in various types with respect to following:

(a) Coverage of population

Ans. According to coverage of population, descriptive research can be classified as follows:

(1) Census Survey: Census survey means gathering pertinent information from the whole population, viz. people institution, householders, etc. Population may consist of persons, institutions, objects, attributes, qualities, families, etc. A population is a well-defined group of many of these. For example, the census survey of Indian Union, which takes place once in ten years each and every household it restricts its scope to the status of people like age, sex, income, education, lands possessed, nature of house, domestic facilities available, etc. The census studies are conducted through quick survey in a stipulated period.

Strength of census survey

The strength of census survey is associated with availing data on whole population. Description of population data acts as a major source of identifying several pertinent questions for research. It is very much useful in making trend analysis of different events. Moreover, hard data base system of entire population is very much useful in development of strategic planning and policy making of education at micro-level as well as at macro-level. The benchmark data on enrolment of students; their background variables, achievement scores, etc. form a major source for planning and development purpose.

Limitations of census survey

Due to the coverage of complete population, data are gathered on limited headings. Moreover, such data are of surface level. Through census survey, one can go for gathering nominal data. The researcher cannot inquire on questions in depth. Many a time such data are gathered mechanically where the investigators are not well trained about cross-examining the evidences at field level. In such cases, the probability of getting valid data is also minimised. Census studies involve employment of huge manpower and monetary resources. It is time consuming too.

(2) Sample Survey: Sample Survey means gathering relevant information about a smaller representation of the population under study. The data gathered through sample survey are generalised to the population of the study. For example, opinion of group of sample students drawn from a particular college or university towards introduction of grading system educational research invariably makes use of sample survey.

You may come across sample survey like:

- Opinion of mothers on compulsory primary education of girl's children in rural area;
- Teachers attitude towards in service education programmes provided by DIETs;
- Attitude of college students towards semester system.

Reasons for conducting sample surveys

Sample surveys are preferred to census survey on following grounds:

- ***Reduced cost:*** Data collected from a small fraction of population involve lesser expenses than that of census survey.
- ***Greater speed:*** Since the size of respondents is smaller than the whole population, the volume of data are smaller. Hence, it is economical in terms of gathering evidences, tabulating them and processing them quickly.
- ***Greater scope:*** Unlike census studies where limited information are gathered from whole population the sample survey cover wide range of data on different dimensions of the study. Moreover, from the point of view of availability researcher or competent researchers it is feasible to conduct sample survey with more vigour then appointing half-baked investigators in census studies. The sample surveys are conducted with full spirit since the conduct of such studies are within the control of the researcher.
- ***Greater accuracy:*** With reduced volume of work using expert and trained personnel, and application of appropriate monitoring mechanism of data collection and analysis, there is, greater chance of gathering valid data and its appropriate processing. Moreover, sampling is particularly more important in obtaining accurate result about phenomena, which are undergoing rapid changes such as opinions about political and social issues and their impacts on education.

(b) Types of events

Ans. According to types of events, descriptive research can be classified as follows:

(1) Cross Sectional survey: Cross sectional survey can be understood as a kind of sample survey where information is gathered from a sample drawn from a cross section of pre-determined population at one point of time. The sample represents different distinct segments of population or stages of development of events. For example, the segments may indicate different stages of education like primary, secondary and higher or different from of education like face-to-face mode and distance mode, etc. It may include the schools covered under a specific scheme and the schools yet to be covered under the scheme. It may also include sample of trained teachers and untrained teachers at primary stage.

(2) Longitudinal survey: Through longitudinal survey, one explores the status of one or more than one variable as investigated on different points of time in order. Through such studies, the changes in the status of the variable over a period of time are explored. Moreover, time-ordered associations of one variable's status at different period of time are studied.

Unlike cross sectional studies where data are gathered at one point in time the longitudinal studies deal with gathering actual evidences at different points in time.

(c) Purpose of Study

Ans. According to the purpose of study, descriptive research can be classified as follows:

(1) Comparative survey: In comparative survey, the purpose is to compare the status of two or more number of variables: institutions, strategies adopted or groups of respondents, etc. For example, you may be interested to compare achievement level of students enrolled in two different institutions assuming that the students of two different institutions belong to the same population. In another case, you may like to compare the reaction of teachers serving in government and private management schools towards leadership behaviour of their principals, or you may be interested to compare the effectiveness of an innovative teaching-learning strategy adopted in certain schools with traditional approach of teaching adopted in same institutions in terms of achievement of learners. In such kinds of studies, you will have to keep the following three points in mind.

Comparison points

Comparative survey involves sensitivity with regard to identification of worthwhile things to compare. The worthwhileness of focus of the study must be identified through view of literature and experiences of experts. For instance, in case of comparing attitude of teachers of different subject groups towards behaviour of principals leadership must be well justified keeping in view the research needs and theoretical framework of study. Moreover, it must be justified that comparison point or the variable on which comparison is done exists in different groups of respondents.

Assumption of similarities

The researcher must be serious about comparability of situations under investigation. For instance, for comparing teacher-training programmes of two types of teacher education institutions you will have to proceed with establishing commonness of student population, admission criteria, faculty norms of institutions, etc. Moreover, comparability of institutional setting, curricular requirements, time schedule, working hours, etc., would lead towards exploring differential practices related to teacher training programmes of different institutions.

Criteria of comparison

The third point to be kept in mind is identifying the criteria of comparison. A researcher will have to delineate criterion variables. The criterion variables must be equally fair to different research situations under investigation. In other words, the criteria of comparison should not bias to a particular kind of institution with a motive to project strong points or to defame with negative points. Fairness in identification of criteria must have its roots in through understanding of researcher. Appropriate tools will have to be identified of criterion variables. Hence, selection of appropriate and valid tools for criterion variables is very much essential in comparative surveys.

(2) Evaluative survey: Such surveys are conducted with the purpose of evaluating a programme, a curriculum, policy, etc. As you know, evaluation means making judgement about "effectiveness", "fruitfulness", "worth", "appropriateness", "suitability" of programme, etc. Hence, when you intend to conduct empirical studies on identifying effectiveness of any programme's functioning or programme's output, you may adopt evaluative survey method. Evaluation studies lead towards arriving at value judgement about the worthwhileness of a programme, a policy or an institution. Two purposes can be served by evaluation of programme through surveys:

- First, it is concerned with the effectiveness of a programme. As a researcher, you make judgement about the effectiveness of a programme.

- Second, it is a decision-oriented study. You may present relevant facts about the status and functioning of a programme through evaluative survey. On the basis of such study, policy makers or decision-making bodies may identify strength and loopholes of a programme and take appropriate decision to improve on the situation.

You may come across a number of evaluative surveys conducted in the field of education. For example, "Impact of study of children's radio broadcast programme on development of general awareness of primary students", "Effectiveness of adult literacy programme in a district", "Impact of mid-day meal programme on enrolment, retention and achievement of primary school", etc.

Evaluation is done with the help of a criterion measure. When we are interested to answer the question "how effective is?", we come to criterion issue: "effective" in terms of what? For example, effectiveness of adult literacy programme need to be judged on the basis of set criteria. The criteria may include rate of participation of adult illiterates in a programme, reaching minimum level of achievement by adult learners, satisfaction of participants about the functioning of programme, etc. Hence, you must take note of identification of appropriate criteria of evaluation. It must follow selection of appropriate measure of criterion variables.

Q10. What do you understand by the documentary research? Differentiate it from historical research. Describe the purpose and limitation of documentary research.

Ans. Documentary research is closely related to historical research since in such surveys we study the existing documents. But it is different from historical research in which our emphasis is on the study of the past; and in the descriptive research we emphasise on the study of the present. Descriptive research in the field of education may focus on describing the existing school practices, attendance rate of the students, health records, and so on.

Documentary research today is a widely used research tool aimed at determining the presence of certain words or concepts within texts or sets of texts. Researchers quantify and analyse the presence, meanings and relationships of such words and concepts, then make inferences about the messages within the texts, the writer(s), the audience and even the culture and time of which these are a part. Documentary research could be defined as a research technique for the objective, systematic, and quantitative description of manifest content of communications. It is a technique for making inferences by objectively and systematically identifying specified characteristics of messages. The technique of documentary analysis is not restricted to the domain of textual analysis, but may be applied to other areas such as coding student drawings or coding of actions observed in videotaped studies, analysing past documents such as memos, minutes of the meetings, legal and policy statements and so on. In order to allow for replication, however, the technique can only be applied to data that are durable in nature. Texts in documentary research can be defined broadly as books, book chapters, essays, interviews, discussions, newspaper headlines and articles, historical documents, speeches, conversations, advertising, theatre, informal conversation, or really any occurrence of communicative language. Texts in a single study may also represent a variety of different types of occurrences. Documentary research enables researchers to sift through large amount of data with comparative ease in a systematic fashion. It can be a useful technique for allowing one to discover and describe the focus of individual, group, institutional or social attention. It also allows inferences to be made which can then be corroborated using other methods of data collection.

Document research is the systematic exploration of written documents or other artefacts such as films, videos and photographs. In pedagogic research, it is usually the contents of the artefacts, rather than say, the style or design, that are of interest.

Purpose of documentary studies

The documentary surveys serve different purposes, which are significant for educational research.

- *To describe the existing structure and functions of educational system or conditions that exists in educational field.* For example, the existing practices of primary education in view of achieving the goals of universalisation of elementary educational or the status of distance education programme in teacher preparation can be included in such category of documentary surveys.
- To discover *the relative importance of certain problems and identifying future trends of different developments in the field education:* The trend analysis of growing demand for certain areas of education, and analysing corresponding need for expansion of education can best fit with such kind of documentary study.
- *To analyse curriculum of different levels of state/country or countries in comparative perspective:* For example you may be interested in analyse curriculum of secondary education adopted by boards

of secondary education of different states *vis-à-vis* Central Board of Secondary Education. Similarly, you may be interested to study logical flow of curriculum of primary education, secondary education and higher secondary education of a particular state of country.

- *To analyse and review study material/evaluation items:* Analysis, review and evaluation of text books, study materials, reference books, examination questions papers, assessment of assignments, internal assessment of students performance, marking procedure of answer books, etc. fall under this category of research. You will come across a number of studies where the researcher has carried out content analysis and evaluation of self-study materials of an open university, question papers of a broad of secondary education, nature of assignments of distance education programme, nature of feedback given by tutors, marking procedure of assignments, etc. Such kind of analysis depends on availability of original documents, adoption of standard parametreof evaluation and researcher's judgement capacity. On many occasions, such kind of evaluation studies are treated as part of formative research, which have major potentials for programme development.
- *To analyse the literacy style, concepts, beliefs, ideology of a writer:* In the case of research in the field of literature, and social science such analysis is given importance. Moreover, in the area of philosophy of education analysis of original text of an author and ideas/comments of others about the author are analysed with significance.

Limitations of documentary studies

While conducting documentary analysis you may find the following limitations inherent in the method itself.

- First, this analysis solely depends on documentary evidences. Conclusions drawn on the basis of documentary data may not give complete picture of the phenomena under investigation. For example, while analysing curriculum, you may depend on text materials. However, the curricular practices as presented in textual form may not reveal complete picture of process dimensions. The investigation remains incomplete without incorporating observation-based evidences.
- Second, data presented in the form of records or publications may not be available in particular order. It may be available in

incomplete form. Moreover, evidences gathered through available documents may not represent the population of study. The views, opinions or reactions of people already available in published documents may not be representative. A particular segment of population who may be expressing their views on certain incidences may not be a good representative sample of population under study. Hence, generalisations of documentary evidences have major limitations.

- Third, you may doubt authenticity of data available in printed text. You may cross-examine information available through one source with that of order. Moreover, you will have to be careful about the trustworthiness of sources of data. Many a time documentary evidences create confusion and lead to complicate the process of investigation. Different records may use different parameters of present data. Unless you trace these parameters of classification of such data it would be difficult to find meaningful base of data analysis. For example, the boundary of some units of analysis, e.g., school districts, age cohorts, dropout radio, etc., can also change from document to document. Different records pertaining to these data may not have used common parametreof classification or definition of terms. Hence, it is always advisable to adopt documentary analysis using internal and external criticism of data, meaningfulness of information and correlating documentary data with other methods of data collection procedures with a view to get total picture of reality (for details of authenticity) of data you may refer the write up on historical research as presented elsewhere.

Q11. Discuss the relevance of descriptive studies in educational research.

Ans. The descriptive research method has undoubtedly been the most popular and the most widely used research method in education. It helps to explain educational phenomena in terms of the conditions or relationship that exist, opinion that are held by the students, teachers, parents and experts, processes that are going on.

(1) The preliminary function of educational research is to understand the nature of phenomena. In other words, the researcher is interested to know the nature of different variables and their interactions constituting the functioning of a system.

Unless you identify the nature of variables or factors and describe their intensity in the context of an event you not proceed further in explaining why the events occurred and how to intervene with events with a view to get desired results. In the initial stage of inquiry, you must have wide database and observations about day-to-day functioning of a system. In the system of education, many events occur because of its dynamism. However, without having base line data on the incidents and corresponding factors you cannot arrive at any conclusion about the cause of the incident. Since in many instances preliminary data are not available you proceed for exploring baseline data from current situations/settings through surveys.

You will come across a large number of surveys studies in almost all areas of educational research, viz. educational psychology, sociology of education, comparative education, educational planning and management, curriculum, teacher education, educational technology examination reforms, adult education, tribal education, women education, special education, etc. The problems like exploring value system of college students, studying achievement pattern of rural students, analysing budgetary provision of school education, identifying coverage of primary education system, identifying coverage of adult literacy programme, exploring needs of distance education learners, etc., are covered under survey research.

(2) Survey research prepares a ground for exploring concomitant relationship between different pertinent variables. The intensity of certain variables is stressed through benchmark investigations. After identifying significant variables and their measurement you may study their correlations with a view to develop empirical ground for explaining significant role of such variables in the prediction of future events. You will come across a number of correlation surveys in different areas mainly concerning psychological aspects of teaching, learning system, achievement, correlates and management of education system. For example, plotting benchmark data concerning two variables in a matrix can indicate whether you can proceed further of studying their relationships or not? or whether you can go for linear relationship study or non-linear study?, etc. Moreover,

the trend data helps you to identify the path of dynamics of certain variables.

(3) In planning and management of education system, it would be worthwhile to develop data base system. Unless you the complexity of a system with its component analysis you cannot ascertain the significance of its components and sub-components in functioning of a system. Hence, you must be vigilant about the dynamics of a system in terms of behaviour or status of various components on a continuous basis. Description of system with factual data on each and every units and sub-unites facilitate decision-making process. Survey of different stages of education system focuses on gathering benchmark data about the characteristics of target group learners, demand for expansions system, expectations of stack holder like learners, parents, employers, teachers, policy makers, available physical and man power resources, existing strategies adopted in tackling teaching-learning problems, dynamics of class room based teaching-learning practices, coverage media and technology in education system, achievement level of learners, utilisation of financial resources, evaluation system, etc. Such data based inquiries help policy makers, administrators and practitioners to develop suitable policies, development of appropriate models/strategies, decision-making, etc.

(4) The relevance of survey research can also be noticed with regard to development and standardisation of varieties of tools for research. More specifically, the behavioural science has been enriched with the contribution of varieties of tools aiming at gathering evidences from different populations. Exploratory studies on identification of status of different variables like intelligence, creativity, motivation, needs, achievement, attitude, aptitude, leadership behaviour, teaching competencies, classroom climate, group dynamics, etc., promoted researchers to construct and standardise suitable and relevant tools with technical accuracy concerning specific population. Over a period of time we have come across emergence of a number of readymade research tools having utility for mass based utilisation for gathering data on different variables.

(5) Survey of current structures and functioning of education system can help us to develop a comparative look of the system

at national and international level. Different parameters like geographic background, culture, economic development, linguistic background, political philosophy are treated as the referent of comparative analysis of education system. The cross-sectional and longitudinal surveys contribute a lot towards development of holistic picture of education system.

(6) Descriptive surveys contribute significantly towards improvement in administrative functions of education. The contribution of evaluation surveys towards policy research and decision-making can also be valued with much more significance. Evaluation surveys help the policy makers, administrators and teachers in making judgements about the merit, value, or worth of educational programmes, products and techniques. Evaluation studies are usually conducted to improve decision-making. A few examples of decision type questions that generate the need for evaluative surveys may read as:

   (i) Which of the portions of existing textbooks need further improvement or modifications?
   (ii) What are the areas in which the in-service teachers fail to perform effectively?
   (iii) Should we maintain our existing set of curriculum objectives or revise them?
   (iv) Is there any need for enhancing financial support to a programme?
   (v) If so, how to generate alternative funding systems?, etc.

   Evaluation research involves the systematic collection of data with a view to help decision-makers. Moreover, it is assumed that the results of evaluation surveys can enable educators to make better judgements and decisions than they could make without having such results available.

(7) Descriptive surveys may provide basis for testing a theory. With the help of descriptive survey, you can examine whether a situation described by some theory exists in reality or not? For instance in Peaget's development theory, the characteristics of each stage of development are described with certain number functions of cognitive development. A number of surveys have been conducted abroad and in India with the help of specific tools for measuring specific development tasks of different stages. Such studies have been conducted in different

populations and culture with a view to verification of certain theoretical questions. However, descriptive surveys have limitations with regard to explaining cause and effect relationships as stated in a theory. Experimental studies may be more relevant to explain causal relationships.

Q12. Discuss the concept of case study as a kind of descriptive research. What are the steps adopted by this approach?

Ans. The case studies in general are classified as descriptive research types. They have sometimes been conducted for purpose of hypothesis testing and taken the form of experimental research. Many case studies, for example, were conducted to investigate the effects of operant conditioning on human behaviour. In a typical study, as reported by Ary *et at.* (1972, p. 288), the researcher identifies a specific behaviour in his subject and systematically records the frequency of this behaviour. Then he introduces an operant conditioning treatment and records the frequency of the specified behaviour during treatment. When a change is observed in the behaviour of the subject as a result of operant conditioning, the researcher begins reversal conditioning; that is, he uses operant conditioning to change the behaviour back to what it was before the original conditioning was instituted.

The case study method was originally used in medicine to examine the patient's previous development, his health and physical state from the beginning and many other factors in the past, besides making a careful study of the patient's present condition and symptoms. Sigmund Freud used case study method to assist his subjects in solving their personality problems. The published detailed accounts of his interviews with patients and his interpretations of their thoughts, dreams and actions provide excellent examples of case studies.

Steps of the case study

The following steps are involved in conducting the case study:

(1) The first step is to determine the present status of the individual or the social unit under investigation through direct observation or measurement. Here the researcher goes for beyond casual observation or superficial description. In addition to a physical examination of the subject, a psychological evaluation designed to determine the general ability level and the emotional maturity of the case is necessary. There are numerous standardised tools that are useful to the researcher in this assessment process. For example, to make a case study of a delinquent child, the first thing the researcher

has to do is to survey the present status of the child by making an assessment of his physique, cognitive and non-cognitive factors through direct observation and administering tests of intelligence, aptitudes and personality.

(2) The next step is to determine the most probable antecedents of the case and to formulate a fruitful hypothesis or a set of hypothesis through the knowledge of similar cases. The researcher, for example, can formulate a hypothesis that the occurrence of delinquent behaviour in a child is due to inadequate home environment, poor teaching in the school, low mental ability or any other factor.

(3) The third step is verification of the hypothesis. The case is then checked for the presence of the antecedents supposed to apply to the situation under investigation. Here the researcher makes use of the knowledge of the present status and the history of the case. He should not overemphasise observational methods and neglect other methods. Van Dalen (1973, p. 209) suggests that a multi-method approach may serve as a more valid test of a hypothesis. The researcher may ask the case to recall past experiences or to experiences or to express present wishes in interviews or questionnaires. Personal documents, such as diaries and letters, and various physiological, psychological or sociological measurements may provide valuable information. Data may be obtained from teachers, friends, parents, brothers, sisters, and other family members.

(4) After verification of the hypothesis, the next step is directed towards further validation of the diagnosis. Some remedial measures in the light of the causes found are suggested.

(5) The last step of the case study is follow up of the case. The case under study is re-examined to ascertain whether any changes have been produced by the treatments introduced. If the change is positive and significant, the diagnosis is taken to be correct.

Q13. Write short notes on the following:

(a) Types of Cross sectional survey

Ans. Cross sectional surveys can be of two types: (i) description of status of **single** variable; and (ii) exploring relationships between **two or more variables.**

Single variable study: In such kind of studies, the researcher is interested to describe the status of any one variable as explored through investigation of sample respondents. For example, in opinion survey the researcher may be interested to explore preference of academic and professional courses by higher secondary school students. Data may be gathered through questionnaire or interview techniques. Data may be analysed descriptively highlighting the preferences of arts, science and commerce stream students. The analysis of data in such kind of study will indicate how characteristics of one sample group are different from another sample group.

Many variables study: A researcher may be interested to study relationships between different variables in the context of different segments of population. In such studies, he will have to pick-up at least two variables for investigation. It may be more than two variables. For examples, one may be interested to explore relationship between achievement and academic achievement level of a group of students and academic interest of same group of students respectively. In exploring relationships of two variables, you are to plot two sets of data, i.e. achievements scores and academic interest scores of same group of sample respondents. Then you will have to employ appropriate statistical techniques for measuring the level of relationships or co-efficient of correlation.

(b) Types of Longitudinal surveys

Ans. There are three kinds of longitudinal surveys, which include the following:

Trend studies: In such kind of studies, data on the variable(s) to be studied are collected at different phases. The population of respondents remains the same for different phases of investigation. Different groups of sample respondents drawn from a population are studied at different phases of investigation. For instance, in the case of impact study in mid-day meal scheme at primary stage the researcher may collect evidences from fresh batch of primary school students on annual basis continuously over a period of a few years. The researcher identifies the trend of response pattern on the basis of the opinion of each batch of fresh students over a period of time. Similarly, the reaction of students of a particular course towards academic activities may be collected on annual basis for five consecutive years from different batch of students. Such data can be used to study the trend of reaction of students towards academic activities.

Panel studies: In such studies, the behaviour pattern or performance level of one group of sample respondents is studied over a period of time. For example, attitude of a particular group of students towards school education is studied over a period of time. In panel study, the sample respondents remain the same for different phases of study.

Cohort studies: In cohort studies, a specific population is studied over a period of time in order to know the effect of a particular event. Different samples are drawn from the specific population at different phases/stage of development of events.

- For example, in a district, prior to introduction of in-service training of teachers through DIETs, teacher's reactions towards in-service education were studied.
- In the second phase, immediately after introduction of in-service education programmes, reactions of teachers were studied.
- In the third phase, the reactions of teachers were studied after completion of 3 years of introduction of in-service education programme.

In this case, the teacher's population was restricted to all the primary schools of a district covered under District Primary Education Project (DPEP). Even though the population of the study was specific the sample respondents representing the population varied from one phase of study to another.

(c) Steps in conducting descriptive research

Ans. The process of descriptive studies is not different from other forms of research. Since such studies, describe and interpret what conditions or relationships exist at present, the researcher may adopt the following steps:

(1) Selection of the Problem: A researcher may be concerned with conditions or relationships that exist, practices that prevail, beliefs, points of view or attitudes that are held, processes that are going on, effects that are being felt or trends that are developing, and may select the problem accordingly from the area or field in which he is interested.

(2) Statement and Definition of the Problem: The researcher must state the problem clearly as it is done in case of other types of research. The statement must identify the variables involved in the study. It should specific clearly whether the study is merely seeking to determine the present status of these variables or whether it will also explore relationships between the variables.

(3) Identification of Data: After stating and defining the problem, the next step for the researcher is to list the data to be collected for the study. He has to specify whether the data are of qualitative or a quantitative nature and whether the data will be collected in the form of counts, test scores, responses to questionnaires, interviews, and so on.

(4) Selection or Development of Tools: The nature of the data to be collected helps the researcher to select the appropriate tools for the study. If the ready-made tools are not available, the researcher has to develop his own tools. Questionnaires, interviews, psychological tests, rating scales, schedules and attitude scales are the most frequently used tools for descriptive research. If the researcher uses ready-made tools, he should satisfy himself about their reliability, validity, and suitability for sample chosen for the study. If the researcher develops his own tools, he should try them out with a small group in order to evaluate them and make modifications if necessary.

(5) Selection of the Sample: The researcher must select the sample about which he wishes to seek information using appropriate sampling techniques. The sample selected should adequately represent the population.

(6) Collection of Data: The researcher should specify the practical schedule for gathering the data from the sample selected for the study with the help of appropriate tools.

(7) Analysis and Interpretation of Data: The data collected are recorded and tabulated in the form of counts, test scores, responses to questionnaires, symbols, field notes, etc. These are analysed and interpreted with the help of appropriate parametric or non-parametric statistical tests and qualitative techniques.

(8) Writing of the Research Report: It is the last stage in the descriptive research as in any other form of research. The researcher should exercise extreme caution in generalising conclusions and reporting them with all the limitations of the study.

(d) Difference between Longitudinal survey and cross sectional survey

Ans. The difference between longitudinal survey and cross sectional survey has been given in the table 5.1:

Table 5.1

	Longitudinal Survey	Cross sectional Survey
(1) Phases of data collection	Data gathered at different points of time covering each stage/phase of phenomena	Data gathered at one point of time covering different stages of phenomena in different locations
(2) Time Required	Very long time	Within limited period
(3) Population and sample	(a) One population (b) Samples of similar nature drawn at different phases.	(a) One population (b) Representing difference stages/phases of events.

contd...

contd...

	Longitudinal Survey	Cross sectional Survey
	(c) Sampling technique is very simple	(c) Complicated techniques of stratified and multistage.
(4) Valid generalisation	(a) More valid and trustworthy since real conditions of different stages are studied (b) Trend of behaviour/ development can be studied	(a) Validity doubted as study is scattered over cross section of population (b) Trend cannot be studied.
(5) Decision-oriented study	Not feasible for quick decision	Quick decision can be possible.

Q14. What is meant by experimental research? Identify basic features of experimental research.

Ans. The experimental research is the application and adaptation of the classical method of experimentation. It is a scientifically sophisticated method. It provides a method of investigation to derive basic relationships among phenomena under controlled condition or, more simply, to identify the conditions underlying the occurrence of a given phenomenon. Experimental research is the description and analysis of what will be, or what will occur, under carefully controlled conditions.

Experimenters manipulate certain stimuli, treatments, or environmental conditions and observe how the condition or behaviour of the subject is affected or changed. Such manipulations are deliberate and systematic. The researchers must be aware of other factors that could influence the outcome and remove or control them in such a way that it will establish a logical association between manipulated factors and observed factors.

Experimental research provides a method of hypothesis testing. Hypothesis is the heart of experimental research. After the experimenter defines a problem, he has to propose a tentative answer to the problem or hypothesis. Further, he has to test the hypothesis and confirm or disconfirm it.

Although, the experimental method has greatest utility in the laboratory, it has been effectively applied non-laboratory settings such as the classroom. The immediate purpose of experimentation is to predict events in the experimental setting. The ultimate purpose is to generalise the variable relationships so that they may be applied outside the laboratory to a wider population of interest.

Characteristics

There are four essential characteristics of experimental research: (i) Control, (ii) Manipulation, (iii) Observation, and (iv) Replication.

(1) Control: Variables that are not of direct interest to the researcher, called extraneous variables, need to be controlled. Control refers to removing or minimising the influence of such variables by several methods such as: randomisation or random assignment of subjects to groups; matching subjects on extraneous variable(s) (s); application of statistical technique of analysis of covariance (ANCOVA); balancing means and standard deviations of the groups.

(2) Manipulation: Manipulation refers to a deliberate operation of the conditions by the researcher. In this process, a pre-determined set of conditions, called independent variable or experimental variable. It is also called treatment variable. Such variables are imposed on the subjects of experiment. In specific terms, manipulation refers to deliberate operation of independent variable on the subjects of experimental group by the researcher to observe its effect. Sex, socio-economic status, intelligence, method of teaching, training or qualification of teacher, and classroom environment are the major independent variables in educational research. If the researcher, for example, wants to study the effect of 'X' method of teaching on the achievement of students in mathematics, the independent variable here is the method of teaching. The researcher in this experiment needs to manipulate 'X', i.e. the method of teaching. In other words, the researcher has to teach the experimental groups using 'X' method and see its effect on achievement

(3) Observation: In experimental research, the experimenter observes the effect of the manipulation of the independent variable on dependent variable. The dependent variable, for example, may be performance or achievement in a task.

(4) Replication: Replication is a matter of conducting a number of sub-experiments, instead of one experiment only, within the framework of the same experimental design. The researcher may make a multiple comparison of a number of cases of the control group and a number of cases of the experimental group. In some experimental situations, a number of control and experimental groups, each consisting of equivalent subjects, are combined within a single experiment.

Q15. Explain the various kinds of variables in experimental research.

Or

Describe dependent, independent and extraneous variables with suitable examples. **[June-2013, Q.No.-3(f)]**

Ans. In experimental study, mainly we deal with two types of variables, viz. independent variables and dependent variables. Besides these variables, we must take care of two more types of variables, viz. extraneous variables and intervening variables. Let us be clear about these terminologies normally used in experimental studies.

(1) Independent variables: Independent variable means the conditions or characteristics, which can be manipulated or controlled to produce certain effects. For instance in classroom setting methods of teaching can be manipulated or controlled to study their effects on learner's achievement. Hence, methods of teaching can be treated as independent variables. Likewise, intelligence, motivation, creative potential, teacher behaviour, learning environment, study habits, etc. can also be treated as independent variables in the context of learner achievement.

(2) Dependent variables: Dependent variable means the conditions or characteristics that undergo as a result of manipulation or control of independent variables in an experiment. For instance, reward or punishment given by teachers may affect learner's achievement in positive or negative direction. Here, achievement is treated as dependent variable. Regular viewing of television programmes may cause change in learner's attitude. Here, learner's attitude is taken as dependent variable.

(3) Extraneous variables: In experimental research, extraneous variables play crucial role. Extraneous variables are those factors, which may have significant effect on dependent variables. In some experimental situation, we may manipulate or control some extraneous variables to minimise their effect on dependent variables.

In an experiment, we are interested in studying the effect of independent variable(s), which is/are the focus of our study. However, there can be a number of outside variables, which can affect the dependent variable. Because of their presence in experimental situations, many experiments get spoiled. Hence, we must be careful about eliminating or minimising the effect of extraneous variables so that the experiment can indicate valid relationship between independent and dependent variables under our study.

For instance, in a study, we may be interested in studying the effect of a particular method of teaching on learner achievement. Our experiment shall focus on controlling/manipulating method of teaching which is an independent variables. However, there are a number of extraneous variables like intelligence, motivation, language comprehension and so on, which may affect learner achievement.

Since our study aims at explaining the relationship between method of teaching and achievement, we must see that the effect of such extraneous variables is eliminated or minimised in the experiment.

(4) Intervening variables: The fourth category of variable taken into consideration is intervening variables. Intervening variables are those variables which influence the experiment but uncontrollable. Moreover, they cannot be measured. In educational setting many such variables intervene between the cause and effect. They may be accidental. They cannot be defined easily in specific context. Only thing is that we may suspect their presence in experimental situation. We may leave them to chance factor. However, these intervening variables must be accounted for. For example, mishappening occurring to certain subjects because of unavoidable circumstances, technology hazards, natural calamities, etc., may come on the way of experiment, which cannot be visualised prior to conduct of experiment. The researcher must take note of occurrence of these situations carefully while dealing with the experiment.

Q16. What is Experimental Research Design? Explain the criteria of a good research design.

Or

What are the methods adopted for controlling various kinds of extraneous variables.

Or

Discuss the criteria of judging the adequacy of experimental research design.

Ans. An experimental research design is to the researcher what a blueprint is to an architect. It provides the researcher an opportunity for the comparison required by the hypothesis of the experiment and enables him to make a meaningful interpretation of the results of the study with the help of statistical analysis of the data. There are three important criteria which researcher must keep in mind while selecting an experimental design for conducting his experiment.

(1) Testing of hypothesis: The first criterion means that the research design must take care of the hypothesis to be tested in the study. The number of variables included in the study, the nature of relationships of be studied and the number of experimental groups/situations to be included must be considered while drawing a research plan/design. For example, the researcher intends to study the effect of experimental variable say; methods of teaching and its interaction with contextual variables say;

learner's family background or mother tongue on learner's achievement, which cannot be studied through a simple research design. It requires appropriate design to study the effects of two different variables on achievement as well as their interaction effect. If the study incorporates questions to study comparative effectiveness of two innovative methods of teaching on learner's achievement, the researcher must go for two experimental group study.

(2) Control of extraneous variable: The control of extraneous factors is crucial to all kinds of experimentation, specifically in social science research where we deal with human beings. Let us examine a few possible alternatives of control in experiments.

(i) **Controlling the subjects:** It is mostly feasible in laboratory studies where physical control is applied to eliminate the presence of one factor in the experiment. In educational research, we must be careful about this type of control. For instance, we may restrict our experiment in rural setting and select only rural subjects to remove residential background (rural urban) as a variable. However, there is caution that all the rural subjects may not have uniform residential background or there cannot be any restriction that some subjects may not have urban exposure at all.

(ii) **Matching the subjects**: In actual sense, it means selecting pairs with identical characteristics. While selecting subjects for experimental group and control we match the groups on the basis of an extraneous variables which may affect the experiment. For instance we know that intelligence affects learner achievement. In case we wish to conduct an experiment on the effect of methods of teaching on achievement, we would like to match the experimental group and control group on their intelligence scores.

(iii) **Randomisation**: This approach is most suitable for experiments concerning social science research. It is suggested that the best satisfactory answer to control extraneous variable is:

- ***Randomise whenever possible:*** Select subjects at random; assign subjects to groups at random; and assign experimental treatments to groups at random.

  Once we select the sample of the study randomly, we go for identifying the subjects to be incorporated in experimental group and control group. Randomisation is one of the best approaches for dividing the sample in two groups randomly. This equalises the group in statistical sense. There is also another approach where randomisation of the groups of subjects is done. For instance, three different groups were included in an experiment to study the effect of three different methods of teaching, viz. 'A', 'B' and 'C'. Ranomisation of the different groups is done to assign each method of teaching to each group of subjects, i.e. Group A, B, and C.

- ***Analysis of co-variance***: Analysis of Co-variance (ANCOVA) is a statistical technique that helps us to control the effect of covariates on dependent variables. On the basis of result of ANCOVA, whatever changes witnessed in the dependent variables are attributed to the experimental variables. Through this technique, the measures of extraneous variables are incorporated for analysis so that the initial differences on several variables between experimental group and control group are eliminated.

(3) Generalisation of findings: The third criterion of research design is concerned with generalisability of results of the experiment. Often we raise questions: to what extent can the results of the study be generalised? or To whom and what can we generalise the results of the study? Such questions are associated with whether the research situation truly represents the conditions for valid generalisations. For example, the sample chosen must truly represent the population. For example, a number of studies are conducted with the help of experimental designs with a view to study effectiveness of specific teaching-learning strategies on student's achievements. The limitations of such kind of studies are observed in the context of experiments conducted on specific group of learners chosen from selected institutions, viz. mostly from urban based English medium schools only. The findings of such studies have limited scope for generalisation even though the design of experiment may be sound from technical point of views. Hence, the researcher must take care of representativeness of sample situations so that generalisation can be made on wider population.

Q17. What are the various steps in experimental research?

Ans. Experimental research provides a logical and systematic method in which the researcher manipulates certain variables, and observes how the condition or behaviour of subjects is affected or changed. The steps generally used by the researcher in such studies are described as under:

(1) Surveying the Literature Relating to the Problem: For a worthwhile research based on experimentation, the researcher like in any other type of research needs to acquire upto date information relating to his problem.

(2) Selecting and Defining the Problem: Experimental research starts with the selection of the problem, which is amenable to experimentation. It needs a rigorous logical analysis and definition of the problem in precise terms. The variables to be studied should be defined in operational terms clearly and unambiguously. It helps the researcher to convert the problem precisely into a hypothesis that can be verified or refuted by the experimental data.

(3) Stating of Hypotheses: The stating of problem hypotheses is one of the distinguishing characteristics of experimental method. Hypotheses are the heart of experimental research, which suggest that an antecedent condition or phenomenon (Independent variable) is related to the occurrence of another condition, phenomenon, event, or effect (dependent variable). To test a hypothesis, the researcher attempts to control all the conditions except the independent variable, which he manipulates. Then he observes the effect on the dependent variable presumably because of the exposure to the independent variable. The researcher, therefore should not only be concerned primarily with experimental plans and statistical procedures, but should give sufficient attention to the formulation of hypotheses. The experimental plans and statistical procedures merely help him in the testing of hypotheses and contribute little in the development of theories or advancement of knowledge. The hypotheses developed or derived from existing theories, however, contribute to the development of new theories and knowledge.

(4) Constructing the Experimental Plan: Experimental plan refers of the conceptual framework within which the experiment is conducted. According to Van Dalen (1973, p. 260) it represents all elements, conditions or phenomena, and relations of consequences so as to:

- (i) identify all non-experimental variables that might contaminate the experiment and determine how to control them;
- (ii) select a research design;
- (iii) select a sample of subjects to represent a given population, assign subjects to groups, and assign experimental treatments to groups;
- (iv) select or construct and validate instruments to measure the outcomes of the experiment;

(v) outline procedures for collecting data and possibly conduct a pilot or 'trial run' and test to perfect, the instruments or design; and

(vi) state the statistical or null hypothesis.

In order to select a suitable research design for conducting the experiment and assign to different experimental treatments to measure the outcomes of experiment, the researcher must be well acquainted with the different types of experimental designs.

Q18. What are different types of experimental research design?

Or

Differentiate between the true experimental design and quasi-experimental design. Illustrate your answer with examples.

[June-2013, Q.No-3(b)]

Ans. Keeping in view the research questions, nature of variables, the context of the study, resources available and scope of the study we go for different kinds of experimental design, such as:

(1) True Experimental design: True experimental designs are mostly used for experimental research in education because they seek to control the main effects of history, maturation, testing, measuring instruments, statistical regression, differential selection, and mortality.

The true experimental designs can be classified into five types:

(i) **Two groups, Randomised Subjects, Post-test only Design:** This design is one of the simplest and powerful experimental designs. The available subjects are assigned to two groups through randomisation, which controls for all possible relevant extraneous variables. No pre-test is used and the random assignment of subjects assures that any initial differences between the groups are attributable only to chance. The two random samples from designed population are obtained in two ways; (1) the subjects may be drawn individually at random and assigned alternatively to the groups; or (2) two different random samples may be selected first and the groups are assigned randomly to the experimental or control condition by the flip of a coin. Only the experimental group is exposed to the experimental treatment. At the end of the experiment, subject of both the groups are measured on the dependent variable T_2. The means of the two groups are compared with the help of appropriate statistical test of significance.

For example, suppose an experimenter wants to ascertain whether a new teaching method will increase reading speed to third grade students. He prepares a list of all the elementary schools of a particular city and assign numbers to all the third grade students. With the help of random number table he may draw a desired sample of 100 students. Then two random samples of 50 subjects each may be selected from the selected sample in two ways: the researcher may select subject individually at random and assign them alternately to the groups, or he may first draw two random samples and then assign groups to the experimental or control condition by tossing a coin.

After assigning the subjects to two groups, the experimental group is taught through the new method and the control group through the conventional method, for a period of time. In all other respects, the researcher will treat the groups alike. After the desired period of time, the subjects of both the groups are compared to determine the effectiveness of new teaching method by using an appropriate statistical test. If the obtained means of the groups are significantly different, the experimenter can be reasonably confident that the use of new teaching method was responsible for the observed difference.

Table 5.2: Paradigm for the Design: Two Groups, Randomness Subjects, Post-Test only Design

Randomly assigned group	**Independent Variable**	**Post-Test**
Experimental	Teaching through new method	T_2
Control	Teaching through conventional method	T_2

(ii) Two Groups, Randomised Matched Subjects, Post-Test Only Design: This design instead of using random assignment of subjects to experimental and control groups, uses a technique of matching. The variables selected for matching must have a significant correlation with the dependent variable and can be measured conveniently. The pre-test scores on the dependent variable or the criterion, if available, can be used very effectively for the matching procedure. The subjects from the desired population are paired so that their scores on the matching variable are as close together as possible. One subject of each pair is randomly assigned to one group and the other to the second group. A coin is tossed to designate the groups as experimental and control groups. The experimental groups is given experimental treatment. After the treatment is over, subjects of both the groups are measured on the dependent variable T_2. The significance of the difference between the two means is ascertained with the help of appropriate statistical technique.

For example, suppose an experimenter is interested in studying the effect of interim tests on the achievement of seventh grade students in general science. He randomly selects 100 students, from the population of seventh grade students studying in the high schools of some city. Intelligence and previous knowledge of general science will be the relevant matching variables that have a significant correlation with the achievement in general science (dependent variable). The experimenter will select the pairs of students from the desired population in such a way that the scores on pre-test (achievement in general science) and intelligence test of the students of each pair are as close together as possible. Then one student of each pair is randomly assigned to a group which will receive instruction with interim tests (i.e. the group which will be administered interim tests at the end of each unit of the selected content in general science) and the other to the second group which will receive instruction without interim tests. At the end of the experiment, students of both the groups will be administered an achievement test on the selected content in general science. The means of the achievement scores for both the groups will be computed to test the significance of the observed difference between them. If the difference comes out to be significant, the experimenter will conclude with confidence that the observed difference in performance is due to the effect of interim tests administered during the classroom instruction.

Table 5.3. Paradigm for the Design: Two Groups, Randomised Matched Subjects, Post-test only Design

Randomly assigned group after matching	Independent Variable	Post-Test
Experimental	Instruction with interim tests	T_2
Control	Instruction without interim tests	T_2

(iii) **Randomised Groups, Pre-test-Post-test Design:** This design is also called as 'Randomised control-group Pre-test-Post-test Design'. In this design, subjects are assigned to the experimental and control groups by random procedures and administered a pre-test T_1 as a measure of the dependent variable *Y*. The experimenter introduces the treatment only to the experimental group for a specified period of time. At the end of the experiment, the experimental and control groups are administered the post-test T_2 as the measure of dependent variable. The difference between means of T_1 and T_2 is found and the difference is tested for significance with the help of an appropriate statistical test in order to ascertain whether the experimental treatment produced a significant effect than the control condition.

For example, suppose an experimenter wants to study the effectiveness of 'Structural Approach' in teaching English on sixth grade students. First he will select subjects from as population of sixth grade students by random methods and then randomly assigns subjects to experimental and control groups. A pre-test measuring dependent variable (performance on an achievement test) will be administered on the group to obtain T_1E scores for the subjects of the experimental group and T_1C scores for the control group subjects. Keeping all the conditions same for the two groups, experimental group will be taught through the structural approach and the control group by conventional method for a stipulated period of time. At the end of the instruction, the experimenter will test the subjects of the groups on the dependent variable to obtain T_1E scores for the experimental group subjects and the T_1C scores for the control group subjects. The difference between the T_1 and T_2 scores for each subject and the mean of these differences for each group, D_E and D_C, will be determined. To ascertain whether the performance in English of the experimental group is sufficiently greater as a result of teaching through structural approach, appropriate statistical test will be applied to test the significance of the difference $(D_E - D_C)$.

Table 5.4: Paradigm for the Design: Randomised Groups, Pre-test Post-test Design

Randomly assigned	Pre-Test	Independent Variable	Post-Test
Experimental group	T_1E	Teaching through structural approach	T_2E
Control group	T_1C	Teaching through conventional method	T_2C

D_E - mean of the difference between experimental subject's pre-test and post-test scores.

D_C - mean of the difference between the control subject's pre-test and post-test scores.

Compare D_E and D_C to ascertain effect of teaching through structural method.

(iv) The Randomised Solomon Three-Group Design

The Randomised Solomon Three-Group Design has been suggested by Solomon. It uses three groups with random assignment of subjects to groups.

This design, in addition to the experimental and control groups of above design employs a second group. The second control group is not pre-tested but is exposed to experimental treatment. It helps the experimenter to overcome the weakness inherent in Pre-test, Post-test Design, i.e. the interactive effect of the pre-testing and the experimental manipulation.

For example, we consider the example again that was used in pre test-post test design. Instead of two groups, the experimenter will frame three groups by randomly assigning subjects to groups from the population of sixth grade students. He will treat one group as the experimental group (E) and the other two as the control groups. The pre-test T_1 will be administered to the experimental group and one of the control groups (C_1) to obtain measures T_{E_1} and TC_1 respectively. The second control (C_2) will not be administered any pre-test.

The experimental group (E) and the second control group (C_2) will be taught through structural approach. The first control group will be taught through conventional method for the stipulated period of time. At the end of the instruction, the subjects of the three groups will be tested on the dependent variable to obtain T_2E scores for the experimental group, and T_2C_1 and T_2C_2 scores for the control group.

To assess the effectiveness of teaching English through structural approach, a comparison of mean scores of $T_2(T_2E, T_2C_1 \text{ and } T_2C_2)$ will be made by using appropriate statistical test. Moreover, this comparison will also help the experimenter to assess interaction effect of pre-testing and experimental treatment (teaching experimental group through structural approach). For example, even though the experimental group has a significantly higher mean on post-test (T_2E) than the first control group (T_2C_1), the experimenter cannot be confident that this difference is due to its teaching through structural approach. However, if the post-test mean of the second control (T_2C_2)is also significantly higher than that of the first control group (T_2C_1), then the experimenter can assume that teaching experimental group through structural approach has produced the difference rather than the interaction due to post-test and experimental treatment, because second control group (C_2) was not administered any pre-test.

Table 5.5: Paradigm for the Design: The Randomised Solomon Three-Group Design

Randomly assigned	Pre-Test	Independent Variable	Post-Test
Experimental group (E)	T_1E	Teaching through structural approach	T_2E
Control group (C_1)	T_1C_1	Teaching through conventional approach	T_2C_1
Control group (C_2)	No pre-test	Teaching through structural approach	T_2C_2

(v) The Randomised Solomon Four-Group Design

In this design, the subjects are assigned at random to the four groups. The experimental group and one of the control groups are administered a pre-test. The other two control groups are not pretested. The design enables the experimenter to control and measure both the main and interaction effect of testing. Moreover, the main effects of a composite of maturation and history are controlled in this design.

For example, in the example considered in pre-test post test, the experimenter will frame four groups instead of two groups. He will designate one group as the experimental group (*E*) and the other three as control groups. The pre-test T_1 will be administered to the experimental group and one of the control groups to obtain the measures T_1E_1 and T_1C_1 respectively. The other two control groups will not be pre-tested.

The experimental group (E) and the second control group will be taught through structural approach. The first and the third control group get instruction through conventional method for a stipulated period of time. At the end of instruction, the subjects of the three groups will be measured on the dependent variable to obtain T_2E scores for the experimental group and T_2C_1, T_2C_2 and T_2C_3 scores for the control groups.

The effectiveness of teaching through structural approach will be ascertained by the comparison of mean scores of T_2, i.e. T_2E, T_2C_1, T_2C_2 and T_2C_3. For this appropriate statistical test will be used by the experimenter.

The experimenter can make several comparison to determine the effect of teaching through structural approach. For example, if the post-test mean (T_2E) of the experimental group (E) is significantly greater than the post-test mean (T_2C_1) of the first control group (C_1), and if the post-test mean (T_2C_2) of the second control group is significantly greater than that of the post-test mean (T_2C_3) of the third control group, the experimenter can conclude that the instruction through structural approach is more effective than the conventional teaching. Moreover, the influence of the instruction through structural approach on a pre-tested group can be determined by comparing the post-test measures T_2E and T_2C_1 of the experimental and first control group respectively or pre-post test changes o these two (E and C_1) groups. The effect of the experimental conditions (instruction through structural approach) on an un-pre-tested group can also be determined by comparing the second and third control groups (C_2 and C_3). If the experimenter finds that the average differences between post-test scores $T_2E - T_2C_1$ and $T_2C_2 - T_2C_3$ are about the same, then he may infer that the experiment has a comparable effect on pre-tested and on un-per-tested groups.

Table 5.6: Paradigm for Design: The Randomised Solomon Four-Group Design

Randomly assigned	Pre-Test	Independent Variable	Post-Test
Experimental group (E)	T_1E	Teaching through structural approach	T_2E
Control group (C_1)	T_1C_1	Teaching through conventional approach	T_2C_1
Control group (C_2)	No pre-test	Teaching through structural approach	T_2C_2
Control group (C_3)	No pre-test	Teaching through conventional approach	T_3C_3

(2) Quasi-experimental Designs: The true experimental designs provide full experimental control through the use of randomisation procedures. There are many experimental situations in which it is not possible for the experimenter to assign subjects randomly to groups or exercise full control over the scheduling of experimental conditions. In such situations, he uses quasi-experimental designs, that provide as much control as possible under the existing conditions. If an experiment use a quasi-experimental design, it is necessary for him to know which of the variables his design may fail to control. He must also be aware of the sources that present threats to both internal validity and external validity and consider them while interpreting the results of the experiment.

Some of the important quasi-experimental designs are designs are discussed as under:

(i) **Non-randomised Control Group, Pre-test-post-test Design:** In a school situation, it is sometimes practically not possible to upset class schedules, to gather subjects for obtaining a sufficiently large sample or to reorganise classes in order to employ randomisation procedures for getting equivalent control and experimental groups. Under these circumstances, therefore, an experimenter may use pre-assembled groups, such as intact classes, for framing experimental and control groups. The pre-assembled groups are selected and are administered pretest. The protest scores are analysed to show that the means and standard deviations of the two groups do not differ significantly. If the pretest scores for the groups are not equivalent, the experimenter may proceed with the conduct of the experiment by using the technique of analysis of co-variance to compensate for this lack of equivalency between the groups. Once the two groups are obtained, it is advisable to use a random procedure to determine which group is to be assigned to experimental treatment and which one to the controlled condition. After determining the groups, the experimental treatment is administered to the experimental group and then the post-test is given to both the groups. The difference between the pre-and posttest scores are compared with the help of appropriate statistical test to ascertain the effect of the independent variable (X).

Table 5.7. Paradigm for Design: Non-randomised Control-group, Pre-test-Post-test Design

Group	Pre-Test	Independent Variable	Post-Test
Experimental	T_1	Experimental treatment	T_2
Control	T_1	Controlled condition	T_2

(ii) Counter balanced Design: When the random assignment of subjects to experimental and control groups is not possible, the counterbalanced design may be used. This design is also known as rotation-group design, crossover design or switchover design.

In a counter balanced design, each group of subjects is exposed to each experimental treatment (X) at different times during the experiment. During the first exposure to the experimental treatment, for example, if group 1 is exposed to treatment X_1, and group 2 to X_2, the second time group 1 is exposed to X_2 and group 2 to X_1. The sums of the scores $(X_1 + X_1)$ and $(X_2 + X_2)$ of the two groups are compared with the help of an appropriate statistical test to ascertain the effect of the experimental treatment. The significant difference between the sums $(X_1 + X_1)$ and $(X_2 + X_2)$ cannot be interpreted as the product of the initial difference between the two groups, for each group affects each X exactly once; nor can the difference be interpreted as the product of the difference between order of testing, for each time to testing affects each X exactly once.

For example, suppose a classroom teacher wants to compare the effectiveness of Method *A* and Method *B* on achievement in social studies of sixth grade students. The teacher could choose two of his classes (group 1 and 2) and two units (unit 1 and unit 2) of social studies equivalent in the complexity and difficulty of the concepts involved. During first replication of experiment, group 1 is taught unit 1 by Method *A* and group 2 is taught the same unit by Method *B*. At the end of instruction, an achievement test on unit 1 is taught unit 2 by Method *B*, group 2 is taught the same unit by Method *A*. An achievement test on unit 2 is administered to both the groups at the end of the instruction.

Table 5.8: Paradigm for the Design: The Counter Balanced Design

Replication	Method A	Method B
Unit 1	Group 1	Group 1
Unit 2	Group 2	Group 2
	Column mean	Column mean

At the end of the experiment, the column means are computed to get the mean achievement for the two groups when taught by the method show by the column heading. The column mean scores are compared to ascertain the effectiveness of the methods upon achievement in social studies.

Q19. Write short notes on the following:

(a) Time series Design

Ans. Unlike true experimental design where experimental and control groups are included in the study, time series design takes into account one group for periodic observations. The observation is applied to a unit consisting of one or more than one subjects. An experimental variable (X) is introduced and its effect is observed by the change or gain in the measurement done at the end of the treatment (X). The following graph indicates the study of experimental input X in course of eight observations spreading over a period of time.

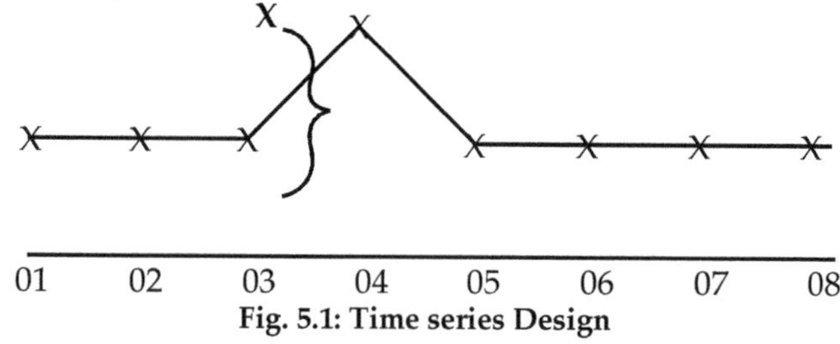

Fig. 5.1: Time series Design

For example, the researcher taught different units of a subject to the students of a particular class and kept on administering unit tests at the end of every unit. He taught students every unit using traditional method except the fourth unit which was taught with the help of computer assisted activities, i.e. experimental treatment X. The differences in the 03 – 04 and 04 – 05 indicate the effect of X. Graphical presentations and qualitative analysis of data are most suitable techniques used for such kind of studies. The researcher must take care of the effects of 'History' and 'Hawthorne effect'. Environmental changes, learner's motivation to use a new method of teaching, teacher's inspiration to use the method, which is different from the usual classroom routine may intervene with the experimental effect.

(b) Validity of Research Design

Ans. Campbell and Stanley (1963) have suggested that there are two general types of validity:

(1) Internal validity: One of the major objectives of the researcher in experimentation is to determine whether the variables that have been identified actually have a systematic effect on the dependent variable and whether the observed results were not affected by the extraneous or situational variables. The extent to which this aim is attained is a measure of internal validity of experiment. This validity is basically a problem of control. The extraneous variables that affect the control of a design contribute to its internal validity.

(2) External validity: The second important objective of the researcher is to determine whether the systematic relationships that have been identified, isolated and measured can be generalised outside the experimental setting. The extent to which this objective is attained is a measure of the external validity of the experiment. This validity is concerned with the generalisability or representativeness of the experimental findings, that is, to what subject populations, settings, experimental, variables and measurement variables can the results of the experiment be generalised.

Q20. Clarify the meaning of ex-post facto research. What are its basic features?

Or

Discuss the concept of ex-post facto research.

Ans. In ex-post facto, study is defined by Kerlinger (1947) as a "systematic empirical inquiry in which the scientist does not have direct control of independent variables because their manifestations have already occurred or because they are inherently not manipulable. Inference about relations among variables are made, without direct intervention, from concomitant variation of independent and dependent variables."

The above definition highlights two major characteristics of ex-post facto research:

One, that the researcher studies the causal relationship between independent and dependent variables without having direct control of independent variable by manipulation or by randomisation, and *two,* that the researcher takes the situation as it is. The causal relationship between two variables is exposed through application of suitable statistical design on given data.

For example, the researcher is interested to know whether normalcy in physical development has its effect on creativity or not. To answer this question, he measures the creativity of a sample of normal's and another sample of differently able or physically challenged children of a particular age group and tests the significance of the difference between the means of two groups. The significant difference between the means of creativity scores of normal children and that of differently abled children shall indicate the casual relationship between normalcy in physical development and creativity. Of course, there may be many other variables that might have produced difference between the creativity scores of the two groups of children. Such questions lead towards adoption of suitable ex-post facto design rather than adopting simple two variable studies. To statistically control, the intervening variable, analysis of variance can be computed with the help of factorial design.

Basic features of ex-post facto studies

We shall examine basic features of ex-post facto studies in the context of problems of study hypothesis, population and sampling, and analysis of data.

Problems of investigation

In ex-post studies the researcher's focus remains on exploring casual relationship between independent and dependent variables in the context of educational setting. Many complex events occur in educational situations. The researcher may be interested to know the factors affecting such events. Different plausible explanations may be available on the basis of our experiences or study of literature. For instance, the phenomenon of school dropouts may be associated with a number of casual factors like parental education, social status, economic position, location of school, and motivation of learners. In order to understand the complex nature of school dropouts we cannot force students to be dropouts and conduct experiment on them to explain the relationship between causes leading to dropout phenomena. Instead, we would like to study probable causes of dropouts in real situation without making any control and make efforts to study the empirical causal relationship between different independent variables and the dependent variables. Hence, the problem is tackled through ex-post facto research. In other words, when we intend to explain a phenomenon that has already occurred, we cannot adopt a design of having controlled observation of plausible causes. Rather, we adopt ex-post facto design to study causal relationship on the basis of available data which are gathered in non-controlled situations.

Hypothesis

Hypothesis in ex-post facto studies have sound rationale. Such rationale may be derived through theoretical analysis or through study of contributions of related studies in the field. Mostly the researcher is interested to study causal relationship between variable without having physical control over the situations. In such cases, the researcher takes into account probable causes of events and tries effects through statistical control. Moreover, the background variables like sex, age, locality, nature of school management, teaching experience and previous achievement are considered as probable factors influencing and educational event. The ex-post facto study takes care of studying the effect of a number of variables on dependent variables. The hypothesis may be stated in the form of testing the effect of such variables independently as well as testing interaction effect of two or more than two variables on dependent variable. Of course, testing of hypotheses is done through statistical control of data. This has been observed that many researchers go for stating hypotheses after data collection, i.e. looking at the nature of data and variables. However, without a theoretical support such kind of statements of hypotheses may lead towards half hazard conclusions. A good ex-post-facto research does not promote such kind of half hazardness in statement of hypotheses.

Population and sample

Unlike experimental studies which are conducted on small groups of subjects ex-post facto studies cover wide range of population. Sample size is also invariably large indicating high probability of generalisation. Cross section of population is well represented in ex-post facto studies.

Different kinds of sampling techniques like simple random sampling, stratified random sampling and multistage sampling are used for wider representation of population. Unlike true experimental studies ex-post facto studies include large size of sample with a view to give better representation of each factor under study. For instance, the ex-post facto study highlighting comparison of low economic, rural, low achiever girls academic motivation with that of high economic, rural, low achiever girls, or comparison of academic achievement of urban, government, school boys with that of rural government school boys would incorporate proper representation of population in the context of variables like locality, economic status, achievement, sex and types of schools. Representation of multifacet population of a study is well accommodated in ex-post-facto research.

Self-selection in ex-post facto research

In ex-post facto research, subjects can be chosen through random procedures. However, since there is no concept of physical control of subjects, the random assignment of subjects to control group and experimental group is not needed. Moreover, random assignment of treatment is also not required in ex-post facto research. What exists in ex-post facto research is 'self-selection' as Kerlinger (1947).

Self-selection occurs in the case of comparison of groups with regard to a particular variable. For example, in the case of study of effect of intelligence on achievement, achievement scores of more intelligent and less intelligent students are compared. Hence, the groups are divided on the basis of intelligence scores such as high intelligent and low intelligent groups. In such cases, the researcher selects subjects on the ground that high or low intelligent students possess achievement, i.e. the dependent variable, in greater or lesser degree. The high intelligent and low intelligent students are identified from amongst a large sample, which might have been drawn randomly. However, the high groups of intelligent students and low intelligent students may not be selected randomly for the study. The major criteria followed in identification of group is the assumption of existence of dependent variable of the study in the context of independent variable. The high intelligent group and less intelligent group are identified on the basis of a rationale that in greater or lesser degree of achievement exists among varied intelligence groups of students. In case the significant difference of achievement scores among these groups is detected, such difference shall be attributed to the independent variable, i.e. intelligence in this case. However, there may be other intervening variable also which might affect the achievement scores. These variables are taken care of by adopting the effect appropriate statistical design.

Statistical design

Ex-post-facto studies may incorporate parametric and non-parametric statistical designs, which may reveal casual relationships of different variables. Depending on the nature of hypotheses appropriate statistical designs are adopted in the study. Multivariate statistical designs are also adopted to study casual relationships of variables and their predictive values through application of statistical controls in the study. Factorial designs of different orders are well accommodated in ex-post-facto research like 2×2×2; 2×3×2 etc.

Q21. What are the steps included in ex-post research?

Ans. The ex-post facto research like the experimental research follows a systematic procedure as is followed in the case of any scientific study. The steps followed in ex-post facto research are the same as are followed in conducting an experimental study. These steps are discussed as under:

(1) Selection of problem: The researcher must identify the problem for investigation after a rigorous exercise. The problem may be identified keeping in view the criteria like originality, newness, critically, and utility of the study. Through study of literature helps the researcher in identification of problem. The researcher must identify the variables under investigation with the support of a sound theoretical framework. The researcher must justify what is the relevance of studying causal relationship between different variables and how does it contribute towards refinement of knowledge and improvement in teaching learning system.

(2) Formulating hypotheses: This step is crucial in ex-post facto research. The researcher must identify independent and dependent variables. Unlike experimental study where relationship between the experimental variables(s) and criterion variables(s) is studied under controlled conditions the ex-post-facto study seeks to study the causal relationship between the numbers of independent variables on a dependent variables in non-controlled situations. The hypotheses must be stated in such a form that they can be tested with the help of suitable designs and statistical techniques. In many cases, the researchers state hypotheses looking at the nature of data variable wise after data collection. Such approach of hypotheses statement may lead to meaningless findings and interpretations for knowledge generation. Such practice needs to be discouraged with a view to make the study scientific. The hypotheses must be stated or formulated before we start collecting data; these need be formulated on the basis of theoretical nature of the relationships to be discovered.

(3) Population and sample of the study: The population of the study must be defined. The sample should be chosen in such a way that all the variables under study can be studied on a sizable number of subjects. For example, a study intending to incorporate different variables the sex, SES, locality, management of school, achievement and intelligence as independent variables must include sample in such a way that every cell of independent variables must have appropriate size of subjects. The number of students in high SES boys from rural private schools group and the number of students in low SES boys from rural private schools must be adequate. Similarly the sample size of high intelligent urban government school girls and low intelligent urban government schools girls must be adequate for comparison purposes. In other words, the cell, values concerning each variable under study must have appropriate number of subjects so that generalisation can be made in that context.

(4) Tools: As in the case of other forms of research, the researcher must develop or use suitable tools for data collection purpose. The readymade standardised tools may also serve the purpose. The criteria of development/adoption of suitable tools must be followed keeping in view their relevance, validity, reliability, and usability in the context of population and variables being studied.

(5) Data collection: Data collection procedures must be planned and designed well in advance so that in specified timeframe data can be gathered from different sources. Since large scale multivariate studies require administration of a number of tools and procurement of data from different sources the timeframe and procedures of data collection must be systematic. Sometimes, the trained field workers are engaged in data collection of large scale ex-post facto studies. The researcher must take care of procuring valid data by employing field workers.

(6) Analysis and interpretation of data: Suitable statistical techniques need to be applied for testing of hypotheses. Different kinds of parametric and non-parametric statistical technique can be applied keeping in view the nature of variables. Usually factorial designs and chi square tests are used to analyse the data with suitable statistical control of independent variable(s). Data need to be statistically processed and results so obtained need to be interpreted in terms of level of confidence for testing of hypotheses. Suitable implications of findings must be derived after analysis of data and interpretation of results.

Q22. Illustrate the nature of ex-post facto studies in education.

Ans. Ex-post facto studies in education are of the following nature:

- A study of teaching success in relation to institutional climate and teaching aptitude of B.Ed. trainees.
- A study of creative thinking, achievement motivation and risk taking behaviour of hearing impaired students in relation to their hearing peers.

- Identification of factors inhibiting introduction of adolescence education in secondary schools.
- Impact of socio-economic diversification on level of aspiration, value pattern, and academic achievement of senior secondary school students.
- Environmental awareness, attitude and interest of the prospective teachers in elementary teacher training institutes.
- A study of normal maturity of elementary school children in relation to parental attitude, school climate and method of teaching.

Detailed presentations of a few small scale and large-scale studies will help you to understand the nature of ex-post facto studies in education.

Small scale ex-post facto study

Effectiveness of zero lecture strategy in teacher training in terms of achievement with teaching aptitude as background variable

In this study, the researcher used the following ex-post facto design.

Table 5.9: Small Scale Ex-Post Facto design

	Achievement scores of	
	Zero lecture group	Traditional method group
High teaching aptitude trainees		
Lower teaching aptitude trainees		

The researcher administered Teaching Aptitude Test and Achievement test to the teacher trainees enrolled in Zero Lecture Group and Traditional Method Group of a teacher education institution.

The researcher aimed at comparing the achievement (criterion variable) levels of different method groups (Independent Variable) so that significant difference observed, if any, shall be attributed to methods of training.

In case the zero lecture group trainees score higher than that of traditional method group on achievement test, it will indicates effectiveness of zero lecture strategy. Teaching aptitude of students was taken as background (independent) variable. It was presumed that the comparison of achievement scores of high teaching aptitude groups and low teaching aptitude groups shall also indicate the effect of teaching aptitude on achievement of trainees exposed to zero lecture group as well as traditional method group. In this study, even though experimental treatment was not given by the researcher, the analogy of experimental treatment existed since the teacher training institution had already introduced the treatment with variation in methods of training. Hence, the independent variable, i.e. methods of training was already manipulated by the institution prior to the study. However, the researcher did not have direct control over the independent variable as he could have done it in case of true experiment.

In the case of background variables, study the researcher bifurcated the groups on the basis of high teaching aptitude and low teaching aptitude. The researcher tested the significant difference of mean achievement scores of high aptitude groups and low aptitude groups with a view to explore the effect of aptitude on achievement.

You will come across a number of studies of ex-post facto type which aim at exploring causal relationships of independent and dependent variable. However, doubts are very often raised about the validity of such results since the differences witnessed in criterion variable/dependent variable might not be attributed to the effect of the independent variable under study and that too in small sample study.

Examples of large-scale ex-post facto research

In a study, the problem was to study impact of socio-economic diversities on level of aspiration, value pattern, and academic achievement of senior secondary school students.

Socio-economic diversities included as many as eight variables, viz. sex, residential areas, family type, parental education background, parental occupation, social categories (caste background), type of school, and streams of education. The researcher intended to study the impact of each of these variables on three dependent variables, viz. aspiration, value pattern and academic achievement of senior secondary school students, respectively.

Moreover, the researcher also aimed at studying the interaction effect of following independent variables on dependent variables, such as:

- Interaction effect of residential area x sex on aspiration, values and achievement.
- Interaction effect of family x sex on aspiration, values and achievement.

- Interaction effect of parental education x sex on aspiration, values and achievement.
- Interaction effect of parental occupation x sex on aspiration, values and achievement.
- Interaction effect of caste background x sex on aspiration, values and achievement.
- Interaction effect of type of schools x sex on aspiration, values and achievement.
- Interaction effect of steams of education x sex on aspiration, values and achievement.

Data were gathered from a sample of 1010 (one thousand ten) +2 level students covering 34 schools of a state using random sampling technique. It was ensured that there must be sizable number of subjects in each cell of independent variables. For instance, under caste background every cell, viz. general caste, OBC, SC and ST had sizable number of representation. For tools were used for collecting, background information, aspiration, Value patterns and achievement in secondary board examinations. The main effects of independent variables on dependent variables were studied with the help of one way ANOVA and 't' tests. Moreover, 2 × 2 and 2 × 3 factorial designs were used for study of interaction effect of independent variables. The factorial design indicating interaction effect of education of parents and sex were studied using the following format:

Table 5.10: Factorial design

	Achievement	
Sex	Boys	Girls
Education of parents	-	-
Primary	-	-
Secondary	-	-
Higher	-	-

In all, as many as 57 hypotheses were formulated and tested to explain main effect and interactions effect of various components of socio-economic diversities on level of aspiration; 57 hypotheses were tested to explain main effect and interaction effect of different components of socio-economic diversities on value pattern; and 57 hypotheses were tested to explain main effect and interaction effect of different components of socio-economic diversities on academic achievement of students.

The advantages of such kind of multivariate large scale studies can be identified with generalisability of findings of ex-post facto studies.

In another case, the problem was to study the effect of institutional climate and teaching aptitude on teaching success of student teachers at B.Ed. level in the context of their background.

The institutional climate included two major variables: institutional status and institutional environment. Institutional status, institutional environment and teaching aptitude were considered as the independent variables. In addition to these variables different background variables like sex, family size, type of residence, medium of instruction and socio-economic status of trainees were also included in the list of independent variables. Student teachers teaching success was treated as dependent variable.

The researcher aimed at studying main effect as well as interaction effect of independent variables on the dependent variable.

Data were collected from 600 B. Ed. Trainees representing 15 colleges affiliated to a university, by administering different tools like Teaching Success Scale, Teaching Aptitude Test, Institutional Environment Scale, Institutional Status Questionnaire and Socio-Economic Status Scale.

The hypotheses concerning main effect and interaction effect of independent variables on teaching success of student teachers were tested with the help of 't' tests and ANOVA employing 2 × 2 and 2 × 3 factorial designs.

The major findings of the study indicated that there were significant effect of institutional environment, institutional status, teaching aptitude and socio-economic status of student teachers on their teaching success where as different background variables like sex, type of family, locality and medium of instruction did not have significant effect on teaching success. There was significant effect of interaction of institutional environment with background variables like sex, locality and medium of instruction on teaching success.

Q23. Explain the significance of action research in education.

Or

Discuss the nature and background of action research in education.

Ans. Action research is a type of research that has been used in many disciplines, including education. Action research, as its name implies, within education is a type of research that aims to enact immediate changes in an educational setting. It has the potential to produce change quickly because the research is carried out by educators in their own work settings. Action research borrows techniques and ideas from all other types of research but differs from the purely quantitative or qualitative approaches in that its orientation combines professional practice, research, and reflection on one's own educational practices (Arhar, Holly, and Kasten, 2001). This means that it simultaneously serves to enhance the professional skills of educators, advance our knowledge, and improve educational processes and outcomes. Educators involved in action research develop both personal knowledge and sensitivity about their practices and contribute to the professional knowledge of their field. Reason and Bradbury (2008) have described action research as a living inquiry that links practice and ideas and creates collaborative learning communities to facilitate ongoing renewal of education. Through action research, practicing educators study themselves and their learning communities as they try to change and improve educational processes and outcomes. Both quantitative and qualitative applied researches aim to improve practice through the knowledge generated by first conducting studies and then reporting their results in journals or at conferences. However, action researchers aim to transform their educational practices as they study them. One metaphor used to describe action research is that educators are making the road while walking it (Reason and Bradbury, 2008, p. 16). Yolanda illustrates this as she studies her own teaching and her students learning at the same time as she is trying to improve it.

Background of action research in education

Promoting democratic principles of management of education

Democratic principle of management ensures participation of stakeholders in decision-making and execution of the system. In school system the teachers, principals, other management personnel like supervisors play a major role in execution of educational programmes and activities. Action research is used as a tool in the hands of such personnel in making improvements in educational practices at grass root level and making it a regular feature for development of school system. Action research provides opportunities for leadership to teachers in analysing critical problems in school set up, identifying measures to overcome them, interventions to solve problems and learning from such experiences to bring improvements in school system. Hence, the gap between knowledge and practices vanish in real situations.

Opportunities for development of scientific thinking among practitioners

The modern age insists on encountering with complex problems scientifically. In other words, we must develop abilities to analyse the problems systematically, try to find out solutions with proper theoretical bases and factual experiences and verify our experiences in real situations so that it contributes towards refinement of ideas and solution of problems scientifically. The teachers and other functionaries of school system need to develop such abilities so that it forms a sound base for development of own environment where they work.

Gap between researches in education and educational practices

It has been noticed that researches conducted at Doctoral degree or Masters level may lead towards generalisation oriented studies. The findings of such studies may be relevant to school system. However, they have not be tried out for bringing expected changes in educational practices. There exists communication gap between researchers, policy makers, administrators and teachers. As a result, contributors of research towards educational development get negligible attention. On the other hand, action research provides opportunities to the practicing teachers and functionaries of school system to link research with development practices of school system.

Motivation of practitioners in problem solution

Psychologically it has been proved that self-initiative and self-participation in dealing with problematic situations can bring fruitful results. Readymade solutions to problems directed from one end to the other does not encourage practitioners to adopt them efficiently. Suggestions or recommendations of commissions or committees on education remain as ideals forever. They are least implemented. Moreover, suggestions resulting from theoretical and large scale applied researches appear to be very much formal in nature. They are not context specific. As an alternative approach of development oriented research, action research provides a platform for teachers and functionaries to get involved in research activities while dealing with school level problems directly.

While justifying the relevance of action research, Corey (1953) had highlighted that, "Our schools cannot keep up with the life they are supposed to sustain and improve unless teachers, pupils, supervisors, administrators and school patrons continuously examine what they are doing. Singly or in groups, they must use their imagination, creativity and constructively to identify the practices that must be changed to meet the needs and demands of modern life, courageously try out those practices that give better promise and methodically and systematically gather evidence to test their worth."

Q24. What are main feature of action research?

Ans. A list of features of action research, put forward by the same authors (2008: 3), states that it:

- It is a set of practices that respond to people's desire to act creatively in the face of practical and often pressing issues in their lives in organisations and communities;
- It calls for an engagement with people in collaborative relationships, opening new 'communicative spaces' in which dialogue and development can flourish;
- It draws on many ways of knowing, both in the evidence that is generated in inquiry and its expression in diverse forms of presentation as we share our learning with wider audiences;
- It is value oriented, seeking to address issues of significance concerning the flourishing of human persons, their communities, and the wider ecology in which we participate;
- It is a living and emergent process that cannot be pre-determined but changes and develops as those engaged deepen their understanding of the issues to be addressed and develop their capacity as co-inquirers both individually and collectively.

Q25. What are differences between action research and other kinds of research in education?

Ans. Research in education is usually carried with a view to solve educational problem and derive theoretical or practical implications, which have wider scope. The case of action research is different from other kinds of research with respect to the following:

Nature of problem

In the concept of theoretical/fundamental research, a researcher is concerned with problems which have theoretical implications and which can yield explanation about the relationship between different variables leading to presentation of systematic view of the educational phenomenon. The applied research deals the problems concerning application of theories and principles in development of educational system. In the case of action research we deal with problems which require immediate solution at the local level. The problems encountered on day to day basis are subject to the inquiry of action research. Such experiences obtained from solution of such problems may contribute towards formation of new knowledge.

Goals of research

Fundamental research aims at generation of new knowledge through evolving/refining theories and principles concerning educational phenomena. It leads towards generalisation of theories and principles that can be verified as and when needed. Action research aims at application of theories and principles in varied situations of education. So as to bring about improvement in educational practices at school level. Its purpose is solely formative/developmental in nature.

Research design

A typical design aims at development of a suitable plan/strategy for testing of hypotheses and arriving at generalisation with respect to a well defined population. It adopts systematic steps for conduct of the study. The internal and external validity of the study are well reflected in its design. In action research flexible design is adopted. The initial design of action research is subject to modification keeping in view the dynamics of situations/context in which the study is conducted. There is scope for modification of hypotheses and methods employed in testing them in the course of conduct of the study. The researcher becomes vigilant about the experiences in the conduct of the study and adopts flexible strategies in dealing with the actual situations.

Nature of population and sample

Generally scientific research deals with generalisation of relationship between variables with respect to a given population. It adopts nomothetic approach where sample units are studied in the context of a well defined population. Hence, appropriate sampling techniques are adopted for ensuring representativeness of population. In the case of action research the researcher (the teacher) deals with his/her own school related problem or situation. The scope of generalisation is limited to one's own work place. The units of the study are chosen from own school. Many a time the sample and population remain same. Generalisation may be made for future course of action provided similar problems appear in future.

Generalisations formulated on the basis of research

The problem of a scientific research is judged in the context of its wider scope. In other words scientific research aims at generation of universal knowledge. As a result the universe, population and sample of the study are well defined. The hypotheses are tested with the purpose of generalisation of results to a specified population. This kind of generalisation is lateral in nature. The aim is to solve the local specific problems and as such they do not have a bigger scope for generalisation to wider population. This type of generalisation is called vertical generalisation findings.

Uses of research

In the case of traditional research, findings are used for generation of new principles and theories so that existing knowledge system gets refined. Moreover, its application through researches help us in solving crucial problems in varied situations. The findings of action research however, indicate how a specific problem is solved through systematic interventions made by practitioners. Hence, action research is used for bringing about the qualitative improvement in one's own working situations directly.

Q26. Explain the steps of action research with the help of an example.

Ans. There are nine steps involved in conducting an action research study, let us consider the following example of an action research study, where each step has been briefly described. Our example begins with the department chair of a high school social studies department who, for some time, has been disappointed in the performance of students in the school's Indian history course. The course has always been taught in a traditional manner—with the content coverage beginning prior to the Indian Revolution and ending with events more recent. The department chair, who teaches multiple sections of the course along with another teacher, believes that there may be some merit in examining a backward" approach to teaching history (i.e. beginning with current events and proceeding back through time in order to end at the Indian Revolution). The chair asks the other history teacher for assistance with this potential action research project, and she agrees.

***Step 1:* Identifying and Limiting the Topic**

The two teachers meet on a couple of occasion over the summer in order to identify the specific topic they hope to address through the examination and trial of this alternative instructional approach. They determine that they believe that their students struggle most in making connections between seemingly unrelated historical events. The department chair argues that perhaps this backward approach (i.e. beginning with more recent historical events with which their students will be more familiar) will have a positive impact on how well they are able to make these types of connections. The teachers decide to focus their attention on any differences that the two instructional approaches have on students' abilities to make these connections.

***Step 2:* Gathering Information**

The teachers decide to talk with the other social studies teachers, as well as teachers in other subject areas, in their building. They want to know what other teachers think about their assumption that students struggle with making connections between historical events, which occurred perhaps decades apart. They ask the others for their initial perceptions about the backward approach to teaching their content. Additionally, the two teachers spend time, independently, over the course of a few days to actually consider why they believe that this is the case for the struggle their students seem to experience. In other they carefully, consider any "evidence" that may have led them to feel this way. They also strongly consider other possible solutions to this dilemma. At their next meeting together, they share what they had reflected on and decide that the backward approach continues to be worthy of investigating.

***Step* 3: Reviewing the Related Literature**

The teachers then decide to collect more formal information—that based on research, in addition to what they had already obtained anecdotally from other teachers of history about the effectiveness of backward approaches to teaching historical, chronological events; how other history teachers may have implemented this type of instruction; and any problems they may have encountered. They decide to split the tasks, with the department chair identifying and reviewing published research studies on the topic and the other teacher contacting history teachers through their professional organisations.

***Step* 4: Developing a Research Plan**

Following the review of published literature and discussions with teachers from other schools and districts that have implemented this type of instruction, the teachers found enough evidence to support the focus of their proposed study (i.e. the backward approach to instruction is effective), although they also found some contradictory evidence (i.e. this approach is less or at least no more effective). The teachers decide on the following researchable question: Is there a difference in instructional effectiveness between a backward approach and a forward approach to teaching Indian history? Furthermore, based on their review of related literature and other information, the teachers state the following predicted hypothesis: Students who are exposed to the background approach will experience higher academic achievement as evidence by their abilities to make connections between historical events, than those exposed to the more traditional forward approach.

Since their hypothesis implies a comparison study, the teachers decide to randomly split the eight sections of Indian history for the coming school year. Each teacher will teach four sections of Indian history—for each teacher, two sections will be taught using the forward approach and two sections will incorporate the backward approach. Achievement data, as well as other teacher-developed assessment data, will be collected from all students enrolled in the Indian history course for this academic year.

***Step* 5: Implementing the Plan and Collecting Data**

Throughout the school year, the two history teachers design performance-based assessments, which examine the extent to which students were able to connect historical events. In addition, students will take an Indian history achievement test in the spring, a portion of which focuses on critical thinking skills as they apply to historical events.

Step 6: Analysing the Data

Immediately following the end of the school year, data analysis is undertaken. Test scores resulting from the administration of the standardised achievement tests are statistically compared for the two groups (i.e. the backward group versus the forward group). It is that the test scores of the students who were taught using the backward instructional approach are significantly higher than those of the students taught in the more traditional manner. In other words, the original research hypothesis has been supported. In addition, scores resulting from the various administrations of classroom-based performance assessments support the results of the standardised achievement tests. Again, the research hypothesis has been supported.

Step 7: Developing an Action Plan

With their findings in hand, the teachers decide to approach their principal and district curriculum coordinator about temporarily revising the Indian history curriculum in order to capitalise on the apparent effectiveness of the backward instructional approach.

They agree that it will be imperative to continue to study the effectiveness of this approach in subsequent academic years. Similar findings in the coming years would provide a much stronger case for permanently changing the approach to teaching Indian history.

Step 8: Sharing and Communicating the Results

The principal and curriculum coordinator are quite impressed with the results of this action research study. They suggest to the department chair that the two teachers make a presentation to the school board and to the entire school faculty at a regularly scheduled meeting at the beginning of the next school year. The two teachers develop and make and effective presentation at the subsequent month's board meeting. A teacher attending the board meeting later suggests that this study might make an interesting contribution at an annual statewide conference on instructional innovations and best practices held each fall.

Step 9: Reflecting on the Process

Over the summer, the two teachers meet in order to debrief and decide on any adjustments to the process that might be beneficial for next year. They consider several questions, including: How well did the process work? Are we sure that the data we collected were the most appropriate in order to answer our research question? Were there additional types of data that could or should have been included in the data collection? Their answers to these questions will help guide next year's implementation of the backward approach to teaching Indian history.

Q27. Write a short note on the scope of action research.

Ans. Action research incorporates all the components of school system operated at grass root level. The area wise specifications are stated in the following Table 5.12:

Table 5.11: Areas of action research

Area of Action Research	Specifications
(1) Learner	Motivation of learners, learning style, attention span, concentration, Learners participation in teaching learning, process, etc. Group dynamics.
(2) Teacher	Level of competencies, Commitment, Teaching style, Motivation, Attitude towards weak students, Dealing with physically challenge learners, Social profile, Teachers communication, Value development of teachers, etc.
(3) Methods of teaching	Activity based teaching, play way approach, child-centred learning, project approach, use of media in class room teaching, positive reinforcement, etc.
(4) Curriculum	Mechanism of curriculum design, mechanism of curriculum construction, mechanism of curriculum revision, curriculum, subject upgradation, intended, transacted and hidden curriculum, teachers role in curriculum design and transaction in context specific situations.
(5) Evaluation	Criterion reference testing, diagnostic testing, formative testing, illuminative testing, achievement testing, objective type testing.
(6) School management	Institutional planning, learners and teachers participation in decision-making, leadership style, class room management, institutional evaluation, accountability of headmasters and teachers, teacher morale, human resource development.
(7) School community interaction	Parental co-operation, PTA, community participation in school activities, community development projects undertaken by school, etc.

6 RESEARCH REPORT AND DISSEMINATION

An Overview

The study conducted by anyone will be of no avail unless it is properly and systematically reported, edited and disseminated to the stakeholders. Research efforts are not of much worth unless the findings results are communicated to the concerned community in a comprehensive manner. Reporting of results makes the process of research activity complete. Research report is a detailed and comprehensive account of research activity. Writing a report involves various criteria and guidelines. The research report must must demarcate and clarify research study was conducted and with what outcomes.

For successful writing of a research report, certain general principles have to be mastered. All research reports; whether doctoral theses or dissertations, follow some standard format chosen from available ones. No research report is complete without adding the essential features of writing footnotes, endnotes and bibliography/reference. This will facilitate the reader or the evaluator of your work to trace your sources for interest or for further examination of your work.

When the draft report is completed from all aspects, the next step is editing of the report so that the document becomes free from all kinds of mistakes and becomes readable.

After completing editing work, the report is disseminated to the stakeholders. The disseminators are individuals or groups that are able to move between one system and another for making use of knowledge obtained through research. Knowledge use occurs when the knowledge obtained through research solves or resolves some problem. Based on this concept of dissemination, a few models of disseminations are extension system model, ERIC model, Regional Laboratory model, and special purpose assistance model.

Q1. What is the meaning of research Report? Give the general format of research report.

Ans. The most important part of the research process is the preparation and presentation of the research report. Research report may be presented orally and in written form depending upon the requirements of situation. Principles of fairness, truth and accuracy along with of researcher's integrity, curiosity and persistence play a big role in enhancing the quality of the research report.

Koul (1984) says, "The researcher is obligated to give a detailed account of all his experiences and thinking involved in the process of research, from identifying the problem to drawing the conclusions. Presentation of the detailed account of research experience is called a research report".

While defining research report, Mohan (2003) remarks "Research report is the presentation of research findings directed to a specific audience to accomplish a specific purpose". In the research report, emphasis is laid on research findings/results, implications and recommendations for future course of action. The research report must reflect what was actually done and how as well as what was initially planned.

General format of research report

A research report generally consists of four to six chapters. The content and the length of the chapters varies but all of the them flow from and are determined by the research theme. A research report comprises five major chapters besides the usual elements such as list of tables, summary and appendices, etc. The content of a research report generally has the following format:

Title Page
Supervisor's Certificate
Acknowledgments
List of Contents
List of Tables

Chapter-I
Introduction
Rationale
Statement of the Problem
Operational Definitions of the Terms Used
Objectives of the Study
Hypotheses
Delimitations

Chapter-II

Review of Literature

Relevant Studies Conducted in one's own country

Relevant Studies Conducted Abroad

Conclusion (based on overview of the related research literature)

Chapter-III

Design of the study

Plant and Procedure

Research Methodology

Population and Sample

Description of Tools and Techniques used

Collection of Data

Scoring Procedure

Statistical Techniques Used

Chapter-IV

Analysis of Data and Interpretation of Results

Chapter-V

Conclusions and Implications

Main Findings

Educational Implications

Suggestions for Further Research

Summary

Bibliography

Appendices

Thus, it is a complete, comprehensive and detailed account of a research study. Research report may be in the form of a thesis or dissertation.

Q2. Why is reporting of research important? Discuss.

Ans. The research report serves various purpose; some of these are discussed below:

(1) Extent of attainment of objectives of the study: A major purpose of the research report is related to the goals of research itself. Primary goals of research can be discussed in terms of its contribution of the existing body of knowledge and providing an acceptable solution to the problem. The research report can enable the researcher as well as others who read it to assess how far the objectives of the research study have been attained and what aspects various undertaken objectives have been overlooked.

(2) **Internal Consistency of the research study:** The critical study of the research report can enable a reader to assess how far the research study is internally consistent. In other words, how far are the objectives of the study relevant to the research problem? Do the hypotheses flow from the objectives and are they based on the review of the related research literature? Was the planned sample the actually used sample? Did substitution of sample unit if any change the defining characteristics of the population? Were the techniques of data analysis relevant of the nature of data and did they meet the assumptions pertaining to the use of a particular technique, e.g. ANOVA, t-test Chi-Square test etc? How far are the conclusions and generalisations based thereon free from possible errors? All of these contribute to the internal consistency of a research study.

(3) **Providing basis for future research:** A research study can yield a number of aspects on which further research may be planned and conducted. Generally, a comprehensive research report provides a list of related topics on which further research can be conducted. Those desirous of conducting research can look up this section in a research report and indentify a problem for their research. Sometime a researcher may go through a research report and decide to replicate the study.

Q3. Discuss the various considerations that you would observe while writing the research report.

Ans. As a researcher, we are required to adhere the criteria, which are helpful in making the research report. The three criteria are objectivity, conciseness and clarity. These are explained below:

Objectivity: Objectivity in the context of research report can be viewed at two levels (a) The research report should be objective in terms of its focus on the research study. It should be free from digressions and it should not include anything that is not relevant to the research study; (b) The style of the research report should be matter-of-fact and free from flowery and idiomatic expression. It should use the vocabulary of the contemporary language be it English or any other language. It should not use obsolete words and archaic phrases.

Conciseness: Conciseness implies the use of fewer words and freedom from verbosity. To use thirty words for what can be equally well expressed in just twelve or fifteen is not conciseness. Conciseness in fact means the use of scientific, i.e. factual style of writing instead of literary writing. Writing concisely requires practice and re-visiting your writing with a view to delete unnecessary words that do not add to meaning. Concise writing promotes plain, non-ornamental writing.

Clarity: Clarity implies the use of simple language for effective communication. A research report is meant for readers other than the researcher and a good research report should communicate rather than miscommunicate. To put it differently, the reader of a research report should be able to get the meaning, precisely the same meaning that the researcher wanted to convey through the research reports. One should avoid the use of long sentences and compound sentences as far as possible because they hinder comprehension. Instead, one should use simple sentences and avoid the use of passive voice as far as possible. One should also avoid the use of ambiguous expressions.

Q4. Write short notes on the following:

(a) Forms of research reporting

Ans. Research report may take various forms depending upon the requirement and the level of research. At a point of time some researchers want to read only the gist of the research work that is being carried out, while other researchers may be in search of a brief presentation of everything that has been undertaken under the research activity.

Research summary: As the name indicates, a research summary is a brief version or condensed form of research report. The important aspects of a thesis or research report are basically provided in a summary form. Since reading the whole research report is time consuming, the prime objective of writing the summary is to enable the reader to understand the research work at a glance. In order to save the time and energy of readers, important parts of a research report are highlighted in a summary form. However, a research summary is no substitute for the proper research report. Ideally, a good research summary should act as an appetiser and motivate the reader to read the proper research report.

Research abstract: A research abstract is a further condensed version of the research summary. The central theme of the research is presented in the form of an abstract. An abstract usually meets the prescribed length in terms of 200 to 500 words. (See figure 6.1)

Abstract*

Dr. B.R. Ambedkar Open University has been telecasting lessons and interactive live teleconference programmes through Doordarshan (television channels of the Government of India) and Mana TV channels since November, 1999. This paper, based on an empirical study, reports the utility of teleconference and telecasting of lessons and their impact on the learning of courses by the MBA students. This paper also identifies the limitations of the use of these media, and provides suggestions to improve the efficacy and utility of these technology-mediated strategies in the process of learning.

* *The above-cited abstract is based on the research paper titled "Role of Teleconference and Tele-lessons in the Instructional Strategy of BRAOU–A Study of Access and Utility," written by V. Venkaiah and published in the IJOL (Vol.15, Nov.1, Jan.2006), IGNOU, New Delhi.*

Fig. 6.1: An example of research abstract

(b) Scope of research report

Ans. Scope of the research report can be discussed from the viewpoint of various types of research. We will discuss educational research from two major points:

- **The intention or the prime goal of the research:** Based on the goals and purposes of research studies, educational research may be of two types–basic and applied research. Basic research (also called theoretical or fundamental research) is targeted towards the expansion, extension or validation of knowledge and is general in nature. Hence, the research report on basic research will focus more on the theoretical aspects of the problem that have been researched. On the other hand, applied research emphasises the solution of a practical problem. In the report writing process, its focus will be on the practical aspects of problem that has been studied.
- **The method of research or the way the research is conducted:** Based on the methods of research–educational research can be broadly categorised into five types, viz. experimental, ex-post facto, survey, historical and ethnographic. Scope of research reports will vary depending upon its purpose. In experimental research, researcher wants to examine the effect of experimental variable and researcher emphasise the process of conducting experiment, controlling the intervening variables in the experimental situation, comparison of results in experimental

and non-experimental situations to determine the effects of experimental variable.

In ex-post facto research, the researcher is interested in determining the relationship among the variables and their possible effects for events after they have taken place. Therefore, there is a need for the researcher to highlight the extent of relationship among variables and their effects in the research report.

In a survey study, the emphasis is laid on examining what exists through the characteristics of variables involved in a situation. This leads to a difference in the focus of the research report. In historical research, the researcher focuses on reconstruction of the past through possible/probable cause-effect relations in order to promote better understanding of the past. Thus, the scope of research report becomes much wider in comparison to reports on other types of research. The scope of a research report on ethnographic study is almost similar to that of historical studies because here too the researcher wants to determine the nature of a given phenomenon.

(c) Writing a research report

Ans. Writing a research report is a scientific task requiring a special training or experience on the part of the researcher. Its basic purpose is to inform the interested audiences of the nature of the problem investigated, the procedure followed in its execution, and the nature of findings and their implications. In this process, the researcher discharges the responsibility of communicating three kinds of information:

- The nature of the study in sufficient details in order to facilitate the replication of the study by another person;
- The nature of findings of the study in sufficient details in order to enable the reader to judge for himself what the conclusions are;
- Processing data and interpretation of results and researcher's own conclusions and recommendations for further research and action.

In addition to a thorough understanding of research process, the report writer must possess good communication skills. A good communication is one, which others can understand and if necessary, use it. The findings of research in education are useful not only for a professional or a specialist in this field but also for practitioners, especially, teachers, administrators and policy planners. All these users of research should be able to understand and interpret the contents of a research report.

Writing a research report is a complex and creative endeavour. It takes weeks and sometimes months in getting started. At times, researchers prefer to write less complex parts of the report first, and then, come to more complex chapters. Instead of beginning with the introduction, which may be conceptually complex and relatively unstructured, students begin with writing the chapter describing the procedure which is not conceptually complex (Fox, 1969), and is relatively structured. But, this is simply a way of getting started. The full report cannot be written effectively in bits and pieces, which are then pasted together. A good research report is characterised by high degree of precision and consistency, which come into being only after a lot of writing, editing and re-writing. It is not generally possible to achieve that level of precision and consistency while preparing the first draft. The investigator must recognise that what he first writes is not the final product, but only the first of several drafts. In short, the best way to get started on writing the research report is to sit down with paper and pencil and write, without much attention, in the beginning, to the fluency and eloquence of what comes through. Fluency and eloquence can be added after the first draft is ready.

Q5. Describe the general principle of writing a research report.

Ans. It would be useful for a researcher to follow a few general principles while writing a research report:

(1) Probably, the foremost rule of research report writing is that the writer must be as objective as possible in reporting the study. Being a scientific document, a research report should not contain subjective statements. The write-up should not reflect overstating or emotional reactions the statements of the kind given below should be avoided:

(i) Obviously, method A is better than method B.

(ii) Wonderful! What a fantastic result!

(iii) Every year many poor and helpless children dropout of school

Such statements reflect some kind of subjectivity and emotional involvement on the part of the author. Therefore, these should be avoided.

(2) A research report should contain an objective, and factual description of past research upon which the study is based. It should not be written in such a way as to justify or prove the researcher's position. The objective reporting demands that the use of personal pronouns, such as I, We and Us, etc., should be kept to the minimum. Instead, impersonal pronouns and the passive voice should be used. Instead of writing "I collected data from rural and urban schools", the researcher should write "the data were collected from rural and urban schools". As far as possible, impersonal pronoun, passive voice, and indirect and reported speech should be used in report writing. The entire report should be written in past tense.

(3) The contents should be presented in a clear, simple, concise and straightforward language. What is to be communicated should be stated in the fewest number of words and simplest possible language. Instead of saying, "the population comprised all the students who graduated in Commerce at the University of Delhi", it would be worthwhile to say, "the population was all Commerce graduates of Delhi University". The research report should reflect researcher's scholarship and literary competence in terms of correct spellings, grammatical construction, and punctuation. For this purpose, the researcher may use a reference book, dictionary or have a spelling and sentence construction programme on the computer. It is advisable to use the services of some expert who is competent in these areas to read the manuscript and correct errors.

(4) There is no unique style or format of writing a research report in fact, there are different style manuals suggesting different rules of writing. However, some rules are common to all formats or manuals. The use of abbreviations and contractions should be avoided. Likewise, instead of writing "MHRD", one should write 'Ministry of Human Resource Development". However, commonly accepted abbreviations such as IQ, UGC, GPA, etc. may be used as exceptions to this rule. Also, the words like 'don't', 'are'nt', 'won't', etc. should not be used in research report writing. If a group of words is used repeatedly in a given sequence to indicate a meaningful concept, it may be abbreviated in bracket at its first use, and thereafter, the abbreviation may be used repeatedly. For example, if "Distance Education Council" is written repeatedly in the report, it may be

written as "Distance Education Council (DEC)" for the first time and as "DEC" at all subsequent uses.

(5) If a sentence starts with a number, the number should be written in terms of words. For example, instead of writing "25 teachers did not return the booklets," one should write, "twenty five teachers did not return the booklets".

(6) The typing of the report should be done with the same scholarship as its writing. The preliminary drafts should be carefully proofread. If the investigator cannot type the report, an efficient typist should be hired for this purpose. The typist should be given the final and correct form of the manuscript. He is not supposed to correct or refine the language of the report. He types what he sees, not what the investigator means. In order to ensure that proper guidelines are followed in typing, the typist may be given a copy of the style manual, which the researcher decides to follow.

(7) These days the word processing software for micros has very much facilitated the preparation of research report. By using this device, the typed material can be displayed on the screen and then stored for making additions, deletions or changes at a later stage. It will be worthwhile if the word processing programme includes the feature of automatic page numbering and heading centering; the ability to rearrange words, sentences and paragraphs and spelling checkers (Gay, 1992).

Q6. Identify the types of research report.

Or

What are the various types of research report?

Ans. Research reports mainly take the form of a thesis, dissertation, journal article and a paper to be prescribed at a professional meeting. Research reports vary in format and style. For example, there are difference found in a research report prepared as a thesis or dissertation and a research report prepared as a manuscript for publication. The dissertation and thesis are more elaborate and comprehensive. While research papers prepared for journal articles and professional meeting are more precise and concise.

For the purpose of sharing research efforts, the researchers publish their articles in professional journals. Preparation of a research report for publication in a professional journal serves the interests of the professional colleagues. Generally, researchers do not read the theses or dissertations of professional colleagues so frequently as the research articles in professional journals. The publication of one's research work in reputed journals also helps in professional development. For this purpose, the researcher selects a reputed journal, prepares the manuscript and submits it for evaluation and publication.

There are a number of professional organisations, which convene annual meetings or conferences at the national or regional level. The major focus of these meetings is to have the members share their views on new knowledge and research findings. While formal and informal exchange of ideas takes place, the major activity in the scheduled timetable is paper presentation. The research reports presented at such conferences follow the same general format as research reports. It is not considered unethical to present the results of a study, which is to be published as long as the date of publication follows that of presentation.

Q7. Discuss the appropriate format and style of writing a research report.

Ans. Format refers to the general pattern of organisation and arrangement of the report. It is an outline that includes sections and subsections or chapters and subchapters or headings and subheadings followed to write research report. All research reports follow a format that is parallel to the steps involved in conducting a study. The format of a research report is generally well spelled out in contents. Different universities, institutions and organisations publishing professional journals follow style manual prepared on their own.

The style, on the other-hand, refers to the rules of spelling, capitalisation, punctuation, and typing followed in preparing the report. Although, specific formats vary in terms of specific headings used, yet all research reports follow a very similar format corresponding to the steps involved in conducting a study. All research reports include a section in which the results of the study are interpreted and discussed whatever be the concerned heading. Similarly, all research reports include a short description of the study, whether under the heading of 'summary' or abstract.

Most institutions of higher education and research have either developed their own format for writing research reports or have adopted any one standard format. In general, a report, whether a thesis, dissertation or a shorter term paper, usually follows a standardised pattern as per the following outlines (Best,1970):

(1) Preliminary sections.

(i) Title page

(ii) Acknowledgements (if any)

(iii) Table of contents
(iv) List of tables (if any)
(v) List of figures (if any)

(2) Main body of the report

(i) Introduction
  (a) Statement of the Problem - specific questions to be answered – hypotheses to be tested.
  (b) Significance of the Problem
  (c) Purposes of the Study
  (d) Assumptions and Limitations
  (e) Definitions of Important Terms
(ii) Review of Related Literature or Analysis of Previous Research
(iii) Design of the Study
  (a) Procedures used
  (b) Sources of Data
  (c) Methods of Gathering Data
(iv) Presentation and Analysis of Data
  (a) Text
  (b) Tables
  (c) Figures
(v) Summary and conclusions
  (a) Restatement of the problem
  (b) Description of procedures used
  (c) Principal findings and conclusions.
  (d) Recommendations for further research

(3) Reference section

(i) Bibliography
(ii) Appendices

Q8. Discuss the different components of research report.

Ans. The various components of research reports are as follows:

Preliminary Section

***The Title Page*:** The first page of the report is the title page and includes the title, author's name, the degree of requirement to be fulfilled, the name of and location of the institution (college or university) awarding degree, the date of the submission of the report, and the signatures of approving committee members. The title should be concise and should indicate the purpose of the study. One should keep in mind its possible usefulness to the reader, who may scan a bibliography in which it may be listed.

Acknowledgement page: Acknowledgements appear as unnumbered footnotes near the bottom of the title page to indicate the basis of a study (e.g., doctoral dissertation), grant support, review of prior draft of manuscript, and assistance in conducting the research.

Table of content: The table of contents includes the major divisions of the report: introduction, the chapters with their sub-sections, the bibliography and the appendix. Page numbers for each of these divisions and sub-divisions are given.

The list of tables: The statistical results are generally represented in tabular form, and usually, there are several such tables in a research report. In order to help the readers to locate these tables, a list of tables along with the serial numbers of pages on which these are located, is provided.

The list of figures: In some reports, a few figures are also included in order to make the presentation and interpretation clearer. A list of such figures is also provided indicating the serial number of pages on which they occur, in order to facilitate the study by the readers.

The main body of the report

Introduction: The introduction of a research report should be lucid, complete and concise. It should be introduce the research problem in the proper context, and arouse and stimulate the reader's interest. If introduction are dull, confused and lacking in precision, direction and specificity, there is little incentive for the reader to continue reading the research report.

In the introduction the researcher defines, analyses and states the nature of the problem. He also reviews the related studies so as to lay a foundation for research. The review of the results of previous researches brings out areas of agreement and disagreement, and shows how the present study arose from contradictions or inadequacies of earlier investigations. The introduction also includes the significance of the problem and the need for conducting the investigation.

Review of related literature: This section is essential to the development of the problem and derivation of effective approach to its solution. The review of the related literature should be exhaustive, analytical, and thorough. It should evaluate the relevance and adequacy of studies reviewed. The various sources must be integrated and synthesised in order to put the research problem in a proper perspective. It should highlight the gaps in the exiting knowledge and help in formulating testable hypotheses, which should emerge from issues that remain un-resolved through previous researches.

Design of the study: This section explains the design of the study in detail. It includes a detailed description of the manner in which decisions have been made about the type of data needed for the study, the tools and devices used for their collection, and the methods by which they have been collected. A researcher may present definition of the population; the size of the sample and the rationale for the size of the sample; the method of sampling; the number of individuals who declined to participate and weeded out, or did not participate in different phases of study and why, when and what types of data were collected; the tools and techniques used for collecting data along with their reliability and validity; the design and method of conducting the experiment giving the full details about the assumptions, classification and manipulation of variables and nature of treatments; directions given to the subjects; the characteristics of interviewers or observers and the type of training provided to them; the types of analyses made; the statistical methods employed and reasons for selecting such methods; and how the data will be organised and presented for analyses and interpretation.

Analysis and interpretation of the data: This section is the heart of the research report. The data analysis and interpretation may either be presented in separate chapters or may be integrated and presented in one chapter. The data are presented in tables and figures accompanied by textual discussions.

The formulae and statistical procedures, which were used in the analysis of the data should be clearly specified and explained in detail. The reasons for selecting a particular test of significance, the assumptions underlying its use and the confidence levels chosen in arriving at the results must be presented carefully. All the unexpected developments in the form of unanticipated relationships or unforeseen trends should be reported fully. Any weakness in the research design, tools, techniques, or population that have come to light the conduct of study should be discussed frankly along with the manner in which factors may have affected the findings of the study.

Summary and Conclusions: This section includes a brief re-statement of the problem, a description of the procedures used, and discussion of the findings and conclusions of the study. The conclusions are presented concisely and related directly to the hypotheses that were tested or to the research questions. They announce whether the findings of the study accept or reject the hypotheses. Conclusions are answers to the questions raised and suggest modification in the existing theory. In addition, the researcher may list unanswered questions that have occurred in the process of study and which require further research beyond the scope of the problem investigated. If no further research would appear to be advantageous in the area investigated and a new approach to the problem is needed, the researcher should make suggestions. In short, the discussions and presentation of the conclusions should leave the reader with the impression of completeness and of positive gain. The summary and conclusion section is the most widely used part of the research report because it reviews all the information that has been presented in its analysis and interpretation sections.

Reference Section

The reference section includes bibliography and appendix. The bibliography follows the main body of the report. In a research article the heading 'references' is used in place of bibliography. The bibliography is a record of those sources and materials that have been used for the study. If the number of references is large, the researcher may divide the bibliography into various sections, one for books, one for periodicals and journals, and possibly one for reports and special documents.

An appendix follows the bibliography. All the relevant supporting unwieldy materials, that are important but not essential to the understanding of the report, are presented in the appendix. These materials include questionnaires, copies of covering letters used, evaluation sheets, checklists, courses of study, long quotations, documents, tests, interview forms, and raw data.

Q9. Describe the utility of tables and figures in the presentation of data in a research report. Construct and interpret tables in terms of rows and columns to represent the results of data analysis.

Ans. Tables are used to convey information. They are used to help readers spot important details, see relationships, get a brief overview of the findings, or grasp the significance of data much more quickly and conveniently than through a long textual discussion. Although the use of the tables in not recommended simply to repeat information adequately covered in the text of the report, the text should contain sufficient details to support the particular argument being put forward. Some readers feel scared of the figures in the tables and prefer to read the evidence presented in the main text. Other readers find tabular presentation easier to follow than written description.

Figures are devices, which are used by a researcher for the purpose of presenting data clearly concisely. When skillfully used, they reveal important trends or relationships that a reader might not grasp when examining complex statistical data. Figures do not replace textural description, but they may help a researcher to explain and interpret complicated data effectively to the reader.

Constructing Tables

Generally, researchers present the descriptive details of data and results of their analysis in tabular and graphical form. Text references should indentify tables by number, rather than by such expressions as, "the above table" or "the following table". If a table has to be continued on the next page, the headings of columns should be repeated on each page. The expression Table is centred between the page margins and typed in capital letters followed by its number. The caption or title is placed two spaces below the word Table, and is brief, clearly indicating the nature of data presented.

As a simple rule, table should not appear physically unless some reference to it is made in the text. This alerts the reader regarding the nature of data to be presented. Such a reference may be made as simple statement like "Table 3 presents the achievement scores of boys and girls at three levels of IQ". After making such a statement the writer can insert the table at an appropriate place. Another important point is that the table should be integrated into the text rather than appearing on separate page. But, the scheme of presentation largely depends on the nature of basic data and the techniques used for their analysis. In behavioural sciences, most of the variables are measured in terms of nominal ordinal and interval scales. Ratio scale is seldom used in behavioural science research.

Q10. Discuss the data on various types of scales of measurement.

Ans. The statistical techniques used for data analysis are mainly determined by nature of data and levels of measurement used. Four different levels of measurement have been clearly identified from lower to higher levels, which are nominal, ordinal, interval and ratio scales of measurement. These are also differentiated in terms of how much can be done in the way of mathematical and statistical operations with numbers applied at different levels of measurement. Higher the level of scale, the more we can do with the numbers we obtain in measurement (Guilford, 1954).

Date on nominal scale

The data on nominal scale are also termed as classicatory data in the sense that such data indicate the classification of objects or responses in two or more categories. It is a process by which the researcher places each observation into one or more of a set of categories so as to know the frequency of occurrence of observations or responses in each category. We may develop the categories ourself or may use categories, which already exist. The categories may be identified before collection of data or may be developed after collecting data, depending on the nature of variables used and purposes of research. For instance, the investigator may classify subjects as 'male' and 'female' as per their inherent characteristics, or he may develop categories such as 'high achievers' and 'low achievers' on the basis of an achievement test. The categories may be two or more. The tabular representation of such data takes the form as shown in table 6.1, which shows the categorisation of 150 residents of a colony by their occupations. The frequencies indicate number of persons belonging to each occupation. These frequencies are also expressed in terms of percentages.

Table 6.1: Distribution of residents by occupation

Category	Occupation	Frequency	Percentage
A	Doctors	15	10.0
B	Engineers	27	18.0
C	Teachers	60	40.0
D	Technicians	30	20.0
E	Labourers	18	12.0
		150	100.0

Sometimes, figures are also used to represent statistical data in a research study. Figures are not used as substitutes for textual description, rather, they are included to emphasise certain significant relationships.

The information presented in table 6.1 may also be given as a bar figure as shown in figure 6.2:

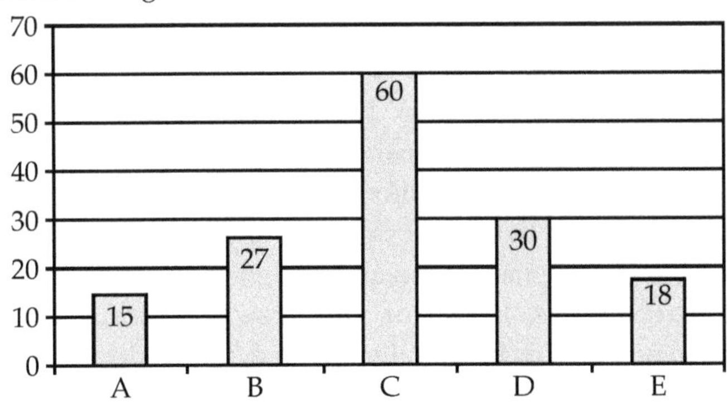

Fig. 6.2: Showing a bar graph for the data given in table 6.1

Sometimes, we have to study the relationship between two nominal or classicatory variables. For this purpose, data have to be tabulated in the form of contingency tables. A contingency table is a two-way classification of nominal data in terms of rows and columns. This kind of presentation of data is also termed as 'crossbreak, representation of data (Kerlinger, 1973). The simplest form of a crossbreak is 2×2 table. If a group of 200 undergraduate students were asked to give their choice for one of the two textbooks A and B, their responses may be shown as follows:

Table 6.2: Male-female preference for Book A and B (frequencies)

	Male	Female	Total
Book A	65	46	111
Book B	50	39	89
Total	115	85	200

Date on ordinal scale

Sometimes, data are not available in quantitative form, but subjects can be ranked from highest to lowest according to the magnitude of trait. Also, situations arise in research when researcher has to rank subjects in ascending or descending order according to the amount of trait they possess. When data are available in terms of ranks or order (such as more or less), we say that data are on ordinal scale. For example, 30 students might be ranked from 1 to 30 with respect to height. The tallest student would be assigned rank 1 and the shortest on would be assigned rank 30.

Although, ordinal scales do indicate that some subjects are higher or better than others, they do not indicate how much higher or how much better (Gay, 1992). In other words, the differences or intervals between ranks are not equal; the difference between rank 1 and rank 2 is not necessarily the same as between rank 9 and rank 10. The statistics that are permissible at the level of nominal-scale are also applicable to measurements on ordinal scale – frequencies, percent, modes and contingency-correlation coefficients. The principle of order makes possible the use of additional statistics including medians, percentiles and rank-order correlation coefficient (Guilford, 1954). The simplest method for reducing raw scores (on interval scale) to rank order is to write the scores in descending order of magnitude and assign ranks 1,2,3,....... etc., from highest to lowest scores. If two or more raw scores are the same, the corresponding ranks may be equally divided. More details may be had from an elementary book on statistics.

Generally, raw scores of subjects are listed as they occur and their ranks are mentioned against them. Table 6.3 presents the weights of 10 subjects along with their ranks:

Table 6.3: Ranking subjects on weight

Subject	Weight (kg.)	Ranks
A	98	2
B	72	8
C	85	4
D	68	9
E	84	5
F	100	1
G	67	10
H	75	6
I	74	7
J	88	3

If there are scores on more than one traits for the same set of subjects, a composite table listing ranks on all the traits may be prepared and further analysis of data may be done.

Data on interval scale

An interval scale also has all the characteristics of a nominal scale and an ordinal scale, but in addition, it is based upon predetermined equal intervals. Most of the tests used in educational research, such as achievement tests, aptitude tests, and intelligence tests, represent interval scale (gay, 1992, p 381). When we talk about scores, we usually refer to interval scale data. When scores have equal intervals it is assumed, for example, that the difference between a score of 30 and a score of 40 is essentially the same as the difference between a score of 50 and a score of 60. However, the interval scale does not have a zero point.

The data on interval scale are normally tabulated in the form of frequency distributions in terms of rows and columns. For example, the IQ scores of 200 children may be tabulated as given in Table 6.4:

Table 6.4: IQ scores of 200 subjects

S. No.	Score
1.	98
2.	105
3.	103
•	•
•	•
.	.
▪	110

However most of the times, raw scores are repeated. Several children may have the same IQ score. The number of times a score occurs, is termed as its frequency. If five children have an IQ score of 115, then we say that frequency of the score 115 is 5. The scores of children may be conveniently tabulated in terms of scores and their frequencies listed in separate columns as shown in Table 6.5.

Table 6.5: IQ distribution of 200 subjects

Scores (X)	Frequency (F)
0.	5
1.	8
6.	12
112	10
.	.
.	.
.	.
.	.
	N = 200

Data on ratio scale

Ratio data are data that can be measured on a scale from zero to infinity, with every possible graduation in between with a potentially unlimited number of decimal places. Measurements of weight, length, time and blood chemistry are all example of continuous/ratio data.

The data on ratio scale has a meaningful zero value and have an equidistant measure (i.e. the difference between 30 and 40 is the same as the difference between 60 and 70). For example, 60 marks obtained in a test is twice of 30. This is so because zero can be measured on the ratio scale.

Q11. Discuss the significance of following in the research report:

(a) Footnotes and Endnotes

Ans. Endnote and footnotes are tools used to show your reader(s) where you found your information. Endnotes are placed at the end of the report, just before or after your bibliography. Footnotes are placed on the bottom of the page where they are introduced. An identifying number or symbol is placed at the end of the material for which the endnote or footnote applies, for the notation.

Both footnotes and endnotes allow the researcher to include additional or parenthetical information that is not otherwise considered part of the regular flow of the report. They enable the writer to validate and substantiate a point, statement or argument; to explain, supplement or expand material that is included in the main body of the report, to provide cross reference to materials appearing in the other parts of the report; to acknowledge and give credit to sources of material that he has quoted directly or indirectly and to provide the reader with sufficient information to enable him to consult sources independently and thus to verify the authenticity and accuracy of material used.

(b) Bibliography

Ans. The bibliography is typed at the end of the main body of the research report. It is preceded by a page bearing the word BIBLIOGRPAHY, capitalised and centered on the page. The first page of the bibliography has the word "Bibliography" as centre heading.

The purpose of a bibliography is quite different from that of a footnote. The purpose of a footnote is to give the specific location of the source of the statement made in the text, including the number of the actual page on which the statement appears in the original source. The purpose of the bibliography, on the other hand, is to identify the whole work rather than a specific part of it. It would be inconvenient to repeat the general reference on each occasion that a source is cited in a footnote, yet the full details of the source need to be included somewhere in the report for the information of the reader. The style of citation and punctuation in a bibliography is quite different from a footnote. For example, in a footnote the author's name is give in the natural order of initials or first name followed by the surname, but in a bibliography the surname precedes the initials of first name.

Q12. Discuss the different styles of writing footnotes/bibliography and reference for research report.

Ans. There are different styles of writing footnotes/bibliography and reference for research reports, viz. the Modern Language Association (MLA) Format, the Chicago Style, the Harvard Style, the American Sociological Association (ASA) Format and American Psychological Association (APA) Format. A brief overview of these different formats is presented as follows:

(1) MLA (Modern Language Association) format

The MLA format is a widely accepted style for writing footnotes, bibliography/reference in most disciplines in humanities. It requires citation within the text rather than endnotes or footnotes. Citation in the text provides information, usually name of the author and page number(s) to lead the reader to the accompanying full bibliographical entry in the *works cited* list, which is placed at the end of the research paper/report.

Parenthetical citations in the text of the research paper/report

Example: At least one other educator has recently quarreled with the traditional division of curriculum into discrete subjects (Moffet 5-10).

Works cited – a section in alphabetical order at the end of the same research paper.

Example: Moffet, James. *Teaching the Universe of Discourse,* Boston: Houghton, 1968

Citation of books, journals, articles and internal resources

Books: In citing books, normally arrange the information in the following order:

- author's name
- title of the book
- name of the editor, translator or compiler
- edition used
- volume No. used
- name of the series
- place of publication, name of the publisher and year of publication
- page number

Examples:

By a single author

Henry, E. Garret. *Statistics in Psychology and Education,* 10th Indian Reprint. Bombay: Vakila Feffer and Simons, 1981.

By two or three authors

Dagar, B.s. and Dull, Indira. *Perspectives in Moral Education, New Delhi:* Uppal Publishing House, 1995.

By corporate author

National Council of Educational Research and Training, Name of the Book, Place of publication.

By anonymous author

Encyclopaedia of Virginia. New York: Somerset, 1993.

An article in a reference book

"Mandarin". The Encyclopaedia American, 1994 ed.

Conference proceedings

Freed, Barbara F., ed. Foreign language Acquisition Research and the Classroom: Proc of Consortium for Language Teaching and Learning Conference, Oct. 1989. University of Pennsylvania, Lexington: Henth, 1991.

Journals and magazines articles: In citing journal and magazine articles, normally the information is arranged in the following order:

- author's name
- title of the article
- *name of the journal*
- series number or name
- volume number
- date of publication
- page number (s)

Examples

From a magazine

Mehta, Pratap Bhanu. "Exploring Myths". New Republic, 6 June, 1988: 17-19.

(2) APA format

The APA style is extensively used in social sciences. It is standardised by the American Psychological Association (APA). In this system, also the citation format requires parenthetical citations within the text rather than footnotes. The citation in the text provides information, the name of the author and the date of publications, to lead to the accompanying bibliography centre. Complete information about what is cited in the text is supplied a "References" given at the end of the research paper. The APA style is used in the double space as was in the case of MLA format.

Example: (cited statement in the text)

Once established, working models are said to be "core features of personality that are then carried into new relationship" (Collins and Read, 1994, p. 56)

Examples of APA style reference citations

Periodicals:

Author, A.A., Author B.B., and Author, C.C. (1999). Title of the article. *Title of the Periodical,* Vol., pp....

Paivi, A. (1975). Perceptional comparisons through the mind's eye. *Memory and Cognition,* 3, 635-647.

Books, reports, brochures (non-periodical)

General form

Author, A.A. (1999). Title of the work. Location: Publisher

By a corporate author **(example)**

American Psychiatric Association (1994). *Diagnostic and statistical manual of mental disorders (4th ed.)* Washington, D.C. : Author

Article in a book (example)

Dagar, B.S. (1997). Evolution of Pedagogy as a Profession. In R.P. Singh (Ed.) *Teacher Education in India-Looking a Head.* (pp.127-143) New Delhi: Federation of Management of Educational Institutions.

Report and Government Printing Office

National Institute of Mental Health. (1990). Clinical Training in Serious Mental Illness (DHHH Publication No. ADM 90—1679). Washington, DC: W.S. Government Printing Press.

Online Periodicals – General Form

Author, A.A., Author, B.B., and Author, C.C. (1999). Title of the Article. *Title of the periodical,* XX, XXX-XXX Retrieved month, year from source.

Examples:

Senior, B. (1957). Team roles and team performance: is there really a link? *Journal of Occupational and Organisational Psychology,* 70, 241-258. Retrieved June, 6, 2001 from ABI/INFORM Global (proquest)

(3) Chicago manual of style

The Chicago style will show you how to create footnotes or endnotes and a bibliography from print and electronic formats. The endnotes/footnotes provide correct bibliographical citation for the sources noted by number in the text. These notes whether footnote or endnote aim at giving an explanation or citation of other works related with the statement in the text, which has been numbered as 1, 2, or 3, etc. It may also indicate some example.

For example

- A similar distinction is made by H. Richard Niebuhr in "The Responsible Self', New York (1963).
- The term 'object' was first used by Freud in *Three Essays on the Theory of Sexuality* (1905) to distinguish objects form sexual aims.

Book (Two authors)

Colby, A. and Kohlberg. L. *Measurement of Moral Judgement: Manual and Results,* Cambridge: Cambridge University Press, 1987.

Corporate author

International Monetary Fund, *Survey of African Economies,* Vol. 7, Algeria, Mali, Morocco, and Tunissa (Washington, D.C.: International Monetary Fund, 1977), 27

Citation in the text

Basic form consists of the author's last name and the year of publication of the work. No punctuation is used between author's name and the date. For example (Dewey 1916)

Articles retrieved in electronic format

Footnotes and endnotes: Author's name in normal order followed by document title, date of Internal publication, <URL> or other retrieval information, date of access.

Peter J. Bryant, "The Age of Mammals", in *Biodiversity Conservation,* April 1999 <http://darwin.bio.uci.edu/~sustain/bio65/index.html? (11th May 1999)

(4) Citing references using 'Harvard' format

Harvard style is one of the most commodity used formats. Whenever, you refer to a document in the text, include the authors, surname, name and year of publication. If there are, two authors both of them should be mentioned. However, in the case of more than two authors, give surname of the first author followed by the abbreviation 'et al' (origin Latin et alii) which indicates that there are at least three authors. This procedure should be followed whether your source is paper or electronic.

Example: Lyons(1983) operationalised the distinction between justice and care in terms of the contrasting/perspectives towards others – the perspective of reciprocity with perspective of response.

Writing a bibliography

At the end of the work, paper, a thesis or a research the bibliography of the authors in alphabetical order in written with surname of the authors(s). If there are more than three authors, give the names of the first, starting with surname and then write the abbreviation 'et al'. The bibliographical details should be taken from the title page of the publication. The title of the work referred to should be in italics. However, in the case of handwritten bibliography the title should be underlined. The pages referred to should also be indicated at the end using pp (e.g. Pp. 79-83). But in the case of journal article, this notation pp is required.

Book by single author

Gilligan, C. (1982). In a *different voice: psychological theory and women's development.* Cambridge M.A: Harvard University Press.

Book by two authors

Fessenden, R. and Fessenden, J. (1988) *Organic chemistry,* 6th ed. London. Brooks/Cole.

Book by a corporate author (e.g. government or some other organisation)

The Economist (1988) *Style guide.* London: Profile Books.

Edited book

Panda, S. (Ed.) (2003). Planning and management in distance education. London and New York: RoutledgeFalmer.

Article in journal

Gilligen, C and Attannci, J. (1988) Two Moral Orientations: Gender Differences and Similarities. *Memil-parlouer quarterly,* 34, pp 223-237.

Dissertation

Willson, Sean (1997). An investigation of physiotherapists working as extends scope practitioners. Unpublished B.Sc. (Hons.) dissertation, Kingston University, Kingston, Survey.

Reference materials dictionaries, encyclopaedias, etc.

Pring, J.T. (Complier) (1986) *The Oxford Dictionary of Modern Greeks: Greek English and English-Greek.* Oxford, Oxford University Press.

On line images

Ostra in Concert, London, 14 March (2002) <www.ostra.net/images.asp> (accessed 25 August 2003).

Q13. What is meant by editing? Discuss its need. What are different types of editing?

Ans. According to IGNOU, the term editing involves making the written material fit for production. It is a process of examining and correcting the written material so that it is suitable for publication or in the case of a research report, fit for submission for evaluation. It is normally done by a senior academic, who may be supervisor or director of the project or some professional editor well versed with subject of research. The editing process involves three aspects–the contents, the format and the language of the research report.

Need

Any research dissertation, before it is sent for evaluation or publication essentially needs to be properly edited in terms of content, format and language.

- Editing involves vetting of the footnotes written at the bottom of different pages or endnotes at the end of the unit for the report itself where some reference is quoted in body of the thesis. It also requires editing of references give at the end of the thesis–those books, journals, dissertation reports of other investigators, proceedings of seminars, symposia, etc., which have been referred to and quoted in the body of the thesis or dissertation/report, etc.

- Second, editing is essential because it improves the academic credibility of the content presented-that is, relevance and adequacy of the content, the method used in the research and literature consulted.
- Third, editing also enhances the readability of the text that it is simple, clear and systematic. And if the editor is responsible for overall quality of the report (supervisor/director of the research project), then s/he will test the veracity and appropriateness of the different facets of research process–objectives, hypotheses, methods and procedures used and the design of the research.

  In this way through editing the overall quality of the research report will be improved considerably.

Types of Editing

The various type of editing is given in the following points:

(1) Content Editing: Content editing of the research report takes cognizance of the nature of research and methodology used for conducting the research. It aims towards exactness or precision in the statement of the problem, its objectives, nature of the research questions or hypotheses, method and procedure, analysis of data and their interpretation, and drawing of inferences and conclusions. Editing must ensure that there is correspondence between the objectives of the study and the results. The details about the tools, techniques and sampling are objectively reported. The findings should be in conformity with the established findings of other researches. In case of any divergence between the established theories or findings, the report must provide proper and convincing explanation.

(2) Format Editing: Format editing ensures that there is no deviation in the format of the research report from the well-accepted format. It is done from the point of (i) structure of the report; (ii) presentation of tables and figures (iii) writing of footnotes and (iv) writing of references or bibliography at the end.

(3) Language Editing: Language editing is to ascertain the proper use of language in the presentation of research report. It is done to vet vocabulary, sentences or structure so that the report becomes comprehensive, interesting, and lucid, with proper use of technical and key terms. The use of idiomatic language, confused expressions and wrong punctuations, etc. is not advisable. Unnecessary repetitions of words and phrases should be avoided. It is advisable to use specific words in place of general and abstract words. Avoid negatives especially double negatives and use of jargon. Due consideration should be given to the linguistic abilities of the users/readers of the research report. Their level of language should match the level of report content.

Q14. What are the features of effective writing/editing?

Ans. The various features of effective editing are as follows:

(1) Avoiding unnecessary repetitions: Unnecessary words and phrases need to be avoided. Phrases such as true facts, definite decisions, grave emerging, free gifts or final ultimatum are redundant.

(2) Specificity: Use of specific words in place of general and abstract words is always better. The difference in the sentences can be seen as given below:

(i) His satisfaction was apparent.

(ii) He was satisfied.

(3) Avoid negatives: Whenever a positive statement can be used instead of a negative one, use it. Use of negatives especially the use of double negative often causes confusion. For example, sentence like, "it was not that I did not appreciate your viewpoint..." requires an extra effort to understand. The same meaning could be more easily and effectively communicated. "His feeling for your view point was...".

(4) Avoid the use of jargon: Lengthy paragraphs or sentences should be avoided. You can break them into small ones, which are manageable and comprehensible. In this context, you may note the following points.

Avoid

- Over punctuation
- Quotation, not very essential to the theme or those which are common place
- Long sentences
- Cliches and worn out phrases.

Use:

- Popular frequently used forms of the words
- British spelling (in the case of English language) as far as possible
- Indian words where equivalents are not available in English
- Proper punctuation

(5) Style: Especially in the case of writing a research report, the conversational personalised style is to be avoided. The use of 'I', 'you', 'we' is not advisable in research report. Here the researcher is supposed to be in the background and, therefore, in such writing the use of third person is always recommended such as "The investigator found", "He, therefore, reached the conclusion ..." instead of "I found ..." and therefore, "I think."

Q15. Explain the need for dissemination of research findings.

Ans. Dissemination of research findings refers to the spreading of knowledge and is an essential step in the research process because knowledge development is wasted unless it becomes known so that it can be used.

The dictionary meaning of the term 'dissemination' is "to scatter or spread widely as though sowing seed, promulgate extensively, broadcast, disperse". However, this dictionary meaning does not adequately reflect the underlying connation as used in social sciences research on dissemination of information (Karen S. Luis and Lisa M. Jones 2001). Lois gives a more appropriate definition.

Dissemination consists of purposive, goal-oriented communication of information or knowledge that is specific and potentially usable, from one social system to another. Pursuant to this definition, the intent of dissemination in education is "not simply to disperse information but to do in ways that promote its use". The goal is to improve and change the organisations and systems as well as the individual practice. To know whether the spread of information was effective, its use, innovation or implementation can be taken as possible parameters. It should, however, does not mean that innovation processes and dissemination are equivalent.

There is another facet of dissemination, which is ignored in the dictionary definition but taken for granted in research *what is being sown.* When we consider the case of research in the field of education, it is reality of educational change, which occurs as a consequence of ideas rather tangible products. Therefore, when we consider dissemination in education, we must focus on new products (ideas, practices) that are designed to stimulate perceptible change that is what impact, the research findings are capable of bringing in the practice of education.

Q16. Define the concept of dissemination and knowledge use.

Ans. Knowledge use occurs when a decision-maker considers the findings of study or a group of related studies, for resolution of a probing problem. (Ricketts, 1982, p. 8) The term 'use' can be defined as the application of a research results to a decision that is relevant to improving the functioning of a system. The use of research findings depends on the way of research findings are disseminated. The research findings, for this purpose need to be presented in a "user-friendly" way. Mere dissemination of knowledge as widely as possible (to promote awareness), may be rather different from those that are intended to encourage its use.

According to National Research Centre for Career and Technical Education (USA), some of the main elements of 'knowledge use' model of dissemination are:

- Provide knowledge usable for practitioners – take the advantage of momentum and typical need for relatively rapid action.
- Create shared understanding of how new ideas could help to improve local practice, encourage potential users to discuss the information are how it can best be used.
- Stimulate increased diffusion of new ideas between and within educational agencies. The more the knowledge flows back and forth regularly, the more likely it is that new ideas from a trusted source will be attended to.
- Combine top-down and bottom-up approaches – dissemination does not need to be either top-down (where dissemination of what is practice is made by policy or by a dissemination agency), or bottom-up (research is collected to respond to the unique needs and situations of the school) instead, the most effective form of dissemination combines some of both.

Educational research is of value when it can be adapted or used by educators to assist students in the learning process.

Educational research is more applicable when it:

- is compatible with existing belief structures;
- diffuses rapidly throughout the organisation's field, so that is becomes legitimised;
- has prima-facie utility in local sites; and
- is presented or discussed within the potential users in ways that make it fit with local preferences.

Relationship between production and consumption of research

If we wish policy research to be used, we need to spend-time working with potential users. There are agencies that commission research and there are scholars (researchers) who conduct it. The members of the Commission publish reviews and even research by noted scholars, but these researches are not used fully unless there is a great deal of interaction between scholar and commission members. Cibulka (1999) raises issues that are central to studies of research utilisation but are not systematically investigator – the politics of research findings and subsequent use for example; Huberman (1994) lays out a theory of relationship between producer and consumer, which highlights a sustained interactivity between the two.

If we wish policy research to be used, we need to spend time working with the potential users.

The nature of knowledge and information that is disseminated is critical in determining use. The information that is transmitted has different characteristics, depending on the context in which it is inserted because research has meaning only when it is interpreted through the human mind. Knowledge is used because it is engaging or compelling and because the person presented with it can imagine how it would apply to him or her.

Socio-economic conditions and dissemination or knowledge use

The dissemination of knowledge use is, in some way, associated with socio-economic status (SES) characteristic of the communities. According to a Study by Garner and Raundenbush in 1991, children in low economic communities perform less well than similarly disadvantaged peers who belong to higher SES parents. It is probably because the parents of higher SES are more exposed to knowledge and information and their use than those parents belonging to low SES. The richness of intellectual and social capital does support education. It implies that the effect of SES factor cannot be ignored by anyone who is interested in the importance of opportunities for all students. The majority of students who could be benefited be implementation of best research belongs to low SES of the communities because before such mentation they were exposed to lesser opportunities.

Organisational learning and knowledge use

The organisational learning perspective, which has its origin in business settings, is now diffusing well in education. According to Senge (1990), we need to look at how schools (i.e. organisations) use knowledge, which may be different from the ways in which individuals use knowledge. The concept "organisational learning" has a social constructivist's perspective according to which knowledge can be used only when it has been "socially processed" (Louis, 1994). Organisations that are more effective in knowledge use usually have more closely linked internal communication networks, and more and more individuals legitimately bring in new ideas from the outside. On the other hand, organisations that do not learn suffer from internal boundaries, competition and excessive individual entrepreneurship (Corwin and Louis, 1982).

In the context of dissemination and improvement theories in education, the organisational learning perspective becomes significant and critical. According to this point, the focus possibility for a school with new knowledge is dependent on social characteristics of the school and its ability to process information. There are, for example, many organisations, which have lot of information at their disposal but they do not know how to use that information. Many schools instead of gathering useable knowledge that would help them improve their importance; they establish a huge store of data, which have little relevance to the quality of their core product.

Based on theory and empirical data organisational learning is best thought of as a conceptual tool for helping schools or other organisations to focus on both the core objectives and the ways of organising how to get there.

Our basic assumption in this regard is: schools do not focus on how to use knowledge about student development and learning because they have:

- limited and ineffective communication systems,
- poor, procedures and strategies for getting information that will help them in their core goals, and
- poor procedures to deal with good and poor information that they do acquire.

Relationship between production and use

According to Huberman (1994) there are five factors in education, which have demonstrated strong empirical relationships with knowledge utilisation. These factors are:

- The context of research including characteristics of the knowledge base and the motivation of the researcher to disseminate to practitioners.
- The user's context including factor ranging from perceived needs to perception of the value of research information.
- Formal mechanisms to link knowledge with intended users.
- The impacts of contexts and linkages on the resources, including attention, time, and acceptability of the research; and
- The amount of effort expended, creating an appropriate environment for use, which includes both the amount and the quality of the dissemination effort, the usability of the

knowledge and the quality of planning and execution in using site.

The dissemination and utilisation research, like Huberman's perspective emphasises the dispersion of knowledge to multiple sites of practice. The researchers and practitioners need to have sustained interactivity and reciprocal influence on each other. Such interactivity will promote research and knowledge utilisation. According, to constructivist approach to teaching practitioner's knowledge is constructed by individuals reflective practice and through a disciplined inquiry, such as action research.

Weiss and Bucuvalas (1980) contended that knowledge produced through rigorous inquiry is required to pass two types of test before it can be used: (i) the truth test, which helps the individual or a group of assertion whether knowledge obtained or the information gathered is a reasonable approximation of "reality"; (ii) utility test, which means whether the knowledge so obtained can be applied under the existing conditions that is whether it is practicable.

Q17. What are the various models of dissemination and knowledge use?

Ans. The US Centre for Career and Technical Education in the 1970s adopted an approach based on the assumption that knowledge is a "thing" that needs to find a good home in the schools. Under such an assumption, dissemination is taken as consisting of four activities: spread, exchange, choice and implementation. However, prior to the 1970s, the primary purpose of dissemination was to cast knowledge out in the world of practice under the view that a good idea will ultimately be used. This latter approach considered ideas about communication as a two way process and extended the dissemination role to support for actual change. It embodies the belief that knowledge comes in definable, usable form and can be placed before the practitioners who will choose something that will solve their problems. The US federal government adopted such a view of dissemination and knowledge use for quite some time. The various models of dissemination and knowledge use are as follows:

(1) Extension system model: Based on the view knowledge US government first of all considered the role of research as a means of improving practice and introduced Land Grant College system that included a link between funded institutions with needs of state agricultural and rural communities through extension services. The motive was that research knowledge could be used to answer specific questions of practice. Under this system, extension officers are appointed who function as a link between the researchers and the users, thus increasing communication between the researchers and the users. This increased a communication between the university and the field. This model proved quite effective, especially in agriculture and related fields over the years. But conceptually it has its own constraints regarding the way we think about dissemination and knowledge utilisation. The extension services until recently have been set up largely to serve the needs of individuals; the problems of educators, however, are invariably associated with the functioning of schools as organised units. As such, the extension technology transfer model does not remain as simple as it looks to be.

(2) Educational resource information centre (ERIC) model: This model is based on the belief that level of knowledge utilisation is low because research is not easily accessible to the users. There is, therefore, a need to start centers where knowledge is available and accessible to the people who want to utilise it. In the US, however, ERIC was designed without giving any thought to as how the educators would actually use the system. For this reason, it never remained user friendly. To make the system effective, efforts should be made for developing more active dissemination strategies, which focus on improving ERIC's use for teachers and administrators.

(3) Regional laboratory system: In the 1960s in the US, the Regional Laboratory System was initiated with the intention that these educational labs would function as research utilising agencies. This system then became the backbone of general-purpose dissemination system of the US government. If this kind of system is adopted in India and made to function in national organisations like the NCERT, NCTE, IGNOU, NIOS, etc. and state organisations like the state institutes of education - SCERT, University Department of Education or some well established colleges of education, it can perhaps better serve the special needs of a target group. These labs are considered as providers of knowledge.

(4) Special purpose assistance: Apart from the general-purpose dissemination, the US government also started special purpose assistance programmes. These programmes were created as assistance centers that provide technical help to special needs recipients. The objectives of these centers were:

- to develop and disseminate curriculum
- to provide training and assistance
- to field test and evaluate new curricula
- to link practitioners and curriculum developers through state curriculum representatives
- to exchange information about curriculum (Smink, 1985)

Smink, (1985) further pointed out that "although promising educational products and practices are increasingly available, relatively few have been implemented by intended users. He proposed the following points regarding dissemination.

We should be clear about:

- What should be developed and disseminated?
- Who is the target audience?
- Who is the dissemination activity needed?
- How should the dissemination activity be designed?
- When and where should dissemination actually occur?

Q18. What are the various strategies used in dissemination of research findings? **[June-2012, Q.No.-3(e)]**

Ans. In the process of reporting the findings of research, some ethical issues also crop up which need to be taken care of. The reporting of findings of research may be done to serve different purposes. For example, you may be required to prepare a policy paper, you may report for the purpose of giving a presentation in a workshop, sometimes you may like to send your findings to the press and the media; or you may like to publish the findings on website. In keeping with the different purposes, there are different strategies or ways to deal with the research findings.

The research report as you have seen presents a detailed account of all the experiences, thinking process involved in the process of research. Unless all the research experiences so obtained are properly communicated, the real purpose of reporting or dissemination cannot be achieved.

In presenting your research findings, you should consider a number of issues – the ethical issues, the recommendations, the format, etc. If you want that your findings should impact policy and practice, you need to plan a comprehensive dissemination strategy. It requires to formulate a dissemination plan, indicating clearly who the user groups are how you can present your findings/report to be usable to the group(s). An example of dissemination plan is given below:

Audience group	**Project director, donors, government local partners**
User group	Agency which is to implement the recommendations, e.g. Government, NGO, community
Possible types of reports	Written report Verbal presentation Public meetings Local media

To demonstrate the above mentioned dissemination plan, let us take the case of Sumit Chaudhary who works with an NGO in Delhi. Sumit has been asked by Director of the Project to study the etiology of girl dropouts in slum and rural areas surrounding Delhi. Sumit has been sanctioned a travel grant to conduct the study. He has been asked to find out the causal factors responsible for dropout of girls living in these areas. Put together a report on his findings and make a presentation on his study in front of the officials of the NGO and representatives from the public who donated funds to carry out the research. The table above shows what kind of Plan Sumit might make.

Written report in the above case may include:

- statement of problem/focus of inquiry
- how Sumit can carry out the research
- description of what he found using both quantitative and qualitative data/barograph, pie charts, vignettes of typical girls/school family and selective quotes.
- Analysis: What patterns of enrolments and dropouts, what key factors emerged?
- Interpretation and discussion: What does this mean in terms of policies, plans, actions, likely barriers and problems, what would have to happen for things to change?
- Recommendations: A plan of action for various stakeholders.

If Sumit was to discuss the findings in a public meeting with communities with agreement of local leaders, officials and representatives of the parents, then he should prepare a two page handout in the local language giving key points from the findings as they can affect the local people.

Similarly, Sumit can manage to hold a radio interview through which he can disseminate his findings to a much wider audience.

He can also send an article in local press.

Ethical contributions: Once the research of this type which is of immediate concern for the stakeholders, the draft of the main findings should be given to the local partners without delay.

And if you have used case studies, pseudonym should be used in place of actual names.

How a particular research experience may be more effectively disseminated depends upon the type of research report. It is, therefore, important to understand, the different types of reports before we can devise appropriate strategy to disseminate the same.

Q19. Explain the classification of research report.

Ans. The nature of a research report may be written, or it may be oral presentation; it may be in print form or it may be broadcast on mass media. Depending on the type of research report, it may have different formats.

The written report

The written report is obviously for academic audience. In such reports formal style of writing is adopted in which the sentences are clear though long. Different terms used are well defined and clarified to the audience. Results are based on pertinent data collected through experiments or surveys, etc. The results are well discussed in detail in the light of supporting theories or findings of other investigators. There is extensive use of references from books, journals, other reports, dissertations or websites.

Oral presentation

Such reports are meant for government officers or the officers of a corporate. These are relatively shorter in size compressing the main points with a series of bullet points. Each point may be a phrase or a long sentence. No references are needed in such reports. Case studies, if any, may be put into the appendix. The purpose of such report is to produce a short, focussed document for busy officials that will enable them to keep the main points in mind. The language used in formal must be very clear.

Print and mass media

The newspaper report is much more punchy and informal in style. It is short and to the point, which aims at a lay audience. It is written in a way that it is salable to the wider community in which the benefits to users are well explained. It is appealing to the national pride by suggesting that such and such initiative will help the country.

Q20. What are the different kinds of ethical issues involved in dissemination of research findings? How can you tackle these issues?

Or

Discuss the ethical issues related to reporting to reporting of research findings. [June-2011, Q.No.-2]

Ans. While going through the process of research, especially the collection of data whether via experimentation or survey essentially involves ethical issues. While conducting research you are advised to take cognizance of such issues. In the process of reporting and dissemination of research findings, also such issues arise. So while reporting you must take care of such issues. Some of these issues are related to the language you use in printing the findings or recommendations of research.

Honesty versus diplomacy

Suppose for example, you conducted a study on organisational climate of an institution and you found that the staff morale is low. You also tried to find out the casual factors responsible for such situation; and you observed that the head of the institution has somewhat autocratic style of functioning. There may be two ways of presenting the same finding. If your findings are critical of some people or institution you have to exercise your judgement about how to present the findings. A point, which is negative in nature, if presented as such, may offend the person concerned and s/he may not like to implement the findings. But the same negative findings may be disseminated in a more positive way. Compare the two versions of the same point relating to the example cited above:

- Staff morale is low because the principal of the institution is autocratic, not easily approachable and unpredictable.
- The principal should use more consultative management style and take care of the needs of the staff and students and respecting their individuality.

In the second way of presentation without being dishonest with the research findings, you have tilted it in a positive direction. In such a presentation, there is much likelihood that the principal without being offended may implement the findings.

Feedback to stakeholders

While conducting experiment or collecting data in other ways, there are many people or subjects involved. Your findings are based on the reaction/observations, etc. of these people. So it will be ethical if the draft report is shown to those involved. Do they consider it fair? Do they wish anything to be taken out or added in? In such situation, you should be able to negotiate for an acceptable compromise. If you have fed back of your findings from those who helped you in collecting data at various stages of the research, you would already be aware of their reactions.

Anonymity

In conducting research, in education, you always choose a sample of individuals called subjects, and obtain their views/reactions about themselves or about others by using some appropriate tool/experiment. The identities of such people you observed/interviewed should be kept secret and should not be divulged to anybody else. The subjects have given the information with a confidence in you and, therefore, it is your ethical duty not to give any clue regarding who the subjects/institutions were. In case study research it may be possible to disguise the context but retain the key information including quotes. For excellent score, read GPH book.

Appendix Tables

Table (A): Binomial Distribution

		p																			
n	**r**	**.01**	**.05**	**.10**	**.15**	**.20**	**.25**	**.30**	**.35**	**.40**	**.45**	**.50**	**.55**	**.60**	**.65**	**.70**	**.75**	**.80**	**.85**	**.90**	**.95**
2	0	.980	.902	.810	.723	.640	.563	.490	.423	.360	.303	.250	.203	.160	.123	.090	.063	.040	.023	.010	.002
	1	.020	.095	.180	.255	.320	.375	.420	.455	.480	.495	.500	.495	.480	.455	.420	.375	.320	.255	.180	.095
	2	.000	.002	.010	.023	.040	.063	.090	.123	.160	.203	.250	.303	.360	.423	.490	.563	.640	.723	.810	.902
3	0	.970	.857	.729	.614	.512	.422	.343	.275	.216	.166	.125	.091	.064	.043	.027	.016	.008	.003	.001	.000
	1	.029	.135	.243	.325	.384	.422	.441	.444	.432	.408	.375	.334	.288	.239	.189	.141	.096	.057	.027	.007
	2	.000	.007	.027	.057	.096	.141	.189	.239	.288	.334	.375	.408	.432	.444	.441	.422	.384	.325	.243	.135
	3	.000	.000	.001	.003	.008	.016	.027	.043	.064	.091	.125	.166	.216	.275	.343	.422	.512	.614	.729	.857
4	0	.961	.815	.656	.522	.410	.316	.240	.179	.130	.092	.062	.041	.026	.015	.008	.004	.002	.001	.000	.000
	1	.039	.171	.292	.368	.410	.422	.412	.384	.346	.300	.250	.200	.154	.112	.076	.047	.026	.011	.004	.000
	2	.001	.014	.049	.098	.154	.211	.265	.311	.346	.368	.375	.368	.346	.311	.265	.211	.154	.098	.049	.014
	3	.000	.000	.004	.011	.026	.047	.076	.112	.154	.200	.250	.300	.346	.384	.412	.422	.410	.368	.292	.171
	4	.000	.000	.000	.001	.002	.004	.008	.015	.026	.041	.062	.092	.130	.179	.240	.316	.410	.522	.656	.815
5	0	.951	.774	.590	.444	.328	.237	.168	.116	.078	.050	.031	.019	.010	.005	.002	.001	.000	.000	.000	.000
	1	.048	.204	.328	.392	.410	.396	.360	.312	.259	.206	.156	.113	.077	.049	.028	.015	.006	.002	.000	.000
	2	.001	.021	.073	.138	.205	.264	.309	.336	.346	.337	.312	.276	.230	.181	.132	.088	.051	.024	.008	.001
	3	.000	.001	.008	.024	.051	.088	.132	.181	.230	.276	.312	.337	.346	.336	.309	.264	.205	.138	.073	.021
	4	.000	.000	.000	.002	.006	.015	.028	.049	.077	.113	.156	.206	.259	.312	.360	.396	.410	.392	.328	.204
	5	.000	.000	.000	.000	.000	.001	.002	.005	.010	.019	.031	.050	.078	.116	.168	.237	.328	.444	.590	.774
6	0	.941	.735	.531	.377	.262	.178	.118	.075	.047	.028	.016	.008	.004	.002	.001	.000	.000	.000	.000	.000
	1	.057	.232	.354	.399	.393	.356	.303	.244	.187	.136	.094	.061	.037	.020	.010	.004	.002	.000	.000	.000
	2	.001	.031	.098	.176	.246	.297	.324	.328	.311	.278	.234	.186	.138	.095	.060	.033	.015	.006	.001	.000
	3	.000	.002	.015	.042	.082	.132	.185	.236	.276	.303	.312	.303	.276	.236	.185	.132	.082	.042	.015	.002

contd.

		p																			
n	r	.01	.05	.10	.15	.20	.25	.30	.35	.40	.45	.50	.55	.60	.65	.70	.75	.80	.85	.90	.95
6	4	.000	.000	.001	.006	.015	.033	.060	.095	.138	.186	.234	.278	.311	.328	.324	.297	.246	.176	.098	.031
	5	.000	.000	.000	.000	.002	.004	.010	.020	.037	.061	.094	.136	.187	.244	.303	.356	.393	.399	.354	.232
	6	.000	.000	.000	.000	.000	.000	.001	.002	.004	.008	.016	.028	.047	.075	.118	.178	.262	.377	.531	.735
7	0	.932	.698	.478	.321	.210	.133	.082	.049	.028	.015	.008	.004	.002	.001	.000	.000	.000	.000	.000	.000
	1	.066	.257	.372	.396	.367	.311	.247	.185	.131	.087	.055	.032	.017	.008	.004	.001	.000	.000	.000	.000
	2	.002	.041	.124	.210	.275	.311	.318	.299	.261	.214	.164	.117	.077	.047	.025	.012	.004	.001	.000	.000
	3	.000	.004	.023	.062	.115	.173	.227	.268	.290	.292	.273	.239	.194	.144	.097	.058	.029	.011	.003	.000
	4	.000	.000	.003	.011	.029	.058	.097	.144	.194	.239	.273	.292	.290	;268	.227	.173	.115	.062	.023	.004
	5	.000	.000	.000	.001	.004	.012	.025	.047	.077	.117	.164	.214	.261	.299	.318	.311	.275	.210	.124	.041
	6	.000	.000	.000	.000	.000	.001	.004	.008	.017	.032	.055	.087	.131	.185	.247	.311	.367	.396	.372	.257
	7	.000	.000	.000	.000	.000	.000	.000	.001	.002	.004	.008	.015	.028	.049	.082	.133	.210	.321	.478	.698
8	0	.923	.663	.430	.272	.168	.100	.058	.032	.017	.008	.004	.002	.001	.000	.000	.000	.000	.000	.000	.000
	1	.075	.279	.383	.385	.336	.267	.198	.137	.090	.055	.031	.016	.008	.003	.001	.000	.000	.000	.000	.000
	2	.003	.051	.149	.238	.294	.311	.296	.259	.209	.157	.109	.070	.041	.022	.010	.004	.001	.000	.000	.000
	3	.000	.005	.033	.084	.147	.208	.254	.279	.279	.257	.219	.172	.124	.081	.047	.023	.009	.003	.000	.000
	4	.000	.000	.005	:018	.046	.087	.136	.188	.232	.263	.273	.263	.232	.188	.136	.087	.046	.018	.005	.000
	5	.000	.000	.000	.003	.009	.023	.047	.081	.124	.172	.219	.257	.279	.279	.254	.208	.147	.084	.033	.005
	6	.000	.000	.000	.000	.001	.004	.010	.022	.041	.070	.109	.157	.209	.259	.296	.311	.294	.238	.149	.051
	7	.000	.000	.000	.000	.000	.000	.001	.003	.008	.016	.031	.055	.090	.137	.198	.267	.336	.385	.383	.279
	8	.000	.000	.000	.000	.000	000	.000	.000	.001	.002	.004	.008	.017	.032	.058	.100	.168	.272	.430	.663
9	0	.914	.630	.387	.232	.134	.075	.040	.021	.010	.005	.002	.001	.000	.000	.000	.000	.000	.000	.000	.000
	1	.083	.299	.387	.368	.302	.225	.156	.100	.060	.034	.018	.008	.004	.001	.000	.000	.000	.000	.000	.000

contd.

		p																			
n	r	.01	.05	.10	.15	.20	.25	.30	.35	.40	.45	.50	.55	.60	.65	.70	.75	.80	.85	.90	.95
9	2	.003	.063	.172	.260	.302	.300	.267	.216	.161	.111	.070	.041	.021	.010	.004	.001	.000	.000	.000	.000
	3	.000	.008	.045	.107	.176	.234	.267	.272	.251	.212	.164	.116	.074	.042	.021	.009	.003	.001	.000	.000
	4	.000	.001	.007	.028	.066	.117	.172	.219	.251	.260	.246	.213	.167	.118	.074	.039	.017	.005	.001	.000
	5	.000	.000	.001	.005	.017	.039	.074	.118	.167	.213	.246	.260	.251	.219	.172	.117	.066	.028	.007	.001
	6	.000	.000	.000	.001	.003	.009	.021	.042	.074	.116	.164	.212	.251	.272	.267	.234	.176	.107	.045	.008
	7	.000	.000	.000	.000	.000	.001	.004	.010	.021	.041	.070	.111	.161	.216	.267	.300	.302	.260	.172	.063
	8	.000	.000	.000	.000	.000	.000	.000	.001	.004	.008	.018	.034	.060	.100	.156	.225	.302	.368	.387	.299
	9	.000	.000	.000	.000	.000	.000	.000	.000	.000	.001	.002	.005	.010	.021	.040	.075	.134	.232	.387	.630
10	0	.904	.599	.349	.197	.107	.056	.028	.014	.006	.003	.001	.000	.000	.000	.000	.000	.000	.000	.000	.000
	1	.091	.315	.387	.347	.268	.188	.121	.072	.040	.021	.010	.004	.002	.000	.000	.000	.000	.000	.000	.000
	2	.004	.075	.194	.276	.302	.282	.233	.176	.121	.076	.044	.023	.011	.004	.001	.000	.000	.000	.000	.000
	3	.000	.010	.057	.130	.201	.250	.267	.252	.215	.166	.117	.075	.042	.021	.009	.003	.001	.000	.000	.000
	4	.000	.001	.011	.040	.088	.146	.200	.238	.251	.238	.205	.160	.111	.069	.037	.016	.006	.001	.000	.000
	5	.000	.000	.001	.008	.026	.058	.103	.154	.201	.234	.246	.234	.201	.154	.103	.058	.026	.008	.001	.000
	6	.000	.000	.000	.001	.006	.016	.037	.069	.111	.160	.205	.238	.251	.238	.200	.146	.088	.040	.011	.001
	7	.000	.000	.000	.000	.001	.003	.009	.021	.042	.075	.117	.166	.215	.252	.267	.250	.201	.130	.057	.010
	8	.000	.000	.000	.000	.000	.000	.001	.004	.011	.023	.044	.076	.121	.176	.233	.282	.302	.276	.194	.07.
	9	.000	.000	.000	.000	.000	.000	.000	.000	.002	.004	.010	.021	.040	.072	.121	.188	.268	.347	.387	.315
	10	.000	.000	.000	.000	.000	.000	.000	.000	.000	.000	.001	.003	.006	.014	.028	.056	.107	.197	.349	.599
11	0	.895	.569	.314	.167	.086	.042	.020	.009	.004	.001	.000	.000	.000	.000	.000	.000	.000	.000	.000	.000
	1	.099	.329	.384	.325	.236	.155	.093	.052	.027	.013	.005	.002	.001	.000	.000	.000	.000	.000	.000	.000
	2	.005	.087	.213	.287	.295	.258	.200	.140	.089	.051	.027	.013	.005	.002	.001	.000	.000	.000	.000	.000

contd.

		p																			
n	r	.01	.05	.10	.15	.20	.25	.30	.35	.40	.45	.50	.55	.60	.65	.70	.75	.80	.85	.90	.95
11	3	.000	.014	.071	.152	.221	.258	.257	.225	.177	.126	.081	.046	.023	.010	.004	.001	.000	.000	.000	.000
	4	.000	.001	.016	.054	.111	.172	.220	.243	.236	.206	.161	.113	.070	.038	.017	.006	.002	.000	.000	.000
	5	.000	.000	.002	.013	.039	.080	.132	.183	.221	.236	.226	.193	.147	.099	.057	.027	.010	.002	.000	.000
	6	.000	.000	.000	.002	.010	.027	.057	.099	.147	.193	.226	.236	.221	.183	.132	.080	.039	.013	.002	.000
	7	.000	.000	.000	.000	.002	.006	.017	.038	.070	.113	.161	.206	.236	.243	.220	.172	.111	.054	.016	.001
	8	.000	.000	.000	.000	.000	.001	.004	.010	.023	.046	.081	.126	.177	.225	.257	.258	.221	.152	.071	.014
	9	.000	.000	.000	.000	.000	.000	.001	.002	.005	.013	.027	.051	.089	.140	.200	.258	.295	.287	.213	.087
	10	.000	.000	.000	.000	.000	.000	.000	.000	.001	.002	.005	.013	.027	.052	.093	.155	.236	.325	.384	.329
	11	.000	.000	.000	.000	.000	.000	.000	.000	.000	.000	.000	.001	.004	.009	.020	.042	.086	.167	.314	.569
12	0	.886	.540	.282	.142	.069	.032	.014	.006	.002	.001	.000	.000	.000	.000	.000	.000	.000	.000	.000	.000
	1	.107	.341	.377	.301	.206	.127	.071	.037	.017	.008	.003	.001	.000	.000	.000	.000	.000	.000	.000	.000
	2	.006	.099	.230	.292	.283	.232	.168	.109	.064	.034	.016	.007	.002	.001	.000	.000	.000	.000	.000	.000
	3	.000	.017	.085	.172	.236	.258	.240	.195	.142	.092	.054	.028	.012	.005	.001	.000	.000	.000	.000	.000
	4	.000	.002	.021	.068	.133	.194	.231	.237	.213	.170	.121	.076	.042	.020	.008	.002	.001	.000	.000	.000
	5	.000	.000	.004	.019	.053	.103	.158	.204	.227	.223	.193	.149	.101	.059	.029	.011	.003	.001	.000	.000
	6	.000	.000	.000	.004	.016	.040	.079	.128	.177	.212	.226	.212	.177	.128	.079	.040	.016	.004	.000	.000
	7	.000	.000	.000	.001	.003	.011	.029	.059	.101	.149	.193	.223	.227	.204	.158	.103	.053	.019	.004	.000
	8	.000	.000	.000	.000	.001	.002	.008	.020	.042	.076	.121	.170	.213	.237	.231	.194	.133	.068	.021	.002
	9	.000	.000	.000	.000	.000	.000	.001	.005	.012	.028	.054	.092	.142	.195	.240	.258	.236	.172	.085	.017
	10	.000	.000	.000	.000	.000	.000	.000	.001	.002	.007	.016	.034	.064	.109	.168	.232	.283	.292	.230	.099
	11	.000	.000	.000	.000	.000	.000	.000	.000	.000	.001	.003	.008	.017	.037	.071	.127	.206	.301	.377	.341
	12	.000	.000	.000	.000	.000	.000	.000	.000	.000	.000	.000	.001	.002	.006	.014	.032	.069	.142	.282	.540

contd.

		p																			
n	r	.01	.05	.10	.15	.20	.25	.30	.35	.40	.45	.50	.55	.60	.65	.70	.75	.80	.85	.90	.95
15	0	.860	.463	.206	.087	.035	.013	.005	.002	.000	.000	.000	.000	.000	.000	.000	.000	.000	.000	.000	.000
	1	.130	.366	.343	.231	.132	.067	.031	.013	.005	.002	.000	.000	.000	.000	.000	.000	.000	.000	.000	.000
	2	.009	.135	.267	.286	.231	.156	.092	.048	.022	.009	.003	.001	.000	.000	.000	.000	.000	.000	.000	.000
	3	.000	.031	.129	.218	.250	.225	.170	.111	.063	.032	.014	.005	.002	.000	.000	.000	.000	.000	.000	.000
	4	.000	.005	.043	.116	.188	.225	.219	.179	.127	.078	.042	.019	.007	.002	.001	.000	.000	.000	.000	.000
	5	.000	.001	.010	.045	.103	.165	.206	.212	.186	.140	.092	.051	.024	.010	.003	.001	.000	.000	.000	.000
	6	.000	.000	.002	.013	.043	.092	.147	.191	.207	.191	.153	.105	.061	.030	.012	.003	.001	.000	.000	.000
	7	.000	.000	.000	.003	.014	.039	.081	.132	.177	.201	.196	.165	.118	.071	.035	.013	.003	.001	.000	.000
	8	.000	.000	.000	.001	.003	.013	.035	.071	.118	.165	.196	.201	.177	.132	.081	.039	.014	.003	.000	.000
	9	.000	.000	.000	.000	.001	.003	.012	.030	.061	.105	.153	.191	.207	.191	.147	.092	.043	.013	.002	.000
	10	.000	.000	.000	.000	.000	.001	.003	.010	.024	.051	.092	.140	.186	.212	.206	.165	.103	.045	.010	.001
	11	.000	.000	.000	.000	.000	.000	.001	.002	.007	.019	.042	.078	.127	.179	.219	.225	.188	.116	.043	.005
	12	.000	.000	.000	.000	.000	.000	.000	.000	.002	.005	.014	.032	.063	.111	.170	.225	.250	.218	.129	.031
	13	.000	.000	.000	.000	.000	.000	.000	.000	.000	.001	.003	.009	.022	.048	.092	.156	.231	.286	.267	.135
	14	.000	.000	.000	.000	.000	.000	.000	.000	.000	.000	.000	.002	.005	.013	.031	.067	.132	.231	.343	.366
	15	.000	.000	.000	.000	.000	.000	.000	.000	.000	.000	.000	.000	.000	.002	.005	.013	.035	.087	.206	.463
16	0	.851	.440	.185	.074	.028	.010	.003	.001	.000	.000	.000	.000	.000	.000	.000	.000	.000	.000	.000	.000
	1	.138	.371	.329	.210	.113	.053	.023	.009	.003	.001	.000	.000	.000	.000	.000	.000	.000	.000	.000	.000
	2	.010	.146	.275	.277	.211	.134	.073	.035	.015	.006	.002	.001	.000	.000	.000	.000	.000	.000	.000	.000
	3	.000	.036	.142	.229	.246	.208	.146	.089	.047	.022	.009	.003	.001	.000	.000	.000	.000	.000	.000	.000
	4	.000	.006	.051	.131	.200	.225	.204	.155	.101	.057	.028	.011	.004	.001	.000	.000	.000	.000	.000	.000
	5	.000	.001	.014	.056	.120	.180	.210	.201	.162	.112	.067	.034	.014	.005	.001	.000	.000	.000	.000	.000

contd.

		p																			
n	r	.01	.05	.10	.15	.20	.25	.30	.35	.40	.45	.50	.55	.60	.65	.70	.75	.80	.85	.90	.95
16	6	.000	.000	.003	.018	.055	.110	.165	.198	.198	.168	.122	.075	.039	.017	.006	.001	.000	.000	.000	.000
	7	.000	.000	.000	.005	.020	.052	.101	.152	.189	.197	.175	.132	.084	.044	.019	.006	.001	.000	.000	.000
	8	.000	.000	.000	.001	.006	.020	.049	.092	.142	.181	.196	.181	.142	.092	.049	.020	.006	.001	.000	.000
	9	.000	.000	.000	.000	.001	.006	.019	.044	.084	.132	.175	.197	.189	.152	.101	.052	.020	.005	.000	.000
	10	.000	.000	.000	.000	.000	.001	.006	.017	.039	.075	.122	.168	.198	.198	.165	.110	.055	.018	.003	.000
	11	.000	.000	.000	.000	.000	.000	.001	.005	.014	.034	.067	.112	.162	.201	.210	.180	.120	.056	.014	.001
	12	.000	.000	.000	.000	.000	.000	.000	.001	.004	.011	.028	.057	.101	.155	.204	.225	.200	.131	.051	.006
	13	.000	.000	.000	.000	.000	.000	.000	.000	.001	.003	.009	.022	.047	.089	.146	.208	.246	.229	.142	.036
	14	.000	.000	.000	.000	.000	.000	.000	.000	.000	.001	.002	.006	.015	.035	.073	.134	.211	.277	.275	.146
	15	.000	.000	.000	.000	.000	.000	.000	.000	.000	.000	.000	.001	.003	.009	.023	.053	.113	.210	.329	.371
	16	.000	.000	.000	.000	.000	.000	.000	.000	.000	.000	.000	.000	.000	.001	.003	.010	.028	.074	.185	.440
20	0	.818	.358	.122	.039	.012	.003	.001	.000	.000	.000	.000	.000	.000	.000	.000	.000	.000	.000	.000	.000
	1	.165	.377	.270	.137	.058	.021	.007	.002	.000	.000	.000	.000	.000	.000	.000	.000	.000	.000	.000	.000
	2	.016	.189	.285	.229	.137	.067	.028	.010	.003	.001	.000	.000	.000	.000	.000	.000	.000	.000	.000	.000
	3	.001	.060	.190	.243	.205	.134	.072	.032	.012	.004	.001	.000	.000	.000	.000	.000	.000	.000	.000	.000
	4	.000	.013	.090	.182	.218	.190	.130	.074	.035	.014	.005	.001	.000	.000	.000	.000	.000	.000	.000	.000
	5	.000	.002	.032	.103	.175	.202	.179	.127	.075	.036	.015	.005	.001	.000	.000	.000	.000	.000	.000	.000
	6	.000	.000	.009	.045	.109	.169	.192	.171	.124	.075	.037	.015	.005	.001	.000	.000	.000	.000	.000	.000
	7	.000	.000	.002	.016	.055	.112	.164	.184	.166	.122	.074	.037	.015	.005	.001	.000	.000	.000	.000	.000
	8	.000	.000	.000	.005	.022	.061	.114	.161	.180	.162	.120	.073	.035	.014	.004	.001	.000	.000	.000	.000
	9	.000	.000	.000	.001	.007	.027	.065	.116	.160	.177	.160	.119	.071	.034	.012	.003	.000	.000	.000	.000
	10	.000	.000	.000	.000	.002	.010	.031	.069	.117	.159	.176	.159	.117	.069	.031	.010	.002	.000	.000	.000

contd.

		p																			
n	**r**	**.01**	**.05**	**.10**	**.15**	**.20**	**.25**	**.30**	**.35**	**.40**	**.45**	**.50**	**.55**	**.60**	**.65**	**.70**	**.75**	**.80**	**.85**	**.90**	**.95**
20	11	.000	.000	.000	.000	.000	.003	.012	.034	.071	.119	.160	.177	.160	.116	.065	.027	.007	.001	.000	.000
	12	.000	.000	.000	.000	.000	.001	.004	.014	.035	.073	.120	.162	.180	.161	.114	.061	.022	.005	.000	.000
	13	.000	.000	.000	.000	.000	.000	.001	.005	.015	.037	.074	.122	.166	.184	.164	.112	.055	.016	.002	.000
	14	.000	.000	.000	.000	.000	.000	.000	.001	.005	.015	.037	.075	.124	.171	.192	.169	.109	.045	.009	.000
	15	.000	.000	.000	.000	.000	.000	.000	.000	.001	.005	.015	.036	.075	.127	.179	.202	.175	.103	.032	.002
	16	.000	.000	.000	.000	.000	.000	.000	.000	.000	.001	.005	.014	.035	.074	.130	.190	.218	.182	.090	.013
	17	.000	.000	.000	.000	.000	.000	.000	.000	.000	.000	.001	.004	.012	.032	.072	.134	.205	.243	.190	.060
	18	.000	.000	.000	.000	.000	.000	.000	.000	.000	.000	.000	.001	.003	.010	.028	.067	.137	.229	.285	.189
	19	.000	.000	.000	.000	.000	.000	.000	.000	.000	.000	.000	.000	.000	.002	.007	.021	.058	.137	.270	.377
	20	.000	.000	.000	.000	.000	.000	.000	.000	.000	.000	.000	.000	.000	.000	.001	.003	.012	.039	.122	.358

Table (B): Normal Area Table

	0.00	0.01	0.02	0.03	0.04	0.05	0.06	0.07	0.08	0.09
0.0	0.0000	0.0040	0.0080	0.0120	0.0160	0.0199	0.0239	0.0279	0.0319	0.0359
0.1	0.0398	0.0438	0.0478	0.0517	0.0557	0.0596	0.0636	0.0675	0.0714	0.0753
0.2	0.0793	0.0832	0.0871	0.0910	0.0948	0.0987	0.1026	0.1064	0.1103	0.1141
0.3	0.1179	0.1217	0.1255	0.1293	0.1331	0.1368	0.1406	0.1443	0.1480	0.1517
0.4	0.1554	0.1591	0.1628	0.1664	0.1700	0.1736	0.1772	0.1808	0.1844	0.1879
0.5	0.1915	0.1950	0.1985	0.2019	0.2054	0.2088	0.2123	0.2157	0.2190	0.2224
0.6	0.2257	0.2291	0.2324	0.2357	0.2389	0.2422	0.2454	0.2486	0.2517	0.2549
0.7	0.2580	0.2611	0.2642	0.2673	0.2704	0.2734	0.2764	0.2794	0.2823	0.2852
0.8	0.2881	0.2910	0.2939	0.2967	0.2995	0.3023	0.3051	0.3078	0.3106	0.3133
0.9	0.3159	0.3186	0.3212	0.3238	0.3264	0.3289	0.3315	0.3340	0.3365	0.3389
1.0	0.3413	0.3438	0.3461	0.3485	0.3508	0.3531	0.3554	0.3577	0.3599	0.3621
1.1	0.3643	0.3665	0.3686	0.3708	0.3729	0.3749	0.3770	0.3790	0.3810	0.3830
1.2	0.3849	0.3869	0.3888	0.3907	0.3925	0.3944	0.3962	0.3980	0.3997	0.4015
1.3	0.4032	0.4049	0.4066	0.4082	0.4099	0.4115	0.4131	0.4147	0.4162	0.4177
1.4	0.4192	0.4207	0.4222	0.4236	0.4251	0.4265	0.4279	0.4292	0.4306	0.4319
1.5	0.4332	0.4345	0.4357	0.4370	0.4382	0.4394	0.4406	0.4418	0.4429	0.4441
1.6	0.4452	0.4463	0.4474	0.4484	0.4495	0.4505	0.4515	0.4525	0.4535	0.4545
1.7	0.4554	0.4564	0.4573	0.4582	0.4591	0.4599	0.4608	0.4616	0.4625	0.4633
1.8	0.4641	0.4649	0.4656	0.4664	0.4671	0.4678	0.4686	0.4693	0.4699	0.4706
1.9	0.4713	0.4719	0.4726	0.4732	0.4738	0.4744	0.4750	0.4756	0.4761	0.4767
2.0	0.4772	0.4778	0.4783	0.4788	0.4793	0.4798	0.4803	0.4808	0.4812	0.4817
2.1	0.4821	0.4826	0.4830	0.4834	0.4838	0.4842	0.4846	0.4850	0.4854	0.4857
2.2	0.4861	0.4864	0.4868	0.4871	0.4875	0.4878	0.4881	0.4884	0.4887	0.4890
2.3	0.4893	0.4896	0.4898	0.4901	0.4904	0.4906	0.4909	0.4911	0.4913	0.4916
2.4	0.4918	0.4920	0.4922	0.4925	0.4927	0.4929	0.4931	0.4932	0.4934	0.4936
2.5	0.4938	0.4940	0.4941	0.4943	0.4945	0.4946	0.4948	0.4949	0.4951	0.4952
2.6	0.4953	0.4955	0.4956	0.4957	0.4959	0.4960	0.4961	0.4962	0.4963	0.4964
2.7	0.4965	0.4966	0.4967	0.4968	0.4969	0.4970	0.4971	0.4972	0.4973	0.4974
2.8	0.4974	0.4975	0.4976	0.4977	0.4977	0.4978	0.4979	0.4979	0.4980	0.4981
2.9	0.4981	0.4982	0.4982	0.4983	0.4984	0.4984	0.4985	0.4985	0.4986	0.4986
3.0	0.4987	0.4987	0.4987	0.4988	0.4988	0.4989	0.4989	0.4989	0.4990	0.4990

Table (C): t-Distribution

df\p	0.40	0.25	0.10	0.05	0.025	0.01	0.005	0.0005
1	0.324920	1.000000	3.077684	6.313752	12.70620	31.82052	63.65674	636.6192
2	0.288675	0.816497	1.885618	2.919986	4.30265	6.96456	9.92484	31.5991
3	0.276671	0.764892	1.637744	2.353363	3.18245	4.54070	5.84091	12.9240
4	0.270722	0.740697	1.533206	2.131847	2.77645	3.74695	4.60409	8.6103
5	0.267181	0.726687	1.475884	2.015048	2.57058	3.36493	4.03214	6.8688
6	0.264835	0.717558	1.439756	1.943180	2.44691	3.14267	3.70743	5.9588
7	0.263167	0.711142	1.414924	1.894579	2.36462	2.99795	3.49948	5.4079
8	0.261921	0.706387	1.396815	1.859548	2.30600	2.89646	3.35539	5.0413
9	0.260955	0.702722	1.383029	1.833113	2.26216	2.82144	3.24984	4.7809
10	0.260185	0.699812	1.372184	1.812461	2.22814	2.76377	3.16927	4.5869
11	0.259556	0.697445	1.363430	1.795885	2.20099	2.71808	3.10581	4.4370
12	0.259033	0.695483	1.356217	1.782288	2.17881	2.68100	3.05454	4.3178
13	0.258591	0.693829	1.350171	1.770933	2.16037	2.65031	3.01228	4.2208
14	0.258213	0.692417	1.345030	1.761310	2.14479	2.62449	2.97684	4.1405
15	0.257885	0.691197	1.340606	1.753050	2.13145	2.60248	2.94671	4.0728
16	0.257599	0.690132	1.336757	1.745884	2.11991	2.58349	2.92078	4.0150
17	0.257347	0.689195	1.333379	1.739607	2.10982	2.56693	2.89823	3.9651
18	0.257123	0.688364	1.330391	1.734064	2.10092	2.55238	2.87844	3.9216
19	0.256923	0.687621	1.327728	1.729133	2.09302	2.53948	2.86093	3.8834
20	0.256743	0.686954	1.325341	1.724718	2.08596	2.52798	2.84534	3.8495

Table (D): Critical Values of F-Ratio (5% level of significance)

df2/df1	1	2	3	4	5	6	7	8	9
1	161.4476	199.5000	215.7073	224.5832	230.1619	233.9860	236.7684	238.8827	240.5433
2	18.5128	19.0000	19.1643	19.2468	19.2964	19.3295	19.3532	19.3710	19.3848
3	10.1280	9.5521	9.2766	9.1172	9.0135	8.9406	8.8867	8.8452	8.8123
4	7.7086	6.9443	6.5914	6.3882	6.2561	6.1631	6.0942	6.0410	5.9988
5	6.6079	5.7861	5.4095	5.1922	5.0503	4.9503	4.8759	4.8183	4.7725
6	5.9874	5.1433	4.7571	4.5337	4.3874	4.2839	4.2067	4.1468	4.0990
7	5.5914	4.7374	4.3468	4.1203	3.9715	3.8660	3.7870	3.7257	3.6767
8	5.3177	4.4590	4.0662	3.8379	3.6875	3.5806	3.5005	3.4381	3.3881
9	5.1174	4.2565	3.8625	3.6331	3.4817	3.3738	3.2927	3.2296	3.1789
10	4.9646	4.1028	3.7083	3.4780	3.3258	3.2172	3.1355	3.0717	3.0204
11	4.8443	3.9823	3.5874	3.3567	3.2039	3.0946	3.0123	2.9480	2.8962
12	4.7472	3.8853	3.4903	3.2592	3.1059	2.9961	2.9134	2.8486	2.7964
13	4.6672	3.8056	3.4105	3.1791	3.0254	2.9153	2.8321	2.7669	2.7144
14	4.6001	3.7389	3.3439	3.1122	2.9582	2.8477	2.7642	2.6987	2.6458
15	4.5431	3.6823	3.2874	3.0556	2.9013	2.7905	2.7066	2.6408	2.5876
16	4.4940	3.6337	3.2389	3.0069	2.8524	2.7413	2.6572	2.5911	2.5377
17	4.4513	3.5915	3.1968	2.9647	2.8100	2.6987	2.6143	2.5480	2.4943
18	4.4139	3.5546	3.1599	2.9277	2.7729	2.6613	2.5767	2.5102	2.4563
19	4.3807	3.5219	3.1274	2.8951	2.7401	2.6283	2.5435	2.4768	2.4227
20	4.3512	3.4928	3.0984	2.8661	2.7109	2.5990	2.5140	2.4471	2.3928
21	4.3248	3.4668	3.0725	2.8401	2.6848	2.5727	2.4876	2.4205	2.3660
22	4.3009	3.4434	3.0491	2.8167	2.6613	2.5491	2.4638	2.3965	2.3419
23	4.2793	3.4221	3.0280	2.7955	2.6400	2.5277	2.4422	2.3748	2.3201
24	4.2597	3.4028	3.0088	2.7763	2.6207	2.5082	2.4226	2.3551	2.3002
25	4.2417	3.3852	2.9912	2.7587	2.6030	2.4904	2.4047	2.3371	2.2821
26	4.2252	3.3690	2.9752	2.7426	2.5868	2.4741	2.3883	2.3205	2.2655
27	4.2100	3.3541	2.9604	2.7278	2.5719	2.4591	2.3732	2.3053	2.2501
28	4.1960	3.3404	2.9467	2.7141	2.5581	2.4453	2.3593	2.2913	2.2360
29	4.1830	3.3277	2.9340	2.7014	2.5454	2.4324	2.3463	2.2783	2.2229
30	4.1709	3.3158	2.9223	2.6896	2.5336	2.4205	2.3343	2.2662	2.2107
40	4.0847	3.2317	2.8387	2.6060	2.4495	2.3359	2.2490	2.1802	2.1240
60	4.0012	3.1504	2.7581	2.5252	2.3683	2.2541	2.1665	2.0970	2.0401
120	3.9201	3.0718	2.6802	2.4472	2.2899	2.1750	2.0868	2.0164	1.9588
inf	3.8415	2.9957	2.6049	2.3719	2.2141	2.0986	2.0096	1.9384	1.8799

10	12	15	20	24	30	40	60	120	INF
241.8817	243.9060	245.9499	248.0131	249.0518	250.0951	251.1432	252.1957	253.2529	254.3144
19.3959	19.4125	19.4291	19.4458	19.4541	19.4624	19.4707	19.4791	19.4874	19.4957
8.7855	8.7446	8.7029	8.6602	8.6385	8.6166	8.5944	8.5720	8.5494	8.5264
5.9644	5.9117	5.8578	5.8025	5.7744	5.7459	5.7170	5.6877	5.6581	5.6281
4.7351	4.6777	4.6188	4.5581	4.5272	4.4957	4.4638	4.4314	4.3985	4.3650
4.0600	3.9999	3.9381	3.8742	3.8415	3.8082	3.7743	3.7398	3.7047	3.6689
3.6365	3.5747	3.5107	3.4445	3.4105	3.3758	3.3404	3.3043	3.2674	3.2298
3.3472	3.2839	3.2184	3.1503	3.1152	3.0794	3.0428	3.0053	2.9669	2.9276
3.1373	3.0729	3.0061	2.9365	2.9005	2.8637	2.8259	2.7872	2.7475	2.7067
2.9782	2.9130	2.8450	2.7740	2.7372	2.6996	2.6609	2.6211	2.5801	2.5379
2.8536	2.7876	2.7186	2.6464	2.6090	2.5705	2.5309	2.4901	2.4480	2.4045
2.7534	2.6866	2.6169	2.5436	2.5055	2.4663	2.4259	2.3842	2.3410	2.2962
2.6710	2.6037	2.5331	2.4589	2.4202	2.3803	2.3392	2.2966	2.2524	2.2064
2.6022	2.5342	2.4630	2.3879	2.3487	2.3082	2.2664	2.2229	2.1778	2.1307
2.5437	2.4753	2.4034	2.3275	2.2878	2.2468	2.2043	2.1601	2.1141	2.0658
2.4935	2.4247	2.3522	2.2756	2.2354	2.1938	2.1507	2.1058	2.0589	2.0096
2.4499	2.3807	2.3077	2.2304	2.1898	2.1477	2.1040	2.0584	2.0107	1.9604
2.4117	2.3421	2.2686	2.1906	2.1497	2.1071	2.0629	2.0166	1.9681	1.9168
2.3779	2.3080	2.2341	2.1555	2.1141	2.0712	2.0264	1.9795	1.9302	1.8780
2.3479	2.2776	2.2033	2.1242	2.0825	2.0391	1.9938	1.9464	1.8963	1.8432
2.3210	2.2504	2.1757	2.0960	2.0540	2.0102	1.9645	1.9165	1.8657	1.8117
2.2967	2.2258	2.1508	2.0707	2.0283	1.9842	1.9380	1.8894	1.8380	1.7831
2.2747	2.2036	2.1282	2.0476	2.0050	1.9605	1.9139	1.8648	1.8128	1.7570
2.2547	2.1834	2.1077	2.0267	1.9838	1.9390	1.8920	1.8424	1.7896	1.7330
2.2365	2.1649	2.0889	2.0075	1.9643	1.9192	1.8718	1.8217	1.7684	1.7110
2.2197	2.1479	2.0716	1.9898	1.9464	1.9010	1.8533	1.8027	1.7488	1.6906
2.2043	2.1323	2.0558	1.9736	1.9299	1.8842	1.8361	1.7851	1.7306	1.6717
2.1900	2.1179	2.0411	1.9586	1.9147	1.8687	1.8203	1.7689	1.7138	1.6541
2.1768	2.1045	2.0275	1.9446	1.9005	1.8543	1.8055	1.7537	1.6981	1.6376
2.1646	2.0921	2.0148	1.9317	1.8874	1.8409	1.7918	1.7396	1.6835	1.6223
2.0772	2.0035	1.9245	1.8389	1.7929	1.7444	1.6928	1.6373	1.5766	1.5089
1.9926	1.9174	1.8364	1.7480	1.7001	1.6491	1.5943	1.5343	1.4673	1.3893
1.9105	1.8337	1.7505	1.6587	1.6084	1.5543	1.4952	1.4290	1.3519	1.2539
1.8307	1.7522	1.6664	1.5705	1.5173	1.4591	1.3940	1.3180	1.2214	1.0000

Table (E): Critical Values of F-Distribution (1% level of significance)

	d_1								
d_2	1	2	3	4	5	6	7	8	9
1	4052	4999.5	5403	5625	5764	5859	5928	5982	6022
2	98.50	99.00	99.17	99.25	99.30	99.33	99.36	99.37	99.39
3	34.12	30.82	29.46	28.71	28.24	27.91	27.67	27.49	27.35
4	21.20	18.00	16.69	15.98	15.52	15.21	14.98	14.80	14.66
5	16.26	13.27	12.06	11.39	10.97	10.67	10.46	10.29	10.16
6	13.75	10.92	9.78	9.15	8.75	8.47	8.26	8.10	7.98
7	12.25	9.55	8.45	7.85	7.46	7.19	6.99	6.84	6.72
8	11.26	8.65	7.59	7.01	6.63	6.37	6.18	6.03	5.91
9	10.56	8.02	6.99	6.42	6.06	5.80	5.61	5.47	5.35
10	10.04	7.56	6.55	5.99	5.64	5.39	5.2	5.06	4.94
11	9.65	7.21	6.22	5.67	5.32	5.07	4.89	4.74	4.63
12	9.33	6.93	5.95	5.41	5.06	4.82	4.64	4.50	4.39
13	9.07	6.70	5.74	5.21	4.86	4.62	4.44	4.30	4.14
14	8.86	6.51	5.56	5.04	4.69	4.46	4.28	4.14	4.03
15	8.68	6.36	5.42	4.89	4.56	4.32	4.14	4.00	3.89
16	8.53	6.23	5.29	4.77	4.44	4.20	4.03	3.89	3.78
17	8.40	6.11	5.18	4.67	4.34	4.10	3.93	3.79	3.68
18	8.29	6.01	5.09	4.58	4.25	4.01	3.84	3.71	3.60
19	8.18	5.93	5.01	4.50	4.17	3.94	3.77	3.63	3.52
20	8.10	5.85	4.94	4.43	4.10	3.87	3.70	3.56	3.46
21	8.02	5.78	4.87	4.37	4.04	3.81	3.64	3.51	3.40
22	7.95	5.72	4.82	4.31	3.99	3.76	3.59	3.45	3.35
23	7.88	5.66	4.76	4.26	3.94	3.71	3.54	3.41	3.30
24	7.82	5.61	4.72	4.22	3.90	3.67	3.50	3.36	3.26
25	7.77	5.57	4.68	4.18	3.85	3.63	3.46	3.32	3.22
26	7.72	5.53	4.64	4.14	3.82	3.59	3.42	3.29	3.18
27	7.68	5.49	4.60	4.11	3.78	3.56	3.39	3.26	3.15
28	7.64	5.45	4.57	4.07	3.75	3.53	3.36	3.23	3.12
29	7.60	5.42	4.54	4.04	3.73	3.50	3.33	3.20	3.09
30	7.56	5.39	4.51	4.02	3.70	3.47	3.30	3.17	3.07
40	7.31	5.18	4.31	3.83	3.51	3.29	3.12	2.99	2.89
60	7.08	4.98	4.13	3.65	3.34	3.12	2.95	2.82	2.72
120	6.85	4.79	3.95	3.48	3.17	2.96	2.79	2.66	2.56
inf	6.63	4.61	3.78	3.32	3.02	2.80	2.64	2.51	2.41

d_1									
10	**12**	**15**	**20**	**24**	**30**	**40**	**60**	**120**	**inf**
6056	6106	6157	6209	6235	6261	6287	6313	6339	6366
99.40	99.42	99.43	99.45	99.46	99.47	99.47	99.48	99.49	99.50
27.23	27.05	26.87	26.69	26.60	26.50	26.41	26.32	26.22	26.13
14.55	14.37	14.20	14.02	13.93	13.84	13.75	13.65	13.56	13.46
10.05	9.89	9.72	9.55	9.47	9.38	9.29	9.20	9.11	9.02
7.87	7.72	7.56	7.40	7.31	7.23	7.14	7.06	6.97	6.88
6.62	6.47	6.31	6.16	6.07	5.99	5.91	5.82	5.74	5.65
5.81	5.67	5.52	5.36	5.28	5.20	5.12	5.03	4.95	4.86
5.26	5.11	4.96	4.81	4.73	4.65	4.57	4.48	4.40	4.31
4.85	4.71	4.56	4.41	4.33	4.25	4.17	4.08	4.00	3.91
4.54	4.40	4.25	4.10	4.02	3.94	3.86	3.78	3.69	3.60
4.30	4.16	4.01	3.86	3.78	3.70	3.62	3.54	3.45	3.36
4.10	3.96	3.82	3.66	3.59	3.51	3.43	3.34	3.25	3.17
3.94	3.80	3.66	3.51	3.43	3.35	3.27	3.18	3.09	3.00
3.80	3.67	3.52	3.37	3.29	3.21	3.13	3.05	2.96	2.87
3.69	3.55	3.41	3.26	3.18	3.10	3.02	2.93	2.84	2.75
3.59	3.46	3.31	3.16	3.08	3.00	2.92	2.83	2.75	2.65
3.51	3.37	3.23	3.08	3.00	2.92	2.84	2.75	2.66	2.57
3.43	3.30	3.15	3.00	2.92	2.84	2.76	2.67	2.58	2.49
3.37	3.23	3.09	2.94	2.86	2.78	2.69	2.61	2.52	2.42
3.31	3.17	3.03	2.88	2.80	2.72	2.64	2.55	2.46	2.36
3.26	3.12	2.98	2.83	2.75	2.67	2.58	2.50	2.40	2.31
3.21	3.07	2.93	2.78	2.70	2.62	2.54	2.45	2.35	2.26
3.17	3.03	2.89	2.74	2.66	2.58	2.49	2.40	2.31	2.21
3.13	2.99	2.85	2.70	2.62	2.54	2.45	2.36	2.27	2.17
3.09	2.96	2.81	2.66	2.58	2.50	2.42	2.33	2.23	2.13
3.06	2.93	2.78	2.63	2.55	2.47	2.38	2.29	2.20	2.10
3.03	2.90	2.75	2.60	2.52	2.44	2.35	2.26	2.17	2.06
3.00	2.87	2.73	2.57	2.49	2.41	2.33	2.23	2.14	2.03
2.98	2.84	2.70	2.55	2.47	2.39	2.30	2.21	2.11	2.01
2.80	2.66	2.52	2.37	2.29	2.20	2.11	2.02	1.92	1.80
2.63	2.50	2.35	2.20	2.12	2.03	1.94	1.84	1.73	1.60
2.47	2.34	2.19	2.03	1.95	1.86	1.76	1.66	1.53	1.38
2.32	2.18	2.04	1.88	1.79	1.70	1.59	1.47	1.32	1.00

Table (F): Critical Values of Chi-square Distribution

df\area	.995	.990	.975	.950	.900	.750
1	0.00004	0.00016	0.00098	0.00393	0.01579	0.10153
2	0.01003	0.02010	0.05064	0.10259	0.21072	0.57536
3	0.07172	0.11483	0.21580	0.35185	0.58437	1.21253
4	0.20699	0.29711	0.48442	0.71072	1.06362	1.92256
5	0.41174	0.55430	0.83121	1.14548	1.61031	2.67460
6	0.67573	0.87209	1.23734	1.63538	2.20413	3.45460
7	0.98926	1.23904	1.68987	2.16735	2.83311	4.25485
8	1.34441	1.64650	2.17973	2.73264	3.48954	5.07064
9	1.73493	2.08790	2.70039	3.32511	4.16816	5.89883
10	2.15586	2.55821	3.24697	3.94030	4.86518	6.73720
11	2.60322	3.05348	3.81575	4.57481	5.57778	7.58414
12	3.07382	3.57057	4.40379	5.22603	6.30380	8.43842
13	3.56503	4.10692	5.00875	5.89186	7.04150	9.29907
14	4.07467	4.66043	5.62873	6.57063	7.78953	10.16531
15	4.60092	5.22935	6.26214	7.26094	8.54676	11.03654
16	5.14221	5.81221	6.90766	7.96165	9.31224	11.91222
17	5.69722	6.40776	7.56419	8.67176	10.08519	12.79193
18	6.26480	7.01491	8.23075	9.39046	10.86494	13.67529
19	6.84397	7.63273	8.90652	10.11701	11.65091	14.56200
20	7.43384	8.26040	9.59078	10.85081	12.44261	15.45177
21	8.03365	8.89720	10.28290	11.59131	13.23960	16.34438
22	8.64272	9.54249	10.98232	12.33801	14.04149	17.23962
23	9.26042	10.19572	11.68855	13.09051	14.84796	18.13730
24	9.88623	10.85636	12.40115	13.84843	15.65868	19.03725
25	10.51965	11.52398	13.11972	14.61141	16.47341	19.93934
26	11.16024	12.19815	13.84390	15.37916	17.29188	20.84343
27	11.80759	12.87850	14.57338	16.15140	18.11390	21.74940
28	12.46134	13.56471	15.30786	16.92788	18.93924	22.65716
29	13.12115	14.25645	16.04707	17.70837	19.76774	23.56659
30	13.78672	14.95346	16.79077	18.49266	20.59923	24.47761

.500	.250	.100	.050	.025	.010	.005
0.45494	1.32330	2.70554	3.84146	5.02389	6.63490	7.87944
1.38629	2.77259	4.60517	5.99146	7.37776	9.21034	10.59663
2.36597	4.10834	6.25139	7.81473	9.34840	11.34487	12.83816
3.35669	5.38527	7.77944	9.48773	11.14329	13.27670	14.86026
4.35146	6.62568	9.23636	11.07050	12.83250	15.08627	16.74960
5.34812	7.84080	10.64464	12.59159	14.44938	16.81189	18.54758
6.34581	9.03715	12.01704	14.06714	16.01276	18.47531	20.27774
7.34412	10.21885	13.36157	15.50731	17.53455	20.09024	21.95495
8.34283	11.38875	14.68366	16.91898	19.02277	21.66599	23.58935
9.34182	12.54886	15.98718	18.30704	20.48318	23.20925	25.18818
10.34100	13.70069	17.27501	19.67514	21.92005	24.72497	26.75685
11.34032	14.84540	18.54935	21.02607	23.33666	26.21697	28.29952
12.33976	15.98391	19.81193	22.36203	24.73560	27.68825	29.81947
13.33927	17.11693	21.06414	23.68479	26.11895	29.14124	31.31935
14.33886	18.24509	22.30713	24.99579	27.48839	30.57791	32.80132
15.33850	19.36886	23.54183	26.29623	28.84535	31.99993	34.26719
16.33818	20.48868	24.76904	27.58711	30.19101	33.40866	35.71847
17.33790	21.60489	25.98942	28.86930	31.52638	34.80531	37.15645
18.33765	22.71781	27.20357	30.14353	32.85233	36.19087	38.58226
19.33743	23.82769	28.41198	31.41043	34.16961	37.56623	39.99685
20.33723	24.93478	29.61509	32.67057	35.47888	38.93217	41.40106
21.33704	26.03927	30.81328	33.92444	36.78071	40.28936	42.79565
22.33688	27.14134	32.00690	35.17246	38.07563	41.63840	44.18128
23.33673	28.24115	33.19624	36.41503	39.36408	42.97982	45.55851
24.33659	29.33885	34.38159	37.65248	40.64647	44.31410	46.92789
25.33646	30.43457	35.56317	38.88514	41.92317	45.64168	48.28988
26.33634	31.52841	36.74122	40.11327	43.19451	46.96294	49.64492
27.33623	32.62049	37.91592	41.33714	44.46079	48.27824	50.99338
28.33613	33.71091	39.08747	42.55697	45.72229	49.58788	52.33562
29.33603	34.79974	40.25602	43.77297	46.97924	50.89218	53.67196

Table (G): Conversion of Person r into a corresponding Fisher's coefficient*

r	z	r	z	r	z	r	z	r	z	r	z
.25	.26	.40	.42	.55	.62	.70	.87	.85	1.26	.950	1.83
.26	.27	.41	.44	.56	.63	.71	.89	.86	1.29	.955	1.89
.27	.28	.42	.45	.57	.65	.72	.91	.87	1.33	.960	1.95
.28	.29	.43	.46	.59	.68	.74	.95	89	1.42	.970	2.09
.30	.31	.45	.48	.60	.69	.75	.97	.90	1.47	.975	2.18
.31	.32	.46	.50	.61	.71	.76	1.00	.905	1.50	.980	2.30
.32	.33	.47	.51	.62	.73	.77	1.02	.910	1.53	.985	2.44
.33	.34	.48	.52	.63	.74	.78	1.05	.915	1.56	.990	2.65
.34	.35	.49	.54	.64	.76	.79	1.07	.920	1.59	.995	2.99
.35	.37	.50	.55	.65	.78	.80	1.10	.925	1.62		
.36	.38	.51	.56	.66	.79	.81	1.13	.930	1.66		
.37	.39	.52	.58	.67	.81	.82	1.16	.935	1.70		
.38	.40	.53	.59	.68	.83	.83	1.19	.940	1.74		
.39	.41	.54	.60	.69	.85	.84	1.22	.945	1.78		

** r's under 25 may be taken as equivalent*

Table (H): Table of critical values of T in the Wilicoxon matched pairs signed ranks test

N	Level of significance for one-tailed test		
	.025	.01	.005
	Level of significance for two-tailed test		
	.05	.02	.01
6	0	-	-
7	2	0	-
8	4	2	0
9	6	3	2
10	8	5	3
11	11	7	5
12	14	10	7
13	17	13	10
14	21	16	13
15	25	20	16
16	30	24	20
17	35	28	23
18	40	33	28
19	46	38	32
20	52	43	38
21	59	49	43
22	66	56	49
23	73	62	55
24	81	69	61
25	89	77	68

Feedback is the breakfast of Champions.

Ken Blanchard

You can Help other students.
"Inform any error or mistake in this book."

We and Universe
will reward you for Your Kind act.

Email at : feedback@gullybaba.com
or
WhatsApp on 9350849407

Question Papers

METHODOLOGY OF EDUCATIONAL RESEARCH : MES-054
June, 2011

Note: *(i) All questions are compulsory.*
(ii) All the questions carry equal weightage.
Answer the following questions in about 600 words.

Q1. Discuss the importance of review of related literature in educational research. Write the names of two Indian and two foreign research journals related to education.

Ans. Refer to Chapter-2, Q.No.-1, and

Examples of Indian Journals: Indian Educational Review and Journal of Psychological Researches.

Examples of Foreign Journals: British Journal of Educational Psychology (UK) and NEA Research Bulletin (USA)

Or

'Historical research has its own place in educational research' Discuss. Explain the main characteristics of Historical research.

Ans. Refer to Chapter-5, Q.No.-5 and Q.No.-4

Q2. Describe briefly positivism in educational research. Also, discuss its assumptions and limitations.

Ans. Refer to Chapter-1, Q.No.-4

Or

Discuss the ethical issues related to reporting of research findings.

Ans. Refer to Chapter-6, Q.No.-20

Q3. Answer any four of the following questions in about 150 words each.

(a) What are the characteristics of a quantitative data?

Ans. Refer to Chapter-4, Q.No.-1

(b) Explain criterion validity with the help of suitable example.

Ans. Refer to Chapter-3, Q.No.-6

(c) **Calculate the SD from following distribution Table.**

Class Internal	Frequencies
40 - 42	05
37 - 39	08
34 - 36	09
31 - 33	10
28 - 30	07
25 - 27	05
22 - 24	04
19 - 21	02
	50

Ans.

Class Interval X	Mid Point x	f	$dx = \frac{(x-32)}{3}$	dx^2	fdx	fdx^2
39.5-42.5	41	5	3	9	15	45
36.5-39.5	38	8	2	4	16	32
33.5-36.5	35	9	1	1	9	9
30.5-33.5	32	10	0	0	0	0
27.5-30.5	29	7	–1	1	–7	7
24.5-27.5	26	5	–2	4	–10	20
21.5-24.5	23	4	–3	9	–12	36
18.5-21.5	20	2	–4	16	–8	32
		50			3	181

$$\sigma = \sqrt{\frac{\sum fdx^2}{N} - \left(\frac{\sum fdx}{N}\right)^2} \times i$$

$$= \sqrt{\frac{181}{50} - \left(\frac{3}{50}\right)^2} \times 3$$

$$= \sqrt{3.61} \times 3$$

$$= 5.7$$

(d) **Differentiate between extraneous and intervening variables citing appropriate examples.**

Ans. Refer to Chapter-5, Q.No.-15

(e) **Discuss the limitations of an educational research.**

Ans. Refer to Chapter-1, Q.No.-8

(f) Discuss the procedure of content analysis as used in educational research.

Ans. Refer to Chapter-4, Q.No.-43

Q4. As a teacher, how could you use sociometric techniques for understanding dynamics in your class.

Ans. Refer to Chapter-3, Q.No.-19

METHODOLOGY OF EDUCATIONAL RESEARCH : MES-054
December, 2011

Note: *(i) All questions are compulsory.*
(ii) All questions carry equal weightage.
Answer the following in about 600 words:

Q1. Describe the nature and scope of research in education. What should be the priority areas of researches according to you?

Ans. Refer to Chapter 1, Q.No.-7, Q.No.-8 and Q.No.-9

Or

Is there a need of hypothesis in philosophical researches? Justify. Discuss null hypothesis with examples.

Ans. The educational researches are designed to achieve the following four objectives:

- To formulate new theory, principles and laws,
- To establish new truth when reality,
- To find out new facts, and
- To suggest new applications.

These objects are achieved by conducting historical, experimental survey and philosophical researches. The philosophical researches are conducted to establish truth or reality. Education has two respects: theoretical and practical. The practical aspect is enriched by scientific researches and conducting philosophical researches can develop theoretical part of education.

Hypotheses are needed because of the following:

- Hypotheses are indispensable research instrument, for they build a bridge between the problem and the location of empirical evidence that may solve the problem.
- A hypothesis provides the map that guides and expedites the exploration of the phenomena under consideration.
- A hypothesis pin points the problem. The investigator can examine thoroughly the factual and conceptual elements that appear to be related to a problem.

- Using hypothesis determines the relevancy of facts. A hypothesis directs the researcher's efforts into a productive channels.
- The hypothesis indicates not only what to look for is an investigation but how to obtain data. In helps in deciding research design. It may suggest what subjects, tests, tools, and techniques are needed.
- The hypothesis provides the investigator with the most efficient instrument for exploring and explaining the unknown facts.
- A hypothesis provides the framework for drawing conclusions.
- These hypotheses simulate-the investigator for further research studies.

Null Hypothesis is a statistical hypothesis which is used in analysing the data. It assumes that observed difference is attributable by sampling error and true difference is zero.

The null hypothesis is used for denying many other forms of researcher hypothesis also. For example,

- If a researcher's hypothesis says that there is a correlation between two variables, the null hypothesis declares that there is no correlation if the entire population is taken; and whatever correlation comes is due to sampling chance.
- If the researcher's hypothesis says that distribution of a trait in a population is not normal, the null hypothesis would say that it is normal and non-normality in the sample taken is merely due to sampling chance.

A null hypothesis challenges the assertion of a declarative hypothesis and denies it altogether. It states that even where it seems to hold good it is due to mere chance. It is for the researcher to reject the null hypothesis by showing that the outcome mentioned in the declarative hypothesis does occur and the quantum of it is such that it cannot be easily dismissed as having occurred by chance. The criteria for rejecting the null hypothesis may differ. Sometimes the null hypothesis is rejected only when the quantity of the outcome is so large that the probability of its having occurred by mere, chance is I time out of 100 or .01 time out of 1. We consider the probability of its having occurred by chance to be too little and we reject the chance theory of the null hypothesis and take the occurrence to be due to a genuine tendency. On other occasions, we may be more bold and reject the null hypothesis even when the quantity of the reported outcome is likely to occur by chance 5 times out of 100 or .05 time out of 1. Statistically the former is known as the rejection of the null hypothesis at .01 level of significance and the latter as the rejection at .05 level.

Q2. Parametric tests are most powerful tests for testing the significance, explain. How inferences will be drawn regarding means of large samples?

Ans. Refer to Chapter-4, Q.No.-21 and Q.No.-22

Or

Discuss the relevance of descriptive research in education.

Ans. The descriptive research method has undoubtedly been the most popular and the most widely used research method in education. It helps to explain educational phenomena in terms of the conditions or relationships that exist, opinions that are held by the students, teachers, parents and experts, processes that are going on, effects that are evident, or trends that are developing. Because of the apparent ease and directness of this method, a researcher can gather information in terms of individual's opinion about some issue, by a simple questionnaire. At times, descriptive survey is the only means through which opinions, attitudes, suggestions for improvement of educational practices and instruction, and other data can be obtained.

The descriptive investigations are of immense value in solving problems about children, school organization, supervision and administration, curriculum, teaching methods and evaluation. There are a number of questions that arise concerning these aspects of education. For example, one may want to know how many of the teachers in a district possess a Bachelors degree in Education. How do these figures compare with the tendency throughout the state? How many minutes per week are normally devoted to the teaching of English spelling? What proportion of total state budget is reasonable to set aside for adult education? What kind of a curriculum do people really want their children to have at the secondary school stage? At what age and grade level do pupils leave school? What happens to students after they leave school? What higher institutions or vocations do they enter? And so on. Such information is useful to teachers and administrators and in understanding the existing educational problems and also in suggesting ways of meeting them. The head of a school may wish to know how other school systems are being run, so that he can compare his practices with theirs. This way he will be able to know what procedures and standards are superior to those of other schools. The teachers will also study the conditions existing in their classrooms and that of other teachers.

The problems in education directly involve people and the situations precipitating these problems are constantly in a state of change. To keep abreast of changes, descriptive studies conducted at different intervals with representative changes, descriptive studies conducted at different intervals with representative groups of people will be immensely helpful.

The descriptive type of research is useful in the development of data gathering instruments and tools like tests, checklists, schedules; questionnaires and rating scales. It also provides the background ideas and data from which many more refined or controlled studies of casual relations are made.

Q3. (a) Explain the Scientific Approach for gaining knowledge.

Ans. Refer to Chapter-1, Q.No.-2

(b) What do you understand by median and when it is used?

Ans. Refer to Chapter-4, Q.No.-6

Whenever a graph falls on a normal distribution, using the mean is a good choice. But if your data has extreme scores (such as the difference between a millionaire and someone making 30,000 a year), you will need to look at median, because you'll find a much more representative number for your sample.

(c) Discuss the assumptions of Normal Probability Curve (NPC).

Ans. Refer to Chapter-4, Q.No.-14

(d) Differentiate between a checklist and a rating scale.

Ans. Refer to Chapter-3, Q.No.-10 and Q.No.-11

(e) Briefly explain the considerations for selecting a good test.

Ans. Refer to Chapter-3, Q.No.-6

(f) Compute the coefficient of rank correlation from the given data.

S.No.	X	Y
1	48	13
2	33	13
3	40	24
4	09	06
5	16	15
6	16	04
7	65	20
8	24	09
9	16	06
10	57	19

Ans.

X	Y	R_1	R_2	$D = R_1 - R_2$	D^2
48	13	8	5.5	2.5	6.25
33	13	6	5.5	0.5	0.25
40	24	7	10	–3	9
09	06	1	2.5	–1.5	2.25
16	15	3	7	–4	16
16	04	3	1	2	4
65	20	10	9	1	1
24	09	5	4	1	1
16	06	3	2.5	0.5	0.25
57	19	9	8	1	1
				$\Sigma D = 0$	41

In this question in X series, the value 16 is repeated thrice. The average rank for the value 16 is 3 (2+3+4)/3. In this case the correlation factor will be $\frac{1}{12}(3^3 - 3)$. In y series, the values 13 and 6 are repeated twice. The average rank for the value 13 is 5.5 (5+6)/2 while for the value 6 is 2.5 (2+3)/2. In both the case, the correlation factor will be $\frac{1}{12}(2^3 - 2)$ and $\frac{1}{12}(2^3 - 2)$.

Applying the formula

$$R = 1 - \frac{6\left[\sum D^2 + \frac{1}{12}(m_1^3 - m_1) + \frac{1}{12}(m_2^3 - m_1) + \frac{1}{12}(m_3^3 - m_1)\right]}{N^3 - N}$$

$\sum D^2 = 41, m_1 = 3, m_2 = 2, m_3 = 2, N = 10$

By substituting values in the above formula, we get

$$= 1 - \frac{6\left[41 + \frac{1}{12}(3^3 - 3) + \frac{1}{12}(2^3 - 2) + \frac{1}{12}(2^3 - 2)\right]}{10^3 - 10}$$

$$= 1 - \frac{6 \times 44}{10^3 - 10}$$

$$= 1 - \frac{264}{999} = 0.735$$

Q4. Suppose you have been given a task to study the attitude of secondary teachers towards the use of ICT of teaching-learning process. Discuss the steps you would undertake while constructing an attitude scale.

Ans. Same as Chapter-3, Q.No.-14

METHODOLOGY OF EDUCATIONAL RESEARCH : MES-054
June, 2012

Note: *(i) All questions are compulsory.*
(ii) All the questions carry equal weightage.
Answer the following question in about 600 words:

Q1. Explain the concept of an attitude scale. Describe the different types of attitude scales and their limitations.

Ans. Refer to Chapter-3, Q.No.-14 and Q.No.-15

Or

Explain the characteristics of normal probability distribution curve. Discuss its uses with suitable examples.

Ans. Refer to Chapter-4, Q.No.-14 and Q.No.-15

Q2. Explain the concept of an experimental research. Discuss various steps involved in conducting an experimental research.

Ans. Refer to Chapter-5, Q.No.-14 and Q.No.-16

Or

Explain the nature and meaning of Ex-post facto research. Describe various steps to be followed while conducting an Ex-post facto research.

Ans. Refer to Chapter-5, Q.No.-20, Q.No.-21 and Q.No.-22

Q3. (a) What do you mean by sampling errors? Explain with examples.

Ans. Refer to Chapter-3, Q.No.-4

(b) Explain the concept of an interview and the stages to be followed in an interview?

Ans. Refer to Chapter-3, Q.No.-18

(c) Explain some of the basic assumptions of analysis of variance.

Ans. Refer to Chapter-4, Q.No.-28

(d) Describe the procedure to find out the reliability of a test.

Ans. Refer to Chapter-3, Q.No.-6

(e) What are the various strategies used in dissemination of research findings?

Ans. Refer to Chapter-6, Q.No.-18

(f) Calculate SD from the following distribution table.

Class Interval	Frequency
45 - 49	2
40 - 44	3
35 - 39	2
30 - 34	6
25 - 29	8
20 - 24	8
15 - 19	7
10 - 14	5
5 - 9	9

Ans.

Class Interval X	f	x	cf	$dx \frac{(x-27)}{5}$	fdx
44.5-49.5	2	47	2	4	8
39.5-44.5	3	42	5	3	9
34.5-39.5	2	37	7	2	4
29.5-34.5	6	32	13	1	6
24.5-29.5	8	27=A	21	0	0
19.5-24.5	8	22	29	–1	–8
14.5-19.5	7	17	36	–2	–14
9.5-14.5	5	12	41	–3	–15
4.5-9.5	9	7	50	–4	–36
					–46

For Mean

$$\bar{X} = A + \frac{\sum fdx}{n} \times i$$

$$= 27 + \frac{-46}{50} \times 5 = 22.4$$

For Median

$$\Rightarrow \frac{n}{2} = \frac{50}{2} = 25^{th}$$

25th, item lies in the class 24.5 – 29.5

Thus,

$$\text{Median} = L + \frac{\frac{n}{2} - cf}{f} \times i$$

$$= 24.5 + \frac{25 - 29}{8} \times 5 = 22$$

Q4. Explain the need for quantification in educational research? Suppose you have to plan an educational study based on the paradigm of quantitative educational research. Discuss the basic assumptions, research design, methods, tools etc as main features of the paradigm.

Ans. Refer to Chapter-1, Q.No.-16 and Q.No.-15

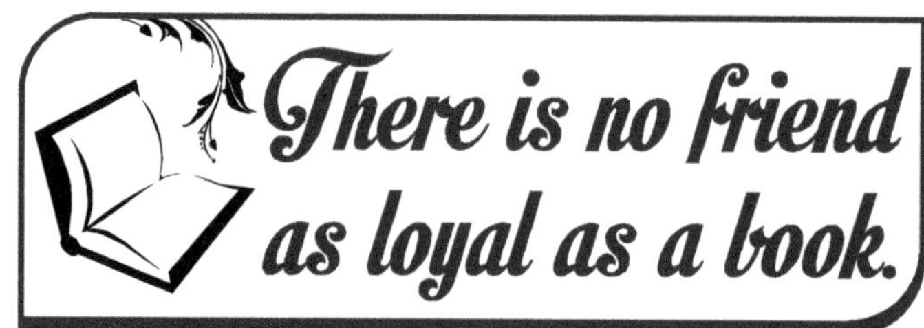

METHODOLOGY OF EDUCATIONAL RESEARCH : MES-054
December, 2012

Note: *(i) All questions are compulsory.*
(ii) All the questions carry equal weightage.
Answer the following questions in about 600 words:

Q1. Define the concept of research. Discuss characteristics and limitations of research.

Ans. Refer to Chapter-1, Q.No.-6

Limitations

Limitations are potential weaknesses in a research and are out of control. We find limitations in almost everything we do. If we are using a conventional oven, food in the middle racks often are undercooked while the food closest to the burner and the top can be too well done. If we are using a sample of convenience, as opposed to a random sample, then the results of your study cannot be generally applied to a larger population, only suggested. If we are looking at one aspect, say achievement tests, the information is only as good as the test itself. Another limitation is time. A study conducted over a certain interval of time is a snapshot dependent on conditions occurring during that time. We must explain how we intend to deal with the limitations we are aware of so as not to affect the outcome of the study.

Or

Explain the nature and meaning of descriptive research. Describe the steps in conducting descriptive research.

Ans. Refer to Chapter-5, Q.No.-8 and Q.No.-13(c)

Q2. Explain the different types of probability sampling with suitable examples.

Ans. Refer to Chapter-3, Q.No.-3

Or

Explain the nature and meaning of questionnaire. What points do you take into consideration while constructing a questionnaire?

Ans. Refer to Chapter-3, Q.No.-8 and Q.No.-9

Q3. Answer any four questions in about 150 words:

(a) What do you mean by 'levels of confidence'?

Ans. The confidence level is the probability value $(1-\alpha)$ associated with a confidence interval. It is often expressed as a percentage. For example, say $\alpha = 0.05 = 5\%$ then the confidence level is equal to (1-0.05) = 0.95, i.e. a 95% confidence level.

Example

Suppose an opinion poll predicted that, if the election were held today, the Conservative party would win 60% of the vote. The pollster might attach a 95% confidence level to the interval 60% plus or minus 3%. That is, he thinks it very likely that the Conservative party would get between 57% and 63% of the total vote.

(b) Differentiate between close ended and open ended questions with examples.

Ans. In asking questions, researchers have two options. They can ask open-ended questions, in which case the respondents is asked to provide his or her own answers to the questions. For example, the respondents may be asked, " What do you feel is the most important issue facing the United States today? and be provided with a space to write in the answer (or be asked to report it verbally to an interviewer). In depth, qualitative interviewing relies almost exclusively on open-ended questions. However they are also used in survey research. These questions enables participants to respond in any way that they please.

In the case of closed-ended questions, the respondents is asked to select and answer from among a list provided by the researcher.

Closed ended questions are very popular in survey research because they provide a greater uniformity of responses and are more easily processed than open-ended ones. A closed ended question is appropriate when the dimensions of a variable are already known it expose all participants to the same response categories and allow standardized quantitative statistical analysis.

(c) Discuss the meaning and characteristics of quantitative data in educational research.

Ans. Refer to Chapter-4, Q.No.-1

(d) What do you mean by ethnomethodology?

Ans. Refer to Chapter-1, Q.No.-5

(e) Explain the need and procedure for dissemination of research findings.

Ans. Refer to Chapter-6, Q.No.-15 and Q.No.-18

To be most effective, dissemination strategies must be incorporated into the earliest planning stages of a research study. In fact, the most successful dissemination processes are typically designed prior to the start of a project.

In creating a dissemination plan, researchers should consider several key questions:

Goal: What are the goals and objectives of the dissemination effort? What impact do you hope to have?

Audience: Who is affected most by this research? Who would be interested in learning about the study findings? Is this of interest to a broader community?

Medium: What is the most effective way to reach each audience? What resources does each group typically access?

Execution: When should each aspect of the dissemination plan occur (e.g. at which points during the study and afterwards)? Who will be responsible for dissemination activities?

When answering these questions, researchers should keep in mind some of the key characteristics of effective dissemination plans:

- Orient toward the needs of the audience, using appropriate language and information levels.
- Include various dissemination methods: written text including illustrations, graphs and figures; electronic and web-based tools; and oral presentations at community meetings and scientific conferences.
- Leverage existing resources, relationships, and networks fully.

(f) Calculate mean and median from the following distribution table.

Class Interval	Frequency
45 - 49	2
40 - 44	3
35 - 39	2
30 - 34	6
25 - 29	8
20 - 24	8
15 - 19	7
10 - 14	5
5 - 9	9

Ans.

Class Interval X	f	x	cf	$dx\frac{(x-27)}{5}$	fdx
44.5-49.5	2	47	2	4	8
39.5-44.5	3	42	5	3	9
34.5-39.5	2	37	7	2	4
29.5-34.5	6	32	13	1	6
24.5-29.5	8	27=A	21	0	0
19.5-24.5	8	22	29	–1	–8
14.5-19.5	7	17	36	–2	–14
9.5-14.5	5	12	41	–3	–15
4.5-9.5	9	7	50	–4	–36
					–46

For Mean

$$\overline{X} = A + \frac{\sum fdx}{n} \times i$$

$$= 27 + \frac{-46}{50} \times 5 = 22.4$$

For Median

$$\Rightarrow \frac{n}{2} = \frac{50}{2} = 25^{th}$$

25th, item lies in the class 24.5 – 29.5

Thus,

$$\text{Median} = L + \frac{\frac{n}{2} - cf}{f} \times i$$

$$= 24.5 + \frac{25-29}{8} \times 5 = 22$$

Q4. Answer the following question in about 600 words:

Explain the nature of action research. Identify a problem, which you face in your classroom teaching and write an action research proposal you would like to conduct to overcome the problem.

Ans. Same as Chapter-5, Q.No.-23 and 26

METHODOLOGY OF EDUCATIONAL RESEARCH : MES-054
June, 2013

Note: *(i) All questions are compulsory.*
(ii) All the questions carry equal weightage.

Q1. Answer the following question in about 600 words.

What are the different paradigms of educational research? Discuss the major characteristics of these paradigms.

Ans. Refer to Chapter-1, Q.No.-16 (a), Q.No.-14 and Q.No.-19

Or

Discuss the importance of review of related literature in educational research, citing different sources of information that can be used for review.

Ans. Refer to Chapter-2, Q.No.-1 and Q.No.-3

Q2. Answer the following question in about 600 words.

What do you mean by probability and non - probability sampling methods? What points should be taken into consideration by a researcher in selecting a sampling method? Explain with examples.

Ans. Refer to Chapter-3, Q.No.-3

Consideration

- **Inappropriate sampling frame:** If the sampling frame is inappropriate i.e., a biased representation of the universe, it will result in a systematic bias.
- **Defective measuring device:** If the measuring device is constantly in error, it will result in systematic bias. In survey work, systematic bias can result if the questionnaire or the interviewer is biased. Similarly, if the physical measuring device is defective there will be systematic bias in the data collected through such a measuring device.

- **Non-respondents:** If we are unable to sample all the individuals initially included in the sample, there may arise a systematic bias. The reason is that in such a situation the likelihood of establishing contact or receiving a response from an individual is often correlated with the measure of what is to be estimated.
- **Indeterminacy principle:** Sometimes we find that individuals act differently when kept under observation than what they do when kept in non-observed situations. For instance, if workers are aware that somebody is observing them in course of a work study on the basis of which the average length of time to complete a task will be determined and accordingly the quota will be set for piece work, they generally tend to work slowly in comparison to the speed with which they work if kept unobserved. Thus, the indeterminacy principle may also be a cause of a systematic bias.
- **Natural bias in the reporting of data:** Natural bias of respondents in the reporting of data is often the cause of a systematic bias in many inquiries. There is usually a downward bias in the income data collected by government taxation department, whereas we find an upward bias in the income data collected by some social organisation. People in general understate their incomes if asked about it for tax purposes, but they overstate the same if asked for social status or their affluence. Generally in psychological survey, people tend to give what they think is the 'correct' answer rather than revealing their true feelings.

Or

Describe the nature and characteristics of a normal probability curve. Discuss its applications with suitable examples.

Ans. Refer to Chapter-4, Q.No.-14 and Q.No.-15

Q3. Answer any four of the following questions in about 150 words each:

(a) What are the strengths and limitations of longitudinal studies in education?

Ans. The strength and limitations of longitudinal studies are as follows:

Strength of longitudinal studies

Longitudinal method is useful in accumulating data for the same subject or subject at various levels and helps in intensive studies of individual or individuals.

Limitations of longitudinal studies

It suffers from the following limitations:

- Longitudinal studies have sampling weaknesses.
- Another limitation of the longitudinal method is that the researcher usually cannot make improvements in his measuring tools or instruments as his study develops without disrupting the continuity of the procedures.
- Sometimes longitudinal studies become unwieldy and unmanageable because of the wide range of behavior to be observed, large number of the subjects in the sample, or less duration of the time period in which the study has to be completed.
- Longitudinal studies required extensive facilities, considerable amount of money and maximum perseverance on the part of research personnel over a number of years. Such studies therefore, may be undertaken by research organizations in the form of projects and not by individual researches.

(b) Differentiate between true experimental design and quasi-experimental design. Illustrate your answer with examples.

Ans. Refer to Chapter-5, Q.No.-18

(c) Explain the concept of standard error of mean.

Ans. Refer to Chapter-4, Q.No.-22

(d) Differentiate between Norm referenced and Criterion referenced tests.

Ans. Refer to Chapter-3, Q.No.-5

(e) What is a chi - square test? Explain its assumptions and the significance in statistical analysis.

Ans. Refer to Chapter-4, Q.No.-32

Assumptions for chi-square tests

The chi-square tests of goodness of fit and for independence do not require the usual assumptions of normal population variances and such. There is, however, one key assumption: Each score must not have any special relation to any other scores. This means that you can't use these chi-square tests if the scores are based on the same people being tested more than once. Consider a study in which 20 people are tested to see if the distribution of their preferred brand of breakfast cereal changed from before to after a recent nutritional campaign. The results of this study could not be tested with the usual chi-square, because the distributions of cereal choice before and after are from the same people.

(f) Describe dependent, independent and extraneous variables with suitable examples.

Ans. Refer to Chapter-5, Q.No.-15

Q4. Answer the following question in about 600 words.

Suppose you are required to conduct an ex-post facto research. Formulate a suitable research topic and develop a research proposal involving the steps of ex-post facto research design.

Ans. Same as Chapter-5, Q.No.-21

Whenever you read a book somewhere in the world a door opens to allow in more light

METHODOLOGY OF EDUCATIONAL RESEARCH : MES-054
December, 2013

Note: *(i) All questions are compulsory.*
(ii) All the questions carry equal weightage.

Q1. Answer the following in about 600 words:

Distinguish between the positivistic and non- positivistic approaches of educational research. Can these approaches be applied together for a research problem? Discuss with suitable examples.

Ans. Positivism can be characterized by various doctrines, such as: knowledge claims can be established only by empirical research; only the observable is researchable; and scientific research is objective, free of value judgment, and is based on testable factual statements. Non-positivist approaches are those that reject at least one of these doctrines.

Now, Refer to Chapter-1, Q.No.-4 and Q.No.-5 and now

Others see a more complex relationship where positivist and non-positivist research enters into some kind of dialectical process whereby higher level knowledge is produced (Klein, Hirschheim & Nissen, 1991). There are few examples of actually mixing positivist and non-positivist research approaches and contrasting the results of doing research on the basis of different ontologies and their resulting choices of epistemology and methodology (cf. Trauth & Jessup 2000).

Nevertheless, most non-positivists seem to imply that positivism and non-positivism can coexist (Lee, 1991; 1994). The frequency of these syncretistic approaches allows Walsham (1995b) to identify four rhetorical figures used in the literature to justify the syncretistic approach.

Or

Discuss the significance to formulating objectives and hypotheses for a research study. Explain various types of hypothesis with suitable examples.

Ans. The objectives of a research project summarise what is to be achieved by the study. Objectives should be closely related to the statement of the problem. For example, if the problem identified is low utilisation of child welfare clinics, the general objective of the study could be to identify the reasons for this low utilisation, in order to find solutions. The general objective of a study states what researchers expect to achieve by the study in general terms. It is possible (and advisable) to break down a general objective into smaller, logically connected parts. These are normally referred to as specific objectives. Specific objectives should systematically address the various aspects of the problem as defined under 'Statement of the Problem' and the key factors that are assumed to influence or cause the problem. They should specify what you will do in your study, where and for what purpose.

Now, Refer to Chapter-2, Q.No.-8 and Q.No.-9

Q2. Answer the following in about 600 words:

Mention various types of probability sampling. Discuss the procedure of selecting a sample using stratified random sampling technique with the help of an example.

Ans. Refer to Chapter-3, Q.No.-3

Procedure of selecting a sample using stratified random sampling

Step 1 Identify all elements or sampling units in the sampling population.
Step 2 Decide upon the different strata (k) into which you want to stratify the population.
Step 3 Place each element into the appropriate stratum.
Step 4 Number every element in each stratum separately.
Step 5 Decide the total sample size (n).
Step 6 Decide whether you want to select proportionate or disproportionate stratified sampling and follow the steps below.

Disproportionate stratified sampling	**Proportionate stratified sampling**
Step 7 Determine the number of elements to be selected from each stratum $= \frac{\text{sample size (n)}}{\text{no. of strata (k)}}$ Step 8 Select the required number of elements from each stratum with SRS technique	Step 7 Determine the proportion of each stratum in the study population (p) $= \frac{\text{elements in each stratum}}{\text{total population size}}$ Step 8 Determine the number of elements to be selected from each stratum = (sample size) × (p) Step 9 Select the required number of elements from each stratum with SRS technique

Or

'A reliable test may not be valid but a valid test is always reliable'. Do you agree with this statement? Give arguments in support of your answer. Also explain various types of validity with suitable examples.

Ans. Perhaps the most important statistical evaluators associated with tests are reliability and validity. These two related criteria are frequently confused. Reliability refers to the consistency of results, that is, the general dependability of a test: A test that produces similar results under similar conditions is said to be reliable. Validity refers to the degree to which a test measures what it purports to measure and what the examiner wishes to measure. Beliability is a prerequisite of validity, but validity is not needed for reliability. To put it another way, a valid test is always reliable, but a reliable test is not necessarily valid.

Consider an everyday analogy: McDonald's hamburgers. McDonald's hamburgers, we suggest, are reliable but not valid. If you walk into a McDonald's anywhere in the world, from Savannah to Hong Kong, you receive precisely the same product. Now that's reliability! But are these sandwiches what you really want when you think of a good hamburger? In our view, they are not. In other words, they are valid examples of "true" hamburgers. To put it in testing terms, there is high reliability and low validity. The same can be true of a test. To use an extreme example, a math test may be highly reliable, but if used to assess reading ability, it would produce results that are clearly invalid.

Now, Refer to Chapter-3, Q.No.-6

Q3. Answer any four of the following questions in about 150 words each.

(a) What is meant by Action Research? Briefly discuss the importance of Action Research citing examples.

Ans. Refer to Chapter-5, Q.No.-23

(b) What do you mean by an ex-post-facto research? Distinguish it from experimental research.

Ans. Refer to Chapter-5, Q.No.-20 and Q.No.-14

(c) Discuss the points that need to be kept in mind while constructing a rating scale for a research study.

Ans. Refer to Chapter-3, Q.No.-12

(d) Explain the concept of parametric and non-parametric tests. State the assumptions for their use.

Ans. Refer to Chapter-4, Q.No.-21 and Q.No.-31

(e) Describe the strategies for validation of qualitative data.

Ans. Refer to Chapter-4, Q.No.-45

(f) Describe the characteristics of a good test.

Ans. Refer to Chapter-3, Q.No.-6

Q4. Answer the following question in about 600 words:

Suppose you have to undertake a study on 'Problems of Dropouts among Distance Learners'. Develop a questionnaire to be administered on the drop-outs of distance education programmes.

Ans. Questionnaire to be administered on the drop-outs of distance education programmes:

(1) Personal Information

Name of student:_____________

Age:____________ Sex: M☐ F☐

Course:__________

(2) What is the structure of the course you took?

☐ Distance learning (i.e., course online only)

☐ Hybrid (i.e., course uses combination of in-class meetings and online activities

(3) Reason for choosing the course structure.

....

....

(4) Thinking back to before the course started, what the thoughts and expectations did you have about the course?

....

....

(5) How did the course meet those thoughts and expectations?

....

....

(6) What three things did you like mast about distance learning?

(i)..

(ii)..

(iii)..

(7) What three things did you not like least about distance learning?

(i)..

(ii)..

(iii)..

(8) What did you find mast challenging about course related to using technology?

....

....

(9) Do you find your study materials at home?

No ☐ Yes ☐ Same time ☐

(10) Do you face any problem related to submitting assignments?

....

....

(11) In terms of time commitments, in what ways is a distance learning course different from face-to-face learning course?

....

....

(12) When comparing a distance learning course with a face-to-face learning, what did you find to be the biggest differences? Similarities?

....

....

(13) What would you tell other students who are considering taking a distance learning course?

....

....

(14) What would tell faculties who are considering teaching a course via distance learning?

....

....

✦✦

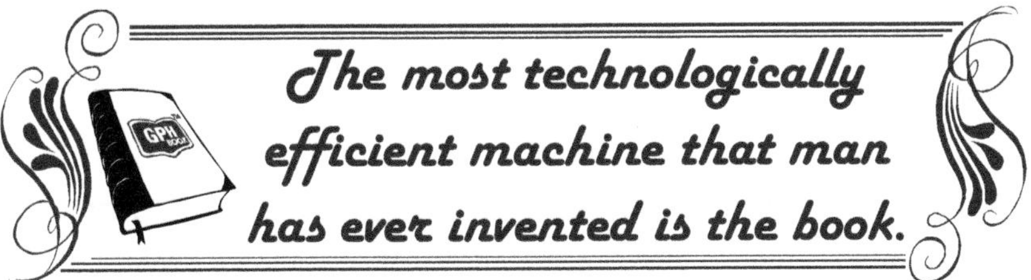

METHODOLOGY OF EDUCATIONAL RESEARCH : MES-054
June, 2014

Note: *(i) All questions are compulsory.*
(ii) All the questions carry equal weightage.

Q1. Answer the following question in about 600 words:

Discuss different types of experimental designs, highlighting their essential features.

Or

What is Normal Probability Distribution Curve? Discuss its applications with suitable examples.

Q2. Answer the following question in about 600 words:

What do you understand by Sampling? Describe its various methods.

Or

What do you mean by Research Tools? Differentiate between questionnaire and schedule.

Q3. Answer any four of the following questions in about 150 words each:

(a) Sources of problem selection

(b) Steps of hypothesis testing

(c) Error in Sampling

(d) Priority areas of Educational Research

(e) Difference between case study and Ex-post facto method

(f) Internal and external criticism

Q4. Answer the following question:

A normal distribution has a mean of 120 and standard distribution of 20. For this distribution:

(a) What scores seperates the top 40% (highest scores) from the rest?

(b) **What scores would you need to be in the top 10% of the distribution?**

(c) **What range of scores would form the middle 60% of this distribution?**

METHODOLOGY OF EDUCATIONAL RESEARCH : MES-054
December, 2014

Note: (i) All questions are compulsory.
(ii) All questions carry equal weightage.

Q1. Answer the following question in about 600 words:

What are the sources of research problem? Discuss in detail the criteria for the selection of a problem.

Or

Define Sampling. Enumerate the characteristics of a good sample and describe the method of estimating the reliability of a sample.

Q2. Answer the following question in about 600 words:

What is the meaning of Hypothesis? Discuss sources and types of hypothesis.

Or

What is the difference between questionnaire and inventory? What are the characteristics of a good questionnaire?

Q3. Answer any four of the following questions in about 150 words each:

(a) Differentiate between Research hypothesis and Null hypothesis.

(b) Differentiate between Independent and Dependent variables.

(c) Differentiate between one-tailed test and two-tailed test.

(d) Differentiate between Type-I and Type-II error.

(e) Differentiate between Case Study and Ex-post Facto Method.

Q4. Answer the following question:

(a) What do you mean by correlation ? Discuss different types of correlation.

(b) Calculate the coefficient of correlation by Rank Difference Method, the scores of a group of students in Maths and Science are as follows:

Maths	**13**	**16**	**11**	**17**	**16**	**12**	**19**	**20**	**20**	**16**
Science	**14**	**19**	**10**	**16**	**15**	**18**	**26**	**29**	**23**	**10**

✦✦

METHODOLOGY OF EDUCATIONAL RESEARCH : MES-054

June, 2015

Note: *(i) All questions are compulsory.*
(ii) All the questions carry equal weightage.

Q1. Answer the following question in about 600 words:

What is meant by 'Experimental Research'? Describe different types of experimental designs with suitable examples.

Or

Discuss the significance of review of related literature in research. Describe the sources of information you would use for review of related literature.

Q2. Answer the following question in about 600 words:

Mention the criteria taken into consideration while constructing a rating scale. Describe different types of rating scales.

Or

Discuss scope of educational research. Explain any four priority areas for research in education in the present Indian context. Illustrate your answer with reasons.

Q3. Answer any four of the following questions in about 150 words each:

(a) Write the characteristics and uses of normal probability distribution curve.

(b) Differentiate between simple random sampling and stratified random sampling.

(c) How do you compute the 'difficulty level' and the 'index of discrimination' of a test item ? Discuss.

(d) Write a short note on 'different types of research reports'.

(e) Explain briefly the various methods of graphic representation of quantitative data.

(f) Describe the steps followed for computing the Analysis of Variance (ANOVA).

Q4. Answer the following question in about 600 words:

Identify a problem for a research study in education using mixed method. Based on your research proposal, prepare a questionnaire with ten items and an interview schedule with ten items for collecting qualitative data.

Whenever you read a book somewhere in the world a door opens to allow in more light

METHODOLOGY OF EDUCATIONAL RESEARCH : MES-054
December, 2015

Note: *(i) All questions are compulsory.*
(ii) All the questions carry equal weightage.

Q1. Answer the following question in about 600 words:

What do you understand by 'Ex-Post-Facto Research'? Discuss the steps followed in conducting.

Or

Describe various methods of finding the reliability of a test with examples.

Q2. Answer the following question in about 600 words:

Discuss different kinds of cross-sectional surveys and longitudinal surveys with suitable examples.

Or

What do you understand by the terms 'Quantitative Research' and 'Qualitative Research' in education? Discuss the steps followed for preparing a research proposal by using qualitative research method.

Q3. Answer any four of the following questions in about 150 words each:

(a) Differentiate between 'Norm-referenced test' and 'Criterion-referenced test'.

(b) Write the formulae for computing Mean, Median and Standard deviation.

(c) What is the need for dissemination of research findings? Explain.

(d) How do you differentiate a checklist from a rating scale?

(e) Write a short note on the use and application of Chi-square (χ^2) test in making statistical inferences.

(f) What is the difference between 'Research hypothesis' and

'Statistical hypothesis'? Illustrate your answer with one example of each.

Q4. Answer the following question in about 600 words:

Discuss the purpose and scope of understanding action research. Identify a problem faced by you in your classroom teaching and prepare an action research proposal to solve the problem.

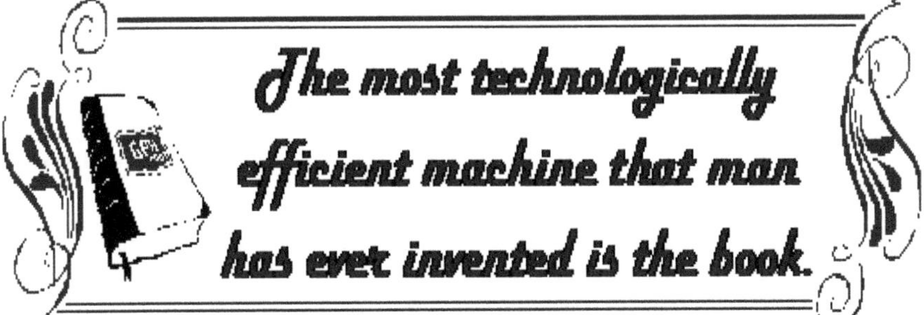

METHODOLOGY OF EDUCATIONAL RESEARCH : MES-054

June, 2016

Note: (i) All questions are compulsory.
(ii) All the questions carry equal weightage.

Q1. Answer the following question in about 600 words.

Explain various approaches to acquiring knowledge. Discuss the contribution of these approaches in educational research.

Or

What is Action Research? How is it different from empirical research? Discuss the procedure of conducting action research.

Q2. Answer the following question in about 600 words.

What do you mean by content analysis? Explain various steps of content analysis with the help of a suitable example.

Or

Discuss the characteristics of a good test. Explain various methods of establishing reliability of a test.

Q3. Answer any four of the following questions in about 150 words each:

(a) Differentiate between checklist and rating scale.

(b) What is Man - Whitney U test and explain its use ?

(c) Discuss various types of interviews used in educational research.

(d) Differentiate between research and null hypothesis with examples.

(e) Discuss the need and significance of review of related literature in educational research.

(f) Differentiate between endnotes/footnotes and bibliography/ references with suitable examples.

Q4. Answer the following question in about 600 words.

Suppose you are required to undertake a historical research, formulate a suitable research topic and develop a research proposal involving steps of historical research.

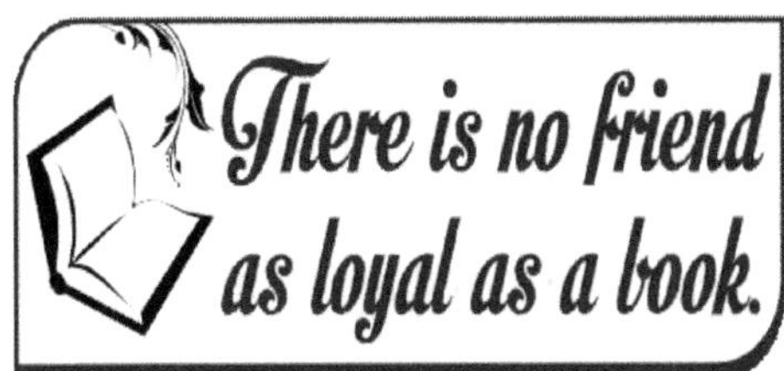

METHODOLOGY OF EDUCATIONAL RESEARCH : MES-054
December, 2016

Note: (i) All questions are compulsory.
(ii) All the questions carry equal weightage.

Q1. Answer the following in about 600 words:

Discuss the characteristics of a good hypothesis. Why should we formulate hypothesis in research? Clarify the different types of hypothesis with examples.

Or

Explain the steps of a research proposal and prepare a brief proposal on any research topic of your choice.

Q2. Answer the following in about 600 words:

Describe the use of questionnaire in research. What points will you take into consideration while constructing a good questionnaire? Explain with examples.

Or

Evaluate qualitative method of educational research. Discuss the procedure for analysing case study of data.

Q3. Answer any four of the following questions in about 150 words each.

(a) Explain the concept of level of significance in educational research with an example.

(b) Discuss the concept of Degrees of freedom. Clarify with examples.

(c) Explain the characteristics of normal probability distribution curve.

(d) Describe the steps of experimental research.

(e) Differentiate between norm referenced test and criterion referenced test.

(f) Discuss the relevance of descriptive studies in educational research.

Q4. Answer the following question in about 600 words:

Explain the components of a research report and Develop an outline of a report your choice.

✦✦

METHODOLOGY OF EDUCATIONAL RESEARCH : MES-054
June, 2017

Note: *(i) All questions are compulsory.*
(ii) All the questions carry equal weightage.

Q1. Answer the following in about 600 words:

Define a research problem. How will you evaluate the selected research problem? Support your answer with suitable examples.

Or

What do you understand by 'Experimental Research'? Explain the characteristics of an experimental research.

Q2. Answer the following in about 600 words:

What do you understand by 'sampling'? Differentiate between 'probability' and 'nonprobability' sampling methods.

Or

Discuss basic assumptions of analysis of variance. Describe the steps to be followed in computing the analysis of variance (ANOVA).

Q3. Answer any four of the following questions in about 150 words each.

(a) Why is writing footnotes, references and bibliography in a research report essential? Discuss.

(b) What do you mean by 'phenomenology' as an alternative method of acquiring knowledge? Explain.

(c) Discuss the importance of 'item analysis' of a test.

(d) What do you mean by an 'observation technique' of data collection? Describe the stages in the process of observation.

(e) Explain sampling errors and their impact on generalization of research findings.

(f) Describe the uses of chi-square and ManWhitney U Test with the help of examples.

Q4. Answer the following question in about 600 words:

What do you understand by an 'action research design? Prepare an action research proposal on a problem faced by you in your school.

++

Believe
you can
&
you're halfway
there.

METHODOLOGY OF EDUCATIONAL RESEARCH : MES-054
December, 2017

Note: *(i) All questions are compulsory.*
(ii) All the questions carry equal weightage.

Q1. Answer the following in about 600 words:

Explain the meaning and characteristics of a hypothesis. Discuss the various types of hypotheses with examples.

Or

Describe the types of descriptive research. Discuss its importance and significance in the field of education.

Q2. Answer the following in about 600 words:

What is historical research? How is historical research relevant to education? Explain with suitable examples.

Or

Discuss the relevance of qualitative research paradigm in the field of education and explain its characteristics.

Q3. Answer any four of the following questions in about 150 words each.

(a) Describe the characteristics of experimental research in education.

(b) Explain the steps to be followed to establish the reliability of a test.

(c) Write a note on the criteria of writing a research report.

(d) What is sampling error ? Explain with the help of examples.

(e) Describe the nature and characteristics of causal-comparative studies.

(f) What are the various sociometric techniques used in the field of education? Discuss.

Q4. Answer the following question in about 600 words:

Explain the objectives of conducting research in the field of education. Discuss the steps of conducting educational research with an example.

✦✦

Life is not about waiting for the storm to pass, it's about learning to Dance in the Rain

METHODOLOGY OF EDUCATIONAL RESEARCH : MES-054
June, 2018

Note: *(i) All questions are compulsory.*
(ii) All the questions carry equal weightage.

Q1. Answer the following in about 600 words:

Differentiate between descriptive and experimental research. Describe the steps of conducting experimental research with an example.

Or

Describe the significance of Review of Related Literature in educational research. Explain the sources of review in the field of education.

Q2. Answer the following in about 600 words:

Differentiate between probability and non-probability sampling techniques. Discuss the types of probability sampling technique.

Or

Explain the nature and characteristics of qualitative research paradigm in education. Discuss its merits and demerits.

Q3. Answer any four of the following questions in about 150 words each.

(a) Explain the characteristics of survey method in education.

(b) Discuss the nature and characteristics of ex-post facto research.

(c) Differentiate between internal and external criticisms in historical research method.

(d) What is observation technique? How is this technique useful in conducting educational research?

(e) Differentiate between directional and non-directional hypothesis.

(f) What are sampling errors? Explain different ways of minimising sampling errors.

Q4. Answer the following question in about 600 words:

Based on the qualitative research paradigm, select a suitable research problem in the field of education. Discuss the research design, method and tools for conducting the selected research.

✦✦

"Whatever the mind of man can conceive and believe, it can achieve".

- W. Clement Stone

METHODOLOGY OF EDUCATIONAL RESEARCH : MES-054
December, 2018

Note: *(i) All questions are compulsory.*
(ii) All the questions carry equal weightage.

Q1. Answer the following in about 600 words:

Explain the concept of normal probability curve and characteristics. A distribution of achievement scores has a mean of 60 and a standard deviation of 12 points. If the distribution is approximately normal, compute the number of candidates who have scored between 45 and 75, out of the whole group of 576 candidates.

Or

Define standard error of mean and discuss its application in statistical inference. A sample of 360 class X students was drawn from a large population. The mean and standard deviation of scores were 48 and 10 respectively. Estimate the population mean in terms of confidence limits.

Q2. Answer the following in about 600 words:

What is qualitative research? How does it differ from quantitative research? Discuss in detail the salient features, of qualitative research and its application in education.

Or

What is a research proposal? How does it differ from a research report? Discuss in detail an outline of a research proposal in education with the help of a concrete example.

Q3. Answer any four of the following questions in about 150 words each.

(a) Explain different methods of acquiring knowledge with examples.

(b) Explain the role of hypothesis in educational research.

(c) What do you mean by reliability and validity of a test? Describe the relationship between reliability and validity of an educational test.

(d) **Explain type I and type II errors in statistical inference with the help of examples.**

(e) **Differentiate between an experimental and an expost-facto study with the help of examples.**

(f) **Describe detailed outline of the format of a doctoral thesis in education.**

Q4. Answer the following question in about 600 words:

Explain the concept of correlation. Show with the help of scattergrams the idea of high, low, positive and negative correlation. How is negative correlation interpreted? Discuss the relation between correlation and causation with examples.

✦✦

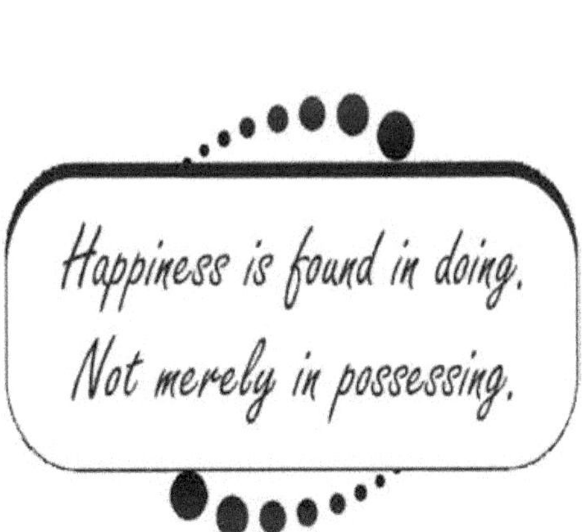

METHODOLOGY OF EDUCATIONAL RESEARCH : MES-054
June, 2019

Note: (i) All questions are compulsory.
(ii) All the questions carry equal weightage.

Q1. Answer the following in about 600 words:

Explain the meaning of "standard error of difference between means" and its application in statistical infeience. An investigator gave a test of reasoning ability to 200 boys and 210 girls aged 15-16 years. The following results were obtained:

	Mean	S.D.
Boys	48	10
Girls	45	9

Examine statistically whether reasoning ability shows gender differences.

Or

What is meant by central tendency? Why is mean considered to be the most dependable measure of central tendency? The mean score of a group of 400 students drawn from a large population was found to be 56 with a standard deviation of 11 points. Estimate the population mean in terms of confidence limits.

Q2. Answer the following in about 600 words:

Define research and describe its characteristics. Discuss in detail the nature and limitations of educational research. Give examples in support of your answer.

Or

What is meant by dissemination of research finding? What are its purposes? Discuss the Major avenues of dissemination of research findings along with their advantages and limitations.

Q3. Answer any four of the following questions in about 150 words each.

(a) Write a note on nature and purposes of science.

(b) Justify the application of null hypothesis in educational research.

(c) Discuss the advantages and disadvantages of projective techniques.

(d) Draw a normal probability curve and list itt characteristics.

(e) Discuss the essential features of a good research design.

(f) Give a brief outline of prebentation of a research report.

Q4. Answer the following question in about 600 words:

What is factorial design in analysis of data? What are its main features? Demonstrate the use of a 2 x 2 x 2 factorial design in terms of number and types of hypothesis tested, its advanttiges over the other designs and interpretation qf results.

++

Whenever you do a thing,
act as if all the world
were watching.

METHODOLOGY OF EDUCATIONAL RESEARCH : MES-054
December, 2019

Note: All questions are compulsory. All the questions carry equal weightage.

Q1. Answer the following in about 600 words:

What do you mean by Paradigm? Discuss various research paradigms, their scope and limitations.

Or

Discuss various types of probability sampling techniques. Give suitable examples to support your answer.

Q2. Answer the following in about 600 words:

What are the characteristics of a good test? Explain various steps of test construction

Or

Discuss the significance of observation as a technique to collect data in research. Explain various types of observations used in various situations with suitable examples.

Q3. Answer any four of the following questions in about 150 words each.

(a) Explain various types of sampling techniques with suitable examples.

(b) Describe sociometric technique of data collection.

(c) Explain the concept of `t-distribution and its relationship with Normal Probability Curve (NPC).

(d) Differentiate between a checklist and a rating scale.

(e) Discuss the conditions in which Chi-square test can be used. Write the formula used for calculating its value.

(f) Explain the concept and significance of usability and objectivity of a test.

Q4. Answer the following question in about 600 words:

Explain the steps of historical research. Discuss as to how the credibility of historical research can be increased with the help of a suitable example.

✦✦

"Do not pray for easy lives.
Pray to be Stronger Men".

- John F. Kennedy

NOTES

www.ingramcontent.com/pod-product-compliance
Ingram Content Group UK Ltd.
Pitfield, Milton Keynes, MK11 3LW, UK
UKHW021932200726
13853UKWH00010B/473